DATE DUE

DE 18 03			

DEMCO 38-296

The Politics and Economics of the European Union

In loving memory of my mother Florence May Jones
and of Alison May Bell

The Politics and Economics of the European Union

An Introductory Text

By

Robert A. Jones
Senior Lecturer in European Studies
Sheffield Hallam University, UK

Edward Elgar
Cheltenham UK • Brookfield, US

JN 30 .J57 1996

Jones, Robert A., 1946-

The politics and economics
of the European Union

8 Lansdown Place
Cheltenham
Glos GL50 2HU
UK

Edward Elgar Publishing Company
Old Post Road
Brookfield
Vermont 05036
US

A catalogue record for this book
is available from the British Library

Library of Congress Cataloguing in Publication Data
Jones, Robert A., 1946–
    The politics and economics of the European Union: an introductory
text / by Robert A. Jones
        Includes bibliographical references and index.
        (acid-free paper)
        1. European Union. I. Title
    JN30.J57   1996   96–18296
    341.24'22—dc20   CIP

ISBN 1 85278 896 8 (cased)
        1 85278 898 4 (paperback)

Printed in Great Britain at the University Press, Cambridge

Contents

SECTION 1 PERSPECTIVES ON THE UNION'S DEVELOPMENT

List of Figures, Maps and Tables

Figures

Maps

Tables

List of Abbreviations and Acronyms

ACP	African, Caribbean and Pacific Countries (signatories to the Lomé Convention)
ACUSE	Action Committee for a United States of Europe
ADAPT	Initiative for the adaptation of the workforce to industrial change
ALTENER	Promotion of renewable energy sources
APEC	Asia-Pacific Economic Co-operation Forum
ARION	Programme of study visits for educational specialists
ASEAN	Association of South-East Asian Nations
BEUC	European Bureau of Consumers' Unions (Bureau Européen des unions de consommateurs)
BRITE/EURAM	Basic Research in Industrial Technologies for Europe
CA	Court of Auditors
CACM	Central American Common Market
CAP	Common Agricultural Policy
Caricom	Caribbean Community
CCP	Common Commercial Policy
CE	Council of Europe
CEDEFOP	European Centre for the Development of Vocational Training
CEECs	Central and East European countries
CEFTA	Central European Free Trade Area
CERN	European Centre for Nuclear Research
CET	Common External Tariff
CFCs	chlorofluorocarbons
CFI	Court of First Instance
CFP	Common Fisheries Policy
CFSP	Common Foreign and Security Policy
CIS	Commonwealth of Independent States
CJTF	common joint task force
CMEA	Council for Mutual Economic Assistance
Comecon	see CMEA

COMETT	Community Action Programme in Education and Training for Technology
COPA	Committee of Professional Agricultural Organisations (Comité des organisations professionnelles agricoles de la CE)
COR	Committee of the Regions
CORDIS	Community Research and Development Information Service
COREPER	Committee of Permanent Representatives
COST	European co-operation on scientific and technical research
CSF	Community Support Framework
CTP	Common Transport Policy
DG	Directorate-General
DIANE	Direct Information Access Network for Europe
EAGGF	European Agricultural Guidance and Guarantee Fund
EBRD	European Bank for Reconstruction and Development
ECB	European Central Bank
ECHO	European Community Humanitarian Office
ECIP	European Community Investment Partners
ECJ	European Court of Justice
ECOFIN	Council of Economic and Finance Ministers
ECSC	European Coal and Steel Community
ECU	European Currency Unit
EDC	European Defence Community
EDF	European Development Fund
EEA	European Economic Area
EFTA	European Free Trade Association
EIB	European Investment Bank
EIF	European Investment Fund
EMCF	European Monetary Co-operation Fund
EMI	European Monetary Institute
EMS	European Monetary System
EMU	Economic and Monetary Union
EP	European Parliament
EPC	European Political Co-operation (later CFSP)
EPU	European Political Union
ERASMUS	European action scheme for the mobility of university students
ERDF	European Regional Development Fund
ERM	Exchange Rate Mechanism
ESA	European Space Agency

ESC	Economic and Social Committee
ESCB	European System of Central Banks
ESDI	European security and defence identity
ESF	European Social Fund
ESP	European Social Policy
ESPRIT	European Strategic Programme for Research in Information Technology
ETUC	European Trade Union Confederation
EU	European Union
Euratom	European Atomic Energy Community
EUREKA	European Research Co-ordination Agency
EURES	European Employment Services Agency
Eurofer	European Confederation of the Iron and Steel Industry
Europol	European Police Office
Eurostat	EC Statistical Office
EUROTECNET	Action programme in the field of vocational training an technological change
EURYDICE	Programme to promote information exchanges on education systems
FAWEU	forces answerable to the WEU
FDI	foreign direct investment
FEU	Full Economic Union
FIFG	Financial Instrument for Fisheries Guidance
FORCE	Action programme for the development of continuing vocational training
G7	Group of Seven leading industrial nations (the US, Canada, Japan, France, Germany, Italy, the UK)
G24	Group of Twenty Four industrial nations (members of the OECD)
GATT	General Agreement on Tariffs and Trade
GSP	Generalised System of Preferences
HELIOS	Action programme for disabled people
HORIZON	Initiative concerning handicapped persons and certain other disadvantaged groups
IBRD	International Bank for Reconstruction and Development (World Bank)
IEGP	Independent European Programme Group
IGC	intergovernmental conference
IGO	international governmental organisation
IMF	International Monetary Fund
IMP	Integrated Mediterranean Programme
INGO	international non-governmental organisation

Interpol	police co-operation centre
INTERREG II	Initiative concerning cross-border co-operation and energy networks
IT	information technology
JESSI	Joint European Submicron Silicon Initiative
JET	Joint European Torus
JHA	Justice and Home Affairs
KALEIDOSCOPE	Programme to support artistic and cultural events having a European dimension
KAROLUS	Training officials in the enforcement of EC regulations
KONVER	Programme to assist areas affected by the rundown of defence industries and of military installations
LEADER II	Initiative for rural development
LEONARDO	Action programme for the implementation of a European Community vocational training policy
LIFE	Financial Instrument for the Environment
LINGUA	Programme to promote the teaching and learning of foreign languages in the European Community
MAGP	multiannual guidance programme
MATTHAUS	Specific common programmes for the vocational training of customs officials
MCA	monetary compensation amount
MEDIA	Action programme to promote the development of the European audiovisual industry
MEP	Member of the European Parliament
Mercosur	a customs union, Argentina, Brazil, Paraguay and Uruguay
MFA	multifibre agreement
MNC	multinational corporation
NACC	North Atlantic Co-operation Council
NAFTA	North American Free Trade Association
NATO	North Atlantic Treaty Organisation
NGO	Non-governmental organisation
NICs	Newly Industrialised Countries
NOW	New Opportunities for Women
OCTs	Overseas countries and territories
ODIHR	Office of Democratic Institutions and Human Rights
OECD	Organisation for Economic Co-operation and Development
OEEC	Organisation for European Economic Co-operation
Official Journal	Official Journal of the European Communities
OPEC	Organisation of Petroleum Exporting Countries

OSCE	Organisation for Security and Co-operation in Europe (formerly CSCE)
OUVERTURE	Co-operation network with East European regions
PCA	Partnership and Co-operation Agreement
PDB	preliminary draft budget
PESCA	Initiative aimed at solving the problems caused by the restructuring of the fisheries sector
PETRA	Action programme for the vocational training of young people and their preparation for adult and working life
PFP	Partnership for Peace
PHARE	Poland and Hungary: Aid for Economic Restructuring
QMV	qualified majority voting
RACE	R&D in Advanced Communications Technologies in Europe
RAPHAEL	Cultural heritage programme
RECHAR II	Initiative concerning the economic conversion of coalmining areas
REGIS II	Initiative concerning the most remote regions
RESIDER II	Programme to assist the conversion of steel areas
RETEX	Initiative for regions heavily dependent on the textiles and clothing sector
RTD	Research and Technological Development
SAVE	Special action programme for vigorous energy efficiency
SCA	Special Committee on Agriculture
SEA	Single European Act
SEM	Single European Market
SIS	Schengen Information System
SME	small and medium-sized enterprise
SOCRATES	Action programme for the development of quality education and training and of a European dimension in studies at all levels
SPRINT	Strategic Programme for Innovation and Technology Transfer
STABEX	System for the stabilisation of export earnings
SYSMIN	System for the stabilisation of export earnings from mining products
TAC	total allowable catch
TACIS	Technical Assistance to the CIS
TEMPUS	Trans-European Mobility Programme for University Studies
TENs	Trans-European Networks

TEU	Treaty on European Union
THERMIE	Programme for the promotion of energy technology
TIDE	Technology initiative for disabled and elderly people
TREVI	Terrorisme, Radicalisme, Extrémisme, Violence Internationale
UCLAF	Unit for the Co-ordination of Fraud Prevention
UNCTAD	United Nations Conference on Trade and Development
UNESCO	United Nations Educational, Scientific and Cultural Organisation
UNHCR	United Nations High Commission (er) for Refugees
UNICE	Union of Industrial and Employers' Confederations of Europe
UNIDO	United Nations Industrial Development Organisation
UNRWA	United Nations Relief and Works Agency
URBAN	Initiative for urban areas
VAT	value-added tax
VER	voluntary export restraint
WEU	Western European Union
WTO	World Trade Organisation
YOUTHSTART	Programme to assist the integration of young people into the labour market

Map 1 Membership of the European Union

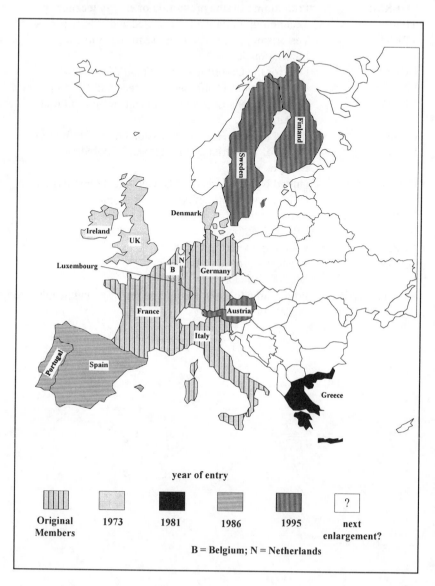

year of entry

Original Members | 1973 | 1981 | 1986 | 1995 | next enlargement?

B = Belgium; N = Netherlands

The Purpose and Plan of the Book

This book seeks to provide students with a clear and topical introduction to the aims, institutions and policies of the European Union in the post-cold war era. The Union is currently undergoing rapid change, rendering it impossible to provide a cut-and-dried exposition of its characteristics or future prospects. Therefore, the book will seek throughout to enhance the reader's understanding of the main issues and controversies surrounding the Union's development.

The first section comprises an introduction to various historical and theoretical perspectives on European integration. By the end of the section, the reader should have a good understanding of the reasons for the formation of the European Union and of the principal factors shaping its development. The section also seeks to identify the Union's distinctive features, by means of a comparative analysis of post-war integration projects. The second section examines the Union's institutional machinery and policy processes. It also seeks to shed light upon the dynamics of institutional change within the Union. The third section examines the main Union policies.

The following ten key points should provide the reader with a preliminary perspective on the Union:

- **It is unique**. The reader should beware of false and misleading analogies. Although the Union shares some characteristics with federal states, with international organisations and with other post-war regional integration projects, it has features which differentiate it from any other political or economic formation.
- **It is unfinished**. The integration process in the European Union has frequently been described as a journey to an unknown destination. Although there is general agreement that the Union is by no means complete, there is no agreement concerning its ultimate purpose, size or shape.
- **It has been an exercise in partial integration**. For much of its history, the European Union project has been confined to Western Europe. The end of the cold war resulted in qualitative changes in the Union's agenda for enlargement and in its relationships with Central and Eastern Europe. The Union has already committed itself to a southward and eastward expansion (Cyprus, Malta and former communist countries in Central and Eastern Europe with 'association' agreements with the Union fully expect to accede

at some point). The West European focus of Union integration is also being challenged by the collaborative links the Union is developing with European countries outside its borders. These links, embracing relationships and activities in diverse fields (including trade, energy, the environment, transport, research and education) are examples of an emerging trend towards the 'pan-Europeanisation' of European integration.

- **Its development has been very uneven.** Far from being a smooth, linear process, the Union's growth has been by fits and starts (with periods of relatively rapid development and of inertia). The range and depth of the Union's policy responsibilities are also very uneven. The strength of the 'integration impulse', as a key factor in the development of the Union, should not, however, be underestimated.

- **It has been an elite project.** Levels of citizen participation in the European Union project have generally been very low. The problem of the Union's 'democratic deficit' surfaces in various forms throughout this book.

- **It involves the intertwining of political and economic objectives.** Although for much of its history, the European Union has been widely interpreted as being primarily an economic formation, its development has been inspired by a combination of political and economic objectives. For example, the political dimension of projects such as the Single European Market Programme and Economic and Monetary Union (EMU) should not be underestimated.

- **It is a product of many influences.** The lack of clarity, coherence or tidiness which have frequently been observed in relation to the Union's goals and institutional structure is due in no small measure to the multiple influences shaping the Union's development. It is therefore probably futile to search for the 'essence' or 'true nature' of the Union.

- **Its central concepts are 'fuzzy'.** Many of the ideas which are regarded as central to an understanding of the Union (such as 'integration', 'federalism', 'subsidiarity' and indeed the term 'Union' itself) are interpreted in many different ways. Indeed, the development of the Union has owed much to the tolerance of ambiguity concerning the interpretation of the Union's goal of an 'ever closer union'.

- **It involves the tension between 'intergovernmentalist' and 'supranational' influences** – that is between the conception of the Union as essentially a 'club of sovereign states' and as a project involving the surrender of state sovereignty to non-state institutions. This tension has crucially influenced the Union's institutional framework and operational characteristics.

- **It is the world's most advanced project in regional integration.** Although many other attempts have been made to forge regional economic and political formations, both within and outside Europe, most have either stalled or failed and none has achieved the degree of integration attained by the Union. Arguably, this degree of success is due to a combination of historical, political and economic circumstances peculiar to post-war Western Europe.

'European Community' or 'European Union'?

Any study of European integration must deal with the problem of nomenclature. Following the entry into force of the Treaty on European Union (the 'TEU' or 'Maastricht Treaty') on 1 November 1993, the term 'European Union' has gained wide currency as a description of what was formerly referred to as the 'European Community'. However, although the Treaty brought into being the 'European Union', it neither abolished the 'European Community' nor explicitly sanctioned the general substitution of the term 'Union' for 'Community'. Nor does the European Union have a legal personality. The subsequent confusion surrounding correct usages is a consequence of various compromises and fudges made at the European Council meeting in Maastricht (at which the TEU was agreed) in December 1991.

The nomenclature problem is by no means due solely to the TEU. Until 1967 (when the 1965 Merger Treaty came into force), there were three separate 'Communities': the European Economic Community (EEC), the European Coal and Steel Community (ECSC) and the European Atomic Energy Community (Euratom). As a result of this merger, these Communities together officially became the 'European Communities'. However, the term 'European Community' has been widely used as a general description of the three Communities for many years, even though they retain their separate identities. The TEU (Article G) formally changed the name of the 'European Economic Community' to 'European Community', the 'EEC Treaty' thereby becoming the 'EC Treaty'. Despite this change, 'European Community' is still used as a general description of the three Communities.

The European Union established by the TEU has a 'temple' structure, comprising three co-existing pillars: firstly, the European Communities pillar, comprising the European Community (formerly known as the European Economic Community), the ECSC and Euratom; secondly, the Common Foreign and Security Policy (CFSP) pillar; and thirdly, the Co-operation in the Fields of Justice and Home Affairs (JHA) pillar.

The second and third pillars involve forms of *intergovernmental co-operation*, due to the unwillingness of most member states to place these core areas of policy within the decisionmaking framework of the European Community. However, the pillars are not entirely separate: decisions on matters within the ambit of the second and third pillars are made by the

Council of the European Union (formerly known, and still widely referred to, as the 'Council of Ministers'), the key decision-taking body within the Community. Moreover, the Commission is 'fully associated' with the work of the Council in relation to CFSP and JHA, even though its implementation role in relation to Community policy does not extend to areas covered by these pillars. The 'roof' of the temple consists of common provisions setting out the Union's broad objectives. The temple's 'plinth' consists of final provisions outlining relationships with existing EC treaties, arrangements for ratification and other matters. In the Treaty, the aims and structure of the Union are set out in various Titles, as shown in Figure 1 below.

Figure 1 The Three Pillars of the European Union

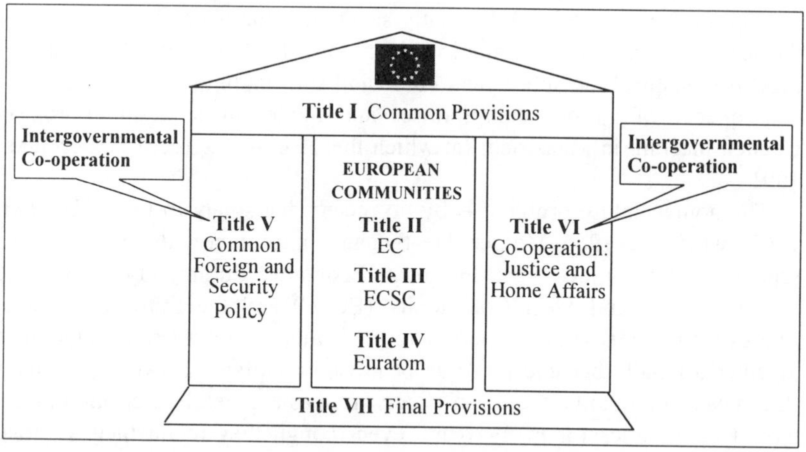

Strictly speaking, when matters relating solely to the European Community are being discussed, the term European Community should still be used. Again strictly speaking, the term 'Union' should be used when referring to all three pillars collectively, or to matters specific to the two 'intergovernmental' pillars. This distinction was confirmed by the UK government in a reply to a parliamentary question put by the leading 'Eurosceptic' MP Bill Cash in December 1993. However, soon after the Treaty came into force, the Council of Ministers took a decision to formally describe itself as the 'Council of the European Union', even when it is discussing European Community affairs, although this nomenclature is not yet widely used. In November 1993, the Secretary-General of the Commission issued a note to all Directors-General and Heads of Service of the Commission stating that the full description of the Commission remains 'Commission of the European Communities', which must be used for legal acts decided by the Commission, although the term 'European Commission' could be used in non-legal documents. It also stated that delegations of the Commission in third countries should continue to be described as delegations of the 'Commission of the European Communities'. However, to underline the Commission's association with the CFSP pillar, the headed notepaper of these delegations would also have the indent: 'European Union Delegation of the European Commission'.

Some opponents of deeper European integration still view the term Union with suspicion, because of its 'federalist' overtones (for similar reasons, they have tended to favour the term 'European Economic Community' over 'European Community'). However, the Union title has already displaced the term European Community in many sections of the European media. Moreover, the term Union is also used extensively in Commission publications. In recognition of this powerful incoming tide, and for reasons of consistency, the term Union is used in this study for current and general references to what was formerly referred to as the Community, even though some of these usages may be technically incorrect. However, although the terms 'Union law' and 'Union budget' are gaining currency, the Commission continues to use the technically correct terms of 'Community law' and 'Community budget'. This pattern of usage is also adopted in this study.

The term Community will be used to describe specific events relating to the three Communities after the 1967 merger until 1 November 1993. In references to specific events prior to the merger, the Communities will be referred to by their separate names. Although both the EEC and Euratom Treaties were signed in Rome in 1957, this study follows conventional usage in referring to the EEC Treaty as the Treaty of Rome.

Section 1

Perspectives on the Union's Development

 **Chapter 1**

The Origins and Development of the European Union

● POST-WAR 'NEW THINKING' ON EUROPEAN CO-OPERATION

○ 'Never Again'

In May 1995, the commemorative ceremonies marking the 50th anniversary of the end of the Second World War in Europe provided moving insights into the origins of the European Union. The 'never again' mood which inspired the ceremonies had also inspired the founders of the Union at the end of the war. The war had once again demonstrated Europe's inability to resolve its disputes peacefully. It had devastated Western Europe's industries and infrastructure. It left Western Europe fearful of Soviet aggression and economically and militarily dependent upon the United States. Although the human and physical destruction wrought by the war was even greater in Eastern Europe, enforced communisation of the Soviet-occupied countries effectively ended any meaningful debate concerning post-war reconstruction in this region. Western Europe, however, was fermenting with radical ideas for reconstruction. By destroying and discrediting the pre-war political and economic order, the war created a fertile climate for fresh approaches to the problem of conflict between West European countries.

The idea which perhaps received the most widespread acceptance in continental Western Europe was that European countries would need to engage in new forms of co-operation in order to achieve their goals of reconstruction. Although each country had its own special motives for seeking co-operation, some reasons were common to all, such as fear of another war in Europe, fear of Soviet aggression and fear of economic collapse. The United States gave both verbal and practical encouragement to European co-operation, notably by insisting that US economic aid for European reconstruction (Marshall Aid) be administered on a Europe-wide basis. The war therefore inspired *new thinking* on approaches to European co-operation. Some variants of this new thinking went beyond ideas for co-operation between the governments of sovereign states and embraced 'supranational' notions for transferring elements of state sovereignty to new European institutions.

○ Rebuilding the Western European States System

In relation to the reform of the West European states system at the end of the war, there were wide differences of view concerning the form 'European co-operation' should take. A rough distinction might be made between *system transformers* and *system menders* (although these labels were not used at the time and need to be applied with caution). The transformers, inspired by supranationalist ideas (of which federalism and functionalism are major forms), regarded the states system as dangerous, out-moded and doomed: for them, the war was no accident, but was a direct consequence of the division of Europe into nation-states. The transformers therefore sought to replace, or at the very least fundamentally modify, the system of independent sovereign states (federalist transformers favoured a frontal assault on the state through the creation of a European government and parliament, whereas functionalist transformers favoured the gradualist strategy of transferring some state functions to supranational authorities). The menders wanted to make the states system work better, through mechanisms of intergovernmental co-operation.

As will be seen, in the buzzing, booming confusion of the real world, the distinction between system menders and system transformers is by no means easy to apply, not least because the participants in European co-operation processes have often been unclear about their ultimate aims. Menders, as well as transformers have used the term European integration in preference to the less radical term European co-operation. Moreover, menders have frequently larded their speeches with the language of transformation (in current terminology, 'Euro-rhetoric'). Similarly, the pursuit of national interest by European governments has often been cloaked in the language of 'Euro-federalism'. Nevertheless, the transformer/mender distinction may still be useful as a means of identifying the main approaches to the reshaping of post-war Western Europe.

It was the system menders who were to have the biggest influence on the shape and character of the new order in early post-war Western Europe, not least because the mending approach found greater favour with West European governments. The inadequacy of the nation-state system was recognised by many menders, but their preferred solution was to seek to make the system less inadequate rather than replace it. Far from leading to the demise of the sovereign state, both world wars led to the creation of more states and to the creation of international institutions designed to bolster rather than undermine the states system. The West European institutions created in the late 1940s – for example, the Organisation for European Economic Co-operation (or OEEC, the body established to administer Marshall Aid) and the Council of Europe were intergovernmental organisations. The North Atlantic Treaty Organisation (NATO), the Euro-Atlantic security alliance, was also founded on 'intergovernmentalist' principles.

The institutional foundations of the European Union were laid in the 1950s, with the creation of the European Coal and Steel Community (ECSC), the European Economic Community (EEC) and Euratom. Although each of these organisations has some supranational features, in their aims and structure they also reflect the powerful influence of intergovernmentalism. Milward, a contemporary economic historian, has argued that the new institutional architecture of post-war Western Europe was largely created to make the states system work better, not as part of a grand design for a federal Europe. In his view, intergovernmental co-operation rescued the European nation-state, by providing a means by which it could perform its security and welfare functions (Milward, 1992). However, the price of this rescue has been an erosion of the ability of states to make independent decisions, because they have been drawn into an expanding and tightening web of co-operation. Moreover, although transformers by no means fully achieved their goals in the early post-war years, their ideas constituted a resilient intellectual current, powerful enough to survive setbacks and to exert a distinctive influence upon the development of the Union.

● CONTENDING APPROACHES TO EUROPEAN UNITY

○ Precursory Ideas

Although, as a geographical concept, the term Europe can be traced back to the writings of the Greek historian Herodotus in the 5th century BC, Europe as a cultural concept – that is as a distinct civilisation, with a history – began to emerge clearly only in the 18th century (den Boer, 1995). By scraping the barrel of history, some nascent ideas for a 'united Europe' can be discerned for example, in the writings of Maximilien Sully (1559–1641), Emmanuel Kant (1724–1804), William Penn (1644–1718), Jeremy Bentham (1748–1841), Jean Jacques Rousseau (1712–68) and Comte Saint-Simon (1760–1825). However, these writers espoused widely different conceptions of European unity: for example, for Sully it meant a union of European sovereigns, for Kant a unity of states and for Saint-Simon a unity of peoples. This confusion about what is meant by a united Europe is as relevant today.

As a powerful political force, the idea of a united Europe emerged only in the 20th century, as a byproduct of the two world wars. In the late 19th century, this idea gained support amongst some European intellectuals, but was hardly part of mainstream political thinking in any European state: other political ideas, for example nationalism and socialism, had far greater popular appeal. The danger of the international anarchy of the states system had been exposed by the horrors of the Great War (1914–18), which provided the stimulus for radical, if often unrealistic, thinking on the recurring problem of European conflict. A Pan-European Union was launched in 1923 by an Austrian count, Richard Coudenhove-Kalergi, but, despite holding a pan-European congress in 1926 and opening branches in most European countries, it never achieved more than fringe group status.

More promisingly for pan-Europeanists, a proposal for a Federal Union of European States was put before the League of Nations by the French Foreign Minister Aristide Briand in 1929. Briand was inspired by the aim of closer co-operation between France and Germany. Although this proposal was made by the representative of a major European government, it was rather vague on detail and in prevailing political conditions stood little chance of adoption (it was referred to a League committee and shelved). In this period, the ideologies of nationalism, and in some countries fascism, were far more potent than pan-Europeanism. Although Fascist movements espoused pan-European ideas, these were based on ideas of dominance and national antagonism. The Versailles Treaty signed in the aftermath of the Great War had reaffirmed the principle of sovereignty and led to the creation of many new states. The League of Nations, established to maintain international peace through collective security was a club of states not a supranational body. Although European powers played the dominant role in the League, it was designed as a global, not a European, organisation.

○ European Federalism and its Alternatives

In the 1930s, neither collective security nor resort to traditional balance of power alliance systems prevented remilitarisation and the slide to another war in Europe. The Second World War gave a boost to federalist ideas in Western Europe, by creating bonds between opponents of fascism, by discrediting aggressive nationalism and by increasing the receptiveness of European elites to new ideas. Federalist groups were active during the Second World War in resistance movements in various occupied countries in Europe. In 1941, Altiero Spinelli and Ernesto Rossi, who were political prisoners confined by Benito Mussolini on Ventotene island in Italy, issued a federalist programme known as the Ventotene Manifesto. In 1944, the European representatives of resistance movements issued a declaration calling for a 'federal union of the European peoples' after the war. The federalist vogue in continental Europe at the end of the war led to the formation of a European Union of Federalists in December 1946. For over four decades after the war Spinelli was a tireless, if often frustrated, champion of federalist ideas.

To what extent were these ideas shared by those in government in this period? Various schemes for Anglo-French union were mooted in the early war years. Jean Monnet, often referred to as the founding father of the European Union, was a French civil servant and businessman who spent the war years in London and the United States. He served as an economic planner in the US during the Second World War and made many contacts with influential US policymakers. In 1940, he drafted a plan for a Franco-British Union, which would have included a common parliament and a common citizenship. The plan was supported by the British Cabinet under Winston Churchill, although for Churchill, this was probably meant as a morale booster rather than a serious proposal. Ideas for federal union gained support amongst governments in exile in London: a plan for close economic links between Belgium, the Netherlands and Luxembourg (Benelux) was agreed in 1943, leading to the Benelux customs union agreement of September 1944.

Support for European federalism again appeared to come from Winston Churchill in September 1946, when he made a speech in Zurich advocating 'a kind of United States of Europe'. However, he was referring to co-operation between states in continental Europe (with the British role limited to that of benevolent sponsor), as a means of reconciling France and Germany. In Churchill's view, Britain's future lay in strong links with the United States and the Empire. In the immediate post-war years, Britain was in a better position than her continental neighbours, both economically and politically: it was the only West European state with representation at the Yalta and Potsdam conferences. It had survived the war with its institutions intact. It had a substantially higher GDP per capita than the continental average. The bulk of its exports went outside Europe. Britain saw itself as a world power, with world responsibilities. From the early 19th century,

Britain had a foreign policy tradition of splendid isolation from continental entanglements (due largely to preoccupation with its Empire). In relation to Europe, it saw its role as a balancer, preventing any one European power from becoming too powerful but avoiding long-standing commitments. The British also had a dislike of grandiose schemes, and preferred pragmatic solutions to practical problems. Prime Ministers Clement Attlee and Winston Churchill, and their foreign ministers Ernest Bevin and Anthony Eden, were all opposed to British participation in European integration projects.

In May 1948, a committee of European federalists (the International Committee of the Movements for European Unity) organised a Congress in The Hague, with the aim of forging a united Europe. The Congress was attended by 750 delegates from 16 countries, including many prominent statesmen and politicians, such as Winston Churchill, Anthony Eden and Harold Macmillan. The sheer diversity of the membership of the Congress (as well as staunch federalists, it also included staunch anti-federalists, such as Churchill and Eden) ensured that there could be no agreed model of a united Europe. The Congress was to prove a great disappointment to the federalists. It did not lead to the creation of a European parliament with strong powers, as they had wanted. Instead, negotiations between European governments after the Congress resulted in the creation of a very weak body, the Council of Europe, in May 1949. The Council's institutional structure comprised a Consultative Assembly of MPs, appointed by national parliaments and with no legislative powers, plus a Committee of Ministers of member states. The UK government adamantly opposed any scheme which would erode national sovereignty, and insisted that the Consultative Assembly be subordinate to the Committee of Ministers. The Council, based in Strasbourg, has subsequently achieved prominence through its Court of Human Rights, but otherwise has remained a rather obscure body. Like most regional and global international organisations created in this period the Council is essentially a form of *intergovernmental co-operation.*

The most significant move towards supranationalism in relation to European co-operation in this period did not come from the 'big bang' approach to the redesign of Europe favoured by the federalists, which required a frontal assault on sovereignty. The outcome of the 1948 Congress showed clearly that the governments of Europe were unwilling to surrender sovereignty to a supranational parliament. The federalist approach was undermined by two elementary political realities: governmental power and the loyalties of citizens to their own nation-states. An alternative approach, developed by Monnet and manifested in the European Coal and Steel Community in 1952, aimed to create a united Europe in a piecemeal, *ad hoc*, way by encouraging technical co-operation between European countries in specific functional areas (known as the *functionalist* or *sectoral integration* approach). This was expected to lead to a gradual erosion of sovereignty and to a gradual shift of loyalties from the national to the European level.

In Eastern Europe, various schemes for regional federations (for example, for a Balkan Union or a Trans-Danubian Federation) were advanced in the early post-war years by Yugoslavia, Bulgaria and other communist regimes. However, these did not receive Joseph Stalin's imprimatur and by January 1948 all federal and confederal plans were being denounced by the Soviets. Stalin's divide and rule policy discouraged collaboration between communist countries, thereby creating a set of 'mini Iron Curtains' within the Soviet bloc. A Soviet inspired and dominated form of *socialist economic integration* was nevertheless created. The Council for Mutual Economic Assistance (CMEA), better known as 'Comecon', was formally established in 1949, to promote economic collaboration between communist countries. It remained largely a paper organisation until the late 1950s, when it was revived by Nikita Khrushchev as a means of strengthening the cohesion of the Soviet bloc. A central objective of the CMEA was the promotion of interstate trade, nominally based on the principle of the socialist international division of labour. From the outset, it was described in communist propaganda as a superior alternative to the EEC, which was demonised as an exploitative capitalist organisation. Four sets of ideas for European unity in the post-war period can therefore be identified (see Table 1.1).

Table 1.1 Approaches to European Unity

The Intergovernmental Co-operation Approach, involving economic and political co-operation between sovereign governments (the degree to which 'intergovernmentalism' constitutes a threat to sovereignty depends upon the extent to which states can opt out of collective decisions).
The Federalist Approach, involving the creation of powerful institutions (an executive, a parliament and a court) above the level of the nation-state. A substantial degree of state sovereignty would be transferred to these supranational institutions.
The Functionalist (Sectoral Integration) Approach, involving the transfer of elements of sovereignty to supranational institutions in specific fields of policy (for example, coal and steel).
Socialist Integration, involving economic collaboration between communist states, based on the principle of the 'socialist international division of labour'.

It will be useful at this point to consider the relevance of these ideas to the three rival economic formations which were to emerge in post-war Europe: the European Community (the main pillar of the European Union); the

European Free Trade Association (EFTA); and Comecon. The Community's development has been influenced (by no means in equal measure) by intergovernmentalist, federalist and functionalist ideas. EFTA was founded in Stockholm in November 1959 as a free trade club firmly based on intergovernmentalist principles and with no supranational aspirations. Its seven members (Austria, Britain, Denmark, Norway, Portugal, Sweden and Switzerland) favoured free trade in industrial goods but not the model of integration pursued by the Community. Despite the exaggerated claims made on behalf of Comecon in communist propaganda, following its revival in the late 1950s it operated on the basis of intergovernmentalism. The Soviet Union was much bigger in size than the other member states, which tended to be suspicious of Moscow's motives in promoting Comecon. To assuage these fears, the Soviet Union insisted that Comecon was not a supranational organisation and posed no threat to the sovereignties of member states. In practice, the sovereignties of these countries were already limited by Soviet political and military dominance. Comecon, wound up in 1991, never had major institutions like the Commission, the European Parliament or the European Court of Justice. Nor did it have a convertible currency and therefore most goods were traded through barter arrangements.

● LAYING THE INSTITUTIONAL FOUNDATIONS

○ The European Coal and Steel Community (ECSC)

Although the primary impetus for European integration was the need to prevent conflict between the European states, from the outset it also had a strong economic rationale. Jean Monnet, who had been appointed by General Charles de Gaulle in 1946 to mastermind France's economic recovery, was the principal architect of the plan for a European Coal and Steel Community. Monnet's ultimate aims in pursuing European co-operation remain a subject of controversy, not least because he was a pragmatist who emphasised that Europe could not be built all at once. He strongly favoured Franco-German co-operation and European links with the US. He favoured projects which went beyond 'mere co-operation' between governments and embraced the idea of a 'fusion of interests' of the European peoples as a long-term goal. But he admitted that he did not know what kind of Europe would emerge. Although he favoured the establishment of a 'United States of Europe' he took no part in the federalist movement of 1945–48, being more at home in the corridors of power than at federalist rallies.

The idea of the Monnet plan was to establish a system of joint regulation of the coal and steel industries of participating states. Cross-border trade barriers would be abolished and the industries would be regulated by a 'supranational' authority. The plan offered practical economic benefits for the participants, by providing coal and steel producers with a larger market for their goods. The initial idea was to link the French and German coal and steel industries, but the Benelux countries and Italy also expressed a desire to participate. The ECSC plan was approved and presented by Robert Schuman, the French foreign minister, in an announcement subsequently known as the Schuman Declaration. Schuman came from the province of Lorraine, which for centuries had been the subject of a territorial dispute between France and Germany. He was strongly committed to Franco-German co-operation. In the early post-war years, the aim of France had been to contain Germany rather than to co-operate with it. However, for various reasons (not least US influence) French policy soon shifted to one of seeking co-operation with its dangerous neighbour. The plan was enthusiastically supported by West Germany's Chancellor Konrad Adenauer and received the backing of the US. From the outset, there was explicit acknowledgement of the political objectives of the ECSC plan. The Schuman Declaration sought to make the possibility of war between the participants unthinkable and impossible, by creating a *de facto solidarity* between them. It was a functionalist experiment, but its stated objectives reflected federalist aspirations as a long-term goal. Thus the plan was described in the Declaration as a first step towards 'a European federation indispensable to the preservation of peace'.

The plan was designed to serve both national and wider European interests. The six original members had their own objectives in pursuing co-operation: for example, without it France feared that its steel industry would not be able to compete with its German counterpart. It reduced the likelihood of German *revanchism* and provided France with an opportunity to play a leading role in European developments. For West Germany, it offered the prospect of gaining full acceptance by the international community. It also offered the German coal and steel industries bigger markets. It gave the Benelux countries a leverage on policy developments which they might otherwise not have had. Some other European countries were primarily agricultural and therefore the ECSC held little interest for them. Some West European countries, including Britain, favoured measures to promote co-operation between states, but opposed 'supranationalist' schemes such as the ECSC and therefore declined to participate. In any case, Britain expected the ECSC to fail.

The ECSC was established by the Treaty of Paris (April 1951) for 50 years. It came into existence in 1952, with Monnet as the first President. The Treaty eliminated trade barriers (duties, quotas and dual pricing) on coal, steel and iron ore. It created a supranational authority (the High Authority). It also had a Council of Ministers, a European Assembly, a Court of Justice and a consultative committee comprising producer, worker and other interests. The High Authority, deriving from French administrative ideas, was an appointed, technocratic executive, with the power to prohibit subsidies and to impose fines. Monnet was adamant that the High Authority should be independent of governments, in other words that it was supranational. But the fact that the ECSC also had a Council of Ministers showed that governments were not willing to surrender full sovereignty over these functions to a supranational authority. The Assembly was not to be directly elected (delegates were designated by national parliaments) and was given only very weak powers. Indeed, the Assembly was added almost as an afterthought.

The establishment of the ECSC demonstrated the feasibility of functional integration, that is the integration of specific sectors of policy previously controlled by national governments. In its early years it was widely regarded as a great success, although national interests later blocked the emergence of fully integrated coal and steel industries. According to Monnet, the ECSC proposals were revolutionary and constituted 'the abnegation of sovereignty in a limited but decisive field'. He saw it as the forerunner of a broader united Europe, because what had been done in the case of coal and steel could be applied to other sectors. The ECSC's structure served as the prototype for the institutional structure of the European Economic Community established five years later (except that the EEC's Commission was given less power than the High Authority and its Council of Ministers more power than that of its ECSC counterpart). In both cases, however, parliamentary control was very weak. It has been argued that the EU's 'democratic deficit' has its roots in the technocratic model of integration first manifested in the ECSC (Featherstone, 1994).

O European Defence Co-operation

The issue of defence was the cause of considerable disagreement between West European governments in the early post-war years. Four contentious security questions required urgent answers: firstly should West Germany be allowed to rearm (and if so under what conditions); secondly, how could Western Europe be effectively defended against a possible Soviet attack; thirdly, what was to be the role of the US in the defence of Western Europe; and fourthly, what was to be the *form* of defence co-operation between European countries? Would co-operation take the form of a conventional alliance system, or would it involve a pooling of defence resources?

The Brussels Treaty signed in 1948 by the UK, France and Benelux, was a conventional alliance and was directed against the prospect of a resurgent Germany. But the most immediate threat to European security came from the

Soviet Union. West Europeans were clearly not capable of defending themselves against a Soviet attack without US support. The Soviet threat led to the creation of NATO, a transatlantic rather than a purely European alliance. Neither the Brussels Treaty nor the NATO Treaty involved a loss of control of member countries' armed forces to a supranational organisation. But some West Europeans were still thinking about how Western Europe could organise its own defence: moreover, some of their ideas went beyond proposals for a conventional alliance, to embrace the prospect of the pooling of military resources. In October 1950, the French Premier Pleven put forward a plan for the creation of a 'European Defence Community', on similar lines to the ECSC. The EDC would have been directed by a European Political Community, embracing a Council of Ministers and a directly elected parliament. A key aim of the plan was to lock Germany into a European defence system in order to limit its capacity for independent action.

Table 1.2 Timeline 1: 1946–54

1946	**September:** Winston Churchill's speech in Zurich advocating a kind of United States of Europe'.
1947	**March:** Belgium, the Netherlands and Luxembourg agree to set up a customs union.
	June: Marshall Plan proposed.
	October: creation of Benelux economic union.
1948	**March:** Brussels Treaty signed by UK, France and Benelux.
	April: Organisation for European Economic Co-operation created, to effectuate the Marshall Plan.
	May: Congress of Europe held in the Hague.
1949	**Spring:** Berlin blockade by Soviet forces.
	April: NATO created.
	May: Council of Europe created , with 10 members.
1950	**May:** Schuman Declaration, proposing that French and German coal and steel be placed under a common Authority.
	October: Pleven Plan for a European Defence Community (EDC).
1951	**April:** Treaty of Paris, establishing the European Coal and Steel Community (ECSC) signed by six states.
1952	**May:** European Defence Community Treaty signed by the six ECSC states.
	July: ECSC High Authority begins work.
1954	**August:** EDC Treaty rejected by the French Parliament.
	October: the Western European Union formed.
	December: UK and ECSC sign an association agreement.

A draft EDC treaty was drawn up by Monnet and by the same team which had drafted the Schuman plan. The plan was signed by the six members of the ECSC in May 1952. It was ratified by four national parliaments, but was rejected by the French parliament in August 1954. France was not ready to relinquish control over its armed forces. Britain had no intention of subordinating its forces in a European army and would have no truck with the Pleven plan. Eden, the British foreign secretary, put forward a counter-proposal for the creation of a conventional alliance, to be known as the Western European Union. The WEU was created in 1954: it was simply an expanded version of the Brussels Treaty and was an indirect way of allowing West Germany into the NATO alliance. It also provided legitimation for German rearmament. The WEU was given its own Parliamentary Assembly and Council, but was clearly based on intergovernmental co-operation, not supranationalism. However, NATO was a far more credible defence organisation than the WEU. Western Europe was not (and perhaps still is not) ready for integration in the field of defence.

O Relaunching the European Unity Idea

Following the failure of the EDC, Monnet and others were seeking ways to maintain the impetus of integration by applying the ECSC model to other sectors, such as atomic energy and transport. Monnet favoured atomic energy as the next sector to be pooled, along the lines of the ECSC. In February 1955, Monnet left the presidency of the ECSC High Authority to become head of the Action Committee for a United States of Europe (ACUSE), a small supranationalist pressure group. The governments of the six members of the ECSC were interested in further economic co-operation, particularly in the area of trade. For example, the Benelux countries had created their own customs union and wished to extend it.

In June 1955, the foreign ministers of the six states of the ECSC met in Messina in Sicily to discuss proposals for a customs union. The chairman was Paul-Henri Spaak, the foreign minister of Belgium. The British sent an official from the Board of Trade rather than a minister to the talks: when discussion at the talks went beyond the idea of co-operation between governments, the official was withdrawn. The British foreign minister, Sir Anthony Eden, made many anti-federalist pronouncements and showed no interest in involving Britain in either the ECSC or in a European customs union. Britain preferred co-operation to take place within the OEEC and within the Council of Europe. The British put forward an alternative scheme for a free trade area as a way of killing off the customs union idea, but without success. Spaak's report on the Messina conference, presented at a foreign ministers' meeting in Venice in May 1956, proposed the creation of a common market and an Atomic Energy Community. This led to the signing of the European Economic Community and European Atomic Energy Community (Euratom) Treaties in Rome in March 1957.

The EEC Treaty (commonly referred to as the Treaty of Rome) was not solely about economics: for example, its preamble contained a reference to a determination 'to lay the foundations of an ever closer union among the peoples of Europe'. The Treaty's main thrust, however, was towards the pursuit of concrete economic objectives: that is, the creation of a common market, a customs union and of various Community policies. Its provisions on economic policy reflected a dual influence of free trade principles and of a belief that economic problems could not be solved by market forces alone. The latter influence was manifested for example in the creation of the European Social Fund (ESF), the European Investment Bank (EIB) and the Common Agricultural Policy (CAP). France insisted that agriculture be included as an integral part of the Treaty, as a means of providing a bigger market for its agricultural exports. The Euratom Treaty sought to promote collaboration between member states and a common market in the nuclear energy sector. Member states were unwilling to relinquish control of their nuclear industries and therefore the Treaty contains various get-out clauses.

Table 1.3 The Main Objectives of the EEC Treaty

- a common market and progressive approximation of economic policies of member states;
- promotion of harmonious economic development and higher living standards;
- closer relations between member states;
- removal of all tariffs and quantitative restrictions on imports and exports between member states;
- a common external tariff and a common commercial policy towards third countries;
- free movement of goods, services, capital and labour;
- common policies for agriculture and transport;
- a European Social Fund;
- a European Investment Bank to finance investment projects in the signatory states.

The institutional structures of the EEC and Euratom were both modelled on that of the ECSC: the EEC and Euratom were given four main institutions: a Commission (equivalent to the ECSC High Authority); a Council of Ministers; an Assembly; and a Court of Justice. The main difference was that the EEC and Euratom Treaties were more intergovernmental than the ECSC

Treaty in that in each case the Council of Ministers had more power and the Commission somewhat less than its ECSC counterpart. The Assembly and Court were common to all three institutions. The Assembly was to be eventually directly elected, but governments were reluctant to invest it with too much power. The 1965 Merger Treaty (in force in 1967) created a single Council and Commission for all three Communities.

In the 1950s and 1960s, West European integration rode on the back of a post-war economic boom. Between 1945 and 1968, Western Europe enjoyed high productivity and low unemployment. Post-war recovery in Western Europe was rapid, due to factors such as high investment rates, US capital and low labour costs. After 1958, there was a big leap in intra-Community trade. EEC timetables for the removal of cross-border tariffs and for the setting of a common external tariff were completed before schedule.

○ **Forms of Economic Integration**

Britain was by no means the only West European country reluctant to commit itself to a customs union. Several favoured the formation of a free trade area, based on a *customs association*, a looser form of organisation which requires neither a common external tariff nor a common external trade policy. Following the signing of the Stockholm Convention in July 1959, a customs association known as the European Free Trade Association (EFTA) was formed between Britain, Denmark, Norway, Sweden, Austria, Switzerland and Portugal, aimed at achieving free trade in industrial goods by 1970. It was conceived as an alternative to the model of economic integration espoused in the Treaty of Rome. The scale below (sometimes viewed as an economic integration continuum) moves from loose to tight economic relationships between states. It should be noted, however, that in the real world these categories have fuzzy boundaries and that it is also possible for participating countries to jump stages.

• **A Customs Association:** barriers to trade, such as customs duties and quotas, between members are removed, but members retain the right to determine their own trade restrictions in relation to non-members. A potential flaw in the customs association idea stems from the freedom it allows members to have different trade policies in relation to non-members. If, for example, member A imposes a 10% tariff on agricultural goods entering its borders from outside the free trade area, whereas member B has only a 5% tariff on the same goods, then there would be a clear incentive for people in country B to import goods for export to country A. To overcome this problem, common rules need to be formulated and enforced.

• **A Customs Union** involves the removal of customs duties and quotas between members, and the introduction of a common external tariff in

relation to non-members. It involves a tighter relationship between members than a customs association, because members lose their individual ability to set their own external tariffs.
• **A Common Market** involves the removal of all impediments to the mobility of factors of production across the borders of member states. Since it is likely to develop from a customs union, it focuses on the removal of non-tariff barriers to trade. An example is the Single European Market, designed to achieve free movement of goods, services, people and capital across the borders of member states. It requires more extensive inter-governmental collaboration than a Customs Union.
• **Economic and Monetary Union (EMU):** its most tangible feature is the harmonisation of monetary and fiscal policies and the replacement of the currencies of the member states by a common currency or by fixed exchange rates (see Chapter 10).
• **Full Economic Union (FEU):** it would involve the merging of large elements of the national economic policies of participating countries into a single economic policy. Some analysts, in particular those opposed to 'deeper' European integration, argue that the implications of EMU are likely to be so profound that EMU and FEU would virtually amount to the same thing. Others, however, argue that EMU would still leave national governments in control of some major economic policies.

○ From Rapid Development to Inertia

After the rapid progress of the 1950s and early 1960s, the Community entered a relatively fallow period. There was a long lull in integration activity which lasted for well over two decades. Many aims of the Treaty of Rome (for example, for a full common market and a common transport policy) existed only on paper. A change in political leadership in France weakened the prospects for rapid integration. Schuman was replaced as French foreign minister by the 'non-federalist' Georges Bidault. De Gaulle, who became president in 1958, was opposed to European federalism and favoured a 'Europe of States', not a 'United States of Europe' or a Europe of 'myths, fictions and pageants'. But although he disliked the supranationalist aspects of the ECSC and Euratom, he was not opposed to political and economic co-operation between European states, especially if France could play a leading role. Moreover, the CAP offered substantial benefits for French agriculture.

Within the EEC, a major crisis developed in 1965, arising from attempts to increase the powers of the Commission and the Council of Ministers. The Commission wanted the EEC to have its own budget, a move strongly opposed by de Gaulle, who also opposed a proposal for majority voting in the Council of Ministers (meaning that states would have to accept the decisions of the majority). France refused to attend Council meetings in this period (the policy of the 'empty chair'). In 1966, this deadlock was ended by the Luxembourg compromise, an agreement which allowed a member state to veto a proposal if it considered it a threat to its vital national interests. The Luxembourg compromise, however, is not enshrined in any Union Treaty and has no legal force (see Chapter 4). The ECSC, Euratom and the EEC were amalgamated on 1 July 1967 to form the 'European Communities'.

Proposals to relaunch the Community had to await the end of de Gaulle's presidency. De Gaulle's abrupt departure from government in April 1969 enhanced the prospects of an agreement on key issues concerning the Community's development, not least in relation to Britain's prospects of entry. De Gaulle's successor as president, Georges Pompidou, soon announced his support for British entry. The Hague summit of December 1969 approved several major measures: the Community was to be given its own budget; the European Parliament's powers were to be increased; foreign ministers were to examine the prospects for economic and monetary union; and negotiations for the entry of new members were to begin. But apart from the decision on enlargement, the summit produced few immediate results.

● BRITAIN'S SLUGGISH AND AMBIVALENT SHIFT TOWARDS MEMBERSHIP

The events leading to Britain's applications for membership of the Community in the 1960s is a story of diminishing options. In the 1950s, it put its faith in the special relationship with the US and in the emerging British Commonwealth. Only when British illusions about these relationships had been shattered did the British seek closer links with the Community. By the early 1960s, the idea of membership had become more attractive to the UK, for several reasons: the Suez crisis dented British faith in the 'special relationship' with the US. The Commonwealth link was not proving as valuable to the UK as its proponents hoped. Trade with EFTA was unbalanced, because whereas the UK had a large market, the other EFTA countries had only small markets to offer UK exporters. Britain's economic performance in the late 1950s was poor in comparison with that of 'the Six'. From the late 1950s, GNP per capita of the Six was substantially higher than the corresponding figure for Britain.

The UK first applied for entry in 1961. It sought special deals to protect its agriculture and its partners in EFTA and the Commonwealth. However, at this time de Gaulle was sceptical of the UK's motives. He vetoed Britain's application in 1963 and again in 1967, on the grounds that Britain was not sufficiently European in outlook (meaning that it was too close to the US and to the Commonwealth) and would, if admitted, be a Trojan horse for the US. Both the Labour and Conservative Parties were divided on the issue, which meant that they were reluctant to dwell on it at election times. For much of the post-war period, the official Labour Party position on European integration veered between hostility and ambivalence. Although a Labour government under Harold Wilson sought entry into the Community in the late 1960s, a powerful group within the Labour Party continued to oppose membership. A Conservative government, returned to office in 1970, negotiated Britain's entry. Following tortuous negotiations, a treaty of accession for membership of the UK, Denmark, Norway and Ireland was signed in Brussels in 1972. After a referendum, Norway opted not to join.

Although various transitional arrangements were agreed (for example the UK got a five-year transition to the CAP) the 1973 entrants were forced to accept the Community as it was, including its budgetary and agriculture policies, neither of which were advantageous to the UK. The Heath government which negotiated Britain's entry possibly hoped that the costs of membership, such as higher food prices and high budgetary contributions, would be offset by increased trade and economic growth. Ironically, the UK entered when the Community's economic boom years had ended. Britain's budgetary contributions were high because, as a large importer, it paid substantial amounts in customs levies. Because it had a relatively small, but efficient, farm sector its contributions were not offset by receipts from the CAP (by far the largest item in the Community budget). The Labour government returned in 1974 sought to renegotiate the entry terms, and held a referendum on entry in June 1975, which resulted in a 67% vote in favour of continued UK membership. Following her victory in the 1979 General Election, Margaret Thatcher (who had replaced the pro-European Edward Heath as Leader of the Conservative Party in 1975) demanded 'Britain's money back' from the Community. Britain received a series of rebates in the early 1980s, but these by no means corrected the imbalance. In 1979 the UK net contribution was almost £1 billion. At the European Council in Fontainebleau in June 1984, Mrs Thatcher negotiated a budget rebate for the UK, but even after the deal Britain remained a substantial net contributor.

It is clear that Britain's troubled relationship with Europe cannot be solely attributed to specific and transient causes such as the 'anti-European' attitudes of particular leaders or disputes about specific issues. It does not explain the longevity of Britain's position as an 'awkward partner' (George, 1990), which has survived several changes of government, or why the European Union has had low public support in Britain, relative to other member states. More fundamental (and less easily correctable) reasons of the difficulties have been suggested. For example, Britain is geographically separate from her European partners – but then so are Ireland and Greece. In the case of these countries, however, their governments could point to tangible material benefits from membership, in the form of substantial net gains from the Community budget. Despite its loss of empire and the declining importance of the Anglo-American special relationship, Britain has continued to view itself as being more than a European power. It has a long and unbroken tradition of parliamentary sovereignty (unlike most other member states). It has an unwritten constitution and tends to dislike the continental 'treaty bound' approach to integration.

Table 1.4 Timeline 2: 1955–72

1955	**June:** Messina Conference on integration attended by the foreign ministers of the six ECSC states. Spaak Committee established to examine options for further integration.
1957	**March:** Rome Treaties signed, establishing the EEC and Euratom.
1958	**January:** Rome Treaties come into force.
1959	**November:** European Free Trade Association convention signed in Stockholm.
1961	**July:** the six EEC members issue the 'Bonn Declaration' aimed at political union.
	August: Ireland applies, and the UK and Denmark request negotiations for EEC membership.
	December: Austria, Sweden and Switzerland apply for association with EEC.
1962	**January:** framework of Common Agricultural Policy agreed.
	April: Norway requests negotiations aimed at membership of EEC.
1963	**January:** EEC negotiations on entry suspended, following opposition by de Gaulle to UK entry.
1965	**April:** treaty merging executives of the three Communities (in force 1 July 1967).
	July: French boycott of institutions begins, over disagreements on budgetary and institutional issues.
1966	**January:** the 'Luxembourg compromise' agreed, ending French boycott.
1967	**May:** UK, Ireland, Denmark and Norway reapply for membership.
1968	**July:** EEC Customs Union completed.
1970	**June:** new negotiations for accession of UK, Ireland, Denmark and Norway.
1972	**January:** signing of treaties of accession for UK, Ireland, Denmark and Norway. Norwegian referendum leads to withdrawal of Norway's application.

The negotiating style of British governments with other member governments has frequently been confrontational and couched in 'us and them' terms. Britain has also perhaps tended to overestimate its importance to other member states and on several crucial occasions has wrongly assumed that integration initiatives could not proceed without British support. Britain has also been accused by other member states of adopting spoiling tactics to impede progress towards deeper integration: for example, in the 1950s, it played a key role in setting up EFTA as a rival to the EEC; at the negotiations leading to the Treaty on European Union (Maastricht Treaty) in December 1991, it put forward its 'hard ECU' plan as an alternative to the plan for a single European currency; in the 1990s it has favoured rapid enlargement of the Union in preference to rapid deepening of integration.

It is now widely recognised that it would have been better for Britain to have participated in the development of the European Union from the start, in order to have shaped this development in a way more in keeping with British preferences. Despite the fact that Britain has been an awkward partner within the Union, it is now so firmly embedded into the Union's political and economic structures that the idea of withdrawal now appears unthinkable. For example, UK business has reoriented its external trade towards the Union, so that most UK exports now go to other member states. The British debate on Europe now centres on what kind of relationship Britain should develop with its European partners.

● THE DEVELOPMENT OF THE SINGLE EUROPEAN MARKET AND THE EUROPEAN UNION: THE 'SECOND RELAUNCH'

A host of factors in the 1970s and early 1980s inhibited the Community's development. A long economic recession, exacerbated by the oil crises of 1973–74 and 1979–80, meant that domestic economic concerns loomed larger than the issue of deeper European integration. The absorption of three new members, and the vexatious issue of Britain's budgetary contributions, also deflected attention away from this issue. The fact that each country had an effective veto on institutional reform was also a major impediment to the launch of new initiatives. This is not to say that the Community was completely 'comatose' in this period. The European Regional Development Fund (ERDF) was set up in 1975. In 1979, the European Monetary System (EMS), including the Exchange Rate Mechanism (ERM) was established (see Chapter 10) and the first direct elections to the European Parliament were held. In 1970, member states established a system of 'European political co-operation', essentially a forum for intergovernmental consultation on foreign policy issues. One of the most significant developments in relation to the institutional balance within the Community was the emergence of the European Council, comprising formal summit meetings of European leaders. These were not provided for in the Treaty of Rome, but came into existence as an offshoot of Council of Ministers' meetings. The European Council came into being in December 1974 and has continued to grow in importance.

In the 1970s and early 1980s, there were many attempts to kick-start the Community's institutional development: in 1972, the Werner plan for economic and monetary union by 1980 was agreed in principle by the member states. The Tindemans report on European Union in 1975 advocated many measures, such as direct elections to the European Parliament (EP), a 'Citizens' Europe' and extension of majority voting in the Council of Ministers, which have subsequently been adopted. A proposal for European Union was launched by the foreign ministers of Germany and Italy in 1981 (the Genscher–Colombo initiative). The European Council in Stuttgart in June 1983 agreed a 'solemn declaration' on European Union. In the early 1980s the 'Crocodile Club' and the 'Kangaroo group', both comprising members of the EP, sought to accelerate the integration process (the Crocodile Club had radical federalist objectives, whereas the Kangaroo group favoured pursuit of a 'single market' programme). The EP approved a 'draft treaty on European Union' in 1984, but had no power to achieve its aspirations.

Although a quantum leap towards European Union did not appear likely, by the mid-1980s a majority of member governments nevertheless supported further integration. The European Council in Fontainebleau in June 1984 established two committees (referred to as the Dooge and Adonnino committees, after their chairmen) to examine the possibilities for further development of the Community. James Dooge focused on institutional questions and Pietro Adonnino on the problem of the Community's democratic deficit. The Dooge committee produced a majority and a minority report which were presented to the European Council in Milan in June 1985. The majority report favoured the strengthening of EC institutions and the establishment of a single European market. The Adonnino committee developed many proposals for a Citizens' (or People's) Europe.

Most reform proposals in this period fell by the wayside because they were too radical and contentious for the time. Others, such as that of a Citizens' Europe were perhaps too fuzzy to catch on. But the idea of a single European market programme commanded a broad measure of support amongst national governments and business groups, for several reasons: it offered a practical solution to the perceived common problem of 'Eurosclerosis' (manifested in widening gaps in the Community's economic performance relative to those of Japan and the US). Even opponents of further integration, such as Mrs Thatcher, could not object to a programme designed to remove barriers to trade between member states. The election of market-oriented governments in several member states in the 1980s also increased the possibility that the Single European Market (SEM) programme would be adopted. Moreover, the aims of the Programme were hardly new, since they sought to fulfil objectives set out in the Treaty of Rome. The rapport between President François Mitterrand of France and Chancellor Helmut Kohl of West Germany provided a favourable political climate for further integration. The appointment of Jacques Delors to the presidency of the Commission in 1984 was also a significant factor, because of his dynamism and determination to achieve a great leap forward in integration.

The institutional and policy implications of the SEM programme were not widely appreciated at the time. Mrs Thatcher viewed the programme as about removing trade barriers, not as a means to deeper integration. But the logic of the programme required that national policies in many sectors be 'harmonised'. Institutional reform was also required in the interests of effective implementation. At the European Council in Milan in 1985, Mrs Thatcher agreed to an extension of majority voting in the Council of Ministers (meaning that on many key issues, members would have to accept majority decisions) and also to an extension of the powers of the European Parliament.

The SEM programme provided the momentum for further attempts at integration, against stiff opposition from Mrs Thatcher, a staunch opponent of proposals for 'ever closer union'. In a speech in Bruges in October 1988, Thatcher outlined her preferred model of the European Community (which was remarkably similar to de Gaulle's vision of a *Union des Patries*) and attacked the idea of a European 'superstate'. Her opposition to Euro-federalism, the CAP and the ERM had strong ideological roots. She opposed policies which would diminish sovereignty or which would lead to more government intervention. She was increasingly at odds with her counterparts in the Community on a wide range of issues, but especially in relation to ideas for a single European currency, for a 'Social Charter' and for a common foreign and security policy.

The European Council in Strasbourg in December 1989 set up an intergovernmental conference on economic and monetary union (EMU), despite Mrs Thatcher's objections. In June 1990, the European Council in Dublin established a parallel intergovernmental conference on political union. The results of the two IGCs, which opened at the European Council in Rome in December 1990, formed the basis of the negotiations on European political and monetary union at the European Council in Maastricht in December 1991. There was little domestic interest in the work of the IGCs.

Ordinary citizens' lack of involvement or interest in integration developments prior to Maastricht has been referred to as a *permissive consensus*. This allowed the policymaking elites (governments, parties, bureaucrats and pressure groups) to set reform agendas and to make decisions without taking too much account of citizens' reactions.

At Maastricht, John Major, who had replaced Margaret Thatcher as British Prime Minister in October 1990, negotiated 'opt-outs' for the UK on monetary union and on the social chapter (see Chapter 3). An increasingly bitter rift on Europe developed within the Conservative Party, reminiscent of the conflicts over Europe which almost tore the Labour Party apart in the 1960s and 1970s. In recent years the Labour Party has done much to shed its 'anti-Europe' image. In 1988, it abandoned its policy to take Britain out of the EC. An indication of the extent of the party's *volte face* is that its former leader Neil Kinnock, for most of his political career a staunch opponent of the EC, is now a Commissioner.

The referenda on the TEU held in Denmark, France and Ireland exposed the extent of public concern about the implications of deeper European integration. In Denmark, 50.7% voted against the Treaty. Ireland and France voted in favour by 69% and 51% respectively. The referenda provided a jolt to governments which had got used to taking decisions on Europe without considering the views of 'ordinary' Europeans. They provided evidence that the era of permissive consensus might be coming to an end. By securing opt-outs and clarification of various issues, the Danish government made the Treaty more palatable to the Danes, who approved it by a narrow majority in a second referendum. In the UK, parliamentary ratification was delayed until after the second Danish referendum. But the crises in the ERM in 1992 and 1993 (see Chapter 10) raised serious doubts about the feasibility of the Maastricht blueprint for economic and monetary union.

An important side-effect of the SEM programme was the effect it had upon EFTA countries, fearful of the effects of the programme upon their trade with the Community. They therefore sought guaranteed access to the SEM through a closer formal link between EFTA and the Community. The Community responded by offering EFTA the opportunity to participate in a 'European Economic Area', a free trade zone embracing the EC and EFTA. Although a European Economic Area (EEA) Treaty was agreed, negotiations proved so tough that four EFTA countries – Austria, Finland, Norway and Sweden – decided to go the whole hog and apply for membership of the Community (or European Union, after the entry into force of the TEU). With the exception of Norway, whose voters rejected a firm offer of EU membership for the second time, these countries acceded to the Union in January 1995. The Swiss people rejected the EEA Treaty in a referendum in December 1992.

Table 1.5 Timeline: 1973–96

1973	**January:** the UK, Denmark and Ireland join the Community.
1975	**June:** Greece applies to join.
1977	**March:** Portugal applies to join.
	July: Spain applies to join.
1979	**March:** the EMS established.
	June: first direct elections to the European Parliament.
1981	**January:** Greece joins the Community.
1984	**February:** EP approves draft treaty on European Union.
1985	**June:** Commission White Paper on the completion of the SEM.
1986	**January:** Portugal and Spain join Community.
1986	**February:** Single European Act signed.
1987	**July:** SEA comes into force.
1988	**June:** European Council instructs a committee to develop proposals for EMU.
1989	**April:** Delors committee presents report on EMU.
	Autumn: revolutions in Eastern Europe.
1990	**June:** European Council convenes intergovernmental conferences (commencing in December) on EMU and political union.
	November: German reunification.
1991	European Economic Area Treaty signed.
	December: Maastricht meeting of European Council agrees TEU.
1992	**February:** TEU signed.
	June: Danish referendum narrowly rejects TEU.
	June: Irish referendum accepts TEU.
	September: withdrawal of UK and Italy from ERM.
	September: French referendum narrowly accepts TEU.
	December: Single European Market programme 'completed'.
1993	**August:** *de facto* suspension of ERM (move to 15% bands).
	November: TEU comes into force.
1994	**February:** terms agreed for entry of Austria, Finland, Norway and Sweden.
	June: elections to the EP. Austrian referendum in favour of entry.
	October/November: Sweden and Finland vote for entry, Norway votes against.
1995	**January:** Austria, Sweden and Finland enter the Union.
	December: Madrid meeting of European Council agrees name of single European currency (the 'Euro') and affirms 1 January 1999 as the launch date for the new currency.
1996	**March:** Intergovernmental conference on reform of the Union opens in Turin.

Both externally and internally, the Union faces major challenges. The civil war in ex-Yugoslavia has damaged the Union's credibility in foreign affairs and has undermined the credibility of the Union's CFSP pillar. The Union's sluggish economic performance, when judged against those of its major global competitors, is also an issue of vital current importance. Despite the increased powers of the European Parliament, the problem of the Union's democratic deficit remains as great as ever. The number of countries seeking entry into the Union has dramatically increased since the end of the cold war. Largely because of the SEM programme and TEU, new members are forced to make stronger commitments to the Union than previous applicants. Even so, there is no shortage of eager candidates for entry. The enlargement issue has intensified the debate in the Union about the speed and direction of integration (that is, should the Union concentrate on deepening integration amongst existing members or on the absorption of new members?). The increased size and diversity of the Union confronts it with major institutional and policy challenges. The capacity of the Union to rise to these challenges will be examined in later chapters.

● A PRELIMINARY EVALUATION

○ The EU in Comparative Perspective

Two waves of regional integration in the post-war period can be identified: from the 1950s, many attempts were made to forge free trade areas or common markets in Europe, Africa, Latin America, the Caribbean and Asia. *First-wave regionalism* largely failed outside Europe. If judged against other attempts at integration in post-war Europe (Comecon and EFTA), the EU must be regarded as a success. Following the departure of Sweden, Austria and Finland, EFTA now comprises four countries with a combined population of only eleven million. Comecon was part of communism's 'grand failure' in Eastern Europe. Even before the cold war officially ended, several Comecon members had announced their intention to leave the organisation and to seek closer links with its flourishing Western rival. *Second-wave regionalism* is a phenomenon of the 1990s: it is more extensive than the first wave, and has possibly been precipitated by increasing international economic interdependence and advances in communications. This second wave involves various attempts to forge regional trading pacts, customs associations, customs unions and common markets.

Of the 109 regional agreements notified to GATT (General Agreement on Tariffs and Trade) between 1948 and 1994, one-third were concluded between 1990 and 1994. However, these second-wave-projects (some of which involve attempts to restart stalled experiments) are still at a fragile stage of development and none approach the level of integration achieved by the EU.

Various regional economic groupings have emerged in post-communist Central and Eastern Europe. The Commonwealth of Independent States (CIS) was formed following the collapse of the Soviet Union in 1991. Several of its members have signed a charter for economic co-operation, although the main thrust of the economic policies of CIS countries seems to be towards increasing national autonomy. Several countries in the region have formed a very loose association called the 'Black Sea Club'. In 1993, its members agreed to establish a trade and development bank and a permanent secretariat. However, the parlous economic state of many member countries seems likely to limit the Club's development. The 'Visegrad Group' (Hungary, Poland, the Czech Republic and Slovakia) have agreed to the mutual elimination of tariffs by the end of the century and have formed the Central European Free Trade Area (CEFTA). It is envisaged that Slovenia, Bulgaria, Romania and the Baltic states may join CEFTA. But all of these countries have already reoriented their trade towards Western Europe and are anxious to enter the EU.

The North American Free Trade Association (NAFTA) embraces the US, Canada and Mexico. It aims to eliminate virtually all restrictions on trade and investment between the three countries over 15 years. The trilateral relationship is obviously unequal. Canada has a slightly lower GNP per capita than the US, but a much smaller population. Mexico's GNP per capita is about one-tenth that of the US. There is a significantly higher proportion of intraregional trade within the EU than between NAFTA countries. NAFTA is not a customs union. Nor does it have 'supranational' institutions.

In Latin America, the most significant recent development in regional integration is the formation of 'Mercosur', a customs union comprising Brazil, Paraguay, Argentina and Uruguay. Mercosur accounts for about 45% of Latin America's population, 33% of its foreign trade and 50% of its GDP. The 'Andean Pact' of 1969 sought to forge links between Venezuela, Colombia, Ecuador, Peru and Bolivia. However, the members agreed to form a free trade area only in October 1992. An agreement came into being in January 1995. In 1960, the Central American Common Market (CACM) was established (Guatemala, El Salvador, Honduras, Nicaragua, Costa Rica and Panama), but as yet has made little progress. The 'Caribbean Community' (Caricom), formed in 1973, has 13 members but a combined population of only 5.5 million. It is seeking the creation of a common market and a monetary union, but has yet to make much progress. The prospect of an 'EC for the Middle East' (initially embracing Israel, Jordan and Palestine) is so far no more than an interesting idea.

In East Asia, the success of 'individualist' economic strategies in recent years has meant that countries see little advantage in pursuing deep economic integration. Regional co-operation in Asia has tended to focus on measures to increase or safeguard market share. The members of ASEAN – the Association of South-East Asian Nations (Singapore, Malaysia, Thailand, Indonesia, the Philippines and Brunei) – have agreed to set up a free trade area by 2003. But these countries currently do the bulk of their trade with other regions rather than with each other. The Asia-Pacific Economic Co-operation Forum (APEC) is an official consultative forum founded in 1989 and aims to increase multilateral economic co-operation between countries in the Pacific rim. Its 15 members are the US, Canada, Japan, South Korea, Australia, New Zealand, Brunei, Indonesia, Malaysia, the Philippines, Singapore, Thailand, China, Hong Kong and Taiwan. However, although members have agreed a draft plan for free trade and investment in the region by 2020, there is no agreement yet on formalising the relationship into a bloc. The diversity of APEC's membership (embracing both very rich and poor countries) is likely to inhibit the group's development.

❍ Why has EU Integration Advanced so Far?

The SEM and TEU are manifestations of another period of accelerated development. What causes these sudden spurts in integration? In the 1950s, the conditions for integration are widely regarded as having been favourable: these included the stimulus of the war, receptive elites, the homogeneity of the original members, US support, and economic growth. But deeper integration also moved ahead in the economically less favourable conditions of the late 1980s. Although many specific causes of 'integration spurts' can be identified, two general factors seem to be at work: firstly, they occur when governments become more receptive to the logic of integration, in that they perceive that positive benefits (not necessarily the same benefits) will flow to their countries from deeper collaboration. Secondly, the logic of integration is given force and urgency by perception of a common threat (of war, invasion and economic weakness in the early post-war years and of economic stagnation in the 1980s and 1990s). These theoretical issues will be explored in the next chapter.

It might be argued that, since the end of the cold war, many of the factors which have been conducive to EU integration no longer apply. For example, the prospect of a war between Western European countries now appears unthinkable. Germany is now significantly larger and more powerful than the second largest member. Enlargement is increasing the diversity of the Union's membership and is diminishing the importance of the factor of geographical proximity. Moreover, the pursuit of political, economic and monetary union is rendering it increasingly difficult to sweep crunch issues under the carpet. Table 1.6 below sets out some possible reasons for the relatively high degree of integration achieved by the EU.

Table 1.6 Factors Conducive to EU Integration

- the impetus for change deriving from the trauma of the Second World War;
- rapid economic growth in Western Europe in the early post-war years meant that the EU got off to a good start;
- the shared characteristics of members: for example, geographical proximity; similar economic and political systems (all are liberal democracies and have market economies); a relatively high level of economic development; perception of a common 'European' identity;
- until German reunification, no one member was much larger than the second largest;
- personalities: at various points, 'change agents' such as Monnet and Delors, have given the Union integration process a powerful boost;
- the pace of enlargement has (up to now) been relatively slow, and therefore the entry question has not crowded out the issue of internal development;
- the perception of the economic benefits to be derived from integration;
- vested interests (that is, the beneficiaries of the CAP and of certain other EU policies) have provided the 'cement', binding the member states together;
- members have been prepared to tolerate ambiguity and incoherence concerning the ultimate aims of integration. The potentially divisive effects of 'crunch' issues has thereby been muted to some degree;
- the Union has developed crisis management and conflict resolution strategies which have helped to prevent disintegration.

○ The Union's Achievements and Failures

Any attempt to assess the successes and failures of the Union so far depends very much on the criteria used and the perspective adopted. From small beginnings, the Union has made substantial progress in integration. It has made a major contribution to the healing of Franco-German conflict. It has had a dynamic effect on trade between members. If judged solely against the progress made by other post-war regional formations, the EU must be regarded as a success.

But serious questions can be raised about the 'successes' of the EU outlined in Table 1.7 below. It would also be easy to advance a counter-case, that the Union's economic performance has failed to match that of its main competitors in recent decades. For example, the economic performance of the EFTA states has been at least as good for much of the post-war period; that of Japan, which has not integrated with any other country, has been even better. The Union has high unemployment relative to the US and Japan. It has a poor record for developing new high-tech industries. Moreover, despite the 'hype' of the Single European Market programme, the aims of the programme are still far from being fully realised. Protectionist policies, notably the CAP, have restricted international trade and arguably have not been to the general benefit of EU citizens. Nor has the European integration project succeeded in exciting, or to any great degree involving, 'ordinary' citizens. Nor does the Union yet have a fully developed portfolio of policies: for example, education, health, welfare and law and order remain very largely national responsibilities. The development of a common foreign and security policy remains at a nascent stage.

Table 1.7 Some Indicators of the Union's Success

- there is a long queue of countries keen to join. Any club which has a waiting list of would-be entrants must be doing something right;
- no member has withdrawn (compare this to EFTA or to the now defunct Comecon);
- it has a strong institutional and policy base;
- it has achieved a deeper level of integration than any other post-war grouping;
- it is very much alive: many of its counterparts are dead, dying or at a nascent stage;
- it has become an international actor in its own right (for example, the Commission negotiates international trade agreements on behalf of all member states);
- it is the largest regional bloc in the world and has by far the highest level of intraregional trade.

○ **Perspectives on the Union's Development**

This chapter has sought to show that there was nothing inevitable about the way the European Union has developed. Moreover, growing international interdependence and the emergence of second-wave regionalism suggests that analyses of the Union's development have to be considered in the context of broader structural changes taking place in the global economy. But in some respects the Union remains unique. Various approaches might be adopted to shed light on the dynamics of change in relation to European integration: for example, we could adopt an *heroic perspective* and focus on the influence of key personalities, such as Monnet, Schuman, Spaak and Delors (as accelerators) and de Gaulle and Thatcher (as would-be decelerators) of integration; we might adopt an *ideological perspective* and attribute European integration to the influence of ideas (such as functionalism, federalism or supranationalism); we could opt for *a situational perspective*, and focus on circumstances and events (such as Europe's parlous situation at the end of the war). In practice, however, these one-dimensional approaches are more misleading than enlightening, because European integration is a product of a dynamic mix of influences, deriving from people, ideas and circumstances.

FURTHER READING

Arter, P., *The Politics of European Integration in the Twentieth Century*, Dartmouth, Aldershot, 1993.

den Boer, P., 'Europe to 1914: the Making of an Idea', in Wilson, K. and Van Der Dussen, J., *The History of the Idea of Europe*, Routledge, London, 1995.

Dinan, D., *Ever Closer Union?*, Macmillan Press, London, 1994.

Featherstone, K., 'Jean Monnet and the "Democratic Deficit" in the European Union', *Journal of Common Market Studies*, vol. 32, no. 2, 1994, pp. 147–70.

George, S., *An Awkward Partner, Britain in the European Community*, Oxford University Press, 1990.

Greenwood, S., *Britain and European Co-operation Since 1945*, Blackwell, Oxford, 1992.

Lipgens, W., *History of European Integration* (2 vols), Oxford University Press, London, 1986.

Mcallister, R., *The European Community: An Historical and Political Survey*, Harvester Wheatsheaf, Hemel Hemstead, 1992.

Milward, A.S., *The European Rescue of the Nation-State*, Routledge, London, 1992.

Stirk, P., *European Unity in Context: The Inter-War Period*, Pinter, London, 1989.

 **Chapter 2**

Theoretical Perspectives on Integration

● IDEAS AND CONCEPTS

○ The Importance of Ideas

There is no 'single currency' of ideas in relation to European integration. Indeed, the subject has inspired a remarkably diverse range of ideas and theories, some of which are *prescriptive* (the authors approve of integration and seek to prescribe integration strategies) and some *descriptive* (the authors are primarily concerned to understand and explain the 'why' and 'how' of integration). In practice, it is difficult to classify integration theories into these two categories, because even the most prescriptive theory has to be supported by description and explanation, and even the most determinedly objective student of integration will make value judgements. Nor does the subject have a 'common language', in that many key terms used in discussions on European integration (such as sovereignty or federalism) are capable of very different interpretations. Two striking features of European integration as a subject of study have been the inability of theory to keep up with events and the ability of events to confound even the most elaborate theory. Nevertheless, neither the origins nor the subsequent development of the Union can be understood without reference to the corpus (more accurately, clash) of ideas which have given direction and shape to European integration processes and to perceptions of these processes.

○ Definitions

Dictionary definitions of integration can never fully encapsulate the various shades of meaning that can be given to this word. In broad terms, it means the coming together of separate units to form a whole. This implies that it goes beyond 'interstate co-operation' (where arguably there is no whole) although the boundary between co-operation and integration is very fuzzy and the two terms are often used as synonyms. Definitions by economists and by political scientists naturally have different emphases. The economist Jovanovic (1992, p. 8) defines international economic integration as 'a process by which the economies of separate states merge in large entities'. Political scientists tend to focus on the implications of political integration processes for national sovereignty and for the behaviour of political actors. From this perspective the integration process involves (1) the voluntary relinquishment by nation-states of the power to make independent decisions in certain policy areas (decisionmaking is shared by the governments of participating states or is transferred to new central institutions) and (2) the shifting of the loyalties, expectations and activities of national political actors to a new centre (see Lindberg, 1963, Chapter 1).

A fundamental distinction is between *voluntary* and *involuntary* integration. There are many examples in history of the involuntary form, such as the forcible incorporation of many newly independent states into the Soviet Federation after the Bolshevik revolution. Similarly, regional economic integration in Eastern Europe during the communist period was by no means fully voluntarist, because of the coercive power exercised over the East European 'People's Democracies' by the Soviet Union. The EU is founded on *voluntarist* principles (no country is forced to join, and no country would be prevented from leaving it). Another fundamental feature of the EU integration process is that, from its inception, it has had explicitly political, as well as economic, goals.

Many other distinctions between types of integration can be made. For example, *positive integration* involves the *building* of common institutions and policies, whereas *negative integration* refers to the *removal* of cross-border barriers of various kinds. In practice, however, this distinction between 'building things up' and 'knocking things down' is difficult to sustain: for example, the Single European Market programme was nominally about knocking down barriers to trade, but entailed major institutional and policy changes amounting to the most significant exercise in positive integration since the 1950s (a fact that at least one of the signatories to the Single European Act, Mrs Thatcher, did not realise until it was too late!). We could also distinguish between *integration 'width'* (the range of subjects covered by integration agreements) and *integration 'depth'* (the extent to which there is a pooling of sovereignty in a particular policy area).

○ Sovereignty

We have already noted the centrality of the sovereignty principle in discussions on European integration. Sovereignty has two principal aspects: firstly an *internal* aspect, meaning supremacy, or authoritative decision-making power, within a state (for example, we speak of the sovereignty of parliament, the supreme law-making body within the UK). Secondly, an *external* aspect, meaning the independence of states in international affairs. The sovereign state is still generally regarded as the chief actor in the international system. It has shown remarkable ability to adjust to new realities, such as increasing international interdependence and the rise of 'non-state actors', such as multinational corporations (MNCs), international governmental organisations (IGOs, such as the International Monetary Fund (IMF)) and international non-governmental organisations (INGOs, such as Oxfam). However, in an increasingly interdependent world, the meaning of sovereignty has to be continually redefined. For example, the internationalisation of modern business, manifested in copious flows of trade, investment, technology and information across state boundaries, means that the old 'billiard ball' model of the state (in which states are assumed to have hard, impenetrable surfaces), is clearly out of date. Sovereignty is not an all-or-nothing condition and therefore it can be gained or lost by degrees.

Integration has also been at least partly inspired by the belief that sovereignty is a malign and dangerous force. According to its critics, it divides humanity into separate units and encourages selfish and insular behaviour. Because it is regarded as a means of uniting human beings, integration tends to be perceived by its proponents as being morally superior to 'non-integration'. But the drive towards integration has also been motivated and justified by the perceived welfare and security benefits of 'going it with others': according to the proponents of integration, these benefits are likely to outweigh the trade-off costs in terms of the erosion of sovereignty. They argue that in an increasingly interdependent world, national sovereignty is being eroded anyway and that countries joining together are likely to have more 'clout' in the international arena. Conversely, opposition to integration generally reflects a desire to defend state sovereignty (which tends to be equated with national independence). Its defenders argue that it enables peoples to govern themselves; that it protects smaller countries against domination by larger countries; and that it remains a focus of national loyalties.

What are the principal integration mechanisms through which the sovereignties of participating states may be eroded?

Firstly, elements of decisionmaking power may be *transferred* from national governments to 'supranational' authorities (see the example in

Figure 2.1). The word 'supra' means 'above', and so literally supranationalism means above the level of nation-states. The High Authority of the ECSC, the European Commission, the European Parliament (EP) and the European Court of Justice (ECJ) are often referred to as supranational, in that they perform functions on behalf of the Union as a whole and do not specifically represent the interests of the individual governments of member states. European governments have not, however, been prepared to commit suicide by transferring power wholesale to supranational authorities. For example, both the SEA and the TEU increased the powers of the EP: but the European Council and the Council of the European Union (both 'intergovernmental' institutions) are, respectively, the key guiding and decisionmaking bodies in the Union. Some analysts (for example, Keohane and Hoffman (1991 p. 16)) deny that the Commission is a supranational entity, because it is not an authoritative decision*maker* above the nation-state, although it clearly has supranational characteristics in the sense referred to above. Many key policy areas, such as foreign affairs, defence, domestic justice and responsibility for direct taxation remain in the hands of the governments of member states.

Secondly, governments of states may participate in shared decisionmaking, in which they agree to be bound by collective decisions. Shared decisionmaking by governments is often referred to as 'intergovernmentalism'. But distinctions which place supranationalism and intergovernmentalism at opposite ends of a spectrum are misleading, because collective decisionmaking by governments is also literally supranational (that is, above the level of individual national governments). Shared decisionmaking in its minimalist form (*loose intergovernmentalism*) constitutes no appreciable threat to sovereignty, because individual governments can veto decisions they find unacceptable. But in its maximalist form (*tight intergovernmentalism*), based on the principle of binding majority voting, it imposes limits on sovereignty, because member states are forced to accept majority decisions. Within the Union, binding majority voting (an example of tight intergovernmentalism) constitutes a greater threat to state sovereignty than the transfer of functions to 'supranational' authorities. Its *raison d'être* is that it enables the Union to move forward, by preventing decisions favoured by the majority from being vetoed.

However, as long as membership of the Union remains voluntary, then it can be argued that sovereignty has been 'lent' rather than lost. The TEU explicitly confirmed the right of any member state to withdraw from the Union. Although the principle that Community law has primacy over national law is well established, this principle is ultimately based on the willingness of national parliaments to accept this. Eurosceptics would retort that, because the issue of withdrawal is not on the political agendas of member states, lent sovereignty is as good as lost (a circular argument!).

Figure 2.1 Two Means of Eroding Sovereignty

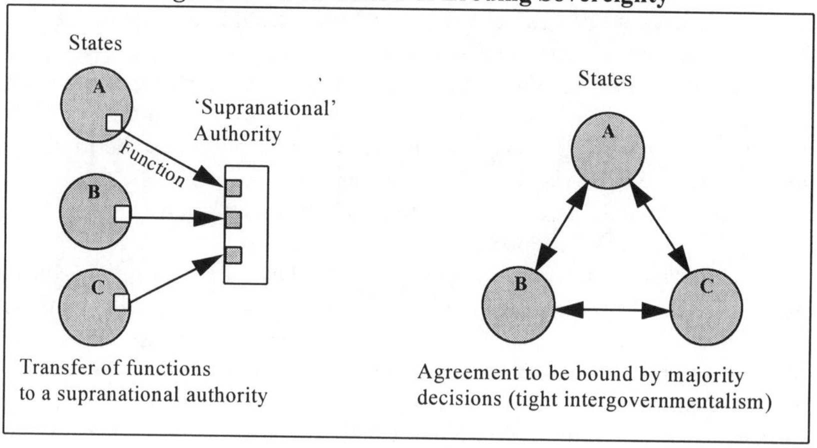
States
A
B
C
'Supranational' Authority
Function
Transfer of functions to a supranational authority
States
A
B
C
Agreement to be bound by majority decisions (tight intergovernmentalism)

• THEORIES OF INTEGRATION

Anyone looking for a definitive explanatory theory of European integration will be disappointed. The trend in integration theory is towards less dogmatic explanations of integration events and processes. Recent approaches tend to disclaim the view that the Union's path of development was inevitable, or that its future can be confidently predicted. They tend to lay greater stress than earlier theories upon the *choices* available to governments and upon the influence of international events and circumstances. The subsections below outline the main theoretical approaches to European integration.

❍ Functionalism

As noted in Chapter 1, 'functionalists' favour the strategy of gradually undermining state sovereignty, by encouraging technical co-operation in specific policy areas across state boundaries. The founding father of the functionalist school was David Mitrany, a Romanian-born scholar who taught for many years at the London School of Economics. He regarded nationalism as the biggest threat to world peace and favoured a shift in human loyalties from the national to the international level through mutually beneficial international co-operation in sectors such as transport, agriculture, science and health. Mitrany's ideas rest on the assumption that governments are less able to meet the welfare needs of their citizens than 'non-political' international authorities. He favoured what he called *technical self-determination* over national self-determination and believed that human loyalties would shift from the nation-state to supranational authorities because of the tangible material benefits these authorities would provide. People would therefore become more committed to transnational co-operation and less nationalistic. Mitrany envisaged the emergence of a spreading web of supranational authorities, to undertake tasks formerly performed by national governments. According to Mitrany, there would be many such agencies, and therefore international power would be diffused rather than centralised. Mitrany thought that these authorities would have a strong managerialist ethos and would be 'above' politics. Mitrany was interested in global rather than regional co-operation (whereas Monnet's ideas had a strong regional focus). For Mitrany, regional integration was nationalism writ large. Therefore, he was opposed to a 'continental union' in Europe, and to the creation of institutions which in his view mirrored those of sovereign states.

The weaknesses of the functionalist approach seem glaring in the light of post-war history: for example, it assumes that functional co-operation can be separated from politics. However, the decisions of technical agencies are often highly political: several, such as the United Nations Educational, Scientific and Cultural Organisation (UNESCO) and the International Labour Organisation, have been torn by political disputes. These agencies have been created by states for their mutual benefit: they remain under the ultimate control of sovereign states and are dependent upon them for their resources. Moreover, the creation of functional authorities has arguably made the states system work better rather than undermining it. There is also scant evidence that loyalties are shifting from the state level to international organisations. Functionalism also left many key questions unanswered, such as how co-ordination of functional authorities would work or how disputes between them would be resolved.

○ Neo-functionalism

This approach is far more realistic than the older functionalism, and less prescriptive: it was developed in the 1950s and 1960s to explain integration processes in the European Community. It is therefore based on intensive study of an actual case. Haas, Nye and Lindberg (all, incidentally, American scholars) are generally acknowledged to be the founders of this approach. Haas (1958) viewed integration as a developing and expanding process involving bargaining and compromise, like other forms of politics. He argued that there could be a learning curve of co-operation between governments, in which the experience of co-operation in some fields could lead of co-operation in others: co-operation was likely to begin in the field of *low politics* (such as coal and steel) and might then be extended to *high politics* (such as foreign and defence policy). In other words, there could be a *spillover* effect from co-operation in one policy area to another. Haas did not, however, believe this spillover process to be automatic or inevitable, not least because it would depend upon choices made by governments and other actors. The principal differences between neo-functionalism and the older type of functionalism are:

1. In neo-functionalism, the political dimension and the role of governments in integration processes are fully accounted for. A central assumption of this approach is that functional co-operation will take place at the behest of governments. Unlike the older functionalism, neo-functionalism accepts the importance of political conflict and the existence of competing interests. It emphasises the importance of elites and elite bargaining rather than mass support for integration in its early stages.

2. Neo-functionalism has a stronger empirical foundation and seeks to explain in some detail how a specific integration process actually works.

3. It focuses upon integration between groups of countries in specific regions or subregions of the world ('regional integration') rather than upon global integration.

After Haas wrote his first book on the subject, there was a lull or plateau in European integration which seemed to undermine the neo-functionalist case. Setbacks in the process of European integration led to the incorporation of the concept of *spillback* (that is, reverse integration) into neo-functionalist theories. In his later writings, Haas acknowledged that the conditions which had provided the driving force for integration in the early period had run out of steam. He noted that there had not been spillover to other areas besides agriculture. He also argued that the power of nationalism and the influence of external factors (international events) had both been underestimated. In addition, he recognised that European integration was too complex to fit neatly into any theoretical model.

Since the mid-1980s, there has been a period of accelerated development of the Union, manifested in the Single European Market programme and the TEU. Was this the result of 'spillover'? Keohane and Hoffman (1991, p. 19) deny that spillover was primarily responsible for the SEM – rather, they attribute it to a combination of factors, in particular to the convergence of national interests, to developments in the global economy and to concern about the poor competitiveness of European industry. Nevertheless, it seems unlikely that recent deepening of integration within the EU could have occurred without a learning curve of collaborative experience. For example, the SEM programme may well have provided the momentum for the TEU's provisions on economic and monetary union.

○ Federalism

Because many countries have federal systems of government, federalism is perhaps the most easily understood (and by the same token misunderstood) of all concepts in integration theory. In a federal system, there is a formal distribution of power between central and regional levels of government. These powers (together with the rights of citizens) are usually defined in a constitutional document. There is usually a federal supreme court to adjudicate in disputes on constitutional issues. The central level invariably has responsibility for foreign and security policy, but many functions are shared with the regional level. In continental Europe, federal systems tend to be associated with *decentralisation* and are viewed as a means by which the powers of the central government can be kept in check, whereas in the UK (which does not have a federal system of government) federalism is often viewed as a *centralising* doctrine, designed to wrest power from national governments and parliaments.

The influence of federalist ideas on European integration processes is difficult to gauge. In Chapter 1 we noted that early post-war federalist groups were essentially fringe movements which had no discernible influence upon the key policymakers in this period. But many of the prime movers in the development of the Union have espoused federalist ideas at some point. In terms of the influence of the federalist movement, parallels might be drawn with the 'environmentalist' movement, which has seen some of its ideas absorbed in a less radical form into mainstream political discourse. 'Euro-federalism' is still regarded as a laudatory idea in many parts of continental Europe. Contemporary federalists (often referred to as *neo-federalists*) tend to be more realistic about the prospects of realising their goals than their predecessors and are prepared to build a federal union in incremental steps rather than all at once (Monnet also espoused an 'incrementalist' approach).

Some commentators believe that the Union is already a federation in all but name (Begg, 1993, p. 162) or is on the way to becoming one (Pinder, 1995, p. 22). The Union already has many federal characteristics – for example: a Union title, some supranational institutions, including an increasingly powerful Parliament, a Court of Justice and a seemingly ever-widening range of common policies. However, there are several major differences between the Union and a 'typical' federation. Firstly, the EU does not have a written constitution and is based upon treaties negotiated by governments. Secondly, the power exercised by member states in EU decisionmaking has no parallel in any existing federation. For example, state governors in the US federal system are not key decisionmakers at central level. Nor, in contrast with EU governments, do they play any significant role in foreign and defence policy. Another approach might be to view the Union as somewhere between a confederation and a federation: a confederation is a looser arrangement than a federation, in that the participating units retain a very high degree of independence. The Union is clearly more than a confederation, but is less than a full federation. There are several reasons why the EU is unlikely to develop into a 'United States of Europe' on the US model: the peoples in the American colonies were more homogeneous than are contemporary Europeans (they had a common language and culture and were largely of British ancestry); the colonies were not fully formed nation-states; nor were their economies fully developed.

⊃ Intergovernmentalism

This approach stresses the role of governments in European integration processes. We have already noted that the term 'intergovernmentalism' tends to be used rather loosely. In addition to the distinction made earlier between tight and loose forms, a further distinction needs to be made between *prescriptive intergovernmentalism* (the view that governments *should* be the dominant actors in the Union) and *descriptive intergovernmentalism* (the view that governments *are*, for good or ill, the key actors in the Union). The Union is clearly different from purely intergovernmental bodies, such as the Organisation for Economic Co-operation and Development (OECD) or NATO, because it contains 'supranational' institutions of considerable importance. Moreover, the extensive use of the binding majority voting principle in the Council of the European Union also differentiates the Union from most other international organisations.

Proponents of descriptive intergovernmentalism cite the important role played in EU policymaking by the Council, the European Council and a support network of intergovernmental committees. According to this approach, which emphasises the importance of intergovernmental bargaining, developments in integration only happen when they coincide with the interests of the governments of member states. For example, it has been argued that the election of more market-oriented governments in member states in the 1980s, and the consequent convergence of 'national interests', was a major factor in the development of the Single European Market programme (Moravcsik, 1991). Descriptive intergovernmentalist theories have frequently emphasised the importance of Franco-German co-operation as the driving force or motor of European integration.

However, intergovernmental bargaining theories need to be qualified and supplemented, by reference to the important roles played by the Commission, the European Court of Justice, the European Parliament, interest groups and domestic politics in the EU policy system. Keohane and Hoffman (1991, p. 13) view the EU as having a 'network' form of organisation. In the *network approach*, EU policy is viewed as the outcome of bargaining and coalition formation between diverse actors, including governments, Union institutions and interest groups: interactions take place within a framework of *mutual interdependency*, although national governments are still considered to play the dominant role in decisionmaking. The 'network' approach combines elements of intergovernmentalist and neo-functionalist perspectives.

The role of domestic politics in intergovernmental bargaining also needs to be acknowledged (Bulmer, 1983). The *domestic politics* approach emphasises the interplay between the national politics of member states and 'European' politics. It assumes that the behaviour of governments at the European level is explicable in terms of their need to take account of both domestic and European pressures and 'audiences'. Thus, in negotiations at European level, governments will seek to protect and foster domestic interests (and thereby bolster their domestic image and standing), but in dealings with their counterparts (the governments of other member states) will not wish to appear to be 'anti-European'. For governments, domestic interests also embrace considerations of party unity on European issues. Balancing these domestic and European pressures is not always possible: the fact that the UK government headed by John Major has seemed out of step with other member states on European issues has been partly attributed to its need to appease a large and voluble group of Eurosceptic Conservative MPs.

Proponents of prescriptive intergovernmentalism seek to oppose attempts to enhance the powers of the Union's 'supranational' institutions. In its maximalist form (for example espoused by British Eurosceptics), prescriptive intergovernmentalism favours a 'club of states' conception of the Union.

● A 'MULTISPEED' UNION?

Multispeed concepts do not constitute a comprehensive theory, but focus on the problem of how European integration processes can proceed, given the increasingly heterogeneous nature of the Union's membership. The central idea of a multispeed Europe is that there will (or should) be variations in the pace of integration pursued by member states. The terms *Europe à la carte* (first developed by the German academic and ex-Commissioner Ralf Dahrendorf), *flexi-Europe* or *variable geometry* are often used to express the same idea. But there is a crucial difference between 'multispeed' and *à la carte* concepts. In a multispeed Europe, member states will be expected eventually to arrive at the same destination. In an *à la carte* Europe, there would always be scope for countries to opt out of specific areas of policy – that is, there would be no common destination. The Commission, in a report prepared for the 1996 Intergovernmental Conference, has accepted the multispeed principle, but remains firmly opposed to an *à la carte* Europe (see Chapter 4).

Yesterday's heresy is often tomorrow's conventional wisdom. The multispeed idea is still viewed with hostility by those who regard it as a cynical ploy to impede the pace of integration. The idea has certainly found support amongst opponents of deeper integration. In May 1994, at a Euro-election rally at Ellesmere Port, John Major outlined a vision of Europe in which the EU's functions 'should be carried out in different ways, often involving different groups of states'. This vision of a 'multitrack, multispeed, multi-layered' Europe was attacked by critics as tantamount to consigning the UK to the slow lane of a two-speed Europe and as incompatible with Major's erstwhile aim to place the UK at the heart of Europe.

However, the multispeed idea has also been adopted by those anxious to ensure that rapid progress towards deeper integration is not impeded by 'laggard' countries: a multispeed Europe has fast lanes as well as slow ones. It had been espoused in a limited form in the Tindemans report on European Union in 1975, but received a generally adverse reaction. In April 1994, Alain Lamassoure, France's European Affairs minister, proposed a 'hard core' of EU members, comprising countries applying all Union policies provided for in the Union treaties. He suggested that this might initially comprise the founder members and would be linked by a political declaration rather than by a new treaty A similar proposal was put forward in Germany by Karl Lamers in a policy report for the Christian Democratic Union in the summer of 1994, fuelling suspicions in some parts of the Union that Germany and France were seeking to create a Union 'premier league'.

In significant ways, however, European integration is already proceeding at multispeed, albeit in an *ad hoc*, piecemeal way rather than as part of a grand design. For example, the agreements reached at Maastricht implicitly sanctioned the multispeed approach in several ways: the UK was allowed to opt out of key aspects of monetary and social policy; Maastricht's intergovernmental pillars provide scope for member states to opt out of joint actions in the fields of foreign and security policy and justice and home affairs; the principle of subsidiarity widens the scope for differences in policy between member countries. The number of countries able to meet the Maastricht criteria for participation in the single currency project due to commence on 1 January 1999 is currently unknown, but it is generally accepted that the project will initially lead to a division of the Union into 'EMU insiders' and 'EMU outsiders' (see Chapter 10).

Some EU states remain unenthusiastic about participation in EU defence structures. But five member countries now participate in the *Eurocorps*, viewed by some as the embryo of the 'European army' of the future. It is possible that, following the entry of Austria, Finland and Sweden, a 'super green' group of countries could emerge. A majority of EU countries have signed the Schengen Agreement, which seeks to abolish virtually all frontier controls between member countries. However, only six countries currently participate in this project (see Chapter 14). Implicit in the Eurocorps and Schengen projects is the assumption that it is legitimate for groups of member states to pursue deeper integration outside the Union framework, providing that these projects are compatible with the Union's goals. Moreover, as the French President Jacques Chirac acknowledged at the European Council meeting in Majorca in September 1995, a future Union with 25 or 30 members will have to allow for different levels of integration.

A multispeed Europe is by no means an unmixed blessing. It increases the complexity of EU institutional structures, rendering them more difficult for ordinary citizens to understand. There is a danger that a multispeed Europe will solidify into an *à la carte* Europe, which could lead to the unravelling or break-up of the Union. It could lead to the creation of several classes of Union membership. On the other hand, it provides a flexible framework for future integration and may be the only way in which an increasingly heterogeneous Union can be held together. Without the UK opt-outs, the TEU would probably not have been signed at all. It could also provide a framework through which the aspirations of East European countries for Union membership might be at least partially met.

FURTHER READING

Begg, D., *Making Sense of Subsidiarity*, Centre for Economic Policy Research, London, 1993.

Bulmer, S., 'Domestic Politics and European Community Policy Making', *Journal of Common Market Studies*, vol. 21, no. 4, 1983, pp. 349–63.

Haas, E.B., *The Uniting of Europe*, Stanford University Press, 1958.

Jovanovic, M.N, *International Economic Integration*, Routledge, London, 1992.

Keohane, R.O. and Hoffman, S. (eds.), *The New European Community*, Boulder, Westview Press, 1991.

Lindberg, L.N., *The Political Dynamics of European Economic Integration*, Stanford University Press, 1963.

Moravcsik, A, 'Negotiating the Single European Act', in Keohane and Hoffman, *op. cit.*, pp. 41–84.

Pinder, J., *European Community*, Oxford University Press, 1995.

 **Chapter 3**

The Treaty on European Union

● ORIGINS

The Treaty on European Union (TEU) was agreed at the European Council in Maastricht in December 1991 and signed in February 1992. The Maastricht summit is widely acknowledged to be a landmark event in the European integration process. All of the issues examined in this book have been affected in some way by the decisions reached at Maastricht. The Treaty is broader in scope, open to a wider range of interpretations and is more controversial than either the Treaty of Rome or the SEA.

The Preamble to the Treaty of Rome refers to the determination to 'lay the foundation of an ever closer union of the peoples of Europe'. Until the 1980s this lofty (and undefined) aspiration remained dormant but not entirely forgotten. In 1983, the European Council in Stuttgart agreed a rather vague 'Solemn Declaration on European Union'. In February 1984, the EP passed a 'Draft Treaty on European Union', although it lacked the power to transform this proposal into reality. The preamble to the Single European Act (signed in February 1986) refers to the 'will to transform relations as a whole among their states into a European Union'. At the time there seemed no certainty that this aspiration would be pursued any more seriously than the 'closer union' goal contained in the Treaty of Rome. However, the Single European Market programme, launched at the European Council in Milan in June 1985, provided the momentum for further integration in three principal ways: it demonstrated the feasibility of a leap forward in integration; the creation of a 'level playing field for business' had very broad-ranging institutional and policy implications; Euro-federalists, inspired by the launch of the SEM, were determined to keep the integration ball rolling.

The progression from the SEA to the TEU provides some support for the 'spillover' theory that integration in one area of activity leads to integration in others. Monetary union and the creation of a 'European social space' were the most obvious next targets for integration, not least because a true level playing field for business could not be fully realised without them. 'One market one money' became a Commission catchphrase in this period. At the European Council in Hanover in June 1988, Delors was asked to chair a committee to examine the practical measures needed to achieve economic and monetary union. The Committee reported in April 1989 in favour of a three-stage transition to EMU. The European Council in Madrid in June 1989 agreed that stage 1 would commence on 1 July 1990. In December 1989, the European Council in Strasbourg agreed that an intergovernmental conference (IGC) would outline the next two stages. At this meeting all member states except the UK adopted the 'Social Charter', in order to develop a 'social space' to match the 'economic space' being created by the SEM. The European Council in Dublin in June 1990 agreed to convene an IGC on EMU in December.

Despite the fact that the SEM programme provided an important impetus for the agreements reached at Maastricht, spillover theory provides only a partial explanation of the events leading to the TEU. Spillover is by no means an inevitable consequence of integration activity. Nor can spillover theory fully explain the peculiar form and content of the TEU. Other possible influences must also therefore be examined. External events are one obvious source of influence. The crumbling of communism in Eastern Europe and the crisis in the Gulf gave added urgency to the need for greater co-operation in the fields of foreign and security policy. The end of the cold war opened up a debate on defence issues, focused on the future of NATO and the Western European Union (WEU). German reunification altered the power balance within the Community, forcing urgent consideration of how potential problems arising from Germany's additional weight could best be dealt with.

The development of the TEU also demonstrates the pivotal role of governments as accelerators and decelerators of integration. A proposal jointly formulated by President Mitterrand and Chancellor Kohl for political union was discussed at the special European Council in Dublin in April 1990. The proposal sought a reduction in the democratic deficit, improved institutional efficiency and the development of CFSP, all to come into force on the same day as the completion of the SEM. It became clear that Kohl in particular was keen to link the goals of monetary union and political union. The Mitterrand–Kohl proposal did not meet with the approval of the UK or Portugal and the decision was postponed until the next European Council in Dublin in June. Discussions at the June summit exposed wide divisions on what political union would mean. Whereas Mitterrand stated that the Union should have a 'federal finality', Mrs Thatcher favoured a 'Europe of states' model quite at variance with federalist schemes for European Union. At the summit Thatcher expressed strong opposition to political union initiatives. Nevertheless, the Dublin summit in June 1990 approved a decision to establish an intergovernmental conference on European political union (EPU) to run in parallel with the EMU conference. It should be noted that these were *intergovernmental* conferences, meaning that neither the EP nor the Commission were full participants in the discussions (although the Commission was a *de facto* participant, without voting rights, and the EP was allowed to make its views known).

Far less preparatory work had been done on EPU than on EMU. The Commission produced an opinion on political union in October 1990, which advocated the creation of European Union leading to 'a federal type organisation', to prevent the Community from degenerating into a 'mere free trade area'. It favoured many of the ideas presented in the Mitterrand–Kohl proposals. In this period, the issue of the institutional architecture of a future Union focused on two alternative models, known as the 'temple' and 'tree' structures. The temple would divide the Union into separate pillars, some of which would be the domain of governments. The tree would give the Union a single, integrated structure. Like a tree it would form an organic unity, with a trunk and various branches. The tree is generally regarded as the more supranationalist option, because unlike the temple it does not restrict or exclude the involvement of Community institutions in key policy areas (notably foreign and security policy and justice and home affairs). It is hardly surprising therefore that the Commission's opinion favoured a tree structure. The IGCs on EMU and EPU opened at the European Council in Rome in December 1990. The European Council asked the conference on EPU to focus on five areas: democratic legitimacy; foreign and security policy; European citizenship; extension and strengthening of Community action; and Community effectiveness and efficiency.

In 1991, the six-month Council presidency was held first by Luxembourg and then by the Netherlands. The Luxembourg presidency produced a draft treaty on political union in June. This was expected to form the basis for a final draft, to be signed in Maastricht in December. The Luxembourg presidency favoured a temple structure, which was disliked by the Commission and Parliament and also by some governments. The initial draft favoured giving the EP powers of 'co-decision' with the Council in some policy areas. Some countries, notably Germany, Belgium, the Netherlands, Luxembourg and Italy, wanted an even stronger role for the EP. France strongly supported monetary union but was lukewarm about political union. The four poorest members pushed for stronger policies on economic and social cohesion (that is, policies to narrow the disparity in wealth between rich and poor regions and countries). A reference to the Union's 'federal vocation' was inserted into the draft at the suggestion of the Commission.

The Dutch presidency put forward its own ideas, in a 96-page 'federalist' document. It favoured a tree structure and considerably enhanced powers for the EP. These federalist proposals were rejected by 10 EC foreign ministers in September 1991 (only Holland and Belgium supported them) in favour of a draft based on the less radical Luxembourg proposals. To further complicate matters, other member states also put forward alternative proposals on specific issues. For example, there were British–Italian and Franco–German proposals on defence, reflecting a difference in emphasis between 'Euro–Atlanticist' and 'Europeanist' approaches to European defence structures. Given these conflicting pressures, it is perhaps surprising that a treaty was agreed at all.

The Treaty covers so many subjects and is so vague and contradictory in places as to be open to various interpretations. The intergovernmental bargaining models of decisionmaking referred to in Chapter 2 may shed light on why the Treaty lacks clarity. Each government came to Maastricht with a shopping list of requirements. No government wanted to be blamed for a breakdown in negotiations. However, each had to keep an eye on its domestic audience (meaning domestic political elites rather than the general public). A deal was only made possible by fudging some contentious issues through liberal use of vague and equivocal formulae, by watering down parts of the draft text and by conceding opt-outs to the UK on monetary union and the social chapter.

Although John Major, who had replaced Mrs Thatcher in October 1990, was viewed as more 'pro-European' than his predecessor, this proved to be more a matter of style than of substance. He was resolutely opposed to a single currency and to the social chapter, both of which were on the Maastricht agenda. The British opt-outs negotiated on these subjects showed that member states were prepared to countenance a multispeed Europe in preference to a breakdown of negotiations. Major also threatened to reject the draft unless references to federalism were removed. The reference to the Union's federal goal was dropped on the first day of the Maastricht summit.

● THE STRUCTURE AND CONTENTS OF THE TEU

○ Structure

The Treaty comprises 7 Titles, 17 Protocols and 33 Declarations. The Protocols are appended to and form part of the Treaty and are justiciable by the ECJ. The most important of these are on social policy, operational aspects of EMU and economic and social cohesion. The 33 Declarations cover a broad range of subjects. For example, there are declarations on the role of national parliaments in the European Union and on the right to access to information. The Declarations are appended to, but do not form part of the Treaty and have no legal force. They are nevertheless part of its context and may be used by the ECJ for interpretation. The Titles, which form the main body of the text, are outlined in Table 3.1.

Table 3.1 The Seven TEU Titles

Title I: Articles A–F. Common Provisions. Articles A and B set out the Union's tasks and objectives. Articles C, D and E deal with the institutional framework and the powers of the major EU institutions. Article F commits the Union to respect for the national identities of member states and of fundamental rights.

Title II: Articles G–G86. Provisions amending the EEC Treaty, with a view to establishing the European Community. The term European Economic Community is replaced by European Community. This Title covers the broadest range of subjects (indeed, it constitutes a 'treaty within a treaty'). It contains 238 articles, including provisions on the powers of Community institutions, Union citizenship and the Community's policy responsibilities. Economic and monetary policy is covered under this Title.

Title III: Articles H–H21. Provisions relating to the ECSC.

Title IV: Articles I–I29. Provisions amending the European Atomic Energy Community (Euratom).

Title V: Articles J–J11. Provisions on a common foreign and security policy.

Title VI: Articles K–K9. Provisions on co-operation in the fields of justice and home affairs (intergovernmental co-operation on immigration, asylum, drugs, terrorism, fraud, civil and criminal matters).

Title VII: Articles L–S. Final provisions, dealing with various institutional and legal issues. Article O states that any European state may apply to join the Union.

○ Contents

Article A of the Treaty's common provisions establishes a Union and states that the Treaty 'marks a new stage in the process of creating an ever closer union among the peoples of Europe, in which decisions are taken as closely as possible to the citizen'. The term Union is only vaguely described. The Union is not a distinct organisation. With the exception of the European Council, it has no institutions of its own and no legal powers. Nor does it replace the EC: indeed, Article A states that the Union is founded on the European Communities (the three Communities are often collectively referred to as the 'European Community'). Most of the Treaty deals with matters falling within the ambit of the Communities. Article B sets out the Union's objectives, viz.:

- *to promote economic and social progress which is balanced and sustainable, in particular through the creation of an area without internal frontiers, through the strengthening of economic and social cohesion and through the establishment of economic and monetary union, ultimately including a single currency in accordance with the Treaty's provisions;*
- *to assert its identity on the international scene, in particular through the implementation of a common foreign and security policy, including the eventual framing of a common defence policy, which might in time lead to a common defence;*
- *to strengthen the protection of the rights and interests of the nationals of member states through the introduction of a citizenship of the Union;*
- *to develop close co-operation on justice and home affairs;*
- *to maintain in full the* acquis communautaire *(that is, Community treaties, legislation, declarations, resolutions, and international agreements) and build on it.*

Article 8 of Title II states that all citizens of member states are citizens of the Union and outlines the rights pertaining to this citizenship. However, this citizenship is complementary to, rather than a replacement for, national citizenship. Most of Title II deals with Community policies: for example, economic and monetary policy, social policy, education, vocational training, culture, public health, consumer protection, trans-European networks, industry, economic and social cohesion, the environment, Research and Technological Development (RTD) and development co-operation. These references collectively constitute a significant extension of the Community's policy responsibilities. The provisions and protocols on EMU arguably constitute the most important single element of the Treaty and will be examined in Chapter 10.

The Treaty also includes important institutional provisions, reflecting the desire to tackle the democratic deficit and to enhance the effectiveness and efficiency of the Union. It gives the EP more power, although far less than it would have liked. Thus the EP was given powers of co-decision with the Council in some policy areas. The range of subjects covered by the co-operation procedure was extended. The 'assent procedure', giving the EP powers of veto on some decisions, was also extended. The EP is also given the power to veto the appointment of the Commission and the power to appoint an Ombudsman. The use of qualified majority voting in the Council is extended. The ECJ is given power to impose fines on states which have not complied with its earlier judgments. The Court of Auditors is upgraded to a full Community institution. The Treaty establishes a Committee of the Regions. These institutional changes are discussed in detail in Chapter 4. The main elements of the treaty are outlined in Table 3.2 below.

Table 3.2 The Main Elements of the TEU

- it creates a European Union;
- it establishes 'European citizenship';
- it establishes a three-pillared structure for the Union;
- it sets out a procedure for economic and monetary union;
- it sets out procedures for intergovernmental co-operation in foreign and security policy;
- it sets out procedures for intergovernmental co-operation in justice and home affairs;
- it deepens and extends the EC's policy portfolio (in some cases this involves the deepening of existing policy and in other cases new policy areas are introduced);
- it establishes the principle of subsidiarity;
- the European Council is identified as responsible for providing the Union with the impetus for development and for defining the Union's general political guidelines;
- it extends the use of qualified majority voting in the Council;
- it increases the powers of the European Parliament;
- it creates a Committee of the Regions;
- it upgrades the Court of Auditors to a full Community institution.

O **Subsidiarity**

The Treaty seeks to clarify the boundaries between national and Community levels of responsibility for policy, by stating that Community action will be in accordance with the principle of 'subsidiarity'. Subsidiarity is now widely regarded as one of the most important of all principles relating to European integration. It is not mentioned in any of the previous treaties, although there is one implicit reference to it in the SEA (Article 11). It was first given prominence in the preamble to the EP's Draft Treaty on European Union in 1984. It is defined in the following way in the TEU:

> **The Community shall act within the limits of the powers conferred upon it by this Treaty and of the objectives assigned to it therein.**
>
> **In areas which do not fall within its exclusive competence, the Community shall take action, in accordance with the principle of subsidiarity, only if and**

in so far as the objectives of the proposed action cannot be sufficiently achieved by the member States and can therefore, by reason of the scale or effects of the proposed action, be better achieved by the Community.

Any action by the Community shall not go beyond what is necessary to achieve the objectives of this Treaty (Article 3b).

Each of the above three paragraphs has been subject to intense scrutiny. The definition is of crucial importance because of its implications for the distribution of power between regional, national and European levels of government. It is a broad principle rather than a clear guide and is open to many different interpretations. A common interpretation is that decisions should be taken at the lowest possible level (that is national, regional or local) rather than at 'European' level, unless there is good reason to do otherwise – that is, it involves the search for the best level of government. It could mean that the EU should not have its finger in every pie and should only do what states cannot do well for themselves. John Major seized on the principle as a kind of talisman against 'federalism', viewing it as moving decision-making back towards the member states in areas where Community law need not, and should not apply. But it has also been interpreted as fitting into the logic of federalism, by allowing for division of responsibilities between levels of government (European, national and regional). Indeed, it has been argued that it only makes sense within a federal context.

But some federalists view the principle with suspicion, fearing that it might be used by national governments as a fig leaf to avoid their commitments. The principle could run counter to the Union's attempts to introduce common standards in many policy areas. Arguably, many EU policies, such as the CAP and social and regional policy, conflict directly with the principle (for example, the Social Chapter requires the harmonisation of employment laws). The European Council in Lisbon in June 1992 favoured the strict application of the subsidiarity principle to legislation and institutions and commissioned studies of how this could be achieved. From September 1992, the Commission implemented a new procedure for reviewing proposals on the grounds of subsidiarity. The Commission's paper on subsidiarity in October 1992 stated that 'a first consequence of the subsidiarity principle is that national powers are the rule and the Community's the exception'. The special European Council in Birmingham in November 1992 called for 'subsidiarity tests' when legislation was being prepared. This led to a set of guidelines, agreed at the European Council in Edinburgh in December 1992, which require the following questions to be put in relation to any proposal:

• *Can the Community act? Does it have a legal basis to do so?*
• *Should the Community act? Can it be achieved by member states, or will it*

be better achieved by the Community?
- *How much should the Community do? Is it using the lightest possible form of legislation, leaving as much as possible for national decision?*

The European Council in Edinburgh also agreed procedures to ensure that these questions were addressed at all stages of the Community's legislative process. Thus all Commission proposals where appropriate would include a subsidiarity declaration and all proposals would be examined by the Council in relation to Article 3b. Any member state could insist that proposals which raise subsidiarity issues be put on a Council agenda. An interinstitutional agreement on subsidiarity was reached between the Council, the EP and Commission in October 1993. The institutions undertook to ensure that they applied 'subsidiarity checks' to their internal procedures. The Commission is required to include a subsidiarity justification in its explanatory memoranda on draft legislation. It is also required to produce an annual report on compliance with subsidiarity. The Council and Parliament must also justify amendments to Commission proposals which involve more intensive or extensive Community intervention. At the European Council in Brussels in December 1993, the Commission set out a programme for the simplification, recasting and in some cases repeal of legislation. Despite these developments, the mechanism for allocating responsibilities between the European and the national (or regional) levels is still rather unclear. It seems likely that the ECJ will be required to make judgments in key test cases on subsidiarity issues.

○ The Intergovernmental Pillars

Titles V and VI create two intergovernmental pillars, excluding the subjects of these pillars from the EC's normal decisionmaking processes. Title V states that general foreign and security policy guidelines will be decided by the European Council. The Council of the European Union will then define and implement the CFSP on the basis of these general guidelines. The Council will take common positions on issues and will decide matters to be taken by joint action by unanimous vote, although it may decide to use qualified majority voting (QMV) in respect of decisions on implementation. The Commission may refer questions on CFSP to the Council. The EP's role is confined to the rights to be consulted, to make recommendations and to be kept regularly informed. The CFSP pillar is outside the jurisdiction of the ECJ. Article J.4 states that the eventual framing of a common defence policy 'might in time lead to a common defence'. The Western European Union is to be developed as the defence component of the Union, working in co-operation with NATO. The role of the WEU and its relations with the European Union and NATO are elaborated in a declaration annexed to the Treaty. Title VI on co-operation in the fields of justice and home affairs identifies nine matters which members were to regard as of common interest (Table 3.3). With regard to these areas, member states are required to inform and consult one another within the Council with a view to adoption of joint positions and joint action. Article K.4 establishes a co-ordinating committee of senior officials (the 'K.4' Committee) to co-ordinate and prepare the Council's work and to give opinions on justice and home affairs matters.

Table 3.3 The JHA Pillar: 'Matters of Common Interest'

- asylum policy;
- rules governing the crossing by persons of the external borders of the member states;
- immigration policy;
- combating drug addiction;
- combating fraud on an international scale;
- judicial co-operation in civil matters;
- judicial co-operation in criminal matters;
- customs co-operation;
- police co-operation to prevent and combat terrorism, drug trafficking and other serious forms of international crime.

○ Social Policy

Because of British objections to the Social Charter, the seven social policy articles form a special protocol. Eleven countries stated their wish to implement the 1989 Social Charter on the basis of the *acquis communautaire.* The signatories use Community institutions to make policy in the areas covered by the protocol. The UK does not take part in deliberations or decisions on these areas. But the social provisions contained in the SEA are still applicable to the UK. The TEU therefore caused two legal bases to coexist: the social chapter of the EC Treaty applicable to all member states and the protocol on social policy under which Community Acts can be adopted for all member states excluding the UK.

● RATIFICATION AND IMPLEMENTATION

○ A Rough Passage

The Treaty was expected to come into force on 1 January 1993 (following ratification by national parliaments and by the EP) but its passage into law proved unexpectedly troublesome. With hindsight, the architects of the Treaty have only themselves to blame, because they had made little effort to engage ordinary citizens in the debates concerning 'European Union'. Public opinion polls exposed widespread ignorance about the content of the Treaty. Moreover, these polls also showed that a substantial proportion of European citizens were at best lukewarm about the goal of European Union.

The 'temple' structure added additional layers of complexity on to an already highly complex institutional structure. The vagueness and contradictory nature of the Treaty meant that anything could be read into it. It could be interpreted as either a defeat or victory for Euro-federalist ideals. Major described the outcome of the summit as 'game, set and match for Britain' (*The Times*, 11 December 1991), because it supposedly halted the centralising trend. Many of his Conservative colleagues in the House of Commons came to different conclusions. An increasingly vocal and well-organised opposition to Maastricht emerged in several member states. Three countries (Denmark, France and Ireland) held referenda on the Treaty. The referenda exposed an unexpected degree of public opposition to the Treaty. The Treaty was narrowly rejected in a Danish referendum in June 1992 (50.7% voted against it). The votes in Ireland in June (69% in favour) and in France in September (only 51.05% in favour) showed the extent of hostility to the Treaty. In debates on the referenda, issues directly relating to the Treaty became mixed up with other issues, such as abortion in Ireland and CAP reform in France.

The credibility of the Treaty was also undermined by internal and external events. The crises in the ERM from the summer of 1992 onwards jeopardised the prospects of rapid progress towards monetary union. There were increasing doubts in Germany as to whether Germans really wanted to exchange their solid Deutschmark for the untried ECU. The inability of the member states to develop a coherent and effective strategy to cope with the civil war in ex-Yugoslavia raised grave doubts about the feasibility of the common foreign and security policy. The Danish government sought to make the Treaty more palatable to the Danish electorate by seeking clarification of certain issues (that it could opt out of the final stage of monetary union; that it was not committed to participation in a common defence policy and that Union citizenship did not replace Danish citizenship). These assurances were given at the European Council in Edinburgh in December 1992, without need for a revision of the Treaty. The second Danish referendum held in May 1993, resulted in a 'yes' vote of 56.8%

In the UK, the Treaty was not a major issue in the April 1992 General Election. The three main parties supported it (the Labour and Liberal Democratic parties criticised the government for not accepting the full Maastricht package). After the election, the UK government's presentation of the Treaty as a victory for the intergovernmentalist, decentralising tendency came under attack from a powerful backbench group of 'Eurosceptic' Conservative MPs, who fought a long rearguard action against ratification. The UK government finally ratified the Treaty in August 1993. It was ratified by Germany in October 1993, following a ruling by the German Constitutional Court. The Treaty came into force on 1 November 1993. Even after ratification, the future of the Treaty (if viewed as a blueprint for the Union's development) remained in doubt: key policy provisions, for example in relation to EMU, social policy and CFSP, are proving far more difficult to put into practice than was envisaged at Maastricht. In many respects, the Treaty is a rather insular document, which gives insufficient weight to current international circumstances (in particular, to the impact of the end of the cold war upon the structure of Europe).

● EVALUATION AND INTERPRETATION OF THE TEU

○ Is the TEU a Federal Treaty?

The TEU is open to too many interpretations for this question to be definitively answered. It is easy to seize on a particular statement in the Treaty in order to justify the worst fears of the anti-federalists. Neither the word 'federal' nor 'supranational' occurs anywhere in the Treaty. Prior to the Maastricht summit, the Commission published a discussion paper which favoured the creation of a Union 'of a federal type'. However, the word federalism was deliberately omitted from the Treaty, at British insistence. The general thrust of the Treaty is towards closer integration (perhaps 'federalising' rather than 'federalist'): its provisions, if realised, would give the Union some of the major features of a federal state, such as a common currency, a central bank and a common foreign and security policy. The EP's report on the Treaty viewed it as 'a step forward, albeit an insufficient one, on the road to a European Union of federal type' (EP, 1992, p. 25).

Conversely, the Treaty has also been viewed as an essentially *intergovernmentalist* treaty, which keeps power firmly in the hands of national governments. The UK government has presented the TEU as constituting a defeat for Euro-federalist ideas, because it confirms the role of governments in Union decisionmaking processes and affirms the 'anti-centralising' doctrine of subsidiarity. The key policy areas of foreign and security policy and justice and home affairs remain largely outside Community decisionmaking structures. Union citizenship is both vaguely defined and limited. British Eurosceptics, however, remain unconvinced and view it as a federalist document which, if fully implemented. would reduce the sovereignties of member states to mere ciphers. The Treaty might also be interpreted as providing a blueprint for a multispeed Europe, in that it effectively sanctions opt-outs on EMU, defence and aspects of social policy.

○ The Case For and Against the TEU

The main arguments in this debate are summarised in Table 3.4.

Table 3.4 The Case For and Against the TEU

For
- it constitutes a logical stage on the road to European integration;
- it sets out a comprehensive approach to European integration;
- it narrows the EU's democratic deficit, by giving more power to the EP;
- it contains many benefits for ordinary people, such as extra voting rights and additional social, diplomatic and consular protection;
- co-ordinated action is required to tackle issues of mutual concern to member states (such as economic policy, crime and foreign policy);
- it complements the SEM, by seeking to remove barriers to cross-border trade not dealt with by SEM provisions (notably currency differences);
- it lays down a foundation for economic and monetary union;
- without further development, the integration process would stall (bicyclists who stop peddling fall off).

Against
- it involves a huge loss of sovereignty by member states: major areas of policy are being removed from the control of national governments and parliaments;
- it is a 'ragbag' of vague commitments and compromises. Virtually anything can be read into it;
- it is a treaty too soon. The SEM process is by no means finished. Enlargement should take priority over further deepening;
- monetary union is by no means a necessary requirement of European integration;
- it is a treaty too far: as the three referenda and subsequent opinion polls have shown, the people of Europe do not want it;
- public knowledge and understanding of the Treaty remains low:
- it is unworkable: many provisions are too ambitious and are proving very difficult to achieve;
- deeper European integration makes it more difficult for other European countries to enter the Union.

○ The 1996 Intergovernmental Conference

The TEU was the first Union treaty to establish a procedure for its own revision. Article N of Title VII provides for an intergovernmental conference (IGC) to be convened in 1996, to examine certain provisions of the Treaty. Because much of the 1996 IGC's deliberations will focus on institutional questions, it will be examined in greater detail in the next chapter.

FURTHER READING

Begg, D., *Making Sense of Subsidiarity*, Centre for Economic Policy Research, London, 1993.

Church, C.H. and Phinnemore, D., *European Union and European Community*, Harvester Wheatsheaf, London, 1994.

Commission, *Treaty on European Union*, 1992.

Coombes, D., *Understanding European Union*, Longman, London, 1994.

Corbett, R., *The Treaty of Maastricht*, Longman, London, 1993.

European Parliament, *Maastricht: the Position of the EP*, Luxembourg, 1992.

Howe, M., *Europe and the Constitution after Maastricht*, Nelson & Pollard, Oxford, 1992.

Laursen, F. and Vanhoonacker, S. (eds), *The Intergovernmental Conference on Political Union*, Martinus Nijhoff, Dordrecht, 1992.

Spicer, M., *A Treaty Too Far*, Fourth Estate, London, 1992.

Section 2

Institutions and Policy Processes

 **Chapter 4**

Institutions and Policy Processes

● KEY FEATURES OF THE UNION'S INSTITUTIONAL STRUCTURE

○ The Structure is Unique

The unique character of the European Union (neither a state nor an international organisation, but with features of both) is reflected in its institutional structure. A key feature of a state is that it has a government with an identifiable head. Within the EU there is no clearly defined 'government' or 'opposition' as such. Nor does the Union's institutional structure fit the conventional model of the three branches of government (executive, legislative and judicial) within a state. Elements of each of the above features of governance can be discerned in the Union's institutional structure, but analogies can be misleading. Perhaps the most misleading analogy of all would be to liken the Union to a smoothly running, elegantly-designed machine comprising neatly fitting interlocking parts and constructed by a single engineer at a particular point in time. The Union system of governance is more like a contraption with many rough and fuzzy edges, consisting of a set of machines with roughly interacting parts designed by many hands, inspired by different ideas, frequently adapted and roughly tuned. The system is composed of a network of interdependent institutions, none of which can function (or indeed makes sense) without reference to others.

○ The Influence of Treaties

Perhaps the single most important feature of the Union is that it is founded on treaties. In the absence of a written constitution, treaties provide the legal foundation of the Union's institutional framework. For example, the roles of the Union's principal institutions, are set out (by no means fully or unambiguously) in the treaties. The institutions are required to act within the powers conferred upon them by the treaties. The treaties also impose legal obligations upon member states. The institutional complexity of the Union is exacerbated by the fact that it is not based on a single treaty (the SEA and TEU amended, but did not replace, the earlier treaties). Nor do the treaties provide a comprehensive and up-to-date guide to the Union's actual institutional structure or activities. For example, one of the Union's most important institutions, the European Council, operated for over a decade before it was even mentioned in a treaty.

○ An Evolving Structure

The Union's somewhat ramshackle structure exemplifies the Union's *ad hoc* approach to institutional change. Unlike many state constitutions, which have a quality of finality about them, the Union's treaties were never meant to be the last word on the Union's institutional arrangements. The Union's 'institutional balance' (the distribution of power between institutions) has undergone significant changes in recent years and is continuing to evolve. For example, the power of the European Parliament has significantly increased in the last decade. The European Council, although not established until 1974 and deriving from informal 'fireside chat' meetings between governmental heads, is a body of first-rank importance. The TEU established a three-pillared institutional framework and also created several new Union agencies. The 1996 IGC will consider further institutional reforms.

○ The Influence of Competing Values and Interests

Both 'intergovernmental' and 'supranational' institutions coexist (not always harmoniously) within the Union. The Council and European Council are intergovernmental bodies, comprising ministerial representatives from member states, whereas the Commission, Court of Justice and Parliament have supranational characteristics, designed to reflect a European interest which transcends the specific interests of member states. This hybrid structure reflects the conflicting influences of intergovernmentalist and supranationalist pressures on the Union's development.

○ A Highly Complex Institutional Framework

Article C of the TEU states that the Union is served by 'a single institutional framework'. But this statement needs to be qualified. As Figure 4.1 below shows, the framework does not fit neatly into the three-pillared Union structure created by the TEU.

Figure 4.1 The Union's Institutional Framework

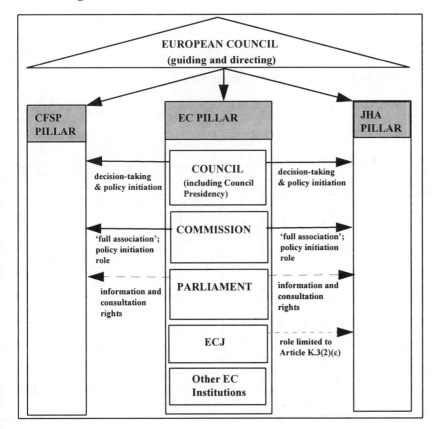

The Union does not (with the exception of the European Council) have institutions of its own but utilises those of the European Community. With the exception of the Council, the role of EC institutions in the inter-governmental pillars is limited. The Commission is 'fully associated' with the work of the CFSP and JHA pillars, but does not have sole right of policy initiative under these pillars. It shares this role with member states (Articles J.8 and K.3). The EP's role in the intergovernmental pillars (Articles J.7 and K.6) is very limited: it has a right to ask questions of, and to make recommendations to, the Council; it must be consulted and have its views considered by the Council presidency; it is kept informed by the Council presidency and by the Commission of developments in the intergovernmental pillars. The ECJ has no role in relation to the CFSP pillar and a very limited role in the JHA pillar (that is, only in relation to Article K.3(2)(c), dealing with conventions). Because of the degree of independence to be granted to the European Central Bank (ECB) under the TEU, arguably the ECB, when established, will constitute a *de facto* fourth pillar. Despite the 1965 Merger Treaty, the ECSC still has a somewhat different institutional structure to that of the European Community and Euratom.

○　The Principle of 'State Representation'

This principle is woven into the institutional fabric of the Union (Table 4.1).

Table 4.1　The Principle of State Representation

	Population	Council	EP	Comm	ECJ	ESC	COR	CA
	1000s	Votes	Seats	App.	App.	App.	App.	App.
Austria	8,006	4	21	1	1	11	11	1
Belgium	10,101	5	25	1	1	12	12	1
Denmark	5,197	3	16	1	1	9	9	1
Finland	5,078	3	16	1	1	9	9	1
France	57,800	10	87	2	1	24	24	1
Germany	81,353	10	99	2	1	24	24	1
Greece	10,390	5	25	1	1	12	12	1
Ireland	3,571	3	15	1	1	9	9	1
Italy	57,154	10	87	2	1	24	24	1
Lux.	401	2	6	1	1	6	6	1
Neth.	15,341	5	31	1	1	12	12	1
Portugal	9,868	5	25	1	1	12	12	1
Spain	39,168	8	64	2	1	21	21	1
Sweden	8,745	4	22	1	1	11	11	1
UK	58,276	10	87	2	1	24	24	1
TOTAL	370,449	87	626	20	15	220	220	15

Comm: Commission; ECJ: European Court of Justice; ESC: Economic and Social Committee; COR: Committee of the Regions; CA: Court of Auditors; App: Appointments.

Member states are allocated votes in the Council, seats in the EP and nomination rights in relation to appointed bodies (although appointees are required to serve the interests of the Union as a whole and do not take orders from any government). The principle extends to language: with the entry of Finland and Sweden, the number of official languages rose from 9 to 11. In 1994, the translation service translated 1,024,000 pages of documents and provided interpreters for more than 10,000 meetings. The rules governing member states' representation in EU institutions give smaller states greater institutional weight than their population sizes justify (Table 4.1).

● CLASSIFICATION OF UNION INSTITUTIONS

The Union now contains so many institutions that some attempt at classification is necessary. The most obvious classification is on the basis of what the institutions do and the roles they perform, as shown in Table 4.2.

Table 4.2 The Main Functions and Roles of the Institutions

Institution	Main Functions and Roles
Commission *(appointed)*	policy initiation; implementation; guardian of treaties; drafting budget; monitoring; troubleshooting; external relations; 'motor' of integration
European Council *(heads of government of member states)*	guidance and strategic direction; decision-taking
Council of the European Union *(ministers of member states)*	main legislative and decision-taking arm; adoption of budget; external relations
European Parliament *(directly elected)*	legislative scrutiny, amendment and (limited) 'co-decision'; assent; supervision; adoption of budget; discussion forum; redress of grievances
European Court of Justice *(appointed)*	judicial interpretation and enforcement
Economic and Social Committee *(appointed)*	advice and representation
Committee of the Regions *(appointed)*	advice and representation
Court of Auditors *(appointed)*	financial auditing
European Investment Bank *(appointed)*	financing Union development projects
Other Institutions *(appointed)*	see below for details

However, the treaties do not provide detailed and comprehensive descriptions of institutional functions and roles. Moreover, the functions and roles of several institutions overlap. A common distinction is between the five 'principal' institutions' (the Commission, Council of the European Union, European Council, Parliament, Court of Justice) and the rest. The principal institutions are regarded as indispensable to the operation of the Union in its present form, although several other institutions form an integral part of the Union's institutional framework. The Union's institutions will now be examined in more detail.

● THE COMMISSION

○ Main Functions and Roles

The Commission is at the heart of the Union's activities and performs major political, executive, legislative, administrative and monitoring tasks. The Commission is sometimes referred to as a 'civil service' but this is misleading. It has considerably more formal power and a much broader range of responsibilities, than, say, the British civil service. It also performs functions which are more directly and overtly political than a public bureaucracy. The Commission was originally conceived as an apolitical, technocratic body, but its guiding, energising and monitoring roles are clearly political (as is its strong impulse towards deeper Union integration). Most Commissioners are prominent career politicians (in the second Delors Commission, only one Commissioner was not a politician. The 1995–99 Commission includes an ex-trades union leader, a professional economist, a 'technocrat' and a diplomat, but several of these have party affiliations). Those appointed tend to be prominent in their own countries, although most have not achieved the highest positions. The Commission's principal functions and roles are:
• **Policy Initiation and Development.** The EC, Euratom and ECSC Treaties bestow upon the Commission primary responsibility for initiating and formulating policy proposals. This responsibility extends to both general and specific proposals, ranging from fundamental ideas concerning the future direction of the Union to technical legislation. Each year its sends proposals, recommendations, drafts, memoranda and reports to the Council for consideration. In 1994, it sent 558 proposals, recommendations or draft instruments to the Council, plus 272 communications, memoranda and reports. The Commission has the sole power to initiate Community legislation (Article 155, EC). Although the Council and EP can request the

Commission to produce legislative proposals, they cannot initiate or draft them. The Council cannot take legislative decisions without a proposal from the Commission. Amendments to Commission proposals by the Council require the Commission's approval, except where the Council puts forward an amendment by unanimous vote. The Commission draws up a legislative programme for each year, which is published in the *Official Journal*. In relation to the Union's two intergovernmental pillars, the Commission shares rights of policy initiative with the Council.

The Commission engages in an extensive network of consultations with Union institutions, governments, and pressure groups prior to the submission of proposals. It is advised by a network of committees, principally by consultative committees (representatives of sectional interests, nominated by industry, unions, consumer groups and so on) and appointed by the Commission; and by committees of experts nominated by national governments. The 'expert' committees tend to meet more regularly than the consultative committees and also tend to be more influential.

• **Implementation.** Its implementation tasks are primarily concerned with rule-making, monitoring and co-ordinating rather than actually delivering policies. It is responsible for ensuring that policies are carried out and provides guidance on implementation to a wide range of organisations in the public and private sectors. It operates the Common Agricultural Policy. It is in charge of the administration of Community funds (including aid programmes for Eastern Europe and the Third World). Its implementation powers derive either directly from the treaties or from powers conferred on it by the Council. It has its own powers under the EC Treaty in relation to competition policy and the control of government subsidies. The treaties give the Commission some direct legislative powers, mainly in relation to the ECSC and the operation of the Common External Tariff (CET). The Council has conferred upon the Commission some legislative powers in specific and technical policy areas, mainly to do with agriculture and the completion of the internal market.

• **The 'Guardian of the Treaties'.** It has a major responsibility to ensure that the provisions of the Treaties and the decisions of Community institutions are properly applied. Its watchdog role give it the power to supervise the day-to-day running of Community policies and to investigate breaches of Community rules. It can investigate possible breaches on its own initiative or as a result of complaints from governments, firms or individuals. Member states are required to notify the Commission of directives incorporated into national law. It can and does take member states to the ECJ for failing to fulfil their treaty obligations. In 1994, it referred 89 cases to the ECJ.

It has well-developed procedures for dealing with breaches of policy or failure to implement policy. It informs the state concerned before initiating infringement proceedings. It sends a letter of formal notice, requiring a reply within two months. If no satisfactory explanation is forthcoming, it issues an opinion stating why the member is in breach of its treaty obligations. Again there is normally a two-month period to reply. This is usually the end of the matter. But if no satisfactory reply is forthcoming, the Commission may refer the matter to the ECJ. It issued infringement proceedings in 974 cases in 1994 (mainly because directives had not been properly incorporated into national law) although the vast majority of these will be settled without resort to the Court.

The TEU gives the Commission the power to recommend that a fine be imposed by the ECJ on a member state which has failed to comply with an earlier judgment of the Court. It can impose fines on firms in breach of Community law on restrictive trade practices. It can require firms breaching rules on 'state aids' (state subsidies for industry) to pay back moneys. It has the power to block large cross-border mergers. It also administers 'safeguard clauses' in the treaties, which allow treaty requirements to be waived in certain circumstances.

• **Financial Responsibilities.** Each year it draws up a draft Community budget and is involved at each further stage of the budgetary process. It manages the budget and is also involved in the management of various programmes which are funded jointly by the EU and other countries or organisations (for example, pan-European research programmes and the PHARE (Poland and Hungary: Aid for Economic Restructuring) programme for Eastern Europe, which it administers on behalf of the OECD).

• **Interinstitutional Brokerage and Troubleshooting.** It performs vitally important mediation and conciliation roles, for example by seeking to find compromise formulae acceptable to all member governments in disputes within the Council and by seeking to broker deals between the Council and Parliament in relation to Community legislation.

• **External Relations.** The Commission has acquired an increasingly prominent international role as a negotiator on behalf of the Union, although the agreements it reaches with other countries and with international organisations are subject to the approval of the Council and in some cases of the EP. It negotiates a wide variety of external agreements. It is a representative or participant on behalf of the Union in meetings of several major international organisations, including the World Trade Organisation (WTO), the OECD and the UN. It maintains delegations in many parts of the world and is the focal point of contact for the diplomatic missions which most countries maintain with the Union. It is 'fully associated' with the work of the CFSP pillar, although in a role which is subordinate and supportive to the Council.

○ Limits on the Commission's Powers

Despite its formidable range of functions, the Commission is by no means all powerful. It has a weaker claim to a democratic mandate than the Council, European Council or Parliament: whereas the Commission is an appointed body, the Council and European Council are made up of the representatives of democratically elected governments and the EP of directly elected members. It must operate within the powers granted to it by the treaties. For example, although it has the power of policy initiation, its proposals can be, and often are, rejected or amended. It has no power to force the Council, European Council or Parliament to accept its proposals. It formulates budgetary proposals, but these are subject to the approval of the Council and Parliament. Moreover, the Council, and European Council exercise directing roles which effectively place limits on the Commission's roles as policy initiator and 'motor' of the Union. Although the Commission plays the key role in formulating rules and procedures for policy implementation, policies are largely carried out by the national, regional and local bureaucracies of member states. All EU policy areas have both national and Union dimensions and it would make no sense to have two sets of bureaucracies to administer measures within a specific policy field.

Devolved policy implementation in the Union is no unmixed blessing. It has resulted in serious problems of uneven and patchy implementation, through non-compliance and foot-dragging. There is considerable scope for policies to be washed out, diluted or delayed at the implementation stage. The diversity of administrative traditions, legal systems and domestic conditions is a formidable obstacle to synchronised policy implementation. The Commission also lacks the resources for effective monitoring.

○ The Commissioners

Collectively known as the 'college', the Commissioners are required to be chosen on the basis of their general competence by common accord of member states. Their independence must be 'beyond doubt' (Article 157, EC) and they are required to give an undertaking neither to seek nor take instructions from any government or body. The complexion of the Commission is, however, determined by national governments, because they choose the Commissioners on the basis of criteria more specific than general competence. Commissioners from smaller member states (which each nominate one Commissioner) are usually associated with the governing party. The governments of states nominating two (see Table 4.3) tend to choose one from the governing party and one from the opposition, although this is not a legal requirement.

Table 4.3 The European Commission (1995–99)

Name, Age, Nationality	Responsibility
Jacques Santer *(54) Luxembourg*	President, common foreign and security policy (with Mr van den Broek), monetary matters (with Mr de Silguy), institutional questions (with Mr Oreja);
Leon Brittan* *(55) UK*	multilateral trade, rels with developed countries, China, Hong Kong, S. Korea Macao, Taiwan, the OECD and WTO;
Neil Kinnock *(52) UK*	transport;
Edith Cresson *(60) France*	science, RTD, human resources, education, training, youth;
Yves-Thibault de Silguy *(46) France*	economic and financial affairs, monetary affairs (with the President);
Monika Wulf-Mathies *(52) Germany*	regional policies, the Cohesion Fund (with Mr Kinnock and Mrs Bjerregaard);
Martin Bangemann* *(59) Germany*	industry, information technology, telecommunications;
Mario Monti *(51) Italy*	internal market, financial services, taxation;
Emma Bonino *(46) Italy*	consumer affairs, EC Humanitarian Office, fisheries;
Marcelino Oreja *(59) Spain*	institutional affairs, culture, media;
Manuel Marin* *(45) Spain*	rels with Latin America, Mediterranean, Middle and Near East, Asia (excluding Japan, China, S. Korea, Hong Kong, Macao, Taiwan);
Joao de Deus Pinheiro* *(59) Portugal*	relations with Africa, Caribbean, Pacific countries. The Lomé Convention;
Karel Van Miert* *(52) Belgium*	competition;
Hans Van den Broek* *(57) Netherlands*	Central and Eastern Europe, Turkey, Cyprus, Malta, other European countries, CFSP (with President);
Ritt Bjerregaard *(53) Denmark*	environment, nuclear safety;
Padraig Flynn* *(54) Ireland*	employment, social policy;
Christos Papoutsis *(41) Greece*	SMEs, energy, tourism;
Erkki Liikanen *(44) Finland*	budget, personnel, translation;
Franz Fischler *(48) Austria*	agriculture and rural development;
Anita Gradin *(51) Sweden*	immigration, home and judical affairs, relations with the Ombudsman, financial control, anti-fraud measures.

* Member of previous Commission.

In the UK a convention has developed that one Commissioner is chosen from the governing party and one from the opposition. Governments can also choose not to appoint Commissioners to a second term. Lord Cockfield was not reappointed by Mrs Thatcher, after a series of disagreements with her about the SEM programme. Although Commissioners are appointed to serve the 'general interest', they nevertheless bring with them valuable national perspectives, which helps to ensure that the Commission is not divorced from national thinking. The fact that Commissioners may wish to return to national politics serves as an incentive for them not to completely disregard national interests, but it would be unwise for them to push the latter too overtly.

Following the entry of Austria, Finland and Sweden in January 1995, the number of Commissioners increased from 17 to 20. Under the TEU, member states are required to collectively choose a nominee for president by unanimous agreement, in consultation with the EP, before nominating the other Commissioners. The Treaty also requires the Council's nomination for this post to be approved by the EP. The EP exercised this right on the re-appointment of Delors and the appointment of Jacques Santer (then Prime Minister of Luxembourg). Member states are required to consult with the nominee for president before nominating the other Commissioners. Each nominated Commission must be approved by a vote of Parliament before it can take office (Article 158, EC). Commissioners serve for a renewable term of five years.

Parliament remains dissatisfied with the dominant role played by governments in the selection process and is seeking to exert a much stronger influence. MEPs would like the Commission to include at least some former MEPs and more women. In January 1995, MEPs cross-examined each of the nominees for the 1995–99 Commission in confirmation hearings (even though the TEU makes no provision for individual hearings). At these hearings, the performances of five Commissioners were judged by MEPs to have been unsatisfactory, but the EP has no power to reject individual nominees. Commissioners can only be removed collectively by the EP. Individual Commissioners can be removed by the ECJ, on application by the Council or Commission, for failing to fulfil conditions for performance of their duties or for serious misconduct. Neither has ever happened.

What criteria determine the choice of president? Although the selection process is by no means fully open, it is possible to identify some key factors shaping choices. The candidates are likely to have held high rank: possible candidates to succeed Delors included four serving prime ministers (Jean-Luc Dehaene, Felipe González, Ruud Lubbers, Santer), a former head of GATT (Peter Sutherland) and a serving Commissioner and former Cabinet Minister (Leon Brittan). Only two Presidents however (Santer and Gaston Thorn) had held prime ministerial office. Many issues surfaced during the selection process for the new president in 1994. The UK government suspected that France and Germany were seeking to foist their preferred candidate

(Dehaene, the Belgian Prime Minister) on other members. At the Corfu European Council in June 1994, the UK government vetoed the nomination of Dehaene on the grounds that he was a federalist and a supporter of 'big government'. Leon Brittan's chances were probably handicapped by his strong views on free trade and his background as a former member of a Thatcher cabinet. Following deadlock on the issue at Corfu, a special summit meeting in July chose Santer as a compromise candidate. Santer had been nobody's first choice. The EP threatened to reject his nomination on the grounds that they had been excluded from the selection process, but endorsed it by 260 votes to 238, with 23 abstentions. The president-designate was questioned at a plenary session of the EP before the vote. Santer's presidency began on 5 January 1995.

Table 4.4 Commission Presidents

Period	President	Country
1958–67	Walter Hallstein	Germany
1967–70	Jean Rey	Belgium
1970–72	Franco Maria Malfatti	Italy
1972–73	Sicco Mansholt	Netherlands
1973–77	François-Xavier Ortoli	France
1977–81	Roy Jenkins	UK
1981–85	Gaston Thorn	Luxembourg
1985–94	Jacques Delors	France
1995–99	Jacques Santer	Luxembourg

It has been suggested that presidents tend to be chosen from big and small countries in rotation (although not invariably so, as Table 4.4 shows). The current holder is the second Luxembourger to have held the post. The performance of the incumbent is another factor shaping preferences. In 1994, there seemed to be wide agreement that the nominee should not be another 'philosopher king' like Delors. Santer is thought to be more of a conciliator and team player than Delors (who was accused of running an 'imperial presidency'). Unlike Delors, Santer does not come from a centralising administrative tradition.

○ The President's Roles

He (always a 'he' so far) plays a major role in distributing Commission portfolios; he performs a guiding and co-ordinating role in relation to the Commission as a whole; he is the main spokesman of the Commission; he is the chief representative of the Commission in its dealings with other EU institutions; he sets out the Commission's annual programme each January in the EP. The President undoubtedly occupies a powerful position, as became apparent during Delors' presidencies. Delors was the first Commission President to become widely known throughout the Union.

However, the President is by no means all powerful. He is not elected and therefore does not have a democratic mandate. He does not appoint the Commissioners, nor can he dismiss them, although member governments are required to consult with the president-designate before choosing the other Commissioners. Officially, the President decides the portfolios of the Commissioners, but in practice selections are heavily influenced by trade-offs between national governments. The Commissioners naturally have their own preferences and therefore also seek to influence the selection process. Larger member states expect that one of their nominees will be given a big portfolio. 'Big' Commission portfolios also tend to go to reappointed Commissioners.

Ten Commissioners in the 1993–95 Commission were retained from the previous Commission, but only seven in the 1995–99 (Santer) Commission. Santer's *Chef de Cabinet* (chief of staff) Jim Cloos played a key role in deciding and demarcating portfolios for the 1995–99 Commission. Santer has sought to break up portfolios, to prevent the 'personal fiefdoms' which developed under Delors and also to improve co-ordination between Commissioners. He decided to have a share in responsibility for CFSP, monetary affairs and institutional questions. In the Santer Commission, there is also more geographical demarcation (that is, responsibility for relations with particular regions or countries).

○ **The Organisation of the Commission**

The Commission is a 'college', meaning that Commission decisions are taken on a collective, basis. It is based in Brussels and has offices in Luxembourg. From January 1995, the term of office of the Commission was extended from four to five years, to make it co-terminous with that of the European Parliament. The TEU gave the Commission the right to designate from its members one or two vice-presidents. Prior to this, no less than six Commissioners were so designated. The new system therefore upgrades the vice-presidential role. In February 1995, Leon Brittan and Manuel Marin were elected vice-presidents of the Commission in a secret ballot of the Commissioners.

Each Commissioner has his or her own private office or Cabinet of six or seven members, headed by a *Chef de Cabinet*. They are the personal staff of the Commissioners, and are normally chosen from the Commissioner's home country (from the civil service, a political party or interest group). A Cabinet gets an extra member if it includes someone who is not a national of the

Commissioner's own country. The *Chefs de Cabinet* meet to prepare proposals for the weekly meeting of the Commissioners. A major part of the Commission's business is agreed by the Cabinets, leaving unresolved issues and broader questions to the Commissioners themselves. There is a network of inter-Cabinet committees, to facilitate co-ordination. The College of Commissioners takes decisions (where necessary) by simple majority vote. The Commission held 46 meetings in 1994. The most important Cabinet is that of the President. The Commission's weekly agenda is prepared by the President's *Chef de Cabinet* and by the Secretary-General of the Commission. The Cabinet, comprising about 11 members, frees up time for the President, deflects conflict from him and feeds him with ideas and information. The Delors Cabinet, headed by the redoubtable Pascal Lamy, was three-quarters French and conducted its business in French. Most Commission business is conducted in French or English.

Below Cabinet level, the Commission is organised into units with specific policy or support responsibilities. The basic unit is the Directorate-General (DG), within which are Directorates and Divisions. There are currently 24 DGs; between 1 and 8 Directorates within each DG and between 5 and 36 Divisions in each Directorate. Some DGs report to more than one Commissioner. Various mechanisms for ensuring effective co-ordination between DGs have been adopted. There are regular meetings of members of the different Cabinets and many inter-DG committees, but the degree of co-ordination between DGs is still widely thought to be insufficient. There are also various specialist units, including a Secretariat-General, a Legal Service, a Spokesman's Service, a Statistical Office, a Translation Service, a European Community Humanitarian Office (ECHO), an Office for Official Publications and an Enlargement Task Force. The Secretary-General, who takes the minutes of the Commission, is the President's main advisor on appointments. There have been only two Secretaries-General so far, Emile Noel and David Williamson. The Legal Service plays a key role in approving major policy initiatives and monitoring breaches of Community law.

The staff of the Commission, excluding the members of the Cabinets and the Commissioners, are known as 'the Services'. These are career officials recruited mainly by open competitive examination from all member states and are usually located in Brussels. In 1994, there were 14,070 permanent posts, and 848 temporary posts, plus 465 permanent posts in the Office for Official Publications. About 15% are engaged in translation services. In actuality, the criterion of 'national balance' as well as merit is a factor in the promotion of Commission staff. For example, there is an informal national quota system for senior Commission posts. The 'quota system' is currently being challenged in the ECJ.

○ **Evaluation**

Arguably, if the Commission did not exist, it would have to be invented, because no other institution is capable of holding the Union together. It has played a powerful role in each major development of the Union. It takes a broader (Union-wide) view on affairs than national governments. Arguably, it can also take a longer view, because it is less likely to be affected by political short-termism than elected officials.

The Commission is a frequent target for criticism. In popular mythology, it is regarded as synonymous with 'Brussels', a shorthand term for bloated, overcentralised, rule-obsessed bureaucracy It has been argued that the Commission has too much power for an unelected body; that it combines too many roles; that its political and administrative functions are inherently incompatible; that there are too many Commissioners, with too many overlapping responsibilities; and that it has insufficient resources to achieve its formidable range of tasks. However, the Commission is clearly not the vast, all powerful bureaucracy of popular legend.

Many possible reforms of the Commission have been suggested: for example, it has been argued that its powers need to be more precisely defined, narrowed or even unbundled. The number of Commissioners might be reduced (perhaps by removing the right of each country to appoint a Commissioner). One suggestion is for big countries to be allocated a senior Commissioner, with other Commission places allocated to small countries on a rotation basis. The Commission could be selected by the Commission President from nominations from member states and approved by both the EP and the Council. Another possibility is that Commissioners could be chosen by the EP. Member states, however, are unlikely to surrender their dominant role in the selection of the Commission.

● THE COUNCIL OF THE EUROPEAN UNION (widely referred to as the Council of Ministers, or as 'the Council')

○ **Main Functions and Roles**

The Council is an intergovernmental institution, comprising ministerial representatives of member states. It is the Union's main legislative arm, having the final say in the adoption of EC law (although it now shares some legislative power with the EP). It takes decisions and confers power on the Commission to act. Together with the EP, it adopts the budget. It is responsible for co-ordinating member states' economic policies (Article 145,

EC). It is responsible for putting the guidelines of the European Council into effect (see below). It is playing an increasingly important role in policy initiation: policy ideas from the Council feed into the Commission through the various contacts between the two institutions. It may request the Commission to undertake studies for the achievement of common objectives (Article 152, EC). The Council has responsibility for intergovernmental co-operation in relation to the CFSP and JHA pillars of the TEU.

The Council meets mainly in Brussels, in its own purpose-built headquarters. In practice, there are many 'Councils' (more than 20), because the ministerial composition of Council meetings depends on the subject matter. For example, meetings on agriculture or transport are attended by transport or agriculture ministers respectively. Meetings of the Council of Economic and Finance Ministers are known as ECOFIN; those of foreign ministers are known as the General Affairs Council. The number of meetings for each Council varies from once or twice a year to every month (excluding August). The General Affairs, ECOFIN and Agriculture Councils each meet monthly (excluding August). At Council meetings ministers are supported by a small team of officials. Large numbers of officials (for example, foreign ministry advisors, permanent representatives, plus other advisors) attend meetings of the General Affairs Council. Items not resolved in other Councils may be referred to the General Affairs Council, but this is not always the case. Unresolved issues may also be discussed by the European Council, but this meets only two or three times a year.

The European Council in Edinburgh in December 1992 agreed that the Council will continue to be based in Brussels, with meetings in April, June and October in Luxembourg. Meetings take place behind closed doors. They are chaired by ministers from the member country holding the six-month presidency of the Council. At least one Commissioner attends these meetings, which usually last for one day. In 1994, the Council held 95 meetings, adopting 46 Directives, 274 Regulations and 148 Decisions.

⊃ Council Voting Methods

Three methods are prescribed in the treaties, viz.:
• **Unanimity:** this used to be the main voting method, but the SEA and TEU narrowed the range of subjects to which it applies. There are nevertheless a large number of specific decisions which require unanimity (in 1995, the Council listed 67 legal bases requiring unanimity or common accord of member states). It is used in relation to matters exclusive to the justice and home affairs and common foreign and security policy pillars. Certain financial and constitutional matters also require unanimity, as do some legislative procedures (see below). The main problem with unanimity is

that it gives each member state a veto over decisions. A possible solution would be to replace unanimity with a 'super majority' requirement (governments voting in favour would need to represent 80% of the Union population).

Another kind of veto, without legal force, is the so-called 'Luxembourg compromise', deriving from a deal in the Council in 1966, to allow discussions to continue until a decision is reached on matters regarded by any member state as affecting its vital national interests. It has been rarely invoked (there were three threats to use it in the 1980s), and many analysts thought that voting provisions in the SEA effectively put paid to it. But in 1994, France threatened to use it in relation to the ratification of the GATT Treaty.

• **Simple Majority:** under this procedure, each member state has one vote and therefore in EU 15, 8 votes are required for a majority. It is restricted mainly to minor procedural matters and to certain measures covered by the Common Commercial Policy (anti-subsidy and anti-dumping tariffs).

• **Qualified Majority (QMV):** under this procedure, each state is given a number of votes, very roughly in accordance with population size. A specific number of votes is required for a positive decision. As a result of the SEA and TEU, QMV covers a very broad range of policy decisions. Until the fourth enlargement (which increased the number of Council votes to 87), 23 votes out of 76 were required to block proposals. Following the fourth enlargement, the adoption of acts requires 62 votes in favour, cast by not less than 10 members, meaning that 26 votes are required to block legislation. There is by no means an exact correlation between population size and voting strength. Luxembourg has two votes, one for every 200,000 citizens whereas Germany has 10, one for every 8 million. In EU 12, the five largest states had 84% of the Union population, and 63% of the Council votes. After the fourth enlargement, the 'big five' had 79% of the population, but their total voting strength decreased to about 55%. If other small countries are admitted, the largest states could find themselves out-voted. One obvious solution would be to change voting weights, to more closely reflect population size. But smaller states might then complain of 'big-state dominance'. Another possibility would be to adopt a 'double majority' system, in which QMV decisions would require the support of at least half of the membership, with a combined population of at least half of the Union total.

In March 1994, a serious dispute arose in the Council over proposals to change the weighting of the QMV system, to take account of the entry of four EFTA countries (Norway was then still in the running for entry). The UK, supported for a time by Spain, opposed proposals to increase the number of votes required to block legislation from 23 to 27 (to retain the blocking minority at about 30% of the votes). Britain argued that the change would weaken sovereignty, because the votes of more countries would be needed to block legislation. However, the British were forced to climb down, due to the resolute stance of 10 other states and a threat from the EP to refuse to ratify the accession treaties unless the blocking threshold was increased. The UK had to accept a deal which promised a 'reasonable delay' (a two-month grace period) on decisions opposed by between 23 and 27 votes) The issue is to be reconsidered at the 1996 Intergovernmental Conference.

Because of a preference for decisionmaking by consensus in Council, reinforced by the fact that under a number of specific legislative procedures unanimity is required, only a small number of Acts are actually adopted with negative votes being cast in Council, as Table 4.5 shows. But without some resort to binding voting procedures, the Council's decisionmaking process would be severely handicapped.

Table 4.5 Total Votes for Legislative Acts (6/12/1993–31/3/1995)

	Total No. of Acts	Acts adopted with negative votes cast
Agriculture	114	17
Fisheries	51	4
Internal Market	50	11
Environment	9	4
Transport	8	–
Social Affairs	3	–
Research	27	1
Education	4	–
Citizenship	2	–
Consumer Protection	1	1
Transparency	2	2
Other	12	–
TOTAL	283	40

Source: Report of the Council on the Functioning of the TEU, Cmnd 2866, HMSO, 1995.

○ **The Council Presidency**

The Council presidency is held for six months by each member state, beginning in January and July. The current and forthcoming presidencies are: 1996: Italy; Ireland; 1997: Netherlands; Luxembourg; 1998: UK; Austria; 1999: Germany; Finland; 2000: Portugal; France; 2001: Sweden; Belgium; 2002: Spain; Denmark; 2003 (first half) Greece.

The presidency (in conjunction with the Commission and the Secretary-General of the Council) organises Union meetings and plays a key role in setting the agenda for the six-month period. It has important external representation roles, acting as spokesman for the Union. The presidency represents the Union on Common Foreign and Security policy issues. Together with the Commission, it is required to keep the EP informed of CFSP developments. It is the representative of the Council in the EP and attends all plenaries. A foreign office minister from the country holding the presidency attends question-time at each plenary to answer questions from MEPs.

Although the presidency chairs Council meetings, it does not give the holder powers of executive decision. The holder is expected to play a constructive, 'consensus-building' role between member states and also to maintain good relations with the EP. Although it grants the holder no licence to blatantly push national interests, it nevertheless provides it with a periodic opportunity to set its stamp on the Union's development and to promote particular policies. There is prestige in running the presidency well, but few holders in recent years have escaped without criticism. For example, the 1994 German presidency was accused by the socialist group in the EP of being 'thin on substance'.

○ Council Support Services

The Council has a General Secretariat based in Brussels with a staff of 2,289 in 1994. It has a Secretary-General, a legal service and seven directorates. There is a close working relationship between the Secretariats of the Council and Commission. The Council is supported in its work by the permanent representatives (the 'Ambassadors') of the member states, collectively known as the Committee of Permanent Representatives and widely referred to by its French acronym COREPER. The Ambassadors are assisted by civil servants from their own countries: about half are from foreign ministries and the rest from various other ministries. They work on behalf of national governments, and endeavour to seek agreement with other representatives. COREPER works behind the scenes by undertaking the groundwork necessary for Council decisions. It prepares the Council's agendas and organises each meeting of the General Affairs Council. The Special Committee on Agriculture (SCA) performs this role in relation to agriculture.

There are two groups within COREPER: 'COREPER 2' deals with 'high policy' and 'COREPER 1' with more technical policy subjects. COREPER 2 is attended by the Ambassadors. COREPER 1 is made up of the deputies of the permanent representatives ('Vice-Ambassadors'). Another group called the Antici Group (named after the Italian official who created it in 1975) is made up of an official from each national ministry (usually the foreign ministry). Anticis help to prepare the ground for meetings of the European Council. The Council, COREPER and the SCA are assisted by a network of working parties and committees made up of senior officials from government departments of the member states. The standing committee on employment has both national officials and interest group representatives. Proposals usually start in working parties and committees. They are then referred to COREPER or the SCA. At Council meetings, items are listed under 'A' or 'B' points. A points have already been agreed and require only formal approval by ministers. B points require further consideration.

❍ **The Main Strengths and Weaknesses of the Council System**

The Council system provides a framework for governments to make binding collective decisions affecting EU citizens. It has a legitimacy which neither the Commission nor the EP yet possesses. Its decisions are likely to be financially realistic, because member states ultimately have to foot the bill for EU policies.

Critics argue that the system is secretive, cumbersome and inefficient. Council agendas, minutes and voting *records* (how specific states cast their votes) are not published. In 1994 the *Financial Times* requested information about voting records on QMV decisions since 1989, but was informed that no such records had been kept. Defenders of the secrecy rule argue that governments would be less willing to take decisions if voting records were published. In October 1993, the Council, Commission and the EP signed an Interinstitutional Declaration on Democracy, Transparency and Subsidiarity. The following December, the Council agreed new procedures to allow the publication of Council votes (although not the individual voting records of states). It also agreed a 'code of conduct' governing public access to documents held by itself or by the Commission. However, by majority vote, it inserted a catch-all clause into the code, allowing the institutions to refuse requests to disclose information. The clause has been used to withhold official records of Council meetings. The Dutch government has started an action in the ECJ to get this clause removed.

In its defence, the Council has stated that it now publishes the results of many of its votes – for example, its votes when acting as a legislator (that is, when it adopts acts which are legally binding for member states) – although it can still choose not to do so. It also states that most requests for access to documents have been granted. In a report written in preparation for the 1996 IGC, the Council stated that up to 31 March 1995, its response to access to Council documents had been 'positive' in 25 cases, 'partially positive' in 20, and 'negative' in 22. One case was referred to the ECJ (Council, 1995).

Another major criticism concerns the disruptive effects of the rotating presidency, which is obviously a threat to policy continuity. *Ad hoc* arrangements have been developed to facilitate the smooth running of the system. The previous, current and next presidencies of the Council work together on some matters to ensure continuity (the 'Troika' arrangement). Ministers from France, Germany, Spain and Italy, which held consecutive presidencies in 1994–96, held meetings in order to develop a common agenda for this period. France and Germany established two working parties to ensure co-ordination of their consecutive presidencies. In order to enhance continuity, the duration of each presidency might be extended to one year. Another possible solution would be to remove the automatic right of each country to hold the presidency. At present, small member states hold the presidency on the same basis as large ones. The current alphabetical system of rotation might be replaced by a 'big state–small state' alternation system, allowing only big states an automatic right to hold the presidency.

● THE EUROPEAN COUNCIL

○ Main Functions and Roles

The European Council is the Union's supreme guiding body. It is concerned with shaping the EU's goals and giving strategic direction to the Union. It has frequently been the launching pad for new Union initiatives. Many landmark decisions in the EU's development have been taken at European Council meetings. It is essentially an executive summit meeting of Union heads of government (in France's case, the head of state). It has developed from informal fireside chats between government leaders to become, according to some assessments, the brains of the Union. The decision to formally establish the European Council was taken at the Paris summit in 1974. The first European Council meeting took place in Dublin in March 1975. The European Council was formally recognised in the Single European Act (Title 1 Article 2), although the Act did not define its powers. Nor were its powers comprehensively defined in the TEU. Article D of the TEU sets out its role, although in general terms (that is, 'to provide the Union with the necessary impetus for development and to define its general political guidelines') and also its composition and frequency of meetings. It is referred to also under Title VI dealing with economic and monetary policy and under Title V (Article J.8) of the CFSP pillar, recognising its responsibility for defining the principles of, and general guidelines for, the CFSP.

○ Operation

A European Council is held at the end of each Council presidency, in June and December. Special meetings may also be held (for example, in

Birmingham in November 1992). European Council meetings, which normally last two days, normally take place in the country currently holding the Council presidency. The meetings are attended by EU heads of government and their foreign ministers, plus the President and one of the Vice-Presidents of the Commission. They are accompanied by officials from the Commission and the Council Secretariat. The idea is to provide opportunities for face-to-face contact between governmental heads, unencumbered by armies of advisors. The Council and Commission Presidents give press conferences at the end of each European Council. The European Council is a political, not a legislative body and therefore the implementation of European Council decisions is left to the Council and to the Commission.

European Council meetings are big events and receive considerable media attention. Each becomes known by the place where it is held – for example, 'Maastricht', 'Edinburgh', 'Madrid'. The types of issue discussed at European Council meetings include the future direction and constitutional development of the Union; the situation of the Union in the world; major foreign policy issues; pressing issues of common concern to member states; and contentious issues which the Council of the European Union has been unable to resolve. Some European Council meetings prove to be damp squibs whereas others are of momentous importance. The Essen summit in December 1994 discussed a range of issues, including action to help the long-term unemployed, Bosnia, enlargement, Eastern Europe, fishing policy, 'Europol' and the environment. It also confirmed the launch of 14 'trans-European network' projects.

O Evaluation

The European Council is firmly established as a heavyweight Union actor, with considerable power to guide and shape the direction ôf the Union. Its significance derives from the importance given to it by the heads of government of member states. Without it, the Union's overall coherence, and its capacity to make fundamental decisions concerning its future, would be seriously weakened. Conversely, it constitutes an additional inter-governmental layer and therefore it has arguably weakened the importance of the Union's supranational elements. The Commission's policy initiation role is weaker in relation to the European Council than to the Council. Because of its decision-taking role, it has also (arguably) weakened the position of the Council, although it meets far too infrequently to usurp the Council's role. The EP has no say in setting European Council agendas and no control over the European Council, although the TEU does require the European Council to submit a report to the EP after each meeting, plus a yearly written report on the progress achieved by the Union. But it should be remembered that both the SEA and the TEU (both of which increased the power of the EP) were agreed at European Council meetings.

● THE EUROPEAN PARLIAMENT

○ Origins

It has its origins in the appointed Assembly established in the ECSC Treaty. The term 'Parliament' was first used in 1962, replacing that of 'Assembly'.

○ The System of Election

The EP is the Union's only directly elected body. Until 1979, when the first direct elections were held, members were appointed from members of national parliaments. Elections take place every five years, in June. Under Article 138(3) of the EC Treaty, there is supposed to be a common electoral system, but this has still not been achieved. All countries, with the exception of the UK (excluding Northern Ireland) use proportional representation, but there is no uniform procedure: there are also differences in voting rights, election days and electoral systems. The number of constituents per Member of the EP (MEP) varies considerably between countries. The number of seats was increased from 518 to 567 for the 1994 elections. From January 1995, this rose to 626 following the fourth enlargement. Within two years of their accession, the new entrants are to hold elections to the EP. In the meantime, they are represented by appointees from their national parliaments.

Table 4.6 Turnouts at Euro-elections in 1989 and 1994

	1994 (%)	1989 (%)
Belgium	90.7	90.7
Denmark	52.5	46.2
France	53.5	48.7
Germany	58.0	62.3
Greece	71.9	79.9
Ireland	37.0	68.3
Italy	74.8	81.0
Luxembourg	90.0	87.4
Netherlands	35.6	47.2
Portugal	35.7	51.2
Spain	59.6	54.8
UK	36.4	36.2

Turnouts tend to be significantly lower than in national elections. It has been frequently argued that the EP needs to be given more power before it is taken seriously by the electorate. Evidence from recent polls seems to belie this assumption. In 1979 63% voted in Euro-elections, but only 56.5% in 1994 (down from 58.5% in 1989), even though both the SEA and the TEU increased the EP's powers. Euro-elections are widely viewed as a series of opinion polls on the performance of national governments. There appears to be little European consciousness amongst voters or even amongst national parties. There are still no 'Euro-parties' as such and national party battles remain paramount. The 'Euro-manifestos' of the main British parties in 1994 actually said little about the role of the EP. Unlike national elections, Euro-elections provide voters with neither clear choices of governmental leadership nor of policies.

○ Backgrounds of MEPs

Few MEPs are nationally known figures, or heavyweights in their own parties. Their calibre is arguably lower than that of national MPs, possibly because MEPs cannot aspire to promotion to the 'government benches'. The parliament elected in 1994 includes 20 former ministers, including four ex-prime ministers – Wilfried Martens and Leo Tindemans (Belgium), Michel Rocard (France) and Poul Schlüter (Denmark), but these 'big names' tend to be past their domestic political peaks. It also includes three former Commissioners. The June 1994 cohort included 110 MEPs with backgrounds in education; 69 in law; 60 in business and finance; 54 in the media; 20 in the trades union movement; 42 in science and engineering; 28 in medicine; 29 in the civil service; and 23 in agriculture. MEPs are not allowed to serve in the governments of member states. Some countries do not allow them to serve in national parliaments. There has been a decline in the number of MEPs who also have seats in national parliaments. There is a mandatory register of MEPs' financial interests, but this is not widely distributed and has many loopholes.

○ Organisation and Procedures

The EP does not have a single headquarters: its plenaries are normally held in Strasbourg; its specialist committees normally meet in Brussels; its Secretariat is in Luxembourg. The Parliament sits for five days in plenary session in a 'hemicycle' (half-circle) chamber every month in Strasbourg, excluding August. Its debates are open to the public. It is not an adversarial debating chamber and lacks the clash of hot opinion to be found in the House of Commons. Most debates are poorly attended and lacklustre. The fact that its business is conducted in 11 official languages is hardly conducive to the free flow of argument. The European Council in Edinburgh December 1992 decided that Parliament is to remain in Strasbourg for 12 plenary sessions (with additional plenary sessions in Brussels) and that the Secretariat would stay in Luxembourg.

The EP has a President (currently the German Social Democrat Klaus Haensch), fourteen Vice-Presidents and a college of five Quaestors, elected by MEPs. Quaestors make administrative and financial decisions affecting MEPs' interests. Its Secretariat, which provides support services, is organised on similar lines to the Council Secretariat. It had 3,249 permanent and 541 temporary posts at the end of 1994. The cost of running the EP in 1994 was around ECU 666 million, about one-quarter of which went on translation costs and another quarter on travelling between sites. The 'Brussels–Strasbourg Euroshuttle' requires lorries to regularly transport documents and equipment 350 miles between the two cities.

○ Political Groups

MEPs sit in political, rather than national, groupings. In order to be recognised as a political group, one of the following minimum criteria must be met:

13 MEPs from at least four countries;
16 from at least three countries;
21 from at least two countries;
26 from one country.

The current range of groups, together with details of the affiliations of British parties, is shown in Figure 4.2 and Tables 4.7 and 4.8. The parties comprising political groups have broad ideological similarities. But party relationships within groups tend to be loose and there is no common organisation outside the EP context. Although parties may agree on a common (usually very broad) manifesto at election times, the national dimension remains strong: MEPs derive legitimacy from national parties and national electorates which select them, not from the political groups. There are two very big transnational political groups: the Party of European Socialists; and the European People's Party. The 'Greens' used to be in the heterogeneous 'Rainbow Group', but since 1989 have been large enough to form their own group. The Nations of Europe is a new anti-federalist grouping. In June 1995, the Forza Europa and European Democratic Alliance groups joined to form the Union for Europe group. The large number of parties (currently over 60) and groups renders it difficult for the EP to act cohesively. There are also cross-party 'issue groups', with a common interest in specific subjects, such as institutional reform.

Figure 4.2 Political Groups in the European Parliament, November 1995

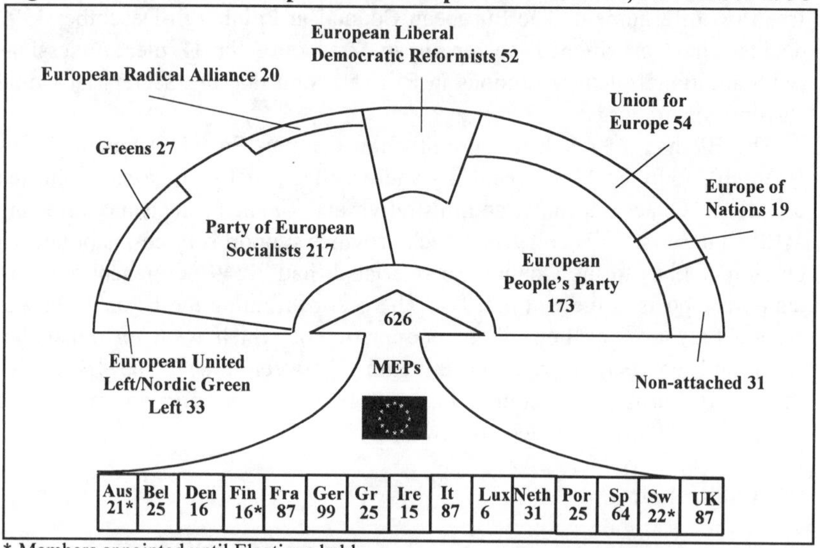

European Liberal
Democratic Reformists 52

European Radical Alliance 20

Union for
Europe 54

Greens 27

Europe of
Nations 19

Party of European
Socialists 217

European
People's Party
173

626

MEPs

European United
Left/Nordic Green
Left 33

Non-attached 31

Aus 21*	Bel 25	Den 16	Fin 16*	Fra 87	Ger 99	Gr 25	Ire 15	It 87	Lux 6	Neth 31	Por 25	Sp 64	Sw 22*	UK 87

* Members appointed until Elections held.

Table 4.7 Political Groups in the EP, November 1995

	Aus	B	Dk	Fn	Fr	G	Gr	Ir	It	Lux	Neth	P	Sp	Sw	UK
PES	8	6	3	4	15	40	10	1	18	2	8	10	22	7	63
EPP	6	7	3	4	12	47	9	4	14	2	10	1	30	5	19
ELDR	1	6	5	6	1	–	–	1	6	1	10	8	2	3	2
EUL/NGL	–	–	1	1	7	–	4	–	5	–	–	3	9	3	–
UFE	–	–	–	–	15	–	2	7	27	–	–	3	–	–	–
Greens	1	2	–	1	–	12	–	2	4	–	1	–	–	4	–
ERA	–	1	–	–	13	–	–	–	2	1	–	–	1	–	2
EN	–	–	4	–	13	–	–	–	–	–	2	–	–	–	–
IND	5	3	–	–	11	–	–	–	11	–	–	–	–	–	1
	21	25	16	16	87	99	25	15	87	6	31	25	64	22	87

Table 4.8 UK MEPs' Political Groups, November 1995

UK Parties	Group	Votes 1994 (%)	Seats	Votes 1989 (%)	Seats
Labour	PES	42.67	62	38.9	45
Con.	EPP	26.85	18	33.0	32
Lib Dem.	ELDR	16.13	2	6.2	0
SNP	ERA	3.08	2	2.6	1
SDLP	PES	1.02	1	0.9	1
OUP	EPP	0.84	1	0.8	1
DUP	NA	1.03	1	1.0	1
Greens	Greens	3.12	0	14.5	0

○ **The Committee System**

Much of Parliament's work takes place in committees and subcommittees. All MEPs serve on one or more of these committees. There are 20 committees, three subcommittees and a temporary committee on employment. Some committees are far more popular than others (for example, foreign affairs and environment policy). Seats are divided on the basis of party group strength. Committee meetings take place in Brussels and are normally open to the public. Their key function is to examine legislative draft laws and policy issues in detail. Committee meetings are frequently attended by Commissioners and other officials. A *rapporteur* (a committee member chosen by other members) draws up the committee report. Committee minutes have to be translated into the Community languages. The EP can set up special committees of inquiry to investigate breaches of Community law.

Table 4.9 Parliamentary Committees

- Foreign Affairs and Security (52);
- Agriculture, Fisheries and Rural Development (45);
- Budgets (33);
- Budgetary Control (18);
- Economic and Monetary Affairs and Industrial Policy (50);
- Energy, Research and Technology (26);
- External Economic Relations (25);
- Legal Affairs and Citizens' Rights (25);
- Social Affairs Employment and the Working Environment (40);
- Regional Policy and Planning, Rels with Reg. and Local Authorities (37);
- Transport and Tourism (28);
- Environment, Public Health and Consumer Protection (44);
- Youth, Culture, Education and the Media (36);
- Development and Co-operation (36);
- Civil Liberties and Internal Affairs (31);
- Institutional Affairs (40);
- Fisheries (22);
- Rules of Procedure, the Verification of Credentials and Immunities (23);
- Women's Rights (36);
- Petitions (27);
- Unemployment (Temporary Committee) (36).

○ **Inter-parliamentary Institutions**

There is an ACP–EU Joint Assembly on which about 70 MEPs serve (see p. 252). There are 22 inter-parliamentary delegations through which MEPs maintain relations with other parliaments and organisations outside the EU.

○   **Main Functions and Roles of the EP**

• **Legislative Powers.** The EP is an integral element of the legislative process, but does not initiate legislation, which is the formal responsibility of the Commission. Since the ratification of the TEU, the EP may (under Article 138b) by absolute majority request the Commission to submit a proposal where it is felt that a 'Community act is required for the purpose of implementing [the] Treaty'. However, this still does not give Parliament the power to initiate legislation (although this depends on the interpretation of the word 'request'). Moreover, absolute majorities are difficult to obtain. It may issue 'own initiative' reports, but the Commission is not required to act on them. However, the informal influence it has on agenda setting and initiation is far from negligible (Judge and Earnshaw, 1994).

Its legislative role used to be solely consultative. However, as a result of provisions in the SEA and TEU, it now has substantial power to amend and, in some areas, veto legislation. About half of the EP's amendments to legislation are accepted. In July 1994 the EP used for the first time its limited powers of veto (the co-decision procedure introduced in the TEU) to reject a Council decision on the liberalisation of the voice telecommunications market. But its legislative powers (even taking into account the new procedures) remain limited in scope. Co-decision does not apply to all categories of legislation and all legislation still requires the Council's approval. Nor does the EP have to be consulted on Commission legislation.

• **The Assent Procedure:** the EP must consent to certain decisions before they can take effect. It has powers of assent in relation to the accession of new members, association and co-operation agreements and agreements with non-EU states having important budgetary implications. For example, the EP has used its assent procedure to block agreements with Turkey and Israel, for alleged human rights violations.

Table 4.10 The Scope of the Assent Procedure

Treaty Article	Subject
8a(2) EC	citizenship
105(6) EC	specific tasks of the ECB
106(5) EC	amendments to the ESCB/ECB statute
130d EC	structural funds and Cohesion Fund
138(3) EC	uniform electoral procedure
228(3) EC	some international agreements
Article O (TEU)	accession of new member states

The TEU extended the scope of parliamentary assent to cover a range of new issues, such as the organisation of the structural funds, changes to the statute of the European system of central banks, the general right of movement and the uniform voting procedure for European elections. The EP has no power to *amend* decisions under the procedure, but it can and does comment on them. The procedure does not cover all EU trade agreements (for example, it does not cover agreements reached under Article 113 of the EC Treaty). The assent procedure was applied in 11 cases in 1994.

• **Supervisory Functions.** A basic function of any parliament is to oversee the work of the executive. However, within the Union, the Council, European Council and the Commission each perform executive roles. Moreover, the rotating Council presidency, and the diversity of views within the European Council and Council, means that the EP does not have a fixed or clear target upon which to focus. The EP does not appoint, nor can it dismiss, the Council or European Council, the members of which are primarily answerable to the national parliaments of member states. Most EU policy is in any case implemented at national level and therefore it is difficult for the EP to supervise the execution of EU policy 'on the ground'.

There is little formal direct contact between the EP and European Council, although the EP presidency is allowed to address the opening session of the European Council. The Presidency of the Council (usually represented by the foreign minister) explains its programme to a plenary session of Parliament at the start of each presidency. At the end of each presidency, the foreign minister returns to summarise the results achieved. Under Article J.7 of the TEU, the presidency is required to consult the EP on the main aspects and basic choices of the CFSP and to ensure that the EP's views are taken into consideration, but there is scant evidence of its influence in this area so far.

Members of the Council attend plenary sessions of the Parliament and are asked to reply to written and oral questions. MEPs may put written questions to the Commission or Council. In 1994, MEPs tabled 2,906 written questions (2,505 to the Commission and 401 to the Council); 166 oral questions (100 to the Commission and 66 to the Council), plus 813 questions during Question Time (565 to the Commission and 248 to the Council). It can ask the Court of Auditors to carry out special enquiries. It debates the Commission's annual work and legislative programmes and also the Commission's annual General Report, but there is little evidence that these debates have much influence.

• **Budgetary Functions.** Together with the Council, it is the budgetary authority of the Community. The EP has the right to propose modifications to compulsory expenditure (spending which arises from treaty obligations, mainly relating to the CAP) and the right to propose amendments to non-compulsory expenditure (that is, expenditure which is not a direct consequence of treaty obligations, such as spending on regional aid or RTD). The modifications it proposes cannot increase expenditure and the Council can reject them by QMV. The Council has the 'last word' on compulsory expenditure whereas the EP has the 'last word' on non-compulsory expenditure (currently accounting for about half of the total). In 1988, an interinstitutional agreement on budgetary discipline increased the non-compulsory elements of the budget. Under Article 203 of the EC Treaty, by majority vote and two-thirds of votes cast, it can reject the draft budget (as it did in 1979 and 1984, due to disagreements over spending priorities). It subsequently adopted revised budgets. Since 1977, the EP has had the exclusive right to grant a discharge of the general budget. However, this occurs after expenditure has been incurred.

• **Involvement in the Appointment and Dismissal of the Commission.** It can dismiss the Commission, by passing a censure motion requiring a two-thirds majority of votes cast, amounting to an absolute majority of members. This right has never been exercised (all 6 motions so far have failed). Moreover, the Council could simply reappoint the same Commissioners. Nor does the EP have the power to dismiss individual Commissioners. However, the TEU gave Parliament powers of approval in relation to the appointment of the Commission and its President (the right of 'investiture'). A new Commission including a President must be approved by the Parliament within 6 months of the election of a new Parliament. In 1994 and 1995, it sought to assert its new powers acquired under the TEU, by engaging in several 'muscle-flexing' episodes (for example, by threatening to veto the Council's nomination for president-designate). Although MEPs were unhappy about the manner of his selection, Santer's nomination for the Commission presidency was endorsed by 260 votes to 238 with 23 abstentions. The vote was non-binding, but Council President in Office Klaus Kinkel said he would abide by the result. The EP questioned each of the nominees for the 1995–99 Commission (giving several a rough ride) but endorsed the new Commission on 20 January 1995. The EP also has the right to be consulted in relation to appointments to the European Central Bank.

• **Forum.** It holds discussions on many important issues and has provided a platform for many world statesmen. Its first annual 'State of the Union' debate took place in November 1995.

• **Redress of Grievances.** The TEU gives the EP formal powers in relation to the redress of grievances. Any citizen of the Union may petition the EP on any matter within the EU's field of responsibility, providing it affects the petitioner directly. It appoints an Ombudsman to receive complaints from any Union citizen, or others resident in a member state, concerning maladministration in the activities of Community institutions, excluding the ECJ and the Court of First Instance (CFI) acting in their judicial roles. The Ombudsman is independent and can only be dismissed by the ECJ. The Ombudsman acts either on his own initiative or on a complaint forwarded by an MEP. However, the Treaty does not commit EC institutions to act on the

Ombudsman's findings. At the request of a quarter of its members, the EP may set up a Committee of Inquiry to investigate alleged contraventions or maladministration in the implementation of Community law.

❍ National Parliaments and the European Union

The relationships between the EP and national parliaments are currently weak. Two declarations on the role of national parliaments were attached to the TEU. One sought to encourage closer contact between national parliaments and the EP and to recognise the importance of rapid information required by national parliaments. The other invited national parliaments and the EP to meet at a 'conference of parliaments', but this has not yet happened. The EP already has some formal contacts with national parliaments: there are conferences of MEPs and MPs (known as 'assizes'); there are annual meetings of the presidents of national parliaments; there are biannual conferences of the European committees of national parliaments and those of the EP.

Although Community legislation is scrutinised by national parliaments, the key issues have usually been decided before national parliaments have had an opportunity to consider them. This does not necessarily mean that national parliaments are of no consequence in EU affairs. For example, the Danish parliament, which has a powerful Common Market Relations committee, initially voted against the SEA in 1986.

In the UK, there are regular debates on European issues in both Houses of Parliament. The big 'European' debates in the House of Commons tend to be of a general nature, providing Eurosceptic MPs with opportunities to assail the Union in general and British membership of the Union in particular. There is a twice-yearly White Paper on developments in the Union, which is debated in parliament. Ministers representing the UK in the Council and European Council are accountable to the UK parliament. Members of either House can ask written or oral questions in parliament on EU matters. Both Houses of Parliament have a Select Committee on European legislation. Such legislation is usually implemented through a statutory instrument laid before the UK parliament. In some cases however, the new Community law is included in a draft bill amending existing legislation. A new system of European standing committees has been in operation since January 1991. There are two, each with 13 members. The select committee on European Legislation refers legislation to one of the two standing committees. The work is divided between them on a subject basis. The committees may require a minister to make a statement or answer questions by members. However, it has been difficult to find enough MPs willing to serve on them.

○ **Evaluation**

The EP is clearly far more than a mere talking shop. Its legislative and assent powers in particular make it a force to be reckoned with. It also has a democratic mandate and is a very open institution. But it still has a formidable public image problem: most European citizens remain ignorant or indifferent about the work of the EP. Its debates are seldom widely reported. It attracts few top-flight politicians from member states. The problem of MEP absenteeism has meant that it has been difficult to secure an absolute majority for some key votes. Unlike elections to the UK parliament, elections to the EP do not lead to the formation of a government. Nor can the EP vote the Council out of office. Nor does it yet have full legislative or budgetary powers. Its supervisory influence over the Council and European Council remains weak. Its organisation on three sites is confusing and wasteful.

The EP had no formal input into the negotiations which led to the TEU, But two MEPs were appointed to the Reflection Group established to prepare for the 1996 Intergovernmental Conference. The EP is seeking a substantial increase in its powers, including the extension of 'co-decision', the right to choose the Commission; the right to agree a five-year programme with the Commission; the right to monitor the Council and the right to raise revenue. Another possible reform would be to establish a bicameral system, by creating a second chamber in the form of a European senate, made up of MPs from national parliaments. This would provide a formal link between the EP and national parliaments. However, a second chamber might be hidebound to national interests and could create a conflict of democratic legitimacies, undermining the EP as a parliament in its own right.

● THE EUROPEAN COURT OF JUSTICE

○ **Functions**

The Court is the Community's judicial institution, with the task of ensuring that Community law is observed (Article 164, EC). It is also the authoritative interpreter and clarifier of Community law. In its first 40 years, the ECJ made nearly 5,000 judgments, including some of crucial importance to the Union's development. For example, the *Cassis de Dijon* judgment (1979) established the principle that goods fit to be sold in one member state are fit to be sold in them all. It is debatable whether the SEM programme would have been launched without this judgment. The Court makes judgments on cases referred to it by Community institutions, national governments, national courts, corporate bodies or individuals. National courts frequently seek preliminary rulings on specific aspects of Community law (there are about 150–200 such cases a year). There is no appeal against the Court's rulings. The Court also gives opinions when requested to do so on the compatibility of international agreements with Community law. Its opinions in such cases are binding. The TEU empowers the ECJ to impose fines for non-compliance with earlier rulings of the Court (Article 171, EC). The Court is also required to rule on 'turf disputes' between Union institutions and member states. For example, in response to a request by the Commission for an opinion, in November 1994, the ECJ ruled that the Commission must share responsibility with member states for some aspects of trade negotiations (for example, for transport, services and intellectual property).

The Commission has brought the most number of actions and has also been taken to the Court more than any other body. For example, the EP took the Commission to the ECJ for failing to put into effect a common transport policy and is currently bringing an action against it for failing to achieve the removal of border checks. The 1980 'Isoglucose judgment' annulled a piece of legislation because the EP had not given an opinion. In this judgment, the Court ruled that if the Commission fails to consult the EP when it is required to do so it is in breach of Community law. In 1994, the Court gave judgment in 30 cases brought under Article 169 of the EC Treaty relating to the failure of member states to comply with their obligations under Community law.

○ Key Principles and Sources of Community Law

The Court operates on the basis of three fundamental principles, which were established before the UK joined the Union:

1) Direct effect. In the *Van Gend en Loos* judgment (1963) the Court ruled that Community law creates rights for citizens which national courts must recognise and enforce. The principle applies to most treaty provisions and secondary legislation.

2) Direct applicability. Regulations (see below) are directly applicable in member states; without need for national legislatures to pass implementing legislation.

NB: it should be noted that the distinction between (1) and (2) is not always made and the terms are sometimes used interchangeably.

3) The primacy of Community law over national law. Community law cannot be overridden by domestic legal provisions (*Costa v. ENAL* (1964)). The ECJ can declare void any legal instruments adopted by the Commission, the Council or national governments which it deems incompatible with Community law. The European Communities Act of 1972 gave legal force to Community law in the UK.

Table 4.11 Sources of Community Law

Primary legislation: that is, the treaties, including annexes, protocols and amendments to the treaties (although elements of the TEU are outside the ECJ's jurisdiction). It also includes treaties of accession.

Secondary legislation: adopted laws made by institutions in accordance with powers granted them by the Treaties.

General principles of law (for example, proportionality and fundamental human rights).

International law, to which the ECJ has referred in its judgments on issues with external implications.

Judicial interpretation (that is, 'case law' – the rulings of the ECJ).

○ **The Limited Jurisdiction of the ECJ**

The Court's remit does not extend to all aspects or facets of the Union. Community law has not supplanted the national law of member states (although it takes precedence if there is a conflict between the two). Nor does it extend to all judicial matters (for example, it excludes criminal law). The Court can only act within the powers given it in the treaties. It is not a 'Supreme Court' on the US model, because the latter is part of a hierarchy of courts (district, state, federal). The EC has no formal connection with the courts of member states, each of which has its own legal traditions.

The remit of the ECJ does nor extend to the organisation and functions of the European Council, or to the CFSP pillar. It covers part of the JHA pillar (Article K.3(2)(c)), dealing with the interpretation and application of conventions (but by May 1995 the Court had not been called upon to deal with a single case pursuant to this subparagraph). For all practical purposes, Article L of the TEU excludes the ECJ from jurisdiction over the CFSP and JHA pillars. In the *Grau Gomis and Others* case (April 1995), the Court held that it had no jurisdiction to interpret Article B of the TEU. The contentious issue of whether Article L should be amended to bring these pillars fully within the Court's jurisdication is likely to be considered by the 1996 IGC.

The ECJ is not to be confused with either the European Court of Human Rights or with the European Commission of Human Rights, both of which are Council of Europe institutions based in Strasbourg. They derive from the Council of Europe's Convention for the Protection of Human Rights and Fundamental Freedoms signed in Rome in November 1950. Article 7 of the TEU requires the Union to respect fundamental rights as guaranteed by this Convention, but human rights in the Community may only be enforced against Community legislation, acts of the Community institutions or acts of a member state in implementing Community law.

O **Structure and Working Methods**

The Court comprises one judge from each member state: when there are an even number of members, the five largest member states take part in a system involving the selection of an additional judge. All are appointed for a renewable term of six years. Every three years there is a partial replacement of judges. One judge is elected president of the Court by the others for a renewable term of three years. Judges are chosen from the legal and academic professions as well as from national judiciaries (few have been top-flight judges in their home countries). Court decisions are by majority vote, but are always announced as unanimous. Sittings are held in public. All of the Union's official languages are used by the Court, although French tends to be used for communication and deliberation between Court members. The Court has six chambers (comprising a president and between two and five judges). The Court is assisted by nine Advocates-General, who make reasoned submissions on cases brought before the Court. The five largest member states each propose one Advocate-General, the others participate in a system involving the rotation of Advocates-General. A British judge currently serving on the ECJ has pointed to the Court's relaxed, non-confrontational way of working as being one of its most impressive features (Edward, 1995).

In order to enable the ECJ to cope with the large volume of cases, a Court of First Instance was established under the SEA and began its work in October 1989. Each member state appoints a judge to the CFI for six years. It has four chambers. It is a second tier of judicial authority, established to enable the Court to concentrate on its essential function, the interpretation of Community law. The CFI deals with administrative disputes within the institutions and disputes between the Commission and firms over competition rules or between the Commission and matters covered by the ECSC Treaty. From March 1994 jurisdiction in respect of trade protection measures was transferred from the ECJ to the CFI. Its judgments are subject to appeal to the ECJ on points of law. The ECJ and CFI had a staff of 750 permanent and 87 temporary posts in 1994.

O **Evaluation**

The ECJ is undoubtedly a formidable institution. The cumulative impact of the ECJ's judgments has crucially influenced the shape and pace of EU integration. The Court has played a key role in ensuring that the Community is based on the rule of law. Eurosceptics tend to view the Court as a centralising force, accusing it of 'judicial activism' and of a keenness to assert the dominance of Community law over national law. They assert that it is a court with a mission to promote the European ideal. It is hardly an impartial judge of the balance of powers between member states and the Community. Moreover, there is no appeal against its decisions. It has been suggested that an additional judicial body should be created, (a 'Union Court of Review') to adjudicate in cases involving disputes about the relative powers of the Union and member states.

As presently constituted, the ECJ is hard pressed to keep up with its workload. There is already a long period between the beginning and end of procedures. It has a heavy caseload, made heavier by the need for documents to be translated into the official languages. Every development in EU integration creates new potential sources of dispute. The Court's workload has increased very significantly as a result of institutional and policy changes resulting from the SEA and TEU. Disputes concerning the interpretation of subsidiarity are likely to further increase the volume of cases.

Table 4.12 The Work of the ECJ and CFI in 1994

	ECJ	CFI
Judgments		
References for a preliminary ruling	119	
Direct actions	53	19
Appeals	16	
Staff cases		41
TOTAL	**188**	**60**
Cases Dealt With		
By judgment	208	70
By order terminating the proceedings	84	372
By an opinion	1	
TOTAL	**293**	**442**
Cases Brought		
References for a preliminary ruling	203	
Direct actions	125	316
Appeals	13	
Opinions/rulings	3	
Special procedures	10	12
Staff cases		81
TOTAL	**354**	**409**
Applications for adoption of interim measures	4	61
Cases pending	494	618
Average length of proceedings (in months)		
References for a preliminary ruling	18	
Direct Actions	21	23
Appeals	21	
Staff cases		15

Source: ECJ Bulletins.

● THE ECONOMIC AND SOCIAL COMMITTEE (ESC)

Based in Brussels, the Committee is a consultative assembly, comprising representatives of employers, workers and other interests drawn from a wide variety of industrial sectors. It was established to involve economic and social interest groups in the development of the Community and to be a formal channel for providing information and advice to the Commission and the Council. Its current term runs from October 1994 to September 1998. It puts forward opinions at the request of the Council, the Commission, and, since 1972, on its own initiative. Under the EC and Euratom Treaties, in some cases it is mandatory, and in other cases optional, for the Commission or the Council to consult with the Committee. The SEA and TEU extended the range of subjects for mandatory referral. In 1994, it adopted 121 opinions on Commission proposals or communications and 23 'own initiative' opinions: its opinion was requested 59 times where this was mandatory. All opinions are published in the *Official Journal*. It can issue majority and minority opinions.

Its members are nominated by national governments and formally appointed by the Council (following consultation with the Commission) for a renewable term of four years. Although members are appointed as individuals, they tend to closely follow views of the organisations they represent. Members are part-time and live and work in their own countries. Members belong to one of three groups:

Group 1: employers (from industry, commerce, public enterprises etc.).
Group 11: workers (mainly from trade unions).
Group 111: various interests (including agriculture, SMEs, the professions, public services and consumer groups).

It has a Chairman and a Bureau (elected by the members for 2 years) and a Secretary-General. It had a staff of 510 permanent posts in 1994, over a third of whom were linguists. It has nine sections or subject groups. Section opinions are drafted by study groups with about 12 members, one of whom acts as a *rapporteur*. Each year there are about 10 plenary sessions, 70 section meetings and 350 study group meetings.

The Committee has produced many useful reports, particularly on technical issues, although its opinions do not have to be accepted by either the Council or the Commission. It was very much involved in the development of the Social Charter, which it claims was heavily influenced by a Committee opinion of 1989. It brings together people from a wide range of occupations and organisations. It provides a vehicle for dialogue between the employers and trades unions. It may promote identification with Europe amongst various business and other groups. It may also provide useful insights into national thinking on various issues. Although there is no constitutional link between the EP and the Committee, there is frequent exchange of information between them. However, the need for the Committee is increasingly being questioned, given that there are now other channels for representation of interests and submission of specialist advice. If the Committee did not exist, it would probably not be recreated.

● THE COMMITTEE OF THE REGIONS (COR)

This is an advisory body established to ensure a stronger voice for the regions in the Union. It was established in the TEU, following a suggestion from Chancellor Kohl. Arguably, the establishment of the COR was a prime example of 'gesture politics', signifying an acknowledgement of the importance of the regional dimension in EU affairs. The COR is consulted on matters affecting regional interests and prior to the adoption of decisions on regional matters. It must be consulted on five policies: education, culture, public health, trans-European networks and economic and social cohesion. It can also issue 'own initiative' opinions. By 31 March 1995, the COR had issued 32 Opinions. Of these, 16 derived from a Council referral, 6 from a Commission referral and 16 were undertaken on the COR's own initiative.

The COR's members (plus an equal number of alternate members) are appointed by member states. There are roughly equal numbers of regional and local government representatives. Members do not have to be elected representatives although most have political affiliations. It has a common organisational structure with the ESC, with which it shares premises and a secretariat. It is, however, independent of the ESC and has no formal connection with the EP. At its inaugural meeting in Brussels in March 1994, the Commission President cautioned it against taking on too much and argued that it should focus its attention on a few crucial items.

● THE COURT OF AUDITORS (CA)

The Court is responsible for the external auditing of the Community's general budget and of the ECSC's operating budget. It has extensive powers to examine whether the EC's receipts and expenditures have been collected and incurred in a sound and lawful manner. The TEU (Article 4, EC) bestows upon the Court the status of a Community institution. It also gives the Court more power to monitor the Community's accounts. Other institutions of the Community are required to furnish the Court with relevant documents. The

Court provides Parliament with valuable information to help it perform its supervisory functions. Based in Luxembourg, the Court was established in 1975 and first met in October 1977. Members are appointed for 6 years by the Council, following consultation with the EP (the EP objected to two nominations in 1989, resulting in one state changing its nomination). Each state proposes one member for appointment. Members must be qualified by virtue of their experience in auditing or a closely related field. The auditors elect a president from their ranks for 3 years. The Court had 360 permanent and 67 temporary posts in 1994, with about 250 engaged in auditing.

The Court issues an annual report on the Community's institutions, divided into a financial audit and a financial management assessment. The report is published in the *Official Journal* at the end of each financial year. Its recent reports have included scathing accounts of financial irregularities concerning Community funds and of poor financial mismanagement by the Commission over many policy areas. Its 1993 report was particularly critical of the administration of the CAP and of the PHARE and TACIS (Technical Assistance to the CIS) programmes for Eastern Europe. The President, André Middelhoek, in his presentation of the report to the EP in November 1994, stated that the Commission has largely failed to achieve the level of financial control needed, pointing out that it had made the same criticism in 1983. The Court also produces reports on Euratom and the ECSC and special reports and opinions on specific subjects. It has frequently been argued that the Court is too small to be able to cope effectively with the magnitude of its monitoring tasks.

● THE EUROPEAN INVESTMENT BANK (EIB)

Founded in 1958 and based in Luxembourg, the EIB is the Union's financial institution. It was established to finance capital investment projects which contribute to the 'balanced development, integration and economic and social cohesion' of member countries. It is both a Union institution and a bank. It is autonomous and has its own legal personality and an administrative structure separate from other EU institutions. It has a board of governors, made up of ministers (usually the finance ministers) of member states. It has a part-time board of directors nominated by the board of governors, plus a member nominated by the Commission. There is a full-time management committee, which controls all current operations. It is organised into seven directorates. It has about 800 staff.

Member states are the shareholders, and contribute to the Bank's capital. It is self-financing. It raises its funds on the financial markets (mainly of member states), and relends money on a non-profit-making basis. Projects supported must be financially viable. It has the top credit rating (AAA) and therefore is able to raise and lend very substantial sums. It is the world's largest multilateral credit institution and, in terms of its equity base, is the largest bank in Europe. It provides long-term loans in 17 currencies, including the ECU. EIB loans may be given to either private or public sector borrowers. It provides funds up to half the cost of projects. Some projects are jointly financed with other EU funds (for example, with the ERDF). In the first half of the 1990s, the EIB supported 36,000 ventures promoted by small and medium sized-enterprises (SMEs).

Balanced regional development is a key priority of the EIB. About two-thirds of its funding is concentrated in regions lagging behind in development, or experiencing redevelopment problems. Trans-European networks and environmental protection are also current priorities. The Bank has made contributions to many well-known projects, including high-speed train networks and the Channel tunnel. All EIB projects now have an environmental dimension and about one-fifth of all lending between 1988 and 1992 went on environmental projects. Since 1988, more than ECU 20 billion has been granted to promote international competitiveness in various industrial sectors. The vast bulk of EIB loans (more than 90%) go to EU countries. In 1994, the EIB granted loans of ECU 19.9 billion, ECU 17.7 billion of which went to member states and the rest to about 130 states outside the Union, principally to ACP states (70 developing countries in Africa, the Caribbean and Pacific with which the EU has a special relationship); and to other countries in the Mediterranean, Latin America, Asia and Eastern Europe. As a result of decisions taken at the Edinburgh European Council, a European Investment Fund (EIF) was set up in 1994. The Fund assists the financing of trans-European networks projects and projects promoted by SMEs. It operates from within the EIB.

● OTHER INSTITUTIONS

The EU has a growing number of specialised functional agencies, most of which are of recent origin. They are located in various member states (so that each state can claim to host a Union institution). Location decisions have led to much horse-trading between member states. In October 1993, the Council decided that these agencies would be sited in the cities shown in Table 4.13. The main justifications for creating these agencies are that they have a sharper focus than general-purpose organisations; that they take the workload off the Commission; and that they enable each member state to have its 'own' EU institution. The main criticisms of them are that that they increase the complexity of the EU policy and implementation system and are insufficiently accountable.

Table 4.13 The Function and Location of Other Institutions

The European Monetary Institute (Frankfurt): to facilitate conditions necessary for transition to stage 3 of EMU. It will eventually be replaced by the European Central Bank.

The European Environment Agency (Copenhagen): to provide objective, reliable and comparable information at European level. The Agency will publish a report on the state of the Union's environment every three years.

The European Ombudsman (Strasbourg, based in the EP): to investigate maladministration.

The European Police Office (Europol) (The Hague): to enable national police and customs to share information on international crime, drugs and terrorism. This includes the 'Europol Drugs Unit'.

The Health and Safety in the Workplace Agency (Bilbao): improving working conditions.

The Office For Harmonisation in the Internal Market (Alicante): to implement Community law in relation to trade marks, designs and models.

The European Medicine Evaluation Agency (London): provides scientific advice to Community institutions and member states concerning authorisation and supervision of medical products.

The European Veterinary Inspection Agency (Dublin): to test animal health. NB: this is part of the Commission and is not a decentralised Union body.

The European Drugs Observatory (Lisbon): to analyse data on drugs.

The European Foundation for Training (Turin): to contribute to the development of the vocational training systems of designated Central and East European countries.

The Foundation for the Improvement of Living and Working Conditions (Dublin): founded in 1975, to contribute to the planning and establishment of better living and working conditions through the dissemination of knowledge).

The European Centre for the Development of Vocational Training (now Thessaloniki): better known as CEDEFOP, it was founded in 1975 to assist the Commission to encourage the promotion and development of vocational and in-service training. In 1993, the decision was taken to move CEDOFOP from Berlin.

The Translation Services Centre for the European Commission (Luxembourg): to meet the translation needs of the new institutions).

● INSTITUTIONAL INTERACTIONS IN THE EU'S POLICY PROCESS

○ Principal Features of the EU's Policy Process

The EU's policy process is very complex, comprising many different formal procedures and requirements. It is not immediately obvious which policy or aspect of policy is covered by which procedure. Figure 4.3 provides an outline of institutional interactions in this process.

Figure 4.3 Institutional Interactions

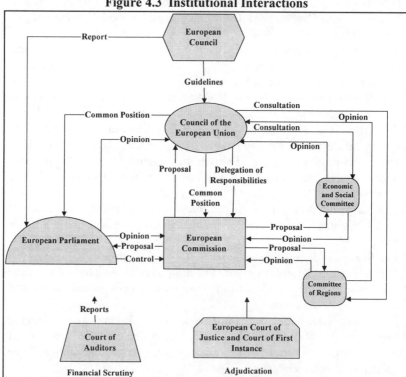

Other key features of this process are:
- the central role played by the Commission;
- legislative power is still unevenly distributed between the Council and EP;
- the Commission, the Council and EP need to work together in order to achieve their legislative objectives;
- policies do not necessarily take legislative form. For example, the CFSP

and JHA pillars lie outside the Community legislative framework. The Council also issues non-legislative pronouncements (resolutions, declarations and agreements etc.);

- the European Council is not directly involved in the legislative process, but exercises considerable influence on policy, through its guiding and directing roles.

○ **The Legislative Process** embraces the following procedures:

- **The Consultation Procedure:** this was the earliest procedure, and was laid down in the Treaty of Rome. The role of the EP under this procedure is purely advisory. A draft is worked out in a Commission DG (in consultation with government officials and other interested parties). When completed, the Commission presents a proposal to the Council. The EP and, in some policy areas, the ESC and COR are then consulted for their opinions. The Commission considers the response of the EP, ESC and COR and may make amendments in the light of their comments. The proposal is then resubmitted to the Council, which refers it to one of its working parties and to COREPER. After discussion in COREPER, the proposal is returned to the Council, which may adopt or reject it. The Commission tends to accept more of the EP's amendments than does the Council (which has the final say).

- **The Co-operation Procedure (Article 189c).** The SEA effectively introduced a parliamentary second reading stage into the legislative process for measures relating to the Single Market, social and economic cohesion and RTD. Some aspects of the SEM regarded as particularly contentious, such as value-added tax (VAT), are not subject to the procedure. But a broad range of legislative measures are within its scope. The TEU (Article 189c, EC) extended the procedure to a wide range of subjects, as Table 4.14 shows. The Treaty deleted RTD specific programmes from the procedure. The first stages are very similar to the consultation procedure. Before making a decision on a proposal submitted by the Commission, the Council must obtain the opinion of the EP. A unanimous vote in the Council is necessary for proposed EP amendments of which the Commission disapproves. In other cases, the Council may agree a common position by QMV. The Council's common position, which must be reached within 3 months, is communicated to the EP, together with an explanation of the Commission's and Council's reasoning. If within 3 months Parliament approves the common position or fails to respond, the Council will adopt the Act. By absolute majority, the EP may reject or propose amendments to the Council's common position. If it rejects the position, the Council can only adopt the Act by unanimity (see Figure 4.4).

Figure 4.4 The Co-operation Procedure (Article 189c)

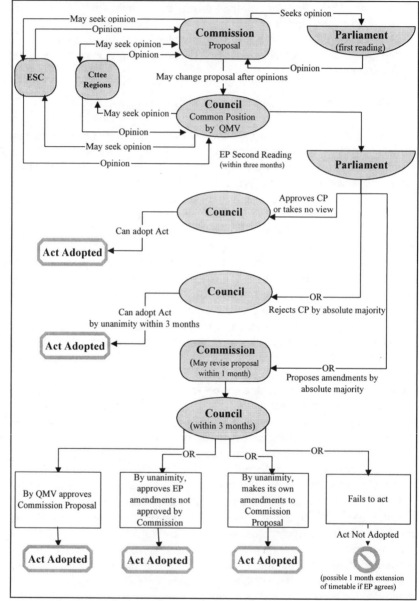

If the EP proposes amendments, the Commission may, within one month, add its opinion before it is sent back to the Council. If the Commission and

Council (by QMV) approve the amendments, the Council can adopt the Act. If the Commission rejects the EP's amendments, the Council can only approve or amend the proposal unanimously. If it does not act within 3 months of receiving the proposal, the Act is not adopted. The procedure substantially increased the legislative role of the EP, but it by no means gave it joint-decisionmaking power with the Council.

Table 4.14 The Scope of Article 189c

Treaty Article		Subject
6	EC	non-discrimination on the basis of nationality
75(1)	EC	transport
84	EC	transport
103(5)	EC	EMU: multilateral surveillance procedure rules
104a(2)	EC	EMU: arrangements for applying 104a(1)
104b(2)	EC	EMU: arrangements for applying 104
105a(2)	EC	EMU: harmonisation measures on circulation of coins
125	EC	Social Fund
127	EC	vocational training
129d	EC	trans-European networks implementation
130e	EC	economic and social cohesion
130o (1&3)	EC	RTD
130w	EC	development co-operation
130s	EC	environment
118a	EC	social policy
2(2) of agreement annexed to the protocol on social policy (TEU)		minimum requirements

- **The Co-decision Procedure (Article 189b).** Under certain circumstances this procedure gives Parliament the power (by absolute majority vote) to block the adoption of legislation by rejecting the Council's common position at second reading. This is sometimes referred to as the power of 'negative assent'. The co-decision procedure means that the EP's views must be taken seriously by the Council because the final text of certain legislation requires the EP's approval (although all legislation still has to be approved by the Council). To some extent therefore, the Council and EP share legislative power, although not an equal basis. Under this procedure (Figure 4.5), after receiving the EP's opinion on a Commission proposal, the Council adopts its common position by QMV – except in the areas of RTD and culture, where unanimity is required. The Council's common position is then submitted to the EP for second reading. Within 3 months the EP can accept, amend, reject or fail to act on, the common position. If it approves the Council's position or fails to act, the Council can adopt the Act. If the Commission and the Council (by QMV) approve the EP's proposed amendments, the Act is adopted. The Council must act unanimously on the proposed amendments on which the Commission has delivered a negative opinion.

The EP can reject the Council's common position by absolute majority. A 'Conciliation Committee' may then be convened by the Presidents of the Council and EP to facilitate agreement. The Committee comprises an equal number of Council and EP representatives. The Commission also participates in the proceedings, seeking to reconcile the positions. The Committee has 6 weeks to achieve an agreed text. If agreement is reached in the Committee, the amended proposal must be approved by the Council (by QMV) and by the EP (by absolute majority) within 6 weeks. If there is no agreement in the Conciliation Committee, the Act is not adopted unless the Council by QMV and (acting within 6 weeks of the expiry of the Committee's 6-week period) confirms its position, possibly with some of the EP's amendments, and the EP does not reject it (it can do so at this stage by absolute majority within 6 weeks of the date of confirmation by the Council). The periods of 3 months and 6 weeks referred to above may be extended by 1 month or 2 weeks respectively, by common accord of the Council and EP.

The areas to which co-decision applies (some of which were formerly covered by the co-operation procedure) are shown in Table 4.15. There are major restrictions on the scope of the procedure. For example, it is not used for the budget, justice, home affairs or EMU. The issue of the scope of Article 189b is likely to figure prominently on the agenda of the 1996 IGC. It is widely predicted that the IGC will widen the scope of Article 189b, although to what extent remains to be seen (some member states favour a substantial widening, although there are significant differences of viewpoint with regard to the areas of policy to which the Article should be extended).

Table 4.15 The Scope of Article 189b

Treaty Article	Subject
49 EC	free movement of workers
54(2) EC	right of establishment
56(2) EC	" "
57(1) EC	" "
57(2) EC	" "
66 EC	services
100a EC	internal market (harmonisation)
100b EC	internal market (national laws)
126 EC	education incentive measures
128 EC	culture*
129 EC	public health incentive measures
129a EC	consumer protection
129d EC	trans-European networks (guidelines)
130I EC	RTD multiannual framework programmes*
130s EC	environment multiannual action programmes

* The items marked with an asterisk require a unanimous vote in the Council.

Figure 4.5 The Co-decision Procedure (Article 189b)

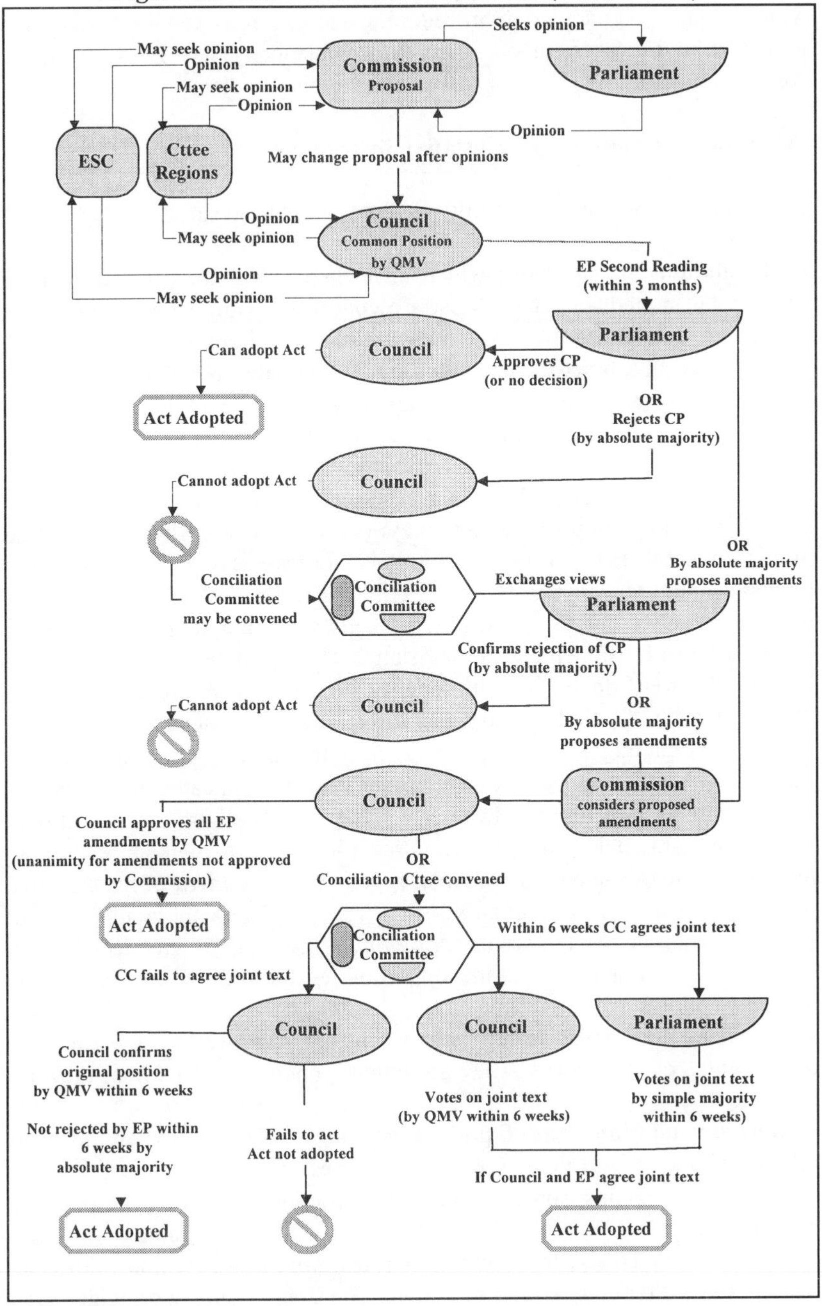

Up to 31 March 1995, 124 proposed acts were subject to co-decision, of which 15 led to a conciliation procedure. Conciliation led to the adoption of a joint text in 11 cases; in one case (voice telephony) the EP rejected the conciliation joint text. The rest still awaited a third reading.

○ Types of Community Legislative Instrument

The following instruments apply to both the European Community and Euratom:

• **Regulations** are decisions which have direct legal force in all member states, with immediate effect. Most are concerned with technical decisions, particularly relating to the CAP. They are of general application, binding in their entirety and directly applicable (that is, they are not subject to national legislative processes) and come into effect as soon as they are published in the *Official Journal*. The main strength of the regulation is that it avoids many of the problems associated with the devolution of legislative responsibilities to national level (for example, foot dragging and differences of interpretation). Its principal weakness (which explains why it is not used more frequently) is that it is rigid and does not take account of variations in national conditions.

• **Directives** set out the principles of legislation, but it is left up to the member states to implement the legislation through national law. The time limit for this to be done is usually set at two or three years. Regardless of the form and methods used to transpose directives into national law, they are nevertheless binding and are expected to have the same results in the member states to which they apply. They are not necessarily applicable to all member states, although they almost always are. They are usually more general than regulations, although some are very specific (for example, in relation to technical standards and environmental protection). The merit of the directive is that it is a means of reconciling the *diversity* of national conditions and structures with the need to secure *uniformity* of Community law. Its principal weakness is that it may provide opportunities for 'policy erosion' at the implementation stage.

• **Decisions** are similar to regulations, but are addressed to governments, undertakings or individuals. They are binding upon those to whom they are addressed.

• **Recommendations and Opinions** are not binding. They are used to provide additional information on specific issues.

The ECSC retains some distinctive institutional features, despite the partial institutional merger of the ECSC, the EEC and Euratom in 1967. Under the Paris Treaty, the Commission has more power within the ECSC than it does within other Union structures. The Commission has a wide range of decisionmaking powers in relation to the operation of the ECSC, which it may exercise without reference to the Council. The ECSC has its own Consultative Committee, comprising interested parties (producers, workers, consumers and retailers) in the coal and steel industries. The ECSC uses a somewhat different nomenclature to that of the EC to describe its legal instruments, viz.:

EC/Euratom	ECSC
Regulations	General Decisions
Directives	Recommendations
Decisions	Individual Decisions
Recommendations and Opinions	Opinions

When the current ECSC treaty expires in 2002, it is probable that the ECSC will be fully integrated into European Community/Euratom structures.

○ **Lobbying in the EU**

The number of pressure groups active at Euro-level is greater now than ever before. In the last twenty years, there has been a population explosion of groups active at Union level, possibly amounting to a tenfold increase. Many professional lobbying firms are located in Brussels. A Commission discussion document published in December 1992 identified about 3,000 special interest groups including 500 European and international federations in Brussels. As the range of Union policies has become more diverse, so too has the range of groups active at Union level. Initially most represented industry and agriculture, but now these constitute less than half of the total. There has been a big growth in lobbying by local and regional councils and by environmental and social groups. There are also numerous sub-industry groups (for example, the motor industry lobby). Many groups are represented in the Union's network of advisory committees. More than 130 non-EU countries also have representation in Brussels.

The Commission has sought to foster the emergence of 'Euro-pressure groups', such as UNICE (Union of Industrial and Employers' Confederations of Europe) and ETUC (European Trade Union Confederation) rather than those favouring exclusively national interests. Other Euro-wide groups include the Committee of Professional Agricultural Organisations (COPA); the European Confederation of the Iron and Steel Industry (Eurofer); the European Chemical Industry Foundation and the European Bureau of Consumers' Unions (BEUC). However most Euro-groups have weak structures. Moreover, many national groups have representation in Brussels.

The EU policy range is very uneven and fragmented. Therefore some groups are more active at European level than others. Groups tend to pursue a dual strategy by lobbying at both the national and European levels. The use of qualified majority voting removed the veto power from national governments on many issues, meaning that lobbying solely at national level is inadequate. As is true of pressure groups at national level, producer groups tend to have stronger representation than consumer groups.

There are very few procedures regulating lobbying in the Union. Nevertheless, a lobbying pattern can be discerned. Like national groups, Euro-groups seek to locate and influence the 'locus of power' and to both obtain and disseminate information. But in the Union system, power is more diffused than at national level, and groups have to adjust their activities accordingly. The Commission is a primary lobbying target, because of its key roles in the policy process The Commission needs to collect information from groups in order to perform its policy initiation and monitoring roles. It may also need the support of groups in its attempts to persuade the Council to adopt its proposals. The EP has also become a major focus of lobbying, which is not surprising given its enhanced role in the legislative process.

● THE 1996 IGC AND INSTITUTIONAL REFORM

○ Preparations for the 1996 IGC

The TEU required an intergovernmental conference to be convened in 1996, to examine a number of specific issues relating to the functioning of the Treaty. The 1996 IGC (sometimes referred to as 'Maastricht 2') opened in Turin on 29 March 1996 and is expected to continue its deliberations until well into 1997. The IGC is the fourth in eleven years and the sixth in the Union's history.

Table 4.16 Previous Intergovernmental Conferences

Date of IGC	Results
1950–51	ECSC Treaty
1955–57	EEC and Euratom Treaties
1985	Single European Act
1990–91 (Economic and Monetary Union)	TEU
1990–91 (Political Union)	TEU

The 1996 IGC will clearly not be a mere tidying up exercise, as may have been originally envisaged, because it will have many unresolved institutional and policy issues to address. Indeed, virtually any issue relating to the Union's objectives can be considered by the IGC. It has already resulted in a wider debate concerning the Union's future than took place prior to the

Maastricht summit. Unlike the two IGCs which preceded Maastricht, the 1996 Conference will give considerable attention to the institutional implications of enlargement.

The IGC is required by the TEU to examine a range of specific provisions – for example, in relation to civil protection; energy; tourism; CFSP; JHA; the powers of the EP; and the scope of the co-decision procedure. The institutional agreement between the EP, Council and Commission in November 1993 added the TEU's provisions on budgetary procedure to the list. In December 1993, the European Council in Brussels agreed that the 1996 IGC would consider many specific institutional reform issues, including the legislative role of the EP, the number of Commissioners and the weighting of votes in the Council. The wider brief of the IGC was confirmed by the European Councils held in Corfu (June 1994) and in Essen (December 1994). The Essen summit agreed on the formation of a Reflection Group to prepare for the 1996 IGC. The summit instructed the Group to consider 'other possible improvements, in a spirit of democracy and openness', such as the Union's options in the light of future enlargement and improvements to institutional efficiency.

The Reflection Group, chaired by the Spanish minister Carlos Westendorp, commenced its work in June 1995. It had 18 members (representatives of the foreign ministers of each member state, a Commission representative plus 2 MEPs). In June 1995, EU foreign ministers and the Reflection Group met in Messina (on the 40th anniversary of the conference which led to the EEC Treaty) to discuss plans for the 1996 IGC. A special 'informal' European Council was held in Majorca in September 1995, to review the Group's progress prior to the presentation of a final report to the European Council in Madrid in December. The Group's Report, published in December 1995, provides the basis for the negotiations in the 1996 IGC. The Report exposed many differences of viewpoint between representatives on a wide range of issues. It is divided into two sections: the first part consists of a 'strategy for Europe' and the second of an analysis of various policy options, categorised under four headings: reform of the Union; the citizen and the Union; efficiency and democracy; and foreign policy.

IGCs are negotiations between governments outside the Union's formal decisionmaking procedures, but the Essen European Council also invited all Union institutions to prepare reports on the operation of the TEU. For example, the Commission's report (spring 1995) focused on the themes of enhancing democracy and effectiveness. The Commission declared itself to be utterly opposed to an *à la carte* Europe and described the TEU provisions on social policy as setting a dangerous precedent. It favoured the removal of the UK's opt-out on social policy. It also warned against dilution of the Union through enlargement. It also favoured a streamlining of the Union's decisionmaking procedures; the replacement of the pillars structure by a single institutional framework; an extension of majority voting; more powers for the EP; a 'genuine' common foreign policy; more effective co-operation in justice and home affairs; and enhanced interinstitutional co-ordination between the Council, Commission and EP. The governments of member states will naturally bring their own shopping lists of preferences to the 1996 IGC. For example, the UK's Conservative government is likely to resist the removal of its opt-out on social policy, or the strengthening of the CFSP. Some governments will no doubt favour substantial deepening of Union integration whereas others are likely to resist this. Some issues which are likely to feature prominently on the IGC's agenda are:

- the complexity of the Union's structures and procedures (how can these be simplified? will the pillars structure survive? how can the Union act more effectively?);
- the institutional implications of an enlarged Union;
- measures to bring the Union closer to its citizens, through increased openness, coherence and accountability;
- the powers of the Union's institutions (for example, will the EP's powers of co-decision be extended? will the EP be granted a bigger role in the appointment of the Commission?);
- voting methods in the Council (will QMV be extended?);
- the size of the Commission (for example, should the number of Commissioners be reduced?);
- CFSP: for example, should there be more use of majority voting? will the WEU be fully incorporated into the Union's structure?
- JHA: how can the procedures and machinery for co-operation in this field be improved?
- clarification of the subsidiarity principle;
- opt-outs: will an *à la carte* Europe be rejected or endorsed (wholly or in part, implicitly or explicitly)?

○ Does the EU Need a Constitution?

Institutional issues are central to the debate about the future direction of the Union. The piecemeal approach to institution building in the EU has resulted in institutional arrangements of labyrinthine complexity. Various reform measures for reducing this complexity have been suggested, such as the consolidation of EU treaties into a single, shorter, more readable treaty; a clearer demarcation between areas of responsibility between the various EU institutions and between the Union and member states.

An alternative would be to formulate a Union constitution. A constitution would provide a much clearer, more comprehensible institutional framework and a clearer definition of Union purposes. Various proposals for a Union constitution have been mooted. In December 1993, the European Constitutional Group produced a draft constitution, emphasising the importance of human rights and individual liberties (perhaps of particular importance, given that these values are not strongly entrenched in some countries currently aspiring to enter the Union). It favoured a clear separation of powers, in which the Council would become the government executive; the Commission the administrative branch; the legislative branch would comprise the EP, the Committee of Regions plus a 'chamber of national parliamentarians'; the ECJ would be the judicial branch. In February 1994, the EP adopted a resolution endorsing a draft constitution on the European Union, which was submitted by its committee on institutional affairs. However, the adoption of a written constitution would antagonise those opposed to a federalist future for the Union. It could impose a framework which would be too rigid to cope with the pressures for change resulting from future enlargement. The only certainty about the EU's institutional structure is that it will continue to evolve.

FURTHER READING

Council, *Report of the Council of Ministers on the Functioning of the Treaty on European Union*, Cmnd 2866, HMSO, May 1995.

Edward, D., 'How the Court of Justice Works', *European Law Review*, vol. 20, no. 5, 1995, pp. 539–58.

European Constitutional Group, *A Proposal for a European Constitution*, European Policy Forum, London, 1993.

Featherstone, K., 'Jean Monnet and the "Democratic Deficit" in the EU', *Journal of Common Market Studies*, vol. 20, no. 2, 1994, pp. 147–70.

Johnston, M.T., *The European Council. Gatekeeper of the European Community*, Westview Press, Boulder, Col., 1994.

Judge, D. and Earnshaw, D., 'Weak European Parliamentary Influence?', *Government and Opposition*, vol. 29, no. 2, 1994, pp. 262–76.

Kirchner, E., *Decision-Making in the European Community*, Manchester University Press, 1992.

Mazey, S. and Richardson, J., *Lobbying in the European Community*, Nuffield European Studies, Oxford University Press, Oxford, 1993.

Nugent, N., *The Government and Politics of the European Union*, Macmillan, London, 1994.

Sbragia, A.M. (ed.), *Euro-Politics: Institutions and Policymaking in the 'New' European Community*, Brookings Institution, Washington DC, 1991.

Weatherill, S. and Beaumont, P., *EC Law*, Penguin, Harmondsworth, 1993.

Chapter 5

The Budget

● PRINCIPAL FEATURES

○ Budgetary Independence

The Community has its own budget, which is independent of the public finances of member states. Between 1958 and 1970, the Community was financed through national contributions, but since April 1970 it has been financed almost exclusively from its *own resources*. The Community has no tax-raising powers and its revenues are collected by member states. But states cannot withhold payment of these revenues, as the ECJ has made clear. The budget is used to finance a wide range of policy commitments and activities. It is the European Community, not the European Union as such, which has a budget. Therefore, the term Community budget is used throughout this chapter.

○ Sources

The Community's own resources comprise four components:
1. **Agricultural, Sugar and Isoglucose Levies:** agricultural levies are imposed on products from outside the Community. Sugar and isoglucose levies are paid by producers to cover market support arrangements and storage costs.
2. **Customs Duties:** levies on imports from non-member states, based on the Common Customs Tariff.
   (NB: for items 1 and 2, member states retain 10% for collection costs).
3. **A Proportion of National VAT:** a notional rate of VAT is applied to an identical range of goods and services in each member state, subject to a

ceiling relating to the size of the state's GNP.

4. **GNP-based Contributions (the 'fourth resource'):** the same proportion of the GNP of each member state. This was introduced in 1988, as a topping up resource to cover expenditure in excess of revenue raised by other means.

The proportions raised from each resource are shown in Figure 5.1. Yields from customs duties and agricultural levies have been falling in recent years as a result of lower tariffs and the Union's increasing self-sufficiency in food. The proportion of national VAT was set at 1% in 1970 and raised to a ceiling of 1.4% in 1985. Until 1995, the base taken into account for this resource could not exceed 55% of a member state's GNP. From 1995, this base was reduced from 55% to 50% for the four poorest states. For other states, it will be reduced in stages between 1995–99. The *fourth resource* contribution increased from 10% in 1988 to 28.6% in 1995. It is arguably the most equitable form of tax, because it is directly related to the GNP of each member state.

Figure 5.1 The Community Budget: Revenue in 1995

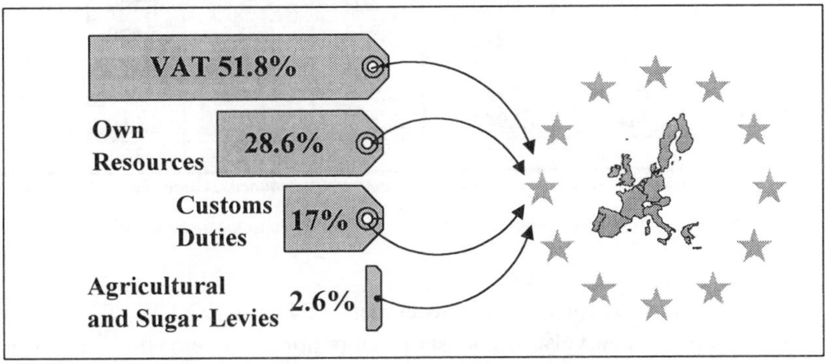

A limit is imposed on the amount of budget revenue raised annually from member states. This is known as the 'Own Resources Ceiling' and is derived from a percentage of the combined GNPs of member states (set at 1.21% in 1995, rising to 1.27% by 1999).

Table 5.1 shows that there are wide variations in both the size and composition of member-states' contributions. The UK contributes a disproportionate amount in customs duties because of its high level of imports. Poorer states are likely to pay disproportionate amounts in VAT contributions because of the consumption patterns of their citizens (they spend proportionately more than the Union average on VAT-rated items). The UK's VAT contribution, estimated at about 10% of total VAT contributions in 1995, is relatively low because of the substantial rebate (or abatement) negotiated by Mrs Thatcher at the European Council in Fontainebleau in 1984 (see below).

Table 5.1 Contributions to Budget Revenues for 1995 (ECU Million)

	Agricultural & Sugar levies	Customs Duties	VAT	GNP-Related	Total	%
Austria	28	295	1,144	585	2,052	2.7
Belgium	118	838	1,223	684	2,863	3.8
Denmark	40	234	700	433	1,407	1.9
Finland	20	171	548	298	1,037	1.4
France	349	1,644	7,644	3,936	13,573	17.9
Germany	398	3,582	12,229	6,087	22,295	29.3
Greece	33	153	599	290	1,075	1.4
Ireland	14	353	320	141	828	1.1
Italy	265	930	4,670	2,978	8,844	11.6
Lux.	0	15	107	47	169	0.2
Neth.	128	1,339	1,950	977	4,393	5.8
Portugal	101	136	605	267	1,109	1.5
Spain	165	515	2,712	1,428	4,820	6.3
Sweden	45	308	953	578	1,885	2.5
UK	260	2,430	3,946	3,022	9,658	12.7
TOTALS	1,964	12,942	39,351	21,752	76,010	100
%	2.6	17	51.8	28.6	100	

Sources: Commission; HM Treasury, European Community Finances, Cmnd 2824, April 1995.

○ Size

The 1995 budget, adopted on 15 December 1994, was ECU 80,893 million. This is still a relatively small sum, amounting to less than 1.2% of Community GNP, or to about ECU 4 a week for each citizen of the Union. The national budgets of states are far larger (in the UK, public expenditure is well over 40% of GNP). Many Community policies do not impose heavy burdens on the budget, because they are regulatory in nature and member states remain largely responsible for carrying them out. Moreover, a substantial amount of budgetary spending would have to be borne by member states if the budget did not exist. Nevertheless, the size of the budget has increased very substantially. Annual per capita expenditure has risen from ECU 19 in 1970 to ECU 219 in 1995 and is set to rise every year during the 1990s. Some key factors accounting for this growth are outlined in Table 5.2 overleaf.

Table 5.2 Some Factors Accounting For the Expansion of the Budget

- the escalating costs of the CAP;
- the extension of the EU's policy responsibilities;
- the accession of Greece, Spain and Portugal;
- economic recession (leading to expansion of regional and social aid);
- the cost of major integration projects (the SEM and TEU);
- ineffective control mechanisms.

Both deepening and widening of Union integration, therefore, have significant budgetary consequences. With the exception of the EFTA countries, all potential future members of the Union would be net beneficiaries from the budget as presently constituted. Indeed, the entry of Central and East European countries into the Union is hardly financially feasible without either a very substantial increase in budgetary resources or an agreement to restrict the access of the new members to these resources.

○ **Allocations**

As Figure 5.2 and Table 5. 3 indicate, *agriculture* takes the lion's share of the budget. The proportion allocated to agriculture has declined from over 80% in 1973 to more than half in 1995. This trend reflects both deliberate policy to restrict the costs of the CAP and the increasing significance of other policies. Apart from expenditure on the CAP, budgetary expenditures are largely directed towards investment in training, infrastructure development and RTD. In 1995, ECU 23 billion was to be spent on 'structural' operations (mainly expenditure on regional and social policies), accounting for 32.5% of the EU's total financial commitments in this year (compared to 18.5% in 1988). Other internal policies, such as energy, transport, education, culture, the environment and consumer protection do not as yet account for a substantial proportion of the budget, although their budgetary significance is increasing. The amount spent on external action (for example, aid for Eastern Europe) has also increased substantially.

The figures below relate to *commitment appropriations*, which are the total cost of legal obligations which can be entered into during the current financial year for activities which will lead to payments in the current and future financial years. *Payment appropriations* refer to the amount available to be spent during the year, taking into account commitments in the current year and preceding years. The difference between the two represents the balance of outstanding commitments. To 'balance the budget', revenue must equal payment appropriations (which for 1995 amounted to ECU 76,527 million). Surpluses are carried forward to the following year. Modest deficits can also be carried forward, but significant deficits require the adoption of a supplementary or amending budget. The entry of Austria, Finland and Sweden increased the 1995 budget by about 5.9% for commitments and 6.1% for payments.

Table 5.3 The 1995 Community Budget (Commitment Appropriations)

	ECU Mn	£ Mn	%
1. Agricultural Guarantee	**37,926**	**29,851**	**46.88**
2. Structural Operations	**26,329**	**20,723**	**32.54**
Agricultural guidance	3,755	2,956	4.64
Regional Development Fund	10,593	8,338	13.10
Social Fund	6,444	5,072	7.96
Cohesion Fund	2,152	1,694	2.66
Other structural operations	3,385	2,664	4.18
3. Internal Policies	**5,056**	**3,980**	**6.25**
Other agricultural operations	208	164	0.26
Other regional operations	51	40	0.06
Social and education policies	731	575	0.90
Energy and environment policies	218	172	0.27
Industry and internal market	729	574	0.90
Research and development	2,969	2,337	3.67
Other internal policies	150	118	0.19
4. External Policies	**4,881**	**3,842**	**6.03**
Food aid	848	667	1.04
Aid to Eastern Europe	1,583	1,246	1.96
Other development aid	1,857	1,462	2.30
Other external policies	594	468	0.73
5. Administration	**4,009**	**3,155**	**4.95**
Commission	2,591	2,039	3.20
Parliament	843	664	1.04
Council	307	242	0.38
Court of Justice	115	91	0.14
Court of Auditors	53	42	0.07
ESC/COR	100	79	0.12
6. Reserves and Repayments	**2,693**	**2,120**	**3.32**
Monetary reserve	500	394	0.61
Emergency reserve	323	254	0.40
Loan guarantee reserve	323	254	0.40
Repayments	1,547	1,218	1.91
TOTAL	**80,893**	**63,670**	**100**

Sources: Commission; HM Treasury, *European Community Finances*, Cmnd 2824, April 1995.

Figure 5.2 Breakdown of Budgetary Expenditure in 1995

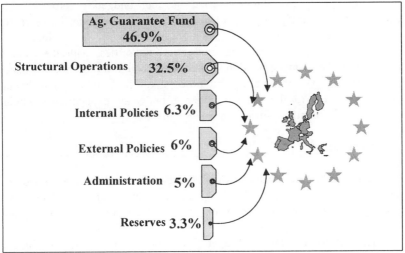

Not all Community financial operations are within the budget. For example, the ECSC has its own budget, derived from loans and a levy on coal and steel production, with budgetary power exercised by its High Authority. The main source of aid to the Third World at Union level is the European Development Fund (EDF) to which members contribute directly. Nor does the budget cover the operations of the European Investment Bank or the European Investment Fund, both of which are concerned with boosting the EU's economies through the provision of finance for investment projects.

● POWERS AND PROCEDURES

○ Powers

Budgetary responsibilities can be roughly categorised as follows:

drafting	Commission
amendment	Council/Parliament
adoption and discharge	Council/Parliament
execution	Commission
control	Commission/Council/Parliament/Court of Auditors
audit	Court of Auditors

Formal power of decision in relation to the budget is shared between the Council and the European Parliament, which together constitute the budgetary authority of the Community. The Commission plays a key preparatory and co-ordinative role in the budgetary process. The categorisation of budgetary responsibilities above should not be taken too literally: for example, there are qualitative differences in the powers of the Council and Parliament as joint budgetary authorities, with the Council generally in the stronger position. Moreover, although the European Council is not formally part of the budgetary process, key financial decisions having major importance for the size and pattern of budgetary expenditure are being made more frequently at European Council meetings.

◯ **Procedures**

The tortuous process through which the budget is drafted, amended and adopted is known as the 'shuttle'. Budgetary procedures are laid down, although by no means exhaustively, in Article 203 of the EC Treaty and comprise the following stages:

• **The Preliminary Draft Budget.** The Commission's DG for Budgets (DGXIX) prepares a preliminary draft budget (PDB) for the following year, based on estimates submitted by the other DGs and by Community institutions. Interest groups also lobby to ensure that their concerns are taken into account in the PDB. The PDB must be agreed by all Commissioners. It must fall within the framework of the current financial perspective agreed by the Council, EP and Commission (see below).

• **Council First Reading.** The PDB is presented in April or May to the Budget Council comprising the Finance Ministers of the member states, who normally meet in July to agree the budget. This meeting is preceded by preparatory work undertaken by a Budget Committee of national officials and by COREPER. The Council usually cuts the PDB, but by only a fraction of the total amount.

The PDB is also forwarded to the EP at the same time as to the Council. There are two broad categories of budgetary expenditure: *compulsory* and *non-compulsory*. Compulsory expenditure is necessary expenditure arising from the EC Treaty or from acts adopted in accordance with it (mainly spending on the CAP). The main non-compulsory items are social policy, regional policy, industry, energy and transport. The distinction is important, because although the EP can propose modifications to compulsory expenditure, the Council can reject them and the EP has no right to a further say on this element of the budget. Even before the EP's first reading, a conciliation procedure involving the Presidents of the Budget Council, the Chairman of the EP's Budget Committee and the Commissioner for Budgets may be established if a dispute seems likely over the categorisation of compulsory and non-compulsory expenditure (the EP naturally wishes as

much as possible to be included in the latter category).
- **EP First Reading.** The draft as amended by the Council is then placed before the EP. Within 45 days of receiving it, the EP must complete its first reading. A key role in examining the draft is played by the EP's Budget Committee, although other parliamentary committees are also involved. Meeting in plenary session in October or November, the EP considers and votes on proposed changes to the budget. Proposed amendments to non-compulsory expenditure require the approval of an absolute majority of MEPs whereas proposed modifications to compulsory expenditure require a majority of votes cast.
- **Council Second Reading.** The Budget Council then considers the draft, as amended and modified by the EP. The Council has 15 days to react to the EP's amendments and proposed modifications. The Council can by QMV modify amendments to non-compulsory expenditure and can reject modifications to compulsory expenditure. It frequently cuts the proposed amendments and rejects the proposed modifications. If it alters the amendments, it then has 15 days to resubmit these to the EP for second reading.
- **EP Second Reading.** This normally takes place in December. The EP has 15 days to act on the Council's alterations. It can reinstate cutbacks made by the Council to non-compulsory spending, by a majority of MEPs and three-fifths of the votes cast. It cannot, however, propose further modifications or changes to compulsory spending. The budget is expected to be adopted no later than 20 December. If no agreement is reached, interinstitutional negotiations take place, involving representatives from the Budget Council, the EP Committee on Budgets and the Budget Commissioner. The EP has the right to reject the Budget as a whole (by a majority of its members and two-thirds of the votes cast), as it did in 1979 and 1984. In these cases, the 'provisional twelfths' system comes into operation, a procedure by which spending is allowed on a monthly basis (based on the monthly figures of the last year's budget), until a new budget is agreed.
- **Control.** There is an elaborate, but by no means fully effective, system of budgetary control. The Commission has a system of internal financial control, which is the responsibility of a Financial Controller, charged with monitoring all budget operations. It also has a Unit for the Co-ordination of Fraud Prevention (UCLAF). The Court of Auditors is responsible for verifying the legality and regularity of Community revenue and expenditure. In November 1994, it presented a scathing report on the Commission's implementation of the 1993 budget. The report stated that much still needed to be done to improve the supervision, accounting and control of Community finances. The audits of the Court, which are retrospective, are used by the EP in its examinations of the implementation of programmes.

● KEY ISSUES

The history of the Community budget is littered with conflicts and crises, many of which have centred on the following issues.

○ Institutional Powers

The budget has been at the centre of the EP's efforts to assert its powers *vis-à-vis* the Council and the Commission, by for example rejecting (or threatening to reject) the draft budget and by proposing budgetary amendments. A *conciliation procedure* has been established to facilitate agreement between the Council and the EP in respect of compulsory expenditure, but if no agreement is reached within the procedure the Council can reaffirm its position. The Council therefore has the 'last word' on compulsory expenditure. However, the EP has the last word on non-compulsory expenditure. It can formulate amendments on non-compulsory expenditure, up to a maximum rate of increase (based on the rate of Community GNP growth, the rate of inflation and the amount of government spending), and calculated by the Commission each year at the start of the budgetary procedure. Any increase in the maximum rate has to be agreed by both the Council and the EP. In its report for the 1996 IGC Reflection Group, the EP proposed that the distinction between compulsory and non-compulsory expenditure should be abolished and that the budget should cover expenditure under the two intergovernmental pillars.

In recent years the establishment of formal and informal mechanisms for dialogue between the Council and EP on budgetary questions has reduced the incidence of major interinstitutional budgetary conflicts. In particular, in 1988 an interinstitutional agreement on budget discipline was signed by the presidents of the Council, Parliament and the Commission (see below). This committed the three institutions to *financial perspectives* for six broad expenditure categories (agriculture, structural actions, internal policies, external action, administrative expenditure and reserves) covering several years. The first perspective (1988–92) committed the institutions to an expansion of the budget, but also contained *ceilings* to ensure tight budgetary discipline (see below).

○ Inadequacy (the failure of resources to keep pace with the demands made on the budget)

There have been many interinstitutional and intergovernmental disputes concerning the adequacy of budgetary resources. In some years, the budget has balanced only by carrying some expenditure items forward to future years. Within the Council, the main source of opposition to large budgetary increases has come from the net contributors amongst the member states. Conversely, the four poorest states have pressed for increases in support of policies aimed at narrowing the development gap between rich and poor states. Both the SEM and the TEU resulted in substantial increases in the size of the European Social Fund (ESF) and the European Regional Development Fund (ERDF). In addition, the TEU established the Cohesion Fund for the four poorest countries. Budgetary issues figured prominently in the negotiations for the fourth enlargement. Spain, in particular, was adamant that wealthy potential entrants would have to agree to provide financial assistance for the poor 'Southern' countries. All three new entrants are net contributors to the budget. It seems likely, therefore, that they will provide additional support for countries seeking to limit budgetary growth. A distinction between *restrainers* and *expanders* also has an institutional dimension: whereas the Council (notwithstanding the views of its poorer members) has frequently sought to limit budgetary expenditure growth, the Commission and the EP have generally sought to expand it.

O **Inequity** (disputes about fairness in revenue and allocation decisions)

Allocations are not based on the *just return* principle, by which states would obtain from the budget roughly what they pay in. The Commission does not publish statistics outlining relative national budgetary contributions and benefits. However, it is well known that there are glaring disparities between member countries in the amounts paid in and received. In the early 1980s, only Germany and the UK were significant net contributors. In recent years, France, the Netherlands and Italy (and now Austria, Finland and Sweden) have joined the 'net contributors' club'. The largest net gainers are the poorer members, especially Greece, Portugal and Ireland. However, three of the richest states are net beneficiaries: Belgium and Denmark receive substantial net benefits from the CAP; Luxembourg benefits from its role as host to several EU institutions.

The UK, the fifth poorest member of EU 15, has been a net contributor ever since it entered the Community. The UK's share of contributions in 1995 was 12.7%, compared with 29.3% for Germany, 17.9% for France and 11.6% for Italy. According to UK government estimates, the UK's annual share of gross receipts is currently about 9% (HM Treasury, Cmnd 2824). In 1980, West Germany was the richest country in the Community. By the early 1990s, Germany had slipped to sixth place (as a result of reunification and the recession), but it remains the largest net contributor, currently providing about 2.5 times as much as it receives from the budget each year. Within Germany, this was a big issue during the 1994 elections to the EP.

○ **The UK's Budgetary Transfers**

Because the UK has a relatively high degree of trade with other countries, it makes relatively high contributions to the budget (derived from high levels of agricultural imports from outside the EU and customs duties). Because it has a relatively small agricultural sector, it receives less from the CAP than several other member states. On the other hand, it currently receives more from the Social Fund than any other member state. On joining the EC, the UK agreed to contribute to the budget on the basis of a fixed percentage of 8.78% of the total, rising to 19.24% in 1977. The incoming Labour government in 1974 sought to renegotiate these terms, on the grounds that the UK's low level of economic growth did not justify such high contributions. An agreement aimed at limiting divergences between contributions and ability to pay, involving partial repayment of VAT contributions (known as the 'clawback mechanism'), was reached at the European Council in Dublin in 1975 and implemented between 1976 and 1980. However, the strict conditions governing repayment rendered it ineffective. The incoming Conservative government in 1979 sought to reduce the UK's contributions by £1 billion, but had to settle for £350 million. In 1983, the UK delayed payment of its contributions to the EU for a month, but the ECJ ruled this to be illegal.

At the European Council in Fontainebleau in 1984, Mrs Thatcher succeeded in negotiating a substantial budget rebate for the UK, known as the Fontainebleau Abatement, which came into operation in 1986 (in 1985, the UK received interim compensation of a reduction in VAT contributions of ECU 1 billion). The abatement is a refund based on a reduction of 66% of the difference between what the UK contributes to the budget and what it receives from it (in terms of EC grants and expenditure). The abatement is deducted from the UK's VAT contribution a year in arrears. Other states make up the difference (because of Germany's position as the main contributor to the budget, it pays only two-thirds of its 'share' – but this still amounts to the largest actual contribution). By the end of 1994, the cumulative value to the UK of the abatement amounted to almost £16 billion. At the Edinburgh summit in 1992, the abatement was fixed until 1999.

Despite the Fontainebleau Abatement, the UK has continued to be a net contributor. There have been significant swings in net contributions from year to year. In 1993, the UK made higher than expected customs duty payments due to higher import costs. Its VAT and fourth resource contributions also rose, largely due to exchange rate movements. The figures shown in Table 5.4 are the UK Treasury's estimates of the UK's contributions and receipts arising from successive Community budgets between 1991 and 1998. The 'unallocated budget' category refers mainly to

contributions to the overseas aid budget. The bulk of the moneys received by
the UK in 1995 derived from the Agriculture Guarantee Fund (ECU 2,757
million), the European Regional Development Fund (ECU 654 million) and
the European Social Fund (ECU 668 million).

Table 5.4 UK Net Contributions to and Receipts from EC Budgets (£m.)

	1991*	1992*	1993*	1994 plans	1995 plans	1996 plans	1997 plans	1998 plans
Gross contribution	5,372	6,500	7,242	8,069	9,049	9,017	9,555	10,259
Gross receipts	2,849	3,168	3,695	4,180	4,571	4,979	4,962	5,148
Net contribution ·	2,523	3,332	3,547	3,889	4,478	4,038	4,593	5,111
UK abatement	2,033	2,139	2,083	2,315	2,848	2,429	2,824	3,097
Net contribution after abatement	490	1,193	1,464	1,574	1,630	1,609	1,769	2,014
Contribution to unallocated budget	320	359	424	510	624	665	715	787

* = Estimated outturn. *Source:* HM Treasury, Cmnd 2817, March 1995.

● REFORMING THE BUDGET

○ Towards Greater Predictability

In recent years, attempts have been made to achieve tighter budgetary
disciplines, a better balance between expenditure categories and vigorous
action against fraud. The Commission has presented two major sets of
proposals on budgetary reform, known as 'Delors 1' (1987–88) and 'Delors
2' (1992). In February 1988, the Council agreed principles of budgetary
discipline based on 'Delors 1'. This set annual ceilings for categories of
expenditure and ceilings for increases in the total budget. It capped increases
in agricultural spending to 74% of average GDP growth. It doubled the
amounts allocated to the structural funds. On the revenue side, it introduced
the 'fourth resource'.

These reforms formed the basis of an Interinstitutional Agreement on
Budgetary Discipline and Improvement of the Budgetary Procedure reached
between the Council Commission and Parliament in June 1988. The
agreement clarified the way the Council, Parliament and Commission
exercised their budgetary responsibilities. It sought to increase the degree of
predictability in relation to budgetary growth, by introducing a 'financial
perspective' which outlined projected expenditures for 1988–92. It therefore
sought to reduce the intensity of the annual conflicts concerning the size and
composition of the budget.

The 'Delors 2' package focused on the financial implications of the TEU.

It favoured orderly, but nevertheless substantial, increases in expenditure to match the objectives of the Treaty. Unlike Delors 1, it included a category for external action. It proposed substantial increases in expenditure on structural policies and 'economic and social cohesion', of particular benefit to the four poorest member states. Richer states initially resisted these proposals, but eventually agreed to budgetary increases, based on the setting of ceilings on six categories of expenditure for the period 1993–99. A new financial perspective for the enlarged Union for 1995–99 was approved at a second reading by the EP in April 1994. Details of the perspective for EU 15 are shown in Table 5.5.

Table 5.5 Financial Perspective for EU 15 for 1995–99 (ECU Million)

	1995	1996	1997	1998	1999
	Current prices			1996 prices	
CAP	37,944	40,807	41,555	42,323	43,110
Structural Funds	24,069	26,579	28,004	28,906	30,790
Cohesion Fund	2,152	2,444	2,715	2,769	2,824
EEA financial mechanism	108	108	108	108	0
Internal policies	5,060	5,337	5,557	5,789	6,010
External policies	4,895	5,264	5,576	5,981	6,465
Administration	4,022	4,191	4,316	4,380	4,445
Reserves	1,146	1,152	1,152	1,152	1,152
Compensation	1,547	701	212	99	0
Total commitments	80,943	86,583	89,195	91,507	94,796
Total payments	77,229	82,202	85,023	87,679	90,428
Payments as % of GNP	1.20	1.20	1.21	1.22	1.23
Own resources ceiling as % of GNP	1.21	1.22	1.24	1.26	1.27

Source: European Parliament Briefing, May 1995.

O The Fight Against Fraud

There has been considerable criticism of overspending, waste and fraud in relation to the budget, although the extent of such fraud is difficult to judge. 4,264 cases of fraud and irregularities were detected by member states and the Commission in 1994 (amounting to ECU 1 billion, or about 1.2% of the total Community budget). About half of detected fraud relates to the agricultural funds. However, some other estimates put fraud as high as 10% of the budget. Moreover, only about 6% of the amounts involved in cases of detected fraud is ever recovered.

The fight against fraud is made particularly difficult by three factors: firstly, the information upon which funding for agricultural and structural policies are based is often difficult to verify; secondly, Union institutions do not have the resources to effectively monitor how allocated moneys are spent; thirdly, the national and regional authorities of member states are responsible for paying out about 80% of Community funds to the final beneficiaries. These authorities are arguably likely to be less diligent in pursuing anti-fraud measures involving Community funds than they are in pursuing frauds on their own budgets. Member states are required to co-ordinate their actions in countering fraud and to take the same measures in countering frauds on the Community budget as they take in matters affecting their own direct financial interests (Article 209a, EC).

In March 1994, the Commission set out an 'anti-fraud strategy', involving a stronger operational presence on the ground, closer partnership with member states, measures to improve the legislative framework and a stronger focus on 'high-risk' sectors. The Commission's anti-fraud unit UCLAF was given 50 new posts in 1994 and the anti-fraud units within the DGs for Agriculture and Customs and Indirect Taxation were transferred to it. The Court of Auditors can now take action against the Commission or member states for failing to act against fraud. However, it seems doubtful if the Union's institutions have sufficient resources, or member states sufficient will, to cope with the magnitude of this problem.

FURTHER READING

Commission, *General Report on the Activities of the European Union (1994)*, Brussels, 1995.

Court of Auditors, *Annual Reports.*

European Journal, Editorial Staff, 'The EC Budget: Winners and Losers', May 1994.

Franklin, M., *The EC Budget: Realism, Redistribution and Radical Reform*, RIIA, London, 1992.

HM Treasury, *European Community Finances*, Cmnd 2824, HMSO, April 1995.

HM Treasury, *Report of the Chancellor of the Exchequer's Department*, Cmnd 2814, HMSO, March 1995.

Shackleton, M., *Financing the European Community*, Pinter, London, 1990.

Strasser, D., *The Finances of Europe: The Budgetary and Financial Law of the European Communities*, Office for Official Publications of the European Communities, Luxembourg, 1992.

Thomson, I., 'The Budget: A Bibliographical Snapshot', *European Access*, 1993/1, pp. 44–8.

Section 3

The Policies of the European Union

Introduction to Section 3

● THE EUROPEAN UNION'S POLICY PORTFOLIO AND POLICY STYLE

○ Overview and Key Characteristics

The rest of the book provides an introduction to the Union's current policy responsibilities. We will begin with an overview of the principal characteristics of the Union's policy portfolio and policy style:

• **Uneven development.** The EU's policy portfolio is both unbalanced and fragmentary. Some EU policies are of long standing and highly developed (notably the CAP and the Common Commercial Policy); some have developed mainly in the last two decades (for example, Regional and Social Policy); some are quite recent and relatively undeveloped (for example, Consumer Policy, Cultural Policy). There are several major policy areas where the Union has at most a minimal role (for example, health, social security) or where its remit does not yet extend (for example, domestic crime). Variations in national conditions, policy traditions and policy priorities render it difficult for the Union to develop 'full' policies in all areas. The range of subjects upon which the Union can justifiably be said to have a policy has nevertheless broadened considerably in recent years, as shown by the large number of policies explicitly referred to in the SEA and TEU.

• **The extensive treatment of policy matters in the treaties** differentiates the EU from the constitutions of most federations. This does not mean that an EU policy requires a strong treaty basis before it can be developed: for example, progress was made in environmental policy from the 1970s, even though there was no explicit mention of the environment in the founding treaties. Similarly, a basis in an EU treaty does not mean that the policy *will* be developed: the Treaty of Rome stipulated a Common Transport Policy (CTP), but this area of policy remained dormant for decades. Policies are set out in great detail in the ECSC Treaty, but references to policies in the later treaties tend to be confined to policy principles (although the TEU outlines the policy on economic and monetary union in great detail). Some policy

131

provisions in the treaties give legal acknowledgement of *de facto* policy developments, such as references to 'European Political Co-operation' in the SEA.

• **The diversity of policy priorities.** Member states by no means have an equal commitment to a strong EU involvement in specific policy areas. For example, some member states are more committed to the development of a common foreign and security policy than others. The UK has traditionally been keen to develop trade policies, but otherwise has tended to be luke-warm about policies leading to deeper integration. EU budgetary allocations for policies are by no means evenly distributed amongst member states and therefore it is hardly surprising that states will have different preferences concerning the EU policy agenda. Both the Commission and the EP have tended to favour extension of the Union's policy responsibilities. The Commission has played a dynamic role as a facilitator, energiser and source of ideas in relation to policy developments. Some Commissions (notably the Delors Commissions of 1984–94) have been far more proactive in this regard than others.

• **The type of EU involvement.** The Union's involvement in policy by no means fits into a homogeneous pattern. For example, foreign and security policy and justice and home affairs are outside the EC policymaking framework. Some policies are referred to in the Treaties as 'common' (agriculture, fisheries, commercial policy, transport, foreign and security policy) meaning that an agreed single policy is expected to replace national policies, at least with regard to major areas of policy. Some are expensive to operate (notably the CAP) whereas others make only small demands on the Community budget. Some are based on a high degree of legal regulation (notably the Common Agricultural, Fisheries and Competition Policies).

• **Policy style.** In some respects, the EU's policy system shares important characteristics with those of national policy systems in liberal democratic states: it is an *elite process*, in that in practice policy decisions are made by a relatively small group of actors; it is a *pluralist process*, in that policy decisions are the outcome of extensive bargaining and compromise between policy actors (principally governments, Union institutions and interest groups); it is *incrementalist*, in that EU policy is constantly adjusted and refined. The Union's policy system also has several distinctive features. It is more complex than policymaking at national level. There are currently more than twenty procedures through which policy decisions are reached. The formulation and implementation of EU policy involves several levels of government and a broader range of institutional actors than national systems. In many respects, the EU's policymaking system is probably more open than those of most national systems (notwithstanding the secrecy surrounding the deliberations of the Council).

- **Implementation remains largely a national function.** The national, regional and local governments of member states are largely responsible for carrying out EU policies. A factor often given insufficient consideration is the variation in the ability (and sometimes the will) of member states to implement policy effectively.

Chapter 6

The Common Agricultural and Fisheries Policies

● THE ORIGINS, AIMS AND OPERATING PRINCIPLES OF THE CAP

○ Origins and Aims

In most parts of the world, agriculture is regarded as a special industry, to be protected and subsidised. The volatility of agricultural markets and the need for security of food supplies has provided a plausible case for government intervention in this sector. The industry has also been widely viewed as part of a nation's cultural heritage. Prior to the creation of the CAP, member states had their own policies for subsidising and protecting domestic agriculture. At the time of the CAP's formation, memories of food shortages during the Second World War were still fresh in many people's minds. The need to increase production and to ensure security of food supplies were therefore regarded as self-evidently desirable goals. Although in the 1950s, 'EC 6' had a farming population of 17.5 million, it produced only 85% of its food requirements. The small size of most farms in EC 6 (average farm sizes in the US were 20 times larger) was hardly conducive to efficiency.

The advantages of a common policy for agriculture were recognised by the Union's founders: it would enable agricultural problems common to all countries to be dealt with by collective action; market stability could be fostered through collective intervention in agricultural markets and through a common policy of external protection; it would provide farmers with new outlets for their produce; it would encourage regional specialisation in food products; it would offer consumers wider choice. The CAP was formally established in the Treaty of Rome (Articles 38–47). Its operational guidelines were agreed at the Stresa conference in 1958 and it came into operation in 1962. From the beginning, it has occupied a central (for many years a dominant) role in Union policy.

Table 6.1 The Principal Aims of the CAP

- to increase agricultural productivity by promoting technological progress;
- to ensure a fair standard of living for the agricultural community;
- to stabilise agricultural markets;
- to ensure the availability of food supplies;
- to ensure stable and reasonable prices to consumers.

O Operating Principles

The CAP is based on the assumption that agricultural markets need to be *managed*. In a free market, the price of any product will rise and fall in accordance with the laws of supply and demand. The CAP was designed to modify the operation of this mechanism in the agricultural sector, through instruments such as price supports, production quotas, production subsidies and import barriers. Recent reforms of the CAP, for example, modifications to price supports, the introduction of direct income supports for farmers and incentives to 'set aside' land for non-agricultural uses, have not changed the system's essential character. In 1960, the Council adopted three principles upon which the CAP is based (see Table 6.2).

Table 6.2 Fundamental CAP Principles

- **Market unity:** free movement of agricultural produce within Community boundaries, meaning the abolition of cross-border barriers to agricultural trade.
- **Community preference:** protection from agricultural imports from outside the Community and promotion of Community agricultural exports, meaning that free trade in agriculture was *not* extended to states outside the Community.
- **Joint financial responsibility:** meaning that the costs of the CAP would be shared amongst member states and would not be based on the 'just return' principle (by which the financial benefits accruing to a member state would be equivalent to its contributions).

The seeds of the main controversies surrounding the CAP are contained within these principles, because each implies a disproportionate distribution of benefits and costs. For example, both consumers and producers should reap benefits from *market unity*. But it also exposes producers to cross-border competition. *Community preference* benefits some producers by shielding them from global competition. But it also restricts consumer choice and results in higher food prices. *Joint financial responsibility* means that producers in some countries probably receive greater financial benefit than they could obtain from their own governments if the CAP did not exist. But it also means that the citizens of some EU countries in effect subsidise the agriculture industries of others. The prime beneficiaries of the CAP, *producer interests*, have proved more powerful, and certainly better organised, than *consumer interests*. Because the costs and benefits of the CAP are distributed very unevenly between member states, some governments have a stronger interest in defending the system than others (although all are subject to strong pressure from producer interests).

● THE OPERATION OF THE CAP

○ Responsibilities

The Agriculture Council is the key decision-taker with regard to the CAP. The EP's powers of co-decision do not apply to agriculture, because it is classified as 'compulsory' expenditure, although the EP subjects the Commission's proposals to detailed scrutiny and suggests many amendments. The dispute between the Council and the EP concerning the classification of agricultural expenditure is currently subject to an action in the ECJ. In its report prepared for the 1996 IGC, the EP has recommended the extension of co-decision to agriculture. Meetings of the Agriculture Council are prepared by the Special Committee on Agriculture (SCA), not by COREPER. There is much horse trading within the Council, because each Agriculture Minister has national agricultural interests to promote and defend.

The Commission has a deeper involvement in the implementation of the CAP than in most other policy areas. The directorate responsible for agriculture, DGVI, is the largest Commission directorate with policy responsibilities. A central role in the management of the CAP is played by a network of management and regulatory committees, comprising agricultural specialists in the Commission and in the agriculture ministries of member states.

○ Finance

The CAP is financed from the Community budget, through the European Agricultural Guidance and Guarantee Fund (EAGGF), which is divided into two sections:

- **The Guarantee Section,** accounting for about 95% of EAGGF spending, finances the price and market support systems. Income aid and 'accompanying measures' are also now included under this heading. As Table 6.3 shows, arable crops (particularly cereals) take the lion's share of the EAGGF.

Table 6.3 EAGGF Guarantee Section Expenditure (1995 Budget Appropriations)

Sector	ECU Million
Arable crops	14,779
Sugar	1947
Olive oil	893
Fruit, veg., wine, tobacco	4,467
Milk and milk products	4,059
Beef, sheep, goat and pigmeat	6,678
Other sectors	1,706
Refunds on processed products	535
MCAs and ACAs	p.m.
Accounts clearance decisions	550
Interest	80
Distribution to the needy	200
Fraud control	85
Rural development	471
Food aid	140
Other measures	23
Total	35,512
Fisheries	47
Income Aid	45
Accompanying measures	1,372
Total	36,976
Enlargement	950
TOTAL	**37,944**

p.m. = *pro memoria. Source:* Commission, *General Report,* 1994.

- **The Guidance Section** provides financial support for adjustment of agricultural structures. Aid from this source is normally co-financed with member states. The EIB and the Union's Structural Funds also contribute. Financing from this section amounted to ECU 3,359 million for commitments and ECU 2,829 million for payments in 1994.

○ Market Intervention Instruments

The CAP has developed a complex array of rules, regulations and operating procedures. Each reform of the CAP has added new layers of complexity to the system. This section focuses on the 'traditional' CAP market intervention instruments. Other, increasingly important, CAP instruments, such as income supports and 'set aside', will be dealt with more fully in the section on CAP reform. The 'traditional' instruments used to implement the CAP are:

• **Price Supports.** In March or April each year, the Agriculture Council sets price levels for a range of agricultural commodities, after receiving proposals from the Commission. In the preceding autumn, the Commission conducts reviews of the state of each agricultural sector and engages in extensive consultations with various interests. The Commission relies heavily on a network of management, advisory and working groups. It is normally expected to submit its proposals to the Council and the EP by mid-January. The Agriculture Council has about 25 working parties to assist in examining the Commission's proposals. Agriculture Ministers are naturally under pressure from their farming lobbies to set high prices.

The price level which should be attainable under normal market conditions is generally referred to as the *target price*. If the price the farmer can obtain in the market is less than the target price, the produce may be sold to an *intervention agency*. These agencies, which operate in all member states, buy in the market when prices for certain agricultural products fall below a certain level. The *intervention* or *buying-in* price is the level at which the intervention agency will buy in the market. Conversely, when commodities are scarce, the agencies release commodities on to the market. About 70% of EU agricultural production is covered by price supports (principally cereals, dairy products, rice, sugar, beef, sheepmeats, certain fruit and vegetables and fishery products). For some products, alternative forms of assistance are provided: for example, pigmeat receives aid only for storage. Table wine receives aid for storage and distillation. For some fruits and vegetables, support for buying in by producer organisations is provided. There are variations in the nomenclature used for these mechanisms. For example, the *guide price* is the target price for beef, veal, wine, fish and some other products; the *basic price* is the basis for calculating the buying-in price for pigmeat and fruit and vegetables; the *withdrawal price* is the level at which certain fruit, vegetables and fish are withdrawn from glutted markets. These operations, plus storage and depreciation costs, are primarily financed through the Community budget. *Threshold prices* are set for agricultural imports when the price of such imports would otherwise be lower than EU prices.

By creating false prices for certain agricultural products, the CAP system has provided farmers with incentives to increase production. This has led to the notorious problem of food surpluses (for example, 'milk lakes' and 'butter mountains'). Dairy, cereals and sugar producers have the worst records for surpluses. Mechanisms have been introduced to reduce support levels when certain production targets are reached. For example, *maximum guaranteed quantities* involve reductions in prices when production exceeds a certain quantity. Production quotas for milk were first introduced in 1984. *Co-responsibility levies* require producers in some sectors (principally milk and cereals) to bear a share of the costs of disposing of surplus production. Surpluses have been disposed of in several ways, such as subsidised sales to non-EU states and handouts to the EU 'needy' (ECU 136 million in 1994).

• **Direct Subsidies.** A few products (for example, oilseeds, olive oil and tobacco) receive supplementary aid, covering a small proportion of production. Some marginal products (principally flax, hemp, silkworms and some seeds) receive flat rate aids by the hectare or quantity produced.

• **Import Barriers.** 'Community preference' (a euphemism for protection) prevents prices for agricultural produce within the Union from falling to world levels. Levies on agricultural imports are imposed at Union frontiers and flow into the Community budget (minus the costs of collection, which accrue to national governments). Non-tariff barriers, such as import quotas, have also been extensively used. About 20% of products for which there is no regime of guaranteed prices (for example, eggs, poultry, some fruit and vegetables, quality wines, flowers) receive protection only from imports, via levies or customs duties. The Union has an extensive network of agreements with developing countries which allow these countries preferential access to EU markets. But, since the bulk of developing countries' agricultural exports consists of tropical products, these concessions offer little threat to the CAP.

• **Export Subsidies (Restitutions):** these are subsidies paid on some agricultural products exported from the EU, aimed at bridging the gap between Union prices and world prices. They encourage agricultural producers in member states to compete in external markets. They have tended to account for about 30% of the EAGGF.

• **The 'Agrimonetary System'.** Without an adjustment mechanism, the fluctuation in the values of Union currencies would defeat the CAP aims of uniform and stable prices. Although CAP prices are fixed in ECU, EU farmers receive payment in their own currencies, calculated at special exchange rates ('green rates') which do not change automatically in line with market exchange rates. Until they were abolished following a Council decision in December 1992, a system of *monetary compensation amounts* (MCAs) was used to cover the difference between 'green' and market rates. MCAs were designed to prevent distortions in trade due to differences between 'green' and market rates. Farmers in countries whose currency had risen were paid compensatory amounts on agricultural exports. Conversely, compensatory amounts were levied on agricultural imports. For countries whose currency had fallen, the reverse would happen (compensatory amounts would be granted on imports and levied on exports).

The MCA system was supposed to be temporary, but turbulence in the currency markets (combined with vested interests) prolonged its use. It is hardly surprising that a strong currency country such as Germany opposed its abolition. Not only was the system very expensive, it was also incompatible with the Single European Market, because in effect MCAs constituted a system of border taxes and subsidies. They were replaced by new agrimonetary arrangements, involving the periodic fixing and adjusting of 'green' rates by the Commission. From February 1995, new rules were introduced which allowed for some degree of currency fluctuation without revaluation of 'green' conversion rates. A new agrimonetary regime was agreed by the Agriculture Council in June 1995. The new regime introduced a dual green currency system, involving fixed rates for strong currency countries and ECU-linked rates for weak currency countries. It also increased the contributions of governments to farmers facing a reduction in farm payments due to currency movements.

● BENEFITS AND COSTS OF THE CAP

○ Benefits

In some respects, the CAP is a victim of its own success, in that it has more than fulfilled some of its original objectives – in particular high agricultural productivity and regularity of food supplies. The Union is now self-sufficient in cereals, wheat, milk, butter, beef, veal, pork, poultrymeat and sugar. The Union is the second largest exporter of agricultural products. It is the world's leading producer of sugar beet and wine (accounting for about 60% of world production). Growth in productivity has been dramatic. Between 1973 and 1989, agricultural output in the Union rose by 29%. Arguably, however, this rise is due at least as much (if not more) to advances in agricultural technology than to the CAP, because dramatic productivity increases have also occurred in many other developed countries.

The principal trends which can be discerned from Table 6.4 and Figure 6.1 are that in the years 1980–92, output has risen by almost a fifth whereas employment has fallen by a third; that productivity (output per employee) has increased by 77%; and that producer prices have fallen by about 30% (consumer prices have fallen by roughly the same amount).

Table 6.4 Trends in EU Agriculture in Real Terms (1980–92)

Year	EAGGF	Final Ag. Output	Employment	Output per employee	Producer prices*
1980	100.0	100.0	100.0	100.0	100.0
1981	88.9	99.0	95.0	104.2	98.7
1982	91.6	104.2	91.8	113.5	98.4
1983	110.2	104.5	90.4	115.6	95.9
1984	120.7	107.8	88.1	122.4	92.8
1985	124.4	107.6	86.0	125.1	88.0
1986	136.1	109.3	83.2	131.4	84.8
1987	138.1	110.6	80.9	136.7	81.5
1988	153.7	112.1	78.1	143.5	79.8
1989	134.8	113.4	74.6	152.0	82.3
1990	132.8	113.8	72.3	157.4	78.3
1991	156.2	115.4	69.6	165.8	76.0
1992	150.7	118.4	67.0	177.3	70.3

*Weighted average. *Source:* Commission.

Figure 6.1 Trends in EU Agriculture in Real Terms (1980–92)

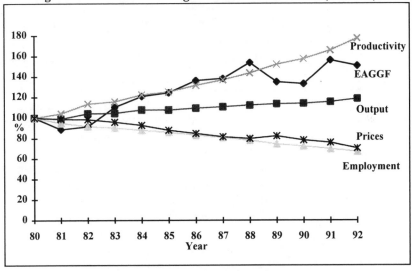

Its proponents argue that the CAP has prevented sharp price swings for agricultural products and has facilitated a fourfold increase in cross-border agricultural trade within the Union. They argue that, without it, both the agriculture industry and rural life within the Union would decline rapidly. Although it has not prevented declines in the incomes of some groups of farmers in recent years, these declines would probably have been even steeper without it. Moreover, food prices have increased by less than consumer prices as a whole. The CAP may well have provided a useful 'cement' in the construction of the Union in the early phases of its development, by providing opportunities for mutually beneficial co-operation between member states in a key economic sector. However, the utility of the CAP as an 'integration cement' has lessened, for two reasons: firstly, the relative importance of agriculture in the economies of most member states has declined. Agriculture as a percentage of Union GDP declined from about 5% in 1973 (EC 9) to about 2.4% in 1993. The numbers employed in agriculture within the Union almost halved between 1973 and 1993, falling from 13.4 million in 1973 to 7.3 million (including east Germany) in 1993. Secondly, enlargement has increased the degree of diversity within this sector, so that the agricultural interests of member states no longer easily converge into a common interest. There are wide variations in the relative importance of agriculture in the economies of the member states and in average farm sizes.

○ Costs

The CAP is an easy target for criticism. It is widely regarded as expensive, wasteful, bureaucratic and fraud-ridden. Not all of the criticisms below are entirely convincing. For example, although agricultural prices in the Union are generally higher than 'world prices', the latter provide an unreliable guide, because quantities traded on world markets are often small in comparison to total production. Moreover, many non-EU exporters also receive subsidies. The CAP is undoubtedly protectionist, but no more so (in some cases considerably less so) than the agriculture policies of many countries. The EU remains the world's largest importer of food. But the defenders of the CAP have, in recent years, found it difficult to present a plausible case against radical reform. The main criticisms of the CAP are:

• **it is an anachronism:** the conditions which led to its creation no longer exist. In particular, food surpluses, rather than food shortages are now the major problem. Since 1973, consumption of agricultural produce within the Union has grown by only 0.5% per year whereas production has grown by about 2% a year;

• **it leads to a gross misallocation of resources,** through interference with market mechanisms;

• **it is very costly to operate** and places severe strains on the Community budget. Moreover, CAP spending has risen considerably faster than Union GDP. The CAP budget will continue to rise throughout the 1990s;

• **consumers pay dearly for the CAP,** through taxation and high food prices;

• **it causes conflicts between member states,** because it benefits some states more than others. For example, France, the Netherlands, Denmark and Ireland with relatively inefficient agricultural sectors have done relatively well out of the CAP, but the UK, with a small but relatively efficient agricultural sector has not;

• **it is inherently inequitable:** according to some estimates, almost half of Union farmers' incomes derives directly or indirectly from subsidies and protection measures of various kinds. Why should farmers be protected, but not coalminers or steel workers? CAP support is far greater for some agricultural products than for others. Moreover, some groups of farmers (particularly the bigger agricultural businesses) obtain more from the CAP than others. About 80% of CAP spending is directed towards about 20% of farmers;

• **it is a source of conflict with other countries:** the EU's principal trade disputes with the US and Australia have centred on the CAP. It is a barrier to the penetration of the EU market by some of the world's poorest countries. Overproduction has led to dumping of agricultural products on world markets;

• **it is difficult to prevent CAP frauds:** the CAP has very complex operating procedures and there are an estimated 3 million farm-related cash transactions a year. National procedures for verifying claims have often been lax. These circumstances providing fertile conditions for fraud: for example, forgery of customs documents to evade customs duties; claims for non-existent produce, livestock or land; the relabelling of imports as Union produce to obtain subsidies; or multiple claims for export refunds for the same goods. Almost half of all detected fraud relates to the agricultural funds. In relation to the EAGGF Guarantee Section 1,623 cases of fraud, amounting to ECU 484 million, were reported for 1994 (1.3% of the Community budget) but this is widely thought to be the tip of a large iceberg;

• **it has damaged the rural environment,** through overproduction.

● REFORM OF THE CAP

○ Pressures For and Against Reform

Until 1992, reform of the CAP largely took the form of limited *ad hoc* adjustments to CAP mechanisms. Although many radical proposals had been made (most notably by the Agriculture Commissioner Sicco Mansholt in 1968) these were blocked by powerful vested interests. The influence of entrenched and tenacious farming lobbies on government policies is often cited as a textbook example of 'institutional capture'. At Union level, farmers are represented by COPA (Committee of Professional Agricultural Organisations) and by more than 100 specialised groups. There are powerful farming lobbies at national level also. Conversely, consumer interests and animal rights lobbies are by no means as well represented in the corridors of power.

In 1985, the Commission sought to place the issue of CAP reform firmly on the Community agenda in a Green Paper (*Perspectives for the Common Agricultural Policy*). A series of *ad hoc* reforms were introduced in the late 1980s. Their main thrust was towards efforts to align production more closely to consumption, through reducing price supports, introducing direct income supports and providing farmers with incentives to set aside land. The *set-aside* scheme adopted in 1988 provided financial assistance to farmers willing to take at least a fifth of arable land out of production for five years (it could be left fallow or used for other purposes, such as tree-planting). Schemes to encourage farmers and farm workers to seek alternative employment were also developed. In 1988, the Council introduced annual ceilings on the growth of agricultural expenditure (limiting it to 74% of GDP growth). Budgetary stabilisers were also introduced for agricultural products, which placed limits on the quantities for which money would be paid. Although in the beginning these reforms appeared to be working, they failed to prevent the accumulation of large surpluses of cereals, dairy products and meat. The reforms were too limited in scope and scale to be fully effective.

By the early 1990s a combination of internal and external pressures proved too powerful for opponents of reform to resist. The main internal pressures were: the mounting cost of the CAP in a period when governments were struggling to control public spending; the demands made by the CAP on the Community budget inhibited the ability of the Union to develop other policy areas; an increasingly vocal environmental lobby pointed to the damage to the countryside wrought by overproduction; exposure of CAP frauds tarnished the reputation of the Union as a whole. The main external pressure came from the US, which threatened trade sanctions against the Union unless it made major changes to the CAP.

○ The MacSharry Reforms

In February 1991, the Commission produced a Reflections Paper on CAP reform. It argued that the Union's self-sufficiency in many agricultural sectors raised questions concerning the need for production incentives. It favoured further reduction of price supports, an increase in income supports and the expansion of accompanying measures, such as 'set-aside'. Six months later it produced more specific proposals, deriving from the

Reflections Paper. The reforms proposed by the Agriculture Commissioner Ray MacSharry in 1992 were based on the Commission's 1991 proposals and pursued five objectives:

- *to maintain the Community's position as a major agricultural producer and exporter;*
- *to bring production in line with demand;*
- *to concentrate support for farmers incomes where it is most needed;*
- *to maintain rural communities;*
- *to protect the rural environment;*
- *to develop the potential of the countryside.*

The main points of the original MacSharry proposals were: a reduction in price supports for cereals, oilseeds and protein crops of 29% over 3 years; an increase in income supports, linked to the withdrawal of land from production (land set aside could be used for other purposes, such as afforestation or tourism); an early retirement scheme for farmers over 55; a compensation scheme for farmers, with small farmers being compensated in full and those with larger farms receiving less; greater emphasis on produce quality; subsidies for agriculture in less-favoured regions and mountain areas; and an environmental action programme, which recognised farmers' role as 'stewards of the countryside'. In addition, there would be measures to combat fraud, such as on-the-spot inspections by the Commission.

The proposals were not *qualitatively* different from the *ad hoc* reforms of the late 1980s. Moreover, they retained the basic features of the CAP. However, they were controversial, for two reasons: firstly, it was estimated that they would lead to 15% of land being taken out of production; secondly, the proposal that compensation arrangements should discriminate between small and large farms provoked strong opposition, not least from the UK. But after considerable wrangling, and some revisions (the compensation scheme was made available to all farm sizes), the plan was agreed by the Agriculture Council in May 1992. The reforms were not designed to effect an immediate cut in the CAP budget, but rather to introduce measures which in the long run should reduce (or at least contain) agricultural spending. Income supports render the costs of the CAP more transparent and will be harder to justify or defend in the long run. The reforms have so far failed to halt rises in milk production. They left some products (for example, sugar and wine) virtually untouched. In the first full year since the adoption of the reforms (1993), set-aside led to an 8.5% reduction in the area under cereals production. In this year, the EU agricultural labour force fell by 4%, compared with an average of 3% in recent years. In 1994, farm incomes increased by 5.7% in real terms and cereals, arable and beef stocks fell significantly. The 1992 reforms paved the way for the GATT deal on agriculture (see below). But the effectiveness and adequacy of the reforms in the longer term remains to be seen.

◯ Agriculture in the Uruguay Round of the GATT

The Commission is mandated to negotiate external trade agreements on behalf of member states, in consultation with a committee appointed by the Council (Article 113, EC). In the Uruguay Round of the GATT talks, the CAP was at the centre of the dispute between the Union, the United States and the 'Cairns group' of agricultural exporting countries (14 members, including Australia and New Zealand). The US farming industry stood to benefit greatly from the liberalisation of trade in agricultural products and US trade negotiators pressed hard for concessions from the Union. Unlike the Cairns group and the poor 'South', the US has a big stick to wield against the Union in the form of trade sanctions. US negotiators sought from the Union improved market and cuts in Union export subsidies for agricultural products.

In 1992, the US threatened sanctions against Union agricultural export subsidies, by announcing its intention to introduce punitive tariffs on a range of Union food and agricultural products by December 1992. These sanctions were averted by a deal between the US and the Commission in November 1992, known as the Blair House Accord. The Accord went further than the MacSharry reforms in several respects: for example, it included sugar and involved 'tariffication' (conversion of protection measures into customs tariffs, which are easier to discern and compare than non-tariff barriers). In addition to 'tariffication', the main points of the deal were: the volume of export subsidies to be reduced by 21% over six years, compared with average annual volumes exported between 1986 and 1990; internal price supports to be reduced by up to 20% (from 1986–88 levels); a safeguard clause, to allow adjustments in tariffs if world market prices fell below the 1986–88 average; and a minimum access clause, allowing importers opportunities to take 3% of the domestic market (rising to 6% in 6 years).

France vociferously opposed the deal. France is the Union's leading agricultural producer, accounting for about a quarter of Union output and is the world's second biggest agricultural exporter. It has about 1 million full-time farmers and powerful farm lobbies (although farmers now constitute only about 5% of France's working population, and agriculture accounts for only 4% of French GDP). The lobbies argued that the deal would result in 30% of French farming land being taken out of production. However, other Union countries were adamant that the Blair House Accord could not be renegotiated, as it would ruin the chances of the Uruguay Round being finalised. A GATT deal was finally agreed in Geneva in December 1993, largely because France could not muster sufficient support within the EU to oppose US demands. The GATT deal (based largely on the Blair House Accord) will cut agricultural subsidies and import barriers over six years. EU consumers should benefit from cheaper agricultural products and lower taxes.

○ The Impact of Enlargements and of Eastern Europe

Each enlargement of the Union has exacerbated the range and complexity of the problems associated with the CAP. For example, enlargement has affected the size and composition of the Union's agricultural labour force. Greece had 935,000 engaged in agriculture in 1981; Spain 1,252,000 in 1986 and Portugal 942,000. The German total increased by about 180,000 following reunification. Although Austria, Finland and Sweden do not have large agricultural sectors, they nevertheless face major problems of adjustment. Farmers in these countries tend to work in harsh or difficult environments. Levels of agricultural support and protection in EFTA are generally higher than in the EU. The new entrants agreed to adjust their agriculture to fit in with the CAP, through transitional arrangements. Subsidies which conflict with the CAP are being phased out and special support arrangements for farmers working in remote or mountainous regions are being introduced. As a result of this enlargement, the 1995 EAGGF Guarantee Section budget was increased by ECU 950 million.

The issue of agriculture has already loomed large in relations between the EU and the transition economies of Eastern Europe, because the latter tend to have large agricultural sectors and a strong comparative advantage in some agricultural products. For example, in 1992, about a quarter of Poland's workforce was engaged in agriculture. East European agriculture could potentially have a major impact on the CAP, even if no states from the region are admitted to the EU, once the association agreements signed with several transition countries enter fully into force. Operational inefficiency, distribution, storage and marketing problems are currently blunting the export capacity of East European agriculture, but the export potential of the region should not be underestimated. The EU currently accounts for over 50% of agricultural exports from Eastern Europe. Conversely, Eastern European countries offer good export markets for high-quality food products from the EU.

○ Should the CAP be Abolished?

The suggestion that the CAP is now more trouble than it is worth, and will become unsustainable with future enlargement, is still regarded as heresy within official circles in the EU. The Commission has repeatedly emphasised that recent CAP reforms do not affect the CAP's basic principles. In 1994, a team of agricultural experts, contracted by the Commission, produced a report on CAP reform. The report reiterated many of the common criticisms of the CAP and recommended the cutting of EU farm prices, the phasing out of farm subsidies over 7 to 10 years and compensation for poorer agricultural regions through the Structural Funds. However, the Commission refused to endorse these recommendations. But, as the power of vested interest agricultural interests weakens, and as the significance of other EU policies increases, the prospects for further major CAP reform is likely to grow.

Some British Eurosceptics favour agricultural *renationalisation*, meaning that each member state would finance its own agriculture industry. This, of course, would be fiercely resisted by those favouring deeper integration. Moreover, it is hardly likely to find favour with those states which benefit most from the CAP. A more likely prospect is a continuation and extension of existing market-oriented reforms, with a stronger emphasis than hitherto upon environmental and consumer considerations. It seems likely that the area under cultivation will continue to decline and that there will be greater emphasis on the quality, rather than quantity, of production.

● THE COMMON FISHERIES POLICY (CFP)

○ Origins and Objectives

Although the CFP derives from the same legal basis as the CAP (Articles 38–43 of the Treaty of Rome), it was not established until 1970. Moreover, due to fierce disagreements between member states concerning how it should operate and on the allocation of quotas, the CFP did not come into being in fully-fledged form until 1983, when major reforms were introduced. Although the CFP shares some basic features with the CAP (a common market, market intervention, Community preference), there are also fundamental differences between the two policies. In particular, the CFP does not involve massive subsidies to fishermen and therefore accounts for less than 1% of the Community budget. The EU fishing industry employs about 300,000 fishermen and 1.5 million in associated industries.

○ The Objectives and Operation of the CFP

The objectives of the CFP are to stabilise fisheries markets, to ensure supply and reasonable prices, to protect and conserve fishing grounds and to obtain maximum economic benefits for fishermen. These objectives have proved far easier to define in broad terms than to achieve.

The operation of the CFP can be divided into four main aspects:

• **Access to fishing waters, and conservation and management of resources.** Each year the Council sets total allowable catches (TACs) for more than 100 fish species. Quotas are then allocated between member countries. There are limits on the minimum size of fish caught. There is a 200 nautical mile Union fishing zone. Union fishermen do not have completely free access to Union waters: when Ireland, Denmark and the UK joined in 1973, a 12-mile limit around national waters was allowed, initially for 20 years. The 1983 reform accepted the principle of 12-mile exclusion zones. The accession of Spain and Portugal (which doubled the number of Union fishermen and increased the Union's fleet tonnage by about 50%) led to further modifications: these countries were granted mutual access, with limits on allowable catches until January 1996. New rules allowing for access of Spanish and Portuguese vessels to the waters of other member states were agreed by the Fisheries Council in December 1994. A Union Inspectorate is formally responsible for surveillance, although national governments actually monitor and enforce Union regulations.

• **Common organisation of fishing markets,** to adjust supply to demand for fish and to guarantee, as far as possible, fair incomes to producers. Compensation may be paid for catches withdrawn from markets, on a decreasing scale. There is a system of guide prices, fixed for most species at the start of each fishing season. A multiannual guidance programme (MAGP) sets targets for reductions in tonnage and motive power of fleets.

• **A programme to promote the fishing industry,** through measures to improve productivity, the modernisation of the fleet and promotion of new activities. In 1994, the Commission announced that ECU 908 million of structural aid was to be granted to the fisheries sector over five years.

• **A common external tariff.** The Council sets minimum import prices for imports from third countries. In 1993, the average tariff was about 11% on fresh, and 20% on processed, fish. There are Union quotas for some products, such as canned tuna. The Commission has negotiated bilateral access agreements with many non-Union countries.

◯ Problems

The EU fishing industry is currently in crisis, due to overcapacity, national rivalries, widespread rule-breaking and cheap imports. Whereas the central CAP problem is 'too many farmers producing too much food', the central CFP problem is 'too many fishermen chasing too few fish', due to the growing capability of fleets and the depletion of fish stocks. The CFP has not succeeded in conserving fish stocks, not least because of ineffective monitoring and enforcement by member states. There are wide variations in the degree of zealousness with which national inspectorates enforce CFP regulations, a situation which has done much to undermine the credibility of the CFP. EU fishermen have had difficulty in accepting that Union fishing grounds constitute a shared resource. They have frequently accused each other of breaking the rules on TACs and of fishing illegally in 'national waters'. The attempt by Spanish fishermen to physically prevent British trawlers from fishing in the Bay of Biscay in 1994 was but one of several recent conflict episodes. Under multiannual guidance programmes for 1993–96, each Union fleet must be decreased by 15–20%. But decommissioning schemes have not been very successful so far. Further restrictions on days at sea and reductions in TACs are currently being mooted.

The problems besetting the EU fishing industry have a major international dimension, due to the depletion of global fish stocks and the intensity of competition between the world's fishing fleets. The joint share of member states in world catches of fish fell from 11% to 7% between 1971 and 1990, whereas the US and Canada maintained their shares. In 1995, a serious dispute developed between Canada and the EU over access to Atlantic fishing grounds. EU fishing industry lobbies are currently campaigning for tighter restrictions on foreign imports (there were riots in Brittany over fish imports from Russia, Poland and elsewhere in 1994). A dispute over access to Norwegian fishing waters for EU vessels almost led to a Spanish veto on the European Economic Area agreement. A compromise deal was eventually agreed, granting the Union an access quota of Norwegian fish, with Spain and Portugal getting the lion's share. The vehemence with which the protagonists in these disputes tend to pursue their arguments is indicative of an industry in crisis.

FURTHER READING

Atkin, M., *Snouts in the Trough: European Farmers, The CAP and the Public Purse*, Woodhead, Abingdon, 1993.
Burnett, J. and Oddy, D., *The Origins and Development of Food Policies in Europe*, Pinter, London, 1994.
Commission, 'EU Agricultural Policy for the 21st Century', *European Economy*, no. 56, 1994.
Commission, *The New Common Fisheries Policy*, Brussels, 1994.
Foders, F., *Reforming the European Union's Common Fisheries Policy*, European Policy Forum, London, 1994.
House of Lords, *The Implications for Agriculture of the Europe Agreements*, Select Committee on the EC, HL Paper 57-11, Session 1993–94, HMSO, 1994.
Swinbank, A., 'CAP Reform 1992', *Journal of Common Market Studies*, vol. 31, no. 3, 1993, pp. 359–72.

 **Chapter 7**

Regional Policy

● JUSTIFICATIONS

Until the creation of the European Regional Development Fund in 1975, regional policy within the Union was very largely the prerogative of member states. Prior to the entry of the UK and Ireland, only Italy was really interested in a Union regional policy, because of its poor Mezzogiorno region. The number of countries with a strong interest in a Union regional policy increased again with the entry of Greece, Spain and Portugal. The accession of Spain and Portugal doubled the number of people living in regions with per capita incomes of less than 75% of the Union average.

In recent years, the case for a Union regional policy has been strengthened by the decline of traditional industries concentrated in specific regions and by increasing recognition of the potential impact of other Union policies on regional disparities. About 50 Union regions now have permanent representatives in Brussels and there are several associations of regions (such as the European Association of Development Agencies and the Association of European Border Regions). The TEU established the Committee of the Regions, to give the regions an institutional voice in the Union. The justifications for a Union regional policy can be summarised as follows:

• **The need for balanced development of the Union as a whole.** The notions of 'Community' and 'Union' imply the acceptance of some form of common interest, transcending the boundaries of member states. A Union policy can be justified on the grounds of *equity* (it is inequitable for living standards to vary so widely between regions) and *efficiency* (the Union's resources are being underutilised in poorer regions).

- **The multidimensional nature of regional problems.** Most Union policies have a regional dimension. Therefore, a Union-wide regional policy can contribute to the achievement of the Union's other policy objectives. The Commission now conducts regional impact assessments for each policy. There is also a need to counteract the tendency of some Union policies to exacerbate regional disparities (see below).
- **The magnitude of regional problems.** Although national regional policies are still operated within member states, national governments (especially in the poorer states) do not have the resources to tackle major regional problems by themselves.

● THE EXTENT OF REGIONAL DISPARITIES WITHIN THE UNION

Wide regional disparities exist not only within the Union as a whole, but also within many member states. Poorer regions tend to have fewer roads, rail lines, telephone lines or other services. According to a Eurostat report published in February 1995 (based on 1992 data), 12 regions in EU 15 have a GDP per capita of less than half the EU average. No region in Greece or Portugal, and only one region in Spain, reached the EU average. Seven regions (Hamburg, Brussels, Darmstadt, Paris, Vienna, Bavaria and Bremen) have a GDP per capita of more than 1.5 times the EU 15 average. Some countries have wider regional disparities than others. Spain, Italy the UK and (since reunification) Germany have the most pronounced interregional variations. Some Spanish regions have made substantial gains in recent years, whereas others continue to stagnate. There are wide disparities between Italy's northern and southern regions. Following reunification, about one fifth of the German population live in regions with GDP per capita of less than 35% of the Union average.

The Union includes an increasingly diverse range of regions – for example, industrial, urban, rural, border and peripheral regions. The Union has recently gained some sparsely populated and remote regions (in Finland and Sweden) and an alpine region (in Austria). Some regions are experiencing dynamic growth, whereas others (for example, many old industrial regions) are in decline. Some inner-city areas are experiencing severe deprivation. Some are industrially diverse whereas others are based on a narrow range of industries. Others have never been industrially developed. Some are adjacent to national borders. Although many of the poorest regions have high unemployment rates, some (mainly in Greece and Portugal) have comparatively low unemployment, even though incomes tend to be low. The main regional problem in the UK is that of declining industrial areas. A strategy for the regions must therefore be flexible enough to address a very broad range of regional problems.

● REGIONAL POLICY FUNDING AND INSTRUMENTS

○ The European Regional Development Fund and other Structural Funds

The ERDF is the principal fund through which Union support for the regions is provided. Because of its long experience in operating a regional policy, the UK played a key role in establishing the ERDF. Between 1975 and 1986, 95% of the Fund was administered on a quota basis, in order to ensure that all member states benefited in some way. The bulk went to Italy, France, the UK, Ireland and Greece. There was also a small non-quota section (5% of the total), which enabled the Union to offer assistance to any region in the form of specific measures or programmes. Following reforms agreed in 1984, quotas were replaced by 'indicative ranges' (minima and maxima), which increased the degree of flexibility in the proportions allocated to each country. The ERDF is one of the Union's *structural funds*, which, together with the *Cohesion Fund*, are the main financial instruments for pursuing the aims of greater economic and social cohesion within the Union. The structural funds comprise:

the European Regional Development Fund (ERDF);
the European Social Fund (ESF);
the Guidance Section of the Agriculture Fund (EAGGF);
the Financial Instrument for Fisheries Guidance (FIFG).

ERDF assistance is provided in the form of *project assistance* (grants for specific projects) and *programme assistance*, which covers a broader range of activities and involves a package of measures targeted at specific problems over several years. More emphasis is now placed on programme, rather than project, assistance. Applications for ERDF moneys are channelled through national ministries. The ERDF has grown from 4.5% of Union spending in 1975 to 13.1% in 1995. The Fund operates on the basis of the *additionality principle*, meaning that allocations should be additional to funding provided by national governments. However, this principle is by no means always observed, because moneys allocated for ERDF programmes and projects have frequently been used for other purposes by national governments once ERDF finance has been secured. There were major reforms of the Fund in 1979, 1984, 1989 and 1993.

○ **The Common Objectives of the Structural Funds**

The 1989 reforms sought to ensure closer co-ordination of structural policies, by setting out common objectives for the Funds. From 1989 until they were revised in July 1993, these common objectives were:

Table 7.1 Structural Fund Objectives until June 1993

Objective 1: promoting the development and structural adjustment of lagging regions (with GDP per capita of less than 75% of the EU average). **Objective 2:** the conversion of regions in industrial decline. **Objective 3:** combating long-term unemployment. **Objective 4:** combating youth unemployment. **Objective 5a:** modernisation and adjustment of agricultural structures. **Objective 5b:** promoting the development of rural areas.

Only three of these objectives (1, 2, and 5b) were strictly regional. Objective 1 areas were given priority. The principal sources of Union finance in support of these objectives are shown below.

Objective 1	ERDF, ESF, EAGGF Guidance Section, FIFG
Objective 2	ERDF, ESF
Objective 3	ESF
Objective 4	ESF
Objective 5a	EAGGF Guidance Section, FIFG
Objective 5b	EAGGF Guidance Section, ESF, ERDF

The revised system of priority objectives (from August 1993) is:

Objective 1 (*lagging regions*). No change was made to this objective, but following intensive lobbying, some additional regions were reclassified as Objective 1 regions. Prior to its extension, this category covered all of Greece, Portugal, Ireland and Northern Ireland, the Italian Mezzogiorno, ten regions in Spain, Corsica, France's overseas departments and the five east German Länder. Until recently, Objective 1 regions were expected to have a per capita income of less than 75% of EU GDP. Under the revised regulations, some regions not fulfilling this criterion were included (the Belgian Hainaut region, the French districts of Valenciennes, Douai and Avesnes, Cantabria, Flevoland, Merseyside and the Highlands and Islands of Scotland). These are mainly industrialised areas where decline in industrial activity is very severe. The UK now has three Objective 1 regions. Austria's Burgenland also qualifies for Objective 1 assistance. Abruzzi, the most prosperous Objective 1 region, will be taken off the list in January 1997.

Objective 2 (*regions in industrial decline*). No fundamental change was made to this objective, although the eligibility criteria were broadened. In addition to well-established criteria (an unemployment rate higher than the Union average; a higher percentage of industrial employment than the Union average; a decline in industrial jobs) other more subjective criteria were added in July 1993, such as the need to rebuild inner cities. Some former Objective 2 regions have been reclassified as Objective 1 regions.

Objective 3. This now embraces the old Objectives 3 and 4. It seeks to combat long-term unemployment and to help young people and others threatened by exclusion from the labour market into work.

Objective 4. This new objective seeks to combat unemployment by facilitating adaptation of workers to industrial change and to changes in production systems.

Objective 5a. No change was made to this objective.

Objective 5b. Adaptation of agricultural and fishery structures. No change was made to this objective, although it now covers areas suffering from a decline in the fishing industry. Priority is given to developing jobs outside farming and fishing, such as tourism and small businesses.

Objective 6. This is a new category, established to provide assistance to remote and sparsely populated regions in Sweden and Finland. It covers regions with outstandingly low population densities (below 8 inhabitants per square km). The regions covered have populations of 450,000 in Sweden (5.3% of the population) and 837,000 in Finland (16.7% of the population, mainly in Lapland and other areas bordering Russia).

Table 7.2 outlines the amounts allocated for these objectives for 1994–99.

Table 7.2 Structural Fund Appropriations for 1994–99 in ECU Million*

	1	2	3 and 4	5a	5b	6	CI	Total
Austria	184	n.d.	n.d.	n.d.	n.d.	–		1,623
Belgium	730	160	465	195	77			1,859
Denmark		56	301	267	54		89	767
Finland		n.d.	n.d.	n.d.	n.d.	511	–	1,704
France	2,190	1,765	3,203	1,932	2,238		1,422	12,750
Germany	13,640	733	1,942	1,143	1,227		1,902	20,586
Greece	13,980		–	–			1,086	15,066
Ireland	5,620	–	–	–	–		384	6,004
Italy	14,860	684	1,715	814	901		1,705	20,679
Lux.		7	23	40	6		13	89
Neth.	150	300	1,079	165	150		241	2,084
Portugal	13,980	–	–	–	664		1,416	15,396
Spain	26,300	1,130	1,843	446	664		2,428	32,810
Sweden		n.d.	n.d.	n.d.	n.d.	230	–	1,420
UK	2,360	2,142	3,377	450	817		1,119	10,265

* = EU 12 at 1994 prices; Austria, Finland and Sweden at 1995 prices;
CI = Community Initiatives (see below); n.d. = not yet determined.
Source: Eurostat, *Europe in Figures*, 1995.

In the early 1990s, economic recession in the Union provided a powerful argument for increases in the amounts allocated to the problem regions. For example, disparities in unemployment rates between the 10 worst-affected and 10 least-affected regions widened in 1992 and 1993. In 1993, unemployment rates in the 10 worst-affected regions were 7 times greater than in the 10 least affected (Commission, *Fifth Periodic Report*, 1994). The European Council in Edinburgh in December 1992 earmarked ECU 141.5 billion for the regions between 1993 and 1999, with 74% going to Objective 1 regions, 11% to Objectives 3 and 4 and the rest distributed roughly evenly amongst other Objectives. Including funding for the 1995 entrants, the total has been increased to about ECU 150 billion between 1994 and 1999. In 1992, the four poorest members received 50% of the funds. Together with the Cohesion Fund (see below), this will rise to 54% by 1999.

○ **The Cohesion Fund**

The Fund was established at the Maastricht summit, due to strong pressure from the four poorest member states. The Fund applies to countries with a GNP per capita of less than 90% of the Union average (Portugal, Spain, Greece and Ireland, with a combined population of 63 million). The TEU includes a protocol on economic and social cohesion and requires the Fund to provide financial support for transport and environmental infrastructure projects. The Edinburgh European Council decided that ECU 15 billion (at 1992 prices) would be allocated to the Fund between 1993 and 1999, with 70% going to Objective 1 regions. The Fund came into existence at the end of 1993 with an annual budget of ECU 1.5 billion, rising to ECU 2.6 billion by 1999. It covers between 80 and 89% of the cost of projects it supports. Whereas the ERDF seeks to reduce *regional* disparities, the Cohesion Fund seeks to reduce disparities between *countries*. Moreover, the Cohesion Fund applies only to four states and is limited to transport and environment infrastructure projects. Fund disbursements are *project-based*, whereas most ERDF funding is *programme-based*. In 1994, the Fund financed 51 projects.

Table 7.3 Cohesion Fund Commitment Appropriations 1993–94

	Environment		Transport		Total	Breakdown
	ECU m.	%	ECU m.	%	ECU m.	%
Greece	198	60	134	40	332	18
Ireland	72	43	96	57	168	9
Portugal	134	40	200	60	334	18
Spain	519	51	499	49	1,018	55
Total	923		929		1,852	100

Source: Commission, *General Report (1994)*, Brussels, 1995.

○ **Policy Instruments**

The Union's regional policy is implemented by means of various mechanisms and procedures, principally:

• **Community Support Frameworks (CSFs).** Member states submit development plans to the Commission, presenting national and regional priorities. The Commission negotiates a Support Framework with national and regional authorities. The CSF defines the priorities of the policy to be implemented. The member states then submit Operational Programmes for the priorities laid down in the CSF.
• **Community Initiatives,** which may target specific areas (for example, border or urban areas), industries (for example, textiles), groups (for example, the disabled) or subjects (for example, defence conversion).

Table 7.4 Community Initiatives

RECHAR II: to assist the economic conversion of the coalmining areas most affected by job losses.
RESIDER II: to facilitate the economic and social conversion of steel areas.
RETEX: to promote economic diversification in areas reliant on the textile and clothing industry.
INTERREG II: to promote co-operation between areas adjoining existing borders and completion of energy networks.
REGIS II: to promote the development of the EU's most remote regions.
Employment and Development of Human Resources: to enhance employment growth and promote social solidarity. It embraces:
NOW: a training initiative for women;
HORIZON: improving access of disabled people to the labour market;
YOUTHSTART: labour market integration of young people without qualifications).
Modernisation of the Portuguese Textile Industry.
SMEs: to assist SMEs to adapt to the SEM and to improve their international competitiveness.
LEADER II: support for 'grass-roots' rural development networks.
KONVER: the defence conversion scheme. The main beneficiaries are Germany, France and the UK.
ADAPT is a new initiative financed from the ESF, to help workers and firms to adapt to industrial change.
PESCA: help for areas dependent upon fishing.
URBAN: to tackle the problems of urban areas.

Between 1989 and 1993, ECU 5.8 billion was allocated to such initiatives (almost 10% of the Structural Funds). The amount to be allocated between 1994 and 1999 is ECU 13.77 billion.

• **Pilot Projects** are exploratory projects on regional problems, such as urban regeneration and traffic congestion.

• **Integrated Mediterranean Programmes (IMPs)** were established in 1985, when Portugal and Spain were about to enter the Union. Grants and loans are provided to facilitate adjustment of Mediterranean regions to enlargement.

● THE REGIONAL IMPLICATIONS OF OTHER UNION POLICIES

The effects, both positive and adverse, of other policies on the regions is potentially very great. For example:

• **The Effects of the Single European Market Programme:** although the precise effects of the SEM are difficult to measure, it is widely acknowledged that the benefits and costs of the programme have not been distributed evenly amongst the regions (see Chapter 9).

• **The Effects of EMU.** Full EMU would exacerbate the economic problems of poorer regions, for several reasons. A common currency would mean that a member country would no longer be able to use its exchange rate as a cushion against external competition. The poorer countries are required to make substantial adjustments to meet the EMU convergence criteria. During the transition to EMU, countries are required to adopt policies to reduce inflation (involving curbs on wages and prices) and budget deficits. This could lead to increased unemployment. Moreover, there is little labour mobility between regions to offset these shocks. The Cohesion Fund is too small to be able to compensate for these adverse economic effects.

• **The Challenge of Enlargement.** Regional issues played an important role during the negotiations for entry into the Union of Austria, Sweden, Norway and Finland. The population density of the two Nordic entrants is only 16 people per sq. km, compared with 145 in EU 12. Unemployment tends to be much higher in the northern regions of these countries. The emphasis in regional policy in the Nordic countries has been on maintaining population, employment and incomes in remote areas. In Austria, the aims have been more varied (for example, to protect the environment in alpine regions and to promote trans-frontier co-operation). The entry of Malta, Cyprus and East European countries would extend the range and complexity of the EU's regional problems. Given the scale of regional problems in Eastern Europe, the EU's current regional policy could not be sustained without a very substantial increase in ERDF funding.

• **The Union's Relations with Eastern Europe.** Fears have been expressed that the opening up of the economies of Central and Eastern Europe, combined with the Union's trade and aid policies towards these countries, may have an adverse impact upon the EU's poorer regions in two principal ways: investment may be diverted from the EU's poorer regions towards the East; moreover, exporters in transition countries have shown an ability to provide stiff competition in certain sensitive industrial sectors such as steel and textiles. But the Commission has argued that these effects have so far been on a comparatively small scale and that increased trade and investment opportunities for EU businesses in transition economies may more than offset any adverse effects (Commission, *Fifth Periodic Report*, 1994).

• **Trans-European Networks.** The Union's aim to create Union-wide transport, telecommunications and energy networks obviously has a major regional dimension (see Chapter 12).

• **Subsidiarity.** The importance given to this principle in current Union thinking raises the fundamental question of where national regional policy ends and Union policy begins.

● THE EFFECTS OF EU REGIONAL POLICY

The effects of EU regional policy are difficult to gauge, for several reasons: firstly, the impact of many programmes and projects, such as infrastructural improvements, can only be judged in the long term; secondly, regional economies, like national economies, are subject to a wide range of influences and it is difficult to assess the impact of specific factors; thirdly, it is difficult to isolate the effects of Union regional policies from those of national policies; fourthly, recipients of ERDF assistance arguably have a vested interest in overestimating its impact; fifthly, there has been little evaluation of the effects of this assistance.

EDRF money has undoubtedly become very significant for local and regional authorities. A Commission report on the regions published in 1994 pointed to evidence of real economic convergence in regional economic performance over the recent past. It estimated that by 1993 the ERDF accounted for about 6% of gross fixed capital formation in the four poorest member states (Commission, *Fifth Periodic Report*, 1994, p. 131). The Report estimated that, in the same year, the structural funds and the Cohesion Fund added 2.3% to the GDP of these countries. It estimated that, since 1986, average economic growth in Spain, Portugal and Ireland has been between

0.75% and 1.75% above the Union average, although this had not resulted in significant falls in unemployment in these areas. Similarly, the Report argued that the rate of net job creation in Objective 2 areas between 1986 and 1993 was up 13%, almost twice the Union average. But convergence is a very slow process: some regions have indeed made progress, but others have stagnated or even declined. Moreover, the effects of Union spending on the regions has been muted to some degree by the economic recession.

Arguably, foreign direct investment (FDI) has had a greater impact upon the economic development of specific regions than either national or European regional policy. FDI brings various benefits to the regions, such as injections of capital, 'know-how' and employment. Between 1986 and 1991, an estimated ECU 120 billion of FDI flowed into the EU. There was an additional ECU 150 billion between member states. For Spain, Portugal and Ireland, FDI has been greater in value than Union regional aid. Greece, however, receives twice as much from the structural funds as from FDI.

Union regional policy has been criticised on several grounds. The amount allocated to the ERDF has been very small, in comparison with the magnitude of the Union's regional problems. National spending on the regions has been substantially greater than EDRF spending. This reflects an unwillingness on the part of the more prosperous member states to agree to large increases in the ERDF. It has also been argued that ERDF moneys are spread too thinly, on too many projects. Another frequent criticism has been that ERDF programmes and projects have been poorly monitored. The 1993 reforms sought to address this problem, although there is no clear evidence as yet of substantial improvements in monitoring. Union regional policies may (to a limited extent) have boosted incomes in recipient regions, but despite significant increases in ERDF funding, regional disparities within the Union remain very large.

FURTHER READING

Armstrong, H.W. and Taylor, J., *Regional Economics and Policy*, Harvester Wheatsheaf, Hemel Hempstead, 1993.

Commission, COM (94), 322, *Fifth Periodic Report on the Social and Economic Situation and Development of the Regions of the Community*, Brussels, 1994.

Commission, *General Report on the Activities of the European Union (1994)*, Brussels, 1995.

Mortensen, J. (ed.), *Improving Economic and Social Cohesion in the European Community,* Macmillan, London, 1994.

Scott, J., *Development Dilemmas in the European Community: Rethinking Regional Development Policy*, Open University Press, Buckingham, UK, 1994.

 **Chapter 8**

Social Policy

● SCOPE AND DEVELOPMENT

○ Scope

Until quite recently, the term 'European Social Policy' (ESP) was virtually synonymous with the employment policies of the Union. Although still largely concerned with employment issues, the scope of ESP has widened considerably in recent years. A Commission Green Paper on ESP in 1993 took it to mean 'the full range of policies in the social sphere including labour market policies' (Commission, 1993). This broadening of policy responsibilities reflects the aim of the Union to be far more than an economic formation. The Commission's White Paper on Social Policy (Commission, 1994) acknowledged the social goals expressed in the TEU (Article 2, EC) – that is, to achieve a high level of employment and of social protection, to raise the standard of living and quality of life, together with economic and social cohesion.

However, ESP remains in many respects undeveloped and lopsided. Although the Union can claim to have policies affecting a wide variety of social groups (workers, the unemployed, women, the disabled, the poor) the social policies of national governments still have the biggest impact on the lives of EU citizens. EU expenditure on social policy is still a very small proportion of national spending on welfare and employment creation. National governments provide pensions, unemployment benefit and other welfare benefits. Even in the field of employment, national governments play the major role. More than 90% of employment legislation is still determined by national governments. A *common* social policy seems unlikely to develop in the foreseeable future for several reasons, notably: the wide variations in the demographic and socioeconomic characteristics of member states; the diversity of social policy regimes; the reluctance of member states to relinquish control over social policy; and the budgetary transfers which a common policy would require.

○ The Diversity of Social Policy Regimes

Various attempts have been made to classify the social policy regimes of member states: for example, distinctions have been made between the 'Bismarck' and 'Beveridge' traditions (the former financing social policy through employment insurance and the latter through general taxation). Similarly, a rough geographical demarcation has been discerned between the social policies of Northern and Southern member states (with the former tending to be far more generous). However, no distinction is watertight. There are wide variations between member states in the relative amounts contributed by governments, employers and individuals to the funding of social policy. There are significant variations in entitlements to, and amounts of, sickness benefit, pensions and family allowances, as shown in Tables 8.1 and 8.2. Average spending on social protection per capita in 1992 ranged from ECU 1,127 in Greece to ECU 6,687 in Denmark (Eurostat, 1994). Unemployment benefit amounts to between 70 and 80% of GDP per capita in some Northern member states, but to about 10% in Italy and 12% in Greece (in Italy only very low rates of unemployment benefit are paid as of right, but other forms of compensation are received).

The Commission has repeatedly stated that there can be no question of fully harmonising social security systems, which derive from the traditions and cultures of each member state. But two factors may be leading to a limited degree of convergence of national social policies:

• *firstly*, member states are affected by common problems, such as rising unemployment, ageing populations, changes in family structures, changes in work patterns and escalating social security and health-care budgets. The capacity of governments to pay for welfare is declining. By the year 2020, the ratio of people aged 65 or older to working age (15 to 64) may have increased by 50% (Commission, 1993, p. 22). In 1992, about four-fifths of all social benefits went on health and pensions. In all countries, therefore, there are pressures to control social spending and to re-examine the efficacy of social policy regimes;

• *secondly*, the objectives of the SEM programme have provided the rationale for attempts to introduce minimum common standards for employees in order to create a more even playing field for labour. In EU 12, five countries had nationally determined minimum wage legislation; in five others, minima were determined by collective bargaining; the UK and Ireland had no minimum wage. The debate in the Union between those favouring social protection and those favouring labour market deregulation has by no means been resolved, not least because it raises contentious ideological issues concerning the role of government in modern market economies. In the early 1990s, economic recession and rising unemployment in the Union increased the intensity of this debate.

Table 8.1 EU Social Protection Benefits by Function in 1991

	Social protection spending as % of GDP	Average Pension as % of GDP per capita	Average Unemp. Benefit as % of GDP per capita	Average Family Allowance as % of GDP per capita	Sickness benefit spending per capita (ECU)	GDP per capita (ECU)
Belgium	26.7	57.4	72.6	8.2	878*	15,167*
Denmark	29.8	68.0	69.1	12.4	1,167	20,444
Germany	26.6	51.2	45.0	7.4	1,486	21,547
Greece	na	78.0	12.2	1.0	104*	5,190*
Spain	21.4	47.3	58.3	0.4	592	10,935
France	28.7	72.8	41.1	8.2	1,204	17,007
Ireland	21.3	43.8	44.2	5.9	550	10,262
Italy	24.4	77.6	9.7	3.5	937	16,392
Lux.	27.5	65.0	23.4	11.0	1,206	19,505
Neth.	32.4	76.4	80.2	6.8	1,036	15,560
Portugal	19.4	42.1	20.5	3.4	283	6,423
UK	24.7	63.9	22.6	8.8	721	14,112

* = 1990. *Sources: Green Paper,* (1993), pp. 42–7; Eurostat.

Table 8.2 Breakdown of EU Welfare Expenditure in 1992 (%)

	Health	Old-age survivors	Maternity leave	Unemployment – promotion of employment	Others	Total
Belgium	34.4	44.7	8.1	11.4	1.4	100
Denmark	28.5	35.1	12.0	17.2	7.2	100
Germany	41.0	40.6	8.9	6.2	3.3	100
Greece	18.7	69.0	1.7	5.3	5.3	100
Spain	36.6	41.3	1.8	18.5	1.8	100
France	34.6	44.1	9.5	7.7	4.1	100
Ireland	36.0	27.2	17.4	14.6	4.8	100
Italy	31.6	62.8	3.9	1.7	0	100
Lux.	39.3	48.4	11.1	0.8	0.4	100
Neth.	45.2	36.9	5.4	8.4	4.1	100
Portugal	45.4	38.8	5.6	5.0	5.2	100
UK	36.4	39.4	10.9	6.0	7.3	100

Source: Eurostat.

○ Development

ESP has a long history, dating back to the formation of the ECSC. Article 46 of the ECSC Treaty sought improvement of the living standards and conditions of workers in the coal and steel industries. A wide range of provisions on employment issues were included in the Treaty of Rome: these covered, for example, free movement of workers, improvement in working conditions and in workers' living standards and equal pay between men and women. The Treaty also established the European Social Fund.

There have been both passive and active periods in the development of ESP. Between 1957 and 1972 the main focus of ESP was on labour mobility. In the 1970s, ESP was expanded to address the growing problem of unemployment, resulting in a quadrupling of the ESF budget between 1973 and 1979. In 1972, member states agreed to establish a Social Action Programme, targeted at employment problems. From the mid-1980s, the notion of *Social Europe* has been promoted by the Commission. Jacques Delors sought to 'sell' the idea of the SEM programme to European trade unions by insisting that the programme had a social dimension and was as much about creating a Europe for workers as for businessmen. The SEA contains provisions to strengthen economic and social cohesion and introduced qualified majority voting with regard to some aspects of social policy. The TEU contains a wide range of social policy provisions. Before the Treaty there was no specific legal competence in public health vested in the Union. The Treaty gives the Union responsibility to take preventive action on public health. The TEU also introduced two sets of social policy provisions: those within the EC Treaty applicable to all member states and the 'Protocol on Social Policy' to which all member states except the UK subscribed. Since 1 January 1994 Community rules on social security also apply to EFTA countries in the European Economic Area.

● THE EUROPEAN SOCIAL FUND

The Fund was established by the Treaty of Rome (Articles 123–8) and was set up in 1960, to promote employment and the geographical and occupational mobility of workers. The bulk of the ESF is now spent on measures to combat unemployment, through the provision of finance for vocational training, resettlement and job creation. The Fund is administered by the Commission, in accordance with guidance by the Council. There is also an advisory committee (the Social Fund Committee) comprising national officials, employers and trades union representatives. The *additionality principle* applies to projects supported by the ESF. In other words, public authorities in member states are required to provide at least as much funding as that sought from the ESF. In the UK the ESF is administered through the Department of Employment. The budget for the ESF is small, relative to the size of the unemployment problem. It has nevertheless increased markedly in both absolute terms and in relation to its share of the Community budget.

In 1983, it was agreed that 75% of the Fund would be directed towards alleviation of unemployment amongst the under 25s. The other main group assisted are over 25s unemployed for more than 12 months. About 40% of the Fund is reserved for the most deprived regions and areas experiencing industrial decline. The scope of the Fund was widened in 1993, following decisions taken by the European Council in Edinburgh in December 1992. Objectives 3 and 4 of the Structural Funds were grouped together to form a single new Objective 3, which was extended to cover those exposed to long-term unemployment. A new Objective 4 was created, to facilitate adaptation of workers to industrial change. Between 1994 and 1999, 9% of ESF appropriations will be earmarked for initiatives to enhance employment opportunities for disadvantaged groups. A European Employment Services agency (EURES) has been established to act as a European employment agency and to provide a discussion forum on employment.

● EMPLOYMENT RIGHTS AND 'SOCIAL EXCLUSION'

In addition to the right to work in any member state (see Chapter 14), ESP seeks to promote a wide range of social rights, particularly in employment.

○ The Social Charter ('The Community Charter of the Fundamental Social Rights of Workers')

The Social Charter reflects the continental approach to industrial relations, based upon the enunciation of employment rights and upon collaboration between 'social partners' (business leaders and trades unions). In 1985, Jacques Delors had sought a new social dialogue between the Commission, UNICE and ETUC (the 'social partners') by arranging a meeting at Val Duchesse, a Belgian chateau. The process which ensued became known as the Val Duchesse Social Dialogue, leading to proposals for strengthening Union employment policies. In 1988, the Marin Report on Social Policy advocated a 'social charter'. The Commission published the first draft of the Charter in May 1989. This was amended largely as a result of British objections, but even the revised draft was unacceptable to the UK government. The Draft was adopted in December 1989 by all member states except the UK. Although enthusiastically welcomed by UK trade unions and by the Labour and Liberal parties, the Charter was regarded by the UK government as an attempt to introduce socialism by the back door. The 'rights' enunciated by the Charter are listed in Table 8.3.

Table 8.3 Social Charter 'Rights'

- the right to work in the EC country of one's choice;
- the freedom to choose an occupation and the right to a fair wage;
- the right to improved living and working conditions;
- the right to social protection under prevailing national conditions;
- the right to freedom of association and collective bargaining;
- the right to vocational training;
- the right of men and women to equal treatment;
- the right of workers to information, consultation and participation;
- the right to health and safety at work;
- protection of children and adolescents;
- a decent living standard for the elderly;
- improved social and professional integration for the disabled.

Although the Charter is a 'solemn declaration' with no direct legal force, its principles are being translated into practice through Community legislation. The Charter is accompanied by a Social Action Programme, comprising 47 specific measures, all of which have now been presented by the Commission. Twenty nine of these required Council approval and more than half have now been adopted. At the Maastricht summit, the UK government reaffirmed its opposition to the Charter and therefore this aspect of social policy forms a separate Protocol of the TEU. The Protocol contains seven articles. Article 1 states that the aims of the Protocol are the promotion of employment, improved living and working conditions, proper social protection, dialogue between management and labour and the development of human resources. Article 2 distinguishes between those areas covered by Article 1 to be decided by QMV and those to be decided by unanimous vote, as shown in Table 8.4.

Article 2(6) excludes questions of pay, the right of association, the right to strike and the right to impose lockouts. Article 3 states that, before submitting social policy proposals, the Commission shall consult with management and labour. Article 4 states that the dialogue between management and labour may lead to contractual relations, including agreements concluded at Union level. In pursuit of the objectives laid down in Article 1, Article 5 requires the Commission to encourage co-operation between member states in the social policy field, and to facilitate co-ordination of national social policies. Article 6 requires each member state to apply the principle of equal pay for male and female workers engaged in equal work. Article 7 requires the Commission to produce an annual report on the progress made in achieving Article 1 objectives.

Table 8.4 Council Voting Procedures on Social Policy

QMV	Unanimity
• health and safety at work	• social security, social protection of workers
• working conditions	• protection of redundant workers
• information and consultation of workers	• representation, collective defence of workers and employers
• equal opportunities between men and women	• employment conditions of third-country nationals
• integration of people excluded from the labour market	• finance for employment generation

The Protocol does not exempt the UK from other commitments on social policy made at Maastricht, or from social policy provisions in the EC Treaty or in the SEA. Social policy is therefore in the unusual position of having two legal bases: that forming an integral part of the *acquis communautaire* (applicable to all member states) and that deriving from the Protocol (applicable to all except the UK). This has created considerable confusion. A Commission communication of December 1993 stated that where possible social proposals will continue to be presented within the terms of the EC Treaty and the SEA, in order to make them binding on all members. The Commission has set out criteria to determine which procedure will be used for proposals (for example, health and safety at work will involve legislation affecting all member states). It was not until June 1994 that an employment law (concerning European Works Councils) was passed under the terms of the Protocol.

Opponents of the Charter argue that it conflicts with the global trend towards more flexible labour markets; that it increases non-wage labour costs, thereby making the goods of EU firms uncompetitive in world markets; and that it is at odds with the principle of subsidiarity. Conversely, the proponents of the Charter argue that there can hardly be a level playing field for business if wide divergences in labour market conditions exist between EU countries. They argue that without social protection and agreed minimum standards, there could be widespread *social dumping*. This has been defined by Padraig Flynn, the Social Commissioner as: 'the gaining of unfair competitive advantage within the Community through unacceptably low social standards' (*Frontier Free Europe*, January 1994), an accusation frequently levelled at the UK because of its rejection of the Social Charter.

○ Equal Opportunities

The principle that men and women should receive equal pay for equal work was laid down in Article 119 of the Treaty of Rome. This Article has been reinforced by various judgments of the ECJ – for example, the *Defrenne versus the Belgian State* judgment on equal pay (1976) and by various directives for example, on equal pay (1975), equal treatment (1976) and on eliminating discrimination in occupational pension schemes (1986). However the Commission has expressed its dissatisfaction with levels of compliance with these directives. The EU also operates equal opportunities 'action programmes', the fourth commencing in 1996. Several EU organisations are concerned with equality. For example, within the Commission, the Equal Opportunities Unit monitors the application of directives and compliance with the action programmes; the Women's Information Service, provides information about developments affecting women; the Advisory Committee on Equal Opportunities represents Equal Opportunities organisations in member states. The EP also has a Women's Rights Committee.

○ Workers' Participation

Forms of employee participation exist in several Union countries. In the 1970s, the Commission proposed several draft directives on company organisation, including workers' participation: the draft *Vredeling* directive of 1972 sought to introduce information and consultation procedures for workers in larger companies, but this was not accepted by the Council. In 1980 and 1983, the Commission drafted directives on worker consultation, but these were blocked by opposition from the UK. Article 118b of the SEA requires the Commission to endeavour to develop a dialogue between management and labour at European level. In 1994, after 13 years of discussion, a directive on worker consultation in EU-wide companies was approved by all member countries, excluding the UK. Because of its social policy opt-out, the UK did not vote on this proposal. The directive requires companies with 1,000 employees or more and 150 staff in a minimum of two member states to consult employees on cross-border decisions. By 22 September 1996, all EU countries except the UK should have passed legislation allowing for the creation of European works councils in multinational enterprises. British firms operating in any other member state must comply with this legislation.

○ **Social Exclusion**

This is the EU term for poverty and marginalization. The Commission estimates that more than 50 million EU citizens live in households with an income of less than half the average for their country. Poverty is a problem largely dealt with at national level, although since 1975 the Commission has operated token poverty programmes. The first three ran from 1975–80, 1984– 88 and 1989–94. Although the 'Poverty 3' budget was twice that of 'Poverty 2', it still only amounted to ECU 121 million, largely because of the reluctance of the richer member states to countenance expansion of the EU's financial responsibilities in this area. In its proposal for a fourth programme, the Commission reiterated that responsibility for fighting social exclusion lay mainly with member states, but affirmed the EU's contributory role. In 1995, adoption of the fourth programme was being blocked by the UK and Germany, which argued that this policy area was a national responsibility.

The EU has also developed policies for the disabled. About 30 million people in the EU have some form of physical or mental handicap. The main EU programme is HELIOS, which seeks to protect and promote the interests of disabled people in employment through measures to prevent discrimination and to provide access to vocational training. The HORIZON programme seeks to create employment for the handicapped, through support for vocational training and business 'start-ups'. The TIDE programme provides funds for development work on technology for the disabled.

● THE 'NEW REALISM': THE GREEN AND WHITE PAPERS ON SOCIAL POLICY

A debate is currently raging in all modern societies concerning the future of public welfare and employment policies. In 1993, the Commissioner for Social Affairs and Employment published a Green Paper (Commission, 1993) on the options for the Union in field of Social Policy, with the aim of stimulating a debate on the future of ESP. The escalating costs of social protection and the growing problem of unemployment made this debate both urgent and necessary. The paper therefore examined a broad range of social policy issues. The Green Paper was prepared and published at roughly the same time as the Delors White Paper on *Growth, Competitiveness and Employment* (see Chapter 9). Both papers addressed the issue of unemployment. In 1994, the Union had an unemployment rate of about 11%, compared with 6% in the US and 3% in Japan. In 1993, long-term unemployment was 42.2% of the total in the EU, compared with 11.2% in the

US. Both papers rejected the 'option' of abandoning EU social protection policies in order to compete with low-wage economies in the Far East. However, both accepted the need for greater flexibility and mobility in EU labour markets, but without abandoning the social ground rules establishing minimum standards. It should be noted that the UK, with a *laissez-faire* labour market has the third highest unemployment in the EU, whereas west Germany and the Netherlands, two of the most regulated labour markets, have amongst the lowest rates of unemployment. The Green Paper advocated a move away from detailed prescriptive employment legislation. It noted that the incoming EFTA countries would seek to improve, rather than lower, minimum standards of social protection – a correct prediction.

Following receipt of 594 comments on the Green Paper from interested parties such as Union institutions, governments, unions, employers and voluntary organisations, the Commission published a White Paper on ESP (Commission, 1994). The White Paper noted the tension in reactions to the Green Paper between those criticising the EU's high labour costs and those arguing that high labour standards are an integral part of the formula for achieving competitiveness. It observed that there was a core of opinion recognising a 'European social model' and supported the need to set minimum standards for social protection in order to avoid social dumping. It favoured the return to a 'single social framework' for social policy (meaning the removal of the UK's opt-out). But it also asserted that subsidiarity was a guiding principle in social policy and that ESP legislation had to be more flexible and less detailed than hitherto. Moreover, it also recognised the need to reconcile high social standards with the capacity to compete in world markets. This approach, labelled the *new realism*, was further developed in the Commission's 5th Social Action Programme (1995–97) launched in April 1995, which gives top priority to job creation. But there is scant evidence so far that the 'new realism' has succeeded in reconciling the conflicting viewpoints on ESP, which remains a highly controversial policy field.

FURTHER READING

Commission COM (93), 551, *Green Paper on European Social Policy*, 1993.
Commission COM (94), 333, *European Social Policy – A Way Forward for the Union*, 1994.
Commission, *Social Europe* (various editions).
Gold, M., *The Social Dimension: Employment Policy in the European Community*, Macmillan, Basingstoke, 1993.
Hantrais, L., *Social Policy in the European Union*, Macmillan, London, 1995.
Whiteford, E.A., 'Social Policy after Maastricht', *European Law Review*, vol. 18, no. 3, 1993, pp. 202–22.

 **Chapter 9**

The Single European Market and the Problem of 'Eurosclerosis'

● WHY THE SEM PROGRAMME WAS ADOPTED

○ Eurosclerosis and the Single Market Prescription

In the mid-1980s, the term *Eurosclerosis* gained wide currency as a description of an illness afflicting the economies of the member states of the Union. Its principal symptoms were economic stagnation, industrial decline, poor productivity, rising unemployment and poor competitiveness in world markets. This perception of weakness was justified by reference to a number of 'gaps' between the performance of the EU economies and those of Japan and the US, viz.: a *trade gap*, a *productivity gap*, an *employment gap*, an *investment gap* and a *technology gap*. The solution adopted to restore the Union to economic health was the Single European Market programme, an ambitious project to abolish remaining trade barriers between member states. The central assumption underpinning the programme was that non-tariff barriers to trade between member states was a major cause of Eurosclerosis. The Union's economic performance gap was thus attributed by the programme's proponents to the fragmentation of the EU economy: whereas the US and Japan each had one market, in 1985 the EU had ten markets, with diverse technical standards, business laws and industrial policies.

On 1 January 1993, the 'completion' of the programme was officially celebrated with bonfires and fireworks displays all over the Union. The previous month in Edinburgh, the European Council declared that the programme had been completed in all essential respects. However, this completion was something of an anti-climax, because the gaps between the economic performance of Japan and the US on the one hand and the EU on the other were as wide (if not wider) in 1993 than in 1985 when the programme had been launched. As further evidence that the programme was no miracle cure for Eurosclerosis, by the end of 1993 the Commission launched another major strategy to deal with the EU's problems of poor economic growth, rising unemployment and unsatisfactory international competitiveness. With hindsight, the assumption that the EU's relatively poor economic performance in this period was *largely* attributable to cross-border trade barriers seems highly questionable. Moreover, it is also now apparent that completing the SEM programme by establishing a framework of laws was not sufficient to create a Single European Market, partly because of omissions in the programme and partly because of incomplete or faulty implementation of SEM measures. But without the hype associated with the programme, it is debatable whether it would ever have been launched.

◯ Relaunching the EC

Several other major developments contributed to the adoption of the SEM programme. The landmark *Cassis de Dijon* ruling by the ECJ in 1979 (which established the principle that if a product was fit to be sold in one member state, it was fit to be sold in them all) provided a juridical underpinning for an ambitious programme of market opening. In the early 1980s there was stronger support amongst the governments of member states for the pursuit of a programme of market-oriented economic liberalisation than hitherto: the Conservative Party was returned to power in the UK in 1979; in 1982, a CDU-dominated coalition came into office in West Germany; in the early 1980s, the Mitterrand government in France largely abandoned its socialist programme. Although the UK government was opposed to forms of integration which would erode sovereignty, it viewed the SEM programme favourably, as being fully in accordance with its free trade principles.

   The appointment of Jacques Delors to the presidency of the Commission in 1984 was also an important contributory factor. Delors' energy and vision secured him a key role as a change agent in the integration process: his initial idea was to pursue the goal of monetary union rather than the SEM programme. However, in the mid-1980s, this seemed a rather impractical goal (not least because Mrs Thatcher would never have agreed to it). It became clear that Delors saw the SEM as a means of accelerating the process of European integration. The SEM programme is frequently characterised as an effort to *relaunch* the Union. By the mid-1980s, it was widely felt that the process of integration in the Community had stalled. A fundamental aim of the Treaty of Rome, to create a common market, had certainly not been achieved because many barriers to the free cross-border movement of goods, persons, services and capital within the Union remained. The SEM programme was therefore designed to kill two birds with one stone: to enhance the EU's economic performance and (more controversially) to kick start the integration process.

○ **Justifying the Single Market Prescription**

The Commission produced a wealth of statistics to prove that internal trade barriers were costing the Union dearly in terms of competitiveness, efficiency and jobs. The expected benefits of 1992 were exhaustively elaborated in the officially commissioned Cecchini Report on the 'costs of non-Europe' published in 1988: according to the Report, stronger competitive disciplines would force 'flabby' companies to become more efficient by means of a 'supply-side shock'; economies of scale would be reaped, as firms expanded into other EU countries; EU firms would also become fitter to compete in global markets. The Report, based on a survey of 11,000 firms, estimated that the creation of an SEM could have the following positive results:

Table 9.1 The Benefits of the SEM (Cecchini Estimates)

- a 4.5% increase in GDP (possibly amounting to 200 billion ECU);
- an increase in employment of between 1.8 million and 5 million (job losses would be more than off-set by job gains);
- lower prices (of between 4.5% and 6.1%);
- more choice for consumers at more competitive prices;
- an improvement of the external trade balance by 1% of GDP.

The Cecchini Report has been widely criticised for being too optimistic in its assessment of the benefits of the 1992 Programme (Grahl and Teague, 1990). The Report was also criticised for giving insufficient weight to the strong possibility that SEM benefits would be distributed very unevenly amongst member states, regions and industries.

● THE MAIN FEATURES OF THE SEM PROGRAMME

The Commission's White Paper entitled *Completing the Internal Market* was approved by the European Council in Milan in June 1985. In December of that year, the Single European Act (which amended the Treaty of Rome) was also approved by the European Council in Luxembourg. The Act was ratified by all national parliaments and came into force on 1 July 1987. The Danish parliament initially rejected the Act, but later accepted it following a referendum. The Act defines the SEM as 'an area without internal frontiers in which the free movement of goods, persons, services and capital is ensured' (these became known as the *four freedoms*). A Commissioner from the UK, Lord Cockfield, a former Chief Executive of 'Boots' and a former UK Trade and Industry Minister, was put in charge of drafting the SEM programme. The programme embraced 289 legislative proposals, many coming into effect at different times, but structured around clear timetables for completion. The legal and institutional framework of the SEM was sought through:

• **Removal of Technical Barriers,** to enable EU producers to sell their products in any member state, without the need to modify these products to conform to different national technical requirements. Given the wide disparities in national regulations and standards within EU 12, it was clearly impossible to suddenly replace these with uniform standards. Two strategies were adopted in relation to technical barriers: firstly, *mutual recognition* of existing national standards, providing essential requirements were met; secondly, *approximation*, through the stipulation of Union-wide 'essential requirements' such as minimum safety and health standards. Instead of product by product harmonisation, which would have been impractical, it was to be pursued by defining product categories. The intended effect of these principles was to prevent national standards from being used as barriers to cross-border trade. A 'CE' marking has been introduced to show that products conform with essential requirements and can be sold anywhere in the Union.

• **Removal of Fiscal Barriers.** Differences in indirect taxes, in particular VAT and excise duties, were regarded as major obstacles to cross-border trade. Given the wide disparities in tax systems within the Union, the aim was to *approximate*, rather than to fully harmonise, indirect taxes. It proved impossible to reach full agreement within the Council on approximation of VAT and the issue is to be discussed again in 1996. New systems for the collection and control of VAT and excise duty payments have nevertheless been introduced.

Excise duties have traditionally been collected by the country where the goods are consumed, not where they originate, leading to substantial differences in prices paid by consumers in different EU countries. Excise duty is now payable when goods are released to retail outlets for consumption. In general, citizens can buy goods in any member state without having to pay extra taxes, providing that they are for personal use and have been bought 'duty paid'. They have the right to buy substantial quantities of alcohol and tobacco for personal consumption. Special rules still apply to some categories of goods such as new cars, motorcycles, boats and planes.

'Duty free' shops should be meaningless in a borderless Union. However, they will exist until 30 June 1999.
- **Removal of Physical Barriers.** For example, customs forms and formalities have been abolished. A Single Administrative Document for goods transported across EU internal borders was introduced on 1 January 1988, replacing over 150 previous documents. From 1 January 1993, even this was abolished. The liberalisation of transport services has been a key element of the programme, involving for example the removal of quota restrictions on road haulage.
- **The Right to Work in Other Member States.** Nationals of any member state have the right to seek and obtain employment anywhere in the Union and to enjoy the same treatment as nationals of the host state in matters of pay, working conditions and trade union rights, subject to certain restrictions (see Chapter 14).
- **Opening Up of the Professions.** Professionals in many occupations (for example, doctors, architects, engineers) now have the right to have their qualifications recognised in other member states.
- **Opening Up of Financial Services.** Cross-border restrictions on the operation of businesses in the services sector, such as banking and insurance, have been largely eliminated.
- **Capital Movements.** Arrangements for free movement of capital now apply throughout the Union. National financial markets have been made open, subject to some national measures and derogations.
- **Opening of 'Public Procurement' Markets.** In the mid-1980s, only about 2% of government contracts went to suppliers from other EU countries. According to Commission estimates, public purchasing amounts to up to 15% of Union GNP. Various public procurement directives have now been introduced. For example, the Supplies Directive enables firms to apply for supplies contracts throughout the Union.

● THE WIDER IMPLICATIONS OF THE PROGRAMME

○ The SEA is not Solely about Trade

The programme is a pivotal event in the development of the Union and has had major internal and external consequences. The SEA embraced highly significant institutional and policy changes which went far beyond technical issues of trade. Partly, this was due to the realisation that internal trade barriers could not be effectively removed without substantial changes in other areas of policy and in the way the Union reached its decisions. The Act therefore involved various flanking (or 'side') measures, for example in the fields of social policy and the environment. In recognition of the danger that removal of barriers would exacerbate the problems of the 'periphery' of the EU, by leading to a further shift of business activity towards the more prosperous industrial regions (the 'golden triangle' of London, Paris and the Ruhr), policies to develop the economies of peripheral regions were to be introduced.

The main institutional changes were the extension of majority voting in the Council and increased powers for the European Parliament. Mrs Thatcher doubted the commitment of some governments to full-blooded trade liberalisation and therefore favoured the use of majority voting in relation to SEM measures. For this reason, she has subsequently been criticised for signing away British sovereignty. However, it is clear that she expected the use of majority voting to be strictly limited to SEM measures. But the broad focus of the SEM programme meant that majority voting covered a wide range of policy areas. 'Integrationists' in the Commission and Council naturally favoured a broad interpretation of the areas to which it applied. The Act also contains references to co-operation between member states in the areas of foreign policy ('European Political Co-operation' (EPC)).

○   Fortress Europe?

Initially, the EU's leading partners (the US, Japan, and EFTA) were fearful that the SEM could lead to the creation of a *Fortress Europe*, protecting EU countries from competition from outside the EU. The EU has consistently denied that the SEM is protectionist, and this view has come to be generally (if not universally) accepted. At the European Council in Rhodes in December 1988 the Council explicitly rejected the term Fortress Europe and instead adopted the term *Partner Europe*. The SEM offers benefits for non-EU exporters, because when it is fully implemented, foreign products will need to conform to one set of trade and technical standards rather than many. However, an anticipated effect of the SEM was that it would result in increased intra-EU trade at the expense of EU trade with other countries – the *trade diversion* effect.

Fears of adverse trade effects provided a stimulus for non-EU companies and countries to seek closer ties with the Union, in order to circumvent potential barriers and thereby gain access to the Union's big market. Circumvention strategies have included foreign direct investment (establishing production bases within the Union); attempts to negotiate new formal relationships with the Union (for example, the European Economic Area agreement and association agreements); and applications for full EU membership.

○ **The European Economic Area (EEA)**

The SEM programme provided a powerful stimulus for EFTA countries, which have strong trading links with the Union, to secure continued access to EU markets and to avoid loss of exports through 'trade diversion'. This led to the formation of the EEA, essentially a vehicle for extending the SEM to EFTA countries. Negotiations for an EEA were set in motion by Jacques Delors in a speech to the EP in January 1989. Delors offered EFTA 'a more structured partnership with common decisionmaking and administrative institutions'. This offer was enthusiastically accepted by EFTA. If Delors' overture was designed to discourage EFTA states from applying for full membership of the Union (by offering them an attractive alternative) it backfired: the Commission's tough negotiating stance in the EEA negotiations probably accelerated the decision of several EFTA countries to apply for full EU membership. Doubts about the ultimate purpose of the EEA hung over the negotiations. Thus the EEA could be viewed either as a transitional arrangement leading gradually but inexorably to EU enlargement, or as a free-standing structure. The EEA Treaty was signed in Opporto in May 1992 and was due to come into force on the same day as the SEM. However, the rejection of the Treaty by the Swiss in a referendum in December 1992 delayed the timetable by a year.

The legal basis of the EEA is the EEA Treaty, plus 12,000 pages of Community legislation appended to it. The EEA is the world's largest free trade zone, accounting for more than two-fifths of world trade. It is a free trade association, not a customs union and therefore there is no common external tariff. It does not embrace political or monetary union. It also excludes the Common Agricultural and Fisheries policies. It came into being on 1 January 1994. The main features of the agreement are: the 'four freedoms' (that is, free movement of goods, services, capital and persons); a competition regime based on EU competition rules; co-operation between the EU and EFTA in many areas, such as RTD, education and the environment; an EFTA financial support mechanism for poorer EU countries; and new institutions to administer the Agreement.

However, by the time it came into existence, its future was already in doubt as a result of the decision by several EFTA countries to apply for full EU membership. But the formation of the EEA can still be regarded as an important development, for three reasons: negotiations for the EEA served as an important economic and psychological preparation for the fourth enlargement; it offers the remaining EFTA countries an alternative to EU membership; it might also provide an intermediate form of EU membership for some East European countries, by serving as the framework for a pan-European trade zone.

● EVALUATION

○ A Qualified Success or a Damp Squib?

It is difficult to disentangle the effects of the programme from other influences on the economies of member states. The global economic recession weakened the positive effects of '1992', because many companies were not strong enough to expand into other EU markets. Moreover, the full impact of the programme will only be apparent when the SEM legislative framework is complete and firmly embedded. For example, public procurement legislation largely came into effect after the official completion of the programme. The achievement of harmonisation of technical standards and the alignment of production systems is also a very protracted process.

The programme proved that member states could develop and carry through an ambitious collaborative project. It created the world's biggest single market, 40% larger than the US market and three times larger than the Japanese market. It provided the momentum for the proposals for European Union agreed at Maastricht. By the end of 1994, states had transposed an average of 89% of SEM legislation into national law (Denmark had the highest figure of 95.9% and Greece the lowest (77.9%)). The Commission's White Paper on *Growth, Competitiveness and Employment* (1993) identified the following tangible achievements of the programme:

Table 9.2 Some Achievements of the SEM (Commission Estimates)

- 70 million customs documents abolished;
- a 3% saving on international transport costs;
- mergers and acquisitions within the EU trebled between 1986 and 1992;
- twice the number of EU firms involved in mergers and acquisitions outside the EU;
- a doubling of trade in sectors previously regarded as sheltered from competition;
- investment up by one-third since between 1985 and 1990;
- 9 million jobs created between 1986 and 1990;
- one half a percentage point extra growth each year.

Ultimately, any project must be judged in relation to its effectiveness in realising its goals. Despite the tangible achievements listed above, the SEM programme has so far not had the impact intended. The Union still suffers from poor competitiveness, poor productivity relative to Japan and the US and high structural employment. US manufacturing output grew twice as fast as that of the EU between 1980 and 1992. The EU's share of manufacturing exports fell from 21.9% in 1980, to 19.4% in 1986 to 17.6% in 1992. There are two possible reasons for the muted impact of the programme so far. It could be due to weaknesses in implementation or to the possibility that the programme is at best a partial solution to the problem of Eurosclerosis. Implementation has certainly been incomplete. In 1994, the Commission disclosed that although about 87% of SEM measures have been transposed into national law, only 119 had been adopted by all members. The implementation of SEM measures in some key sectors, such as intellectual property and public procurement had been generally poor. Temporary deferrals have also contributed to incomplete implementation (for example, until July 1994 insurance companies were not able to set up and do business anywhere in the EU; stockbrokers were not able to operate anywhere in the EU until 1996; vocational qualifications were not valid throughout the Union until June 1994).

Other forms of foot-dragging by governments has been a major problem: for example, the service sector, now the largest source of employment and output, has proved difficult to deregulate. Even when legislation has been passed by governments, it has by no means always been put into practice. The removal of non-tariff barriers to trade is hardly sufficient if major physical impediments to cross-border movement, such as transport, energy, telecommunications and postal service bottlenecks, remain. The liberalisation of basic telephone services has been postponed until 1998. Moreover, the programme left several other major obstacles to the achievement of a level playing field for business untouched (for example, state subsidies for industry and the existence of separate currencies).

The emphasis in the SEM programme is shifting towards more effective implementation. In June 1993, the Commission published its *Strategic Programme for the Internal Market*, which gives priority to monitoring, enforcement and evaluation. In February 1994, it began a large-scale study of the effects of the SEM, which will be available in 1996. It already produces an annual report on the operation of the SEM. The Commission's 1995 work programme included a new SEM offensive, aimed at stricter monitoring and enforcement. The Commission has launched initiatives to develop closer links between national enforcement bodies: for example, the MATTHAUS and KAROLUS programmes involve vocational training and exchanges of officials engaged in implementation of SEM programmes. It also emphasises the need to fill gaps in the original programme, by upgrading flanking policies such as Trans-European Networks (TENs). A level playing field for business cannot be fully realised as long as separate currencies exist. The Commission therefore argues that a single currency would be 'the capstone of the internal market' (*Frontier Free Europe*, no. 3, 1993).

○   **Was the SEM Programme a False Panacea?**

In the 1990s, the EU's continuing economic malaise has led to a search for other possible solutions to this problem, such as high labour costs, low labour market flexibility and technological backwardness. The EU's policy of social protection, according to its critics, results in high unit labour costs and low labour market flexibility. For example, it has been suggested that less ought to be spent on 'passive benefits' (unemployment pay) and more on active labour market measures, such as retraining. In 1992, average labour costs were 20% higher in the EU than in Japan or the US. Moreover, there are now many countries around the world (particularly in the Far East and Eastern Europe) capable of producing high-quality goods at a fraction of average labour costs in Western Europe.

Another possible cause has been failure to adapt to rapid changes in technology. For example, high-tech exports account for almost one-third of US exports, but for less than a fifth of Western Europe's. Of US manufacturing exports to the EU in 1993, 51% comprised high-tech, 29% medium-tech and 20% low-tech goods; however, of EU exports to the US, only 23% were high-tech. These explanations of the EU's current economic malaise have given rise to various ideas for dealing with the problem, such as labour market deregulation, reskilling, investment in infrastructure and RTD, lower taxes and protection from 'unfair' competition.

Current ideas for tackling Eurosclerosis seem to be based on less dogmatic, more tentative, appraisals of the problem. However, these ideas tend to have two features which may prevent their full adoption: they tend to have high price tags (requiring substantial new investment and new policy commitments); and they tend to raise contentious ideological issues, not least concerning the role of government in business and industry and the problem of reconciling national and Union level policies.

● THE STRATEGY FOR GROWTH, COMPETITIVENESS AND EMPLOYMENT

At the European Council in Copenhagen in June 1993, the Commission was asked to prepare a White Paper on the EU's jobs crisis. The White Paper, on the theme of *Growth, Competitiveness and Employment*, was adopted by the European Council in Brussels in December 1993. The paper put forward proposals to create 15 million new jobs by the year 2000, thereby reducing EU unemployment rates from the current 10.4% to 5%. It argued that EU economic growth needed to be boosted by at least 3% a year. It rejected various solutions, including a resort to protectionism; a 'dash for growth' (meaning a big increase in government spending and consequent inflation)'; a generalised reduction in working hours and job sharing; or drastic cuts in wages. It argued that there was no way the EU could reduce its labour costs to the level of Eastern Europe or China. Its major proposal in relation to the EU's international trading position was that European firms should be encouraged to 'trade up' to higher added value activities, such as the new information technology and biotechnology industries. The White Paper did not propose another major legislative programme linked to the SEM. It emphasised that its strategy was complementary to the SEM rather than an alternative. It also recommended many other specific measures (Table 9.3).

Table 9.3 The Commission's Growth Strategy: Specific Measures

- new incentives for part-time work;
- tax incentives for small firms to create jobs;
- training schemes for unqualified school leavers ;
- switching some labour costs from employers to general taxation;
- non-wage social security costs to be made more progressive, to encourage more jobs for the less skilled;
- enabling social security to 'top up' income from work;
- greater wage flexibility;
- promoting training and 'know-how';
- increased investment in industry and in infrastructure;
- a higher investment rate of 23–24% of GNP (the current rate is about 19%);
- a target of 3% of GNP to be spent on RTD;
- reorienting government support for industry towards growth sectors;
- increases in spending on transport and energy networks;
- the creation of 'information highways' for telecoms;
- new environmental projects;
- a network of European science parks.

The plan would be financed through a mixture of private sector funding and public sector loans, via the Community budget, the EIB and 'Union bonds' issued by the Commission on behalf of the Union. The Union bonds proposal (which would have given the Commission its own fund-raising powers) was vetoed by the European Council. It would have increased public spending and might also have undermined the EIB's role. The European Council did, however, accept the broad thrust of the Commission's growth strategy. It also agreed to the creation of a new financial institution, known as the European Investment Fund to bring together investors from the public and private sectors. The Fund has so far been too small to have much impact on the problem. Several recent European Councils (notably Essen and Cannes) have re-emphasised the need for urgent action to deal with the unemployment problem. In February 1995, the Commission set up a 'Competitiveness Advisory Group' comprising experts from industry, finance and unions to provide reports every six months with ideas for new EU initiatives. Some member states (and also the Commission and EP) would like to go further and add a clause or chapter to the TEU, committing the Union to the pursuit of more effective employment policies. But translating such legally binding commitments into effective policies would be a formidable task indeed, as the recent history of the Union's efforts to devise and implement an effective solution to the problem of unemployment so clearly demonstrates.

FURTHER READING

Cecchini, P., *The European Challenge: 1992 The Benefits of a Single Market*, Wildwood House, Aldershot, 1988.

Cockfield, Lord, *The European Union: Creating the Single Market*, Wiley, London, 1994.

Colchester, N. and Buchan, D., *Europe Relaunched: Truths and Illusions on the Way to 1992*, Economist Books, London, 1990.

Commission, *Growth, Competitiveness and Employment*, White Paper, 1993.

Commission, COM (93), 314, *Employment in Europe*, 1993.

Grahl, J. and Teague, P., *1992 – The Big Market*, Lawrence & Wishart, London, 1990.

Sachwald, F. (ed.), *European Integration and Competitiveness*, Edward Elgar, Cheltenham, 1994.

Tsoukalis, L., *The New European Economy*, Oxford University Press, 1993.

Wise, M. and Gibb, R., *Single Market to Social Europe*, Longman, London, 1993.

Chapter 10

Economic and Monetary Union

● BACKGROUND

The ultimate goal of economic and monetary union (EMU) is the replacement of the currencies of member states by a single currency. The achievement of EMU will have profound institutional and policy implications for the European Union. For Euro-integrationists, a single currency is viewed as a logical corollary of the Single European Market programme and as an essential feature of a fully developed Union. For Eurosceptics, EMU constitutes a nightmare scenario, confirming their worst fears about the threat to state sovereignty of deeper European integration. It is perhaps not surprising that Euro-integrationists have pursued the goal of EMU with such dogged determination, or that Eurosceptics are so resolutely opposed to it. The provisions and protocols relating to EMU are widely regarded as the most important element of the TEU. In spite of the current inability of member states to fulfil all conditions for full monetary union as laid down in the Treaty, and in spite of current uncertainties concerning the feasibility of the Maastricht timetable for EMU, it seems virtually inevitable that a single currency will be introduced at some point. However, the new currency zone, when first established, is most unlikely to embrace all member states of the Union.

The Treaty of Rome did not refer to the goal of a single currency, nor indeed to a system for co-ordinating monetary policy. But from the late 1960s, the need to secure greater monetary stability became increasingly apparent, following recurring crises in the international monetary system. The 'Bretton Woods' system of fixed exchange rates finally collapsed in 1971. In 1969, the Commission proposed the Barre Plan (named after the Commissioner who produced it) for greater co-operation and mutual assistance in financial crises. The following year, the Werner Report (named after its main author, the Prime Minister of Luxembourg) proposed a phased economic and monetary union by 1980. But this was an idea ahead of its time, not least because of the low priority accorded by member states to deeper integration in this period. An agreement to restrict fluctuations between member currencies within a range of ±2.25%, known as the 'Snake', was introduced in 1972. But the Snake was a venomless beast, quite unable to cope with the turmoil in the currency markets. The UK and Ireland left the Snake soon after joining and by 1977 only Germany, Denmark and the Benelux countries remained. Nevertheless, efforts to enhance monetary co-operation between member states continued.

Following decisions taken at the European Council in Brussels in December 1978, a European Monetary System (EMS) was established in March 1979. The EMS was designed to create a zone of monetary stability, by reducing fluctuations in the exchange rates of member currencies. It also sought to impose greater disciplines on members by inhibiting resort to unilateral devaluations.

● THE EUROPEAN MONETARY SYSTEM (EMS)

The EMS currently comprises: the European Currency Unit (ECU), the Exchange Rate Mechanism (ERM) and – since 1 January 1994 – the European Monetary Institute (EMI). The EMI took over the tasks of the European Monetary Co-operation Fund (EMCF) which had operated since 1973.

○ The ECU

The ECU was introduced in 1975, replacing the book-keeping unit known as the 'European Unit of Account'. It is a nominal currency, made up of a basket of all EC currencies, weighted according to the economic strengths of the economies of member states. These 'weights' are defined in units per ECU. The currency composition of the ECU had been reviewed every five years, but was 'frozen' when the TEU came into effect. Governments have not made the ECU legal tender and it does not exist in note or coin form, although several countries have minted symbolic ECU coins. But in other respects it is regarded as a currency and can be used in settlements between organisations or even between individuals. It is the unit of account for the Community budget. It is traded on foreign exchanges and there is a substantial ECU bond market. In 1988, the UK government began issuing some treasury bills in ECUs. It is used far more in financial settlements than in trade transactions (only about 1% of trade transactions are settled in ECU). Individuals can buy travellers' cheques, unit trusts and mortgages in ECU because it is recognised by EU banks, although these uses have been very limited. In December 1995, the European Council in Madrid opted for the title 'Euro' instead of ECU as the name of the future European single currency (see below).

○ The European Monetary Co-operation Fund (EMCF)

The EMCF was established in 1973, to facilitate currency transactions between member states. The EMCF's credit facilities were used to settle obligations deriving from interventions in the foreign exchange markets by the central banks of member states. Participants deposited 20% of their gold reserves and 20% of their dollar reserves in return for ECUs of the same value. In accordance with the TEU's provisions for Stage 2 of economic and monetary union, the EMCF has been dissolved and its tasks taken over by the European Monetary Institute (see below).

○ The Exchange Rate Mechanism (ERM)

The ERM was established in 1979 as a mechanism for reducing fluctuations in the relative values of member currencies. It operates on the basis of mutual support and collective action by the central banks of the member states. The central banks intervene in the currency markets, by buying or selling member currencies to influence their value. Intervention is based on the laws of supply and demand: when a currency rises or falls in value to above or below an agreed level (known as a fluctuation margin or band) the central banks are expected to act to restore the value of the currency to within the prescribed limits. At the time of the ERM crises in the summer of 1992, the ERM had 10 members. Spain joined in June 1987, the UK in October 1990 and Portugal in April 1992. Greece has never participated (its economy is too weak) and Luxembourg bases its franc on the Belgian franc.

The ERM is based on a parity grid system, meaning that each member currency is allowed to fluctuate by a limited amount from a fixed par value with regard to every other currency in the system. An ECU central rate is determined for each currency, which enables the central rates between all currencies to be calculated. When the upper or lower limit between two currencies is reached, the bank with the strong currency sells its own currency in exchange for the weak currency and vice versa. The most common measure of divergence has been deviation from bilateral deutschmark (DM) central rates, because of the strength of the DM.

Before the crises of 1992–93, ERM members kept their currencies within a set margin of fluctuation against a central rate established for each currency: ±2.25% within the normal (or narrow) band, or ±6% within the wide band. These rates were agreed at meetings of ECOFIN (comprising the finance ministers of member states). The wide band was regarded as provisional, in that all countries were expected to enter the narrow band as soon as circumstances permitted. The UK, Spain and Portugal were in the wide band in August 1992. Italy had moved from the wide to the narrow band in January 1990. In practice, interventions took place before currencies reached their upper or lower bands. Divergence indicators signalled that a currency was deviating too much from the average and were designed to provoke a timely response before a currency reached its permitted limit. As soon as a currency reached 75% of its deviation against the average of all other currencies, appropriate action was expected. Currencies could also be realigned by common agreement. There were 12 realignments of central rates between 1979 and 1991, although most of these were in the early years of the system. In the later years realignments were fewer and smaller in scale. This served to further strengthen confidence in the effectiveness and soundness of the mechanism.

The ERM came into operation in the year Mrs Thatcher came to power in the UK. She opposed the ERM on the grounds that it distorted market forces and limited the capacity of governments to make decisions appropriate to domestic conditions. However, by the late 1980s, there was a strong groundswell of opinion in the UK in favour of entry, not least because the ERM was widely perceived to have played a key role in securing monetary stability and low inflation within the ERM zone in the 1980s. By contrast, the UK experienced wide sterling fluctuations throughout this decade. The ERM issue caused a rift between Mrs Thatcher and Chancellor Nigel Lawson, who came to favour UK membership, as did several other prominent Cabinet members. Chancellor Lawson had informally linked sterling to the DM from 1987. The critical mass of support for entry proved too strong for Mrs Thatcher to resist, even though Lawson had resigned from the Cabinet in 1989. Lawson's successor as Chancellor, John Major, took the UK into the ERM in October 1990.

The main benefits of entry for the UK were perceived to be the counter-inflationary discipline the ERM would impose and reduction in currency risks for UK businesses. The DM was the linchpin of the ERM, because of the strength of the German economy and the reputation of the Bundesbank for financial prudence. Ironically, the UK entered in the month when Germany was reunified, an event which was to place severe strains on the mechanism. Sterling entered the wide band of the system at a rate of DM 2.95, which most analysts now agree was too high to sustain in the long term because of the weakness of the UK economy.

○ The Faultlines in the ERM Exposed: 'Black Wednesday'

The crises of 1992–93 (leading to 2 withdrawals, 5 realignments and a move to 15% fluctuation bands) ended 13 years of relative stability within the ERM. Because the ERM was regarded as fundamentally sound, it figured prominently in the Maastricht blueprint for monetary union. However, on 16 September 1992 ('Black Wednesday'), both sterling and the lira were forced out of the ERM by currency speculation: the Spanish peseta was devalued by 5%, and by another 6% in November, together with the Portuguese escudo (also by 6%). The Irish punt, the Danish krone and the French franc also came under attack from currency speculators. By the end of 1992, sterling and the lira had depreciated by about 15% and 16% respectively. In January 1993, the punt was devalued by 10% and in May the peseta and escudo were again devalued. In July 1993, five ERM currencies (the French and Belgian francs, the Danish krone, the peseta and escudo) came under renewed speculative attack. This forced a move to broader fluctuation bands of ±15% on 2 August 1993 for eight currencies (the exceptions being the DM and guilder). Other than as a face-saving exercise, and as a symbol of a refusal to admit that the ERM was effectively suspended, the bands were so wide as to appear meaningless.

Why did these crises occur? Apprehension over the future of the TEU (following the outcome of the first Danish referendum and the looming French referendum) has been cited as a precipitating factor of the 1992 crisis. But this does not explain why the mechanism proved too fragile to withstand uncertainties concerning the TEU. German economic and monetary policy was widely regarded as a fundamental cause of the 1992–93 crises. Because the DM was the linchpin of the system, the fate of the ERM was greatly influenced by developments in the German economy. In order to finance reunification, the German government chose a policy of borrowing rather than raising taxes or revaluing the DM. The Bundesbank was determined to maintain a tight monetary policy. To stem rising inflation, German interest rates were kept high. To prevent their currencies depreciating against the DM, the interest rates of other members had to maintained at a high level. According to British Eurosceptics, the consequences of the UK's ERM membership were high interest rates, economic stagnation, bankruptcies and higher unemployment (although the underlying weakness of the UK economy obviously pre-dated UK entry into the ERM).

The cause of the crises in 1992–93 has also been attributed to insufficient co-operation between member countries and to the inflexible manner in which the mechanism was operated. It has been argued that parities ought to have been adjusted more frequently. By contrast, Eurosceptics have argued that the very principle of the ERM, which centres on government intervention to counteract market forces, is fundamentally flawed. Arguably, global currency markets are now far too large to be 'bucked', even by collective government intervention: about $1 trillion is traded daily on world currency markets, which is estimated to be about 2.5 times the total official reserves of the ten leading industrialised nations.

Table 10.1 The ERM Debate

Advantages of the ERM

(as frequently mentioned by its proponents prior to the 1992–93 crises)

- a more stable financial environment: it provides a semi-fixed exchange rate system which reduces the risks faced by businesses when engaged in cross-border trade;
- collective action: countries do not have to rely solely on their own efforts to maintain the relative value of their currencies;
- it imposes counter-inflationary disciplines, by limiting the extent to which a currency is allowed to depreciate. If firms in one member country raise their prices above those of competitors in other EU countries, they will not be able to sell their goods (firms would price themselves out of business if they paid excessive wage rises).

The Weaknesses of the ERM

(according to its detractors)

- it is based on the dubious assumption that currency values can be maintained through collective government intervention – that is, that governments can buck the market. National banks do not have sufficient reserves to prop up a currency, given the tremendous strength and mobility of international capital markets;
- it is based on the equally dubious assumption that, when the chips are down, central banks will defend other countries' currencies;
- it is a fair weather system: although there was a long period when the ERM seemed to work (that is, currencies in the system were relatively stable and inflation was relatively low), it could not cope with the economic consequences of German reunification;
- it provides rich pickings for currency speculators, who have a guaranteed buyer of weak currencies in the system – the central banks of member countries;
- loss of monetary sovereignty: national governments cannot set interest rates in accordance with national economic requirements, because the economic policies of weak currency countries are dominated by those of the strongest currency.

○ The Effects of 'Black Wednesday'

The near collapse of the ERM threatened the plan for EMU as laid down in the TEU. Although the day of the UK's exit from the ERM was dubbed 'Black Wednesday', it enabled the UK government to lower interest rates by half in order to boost economic recovery. Sterling was also devalued, making British exports cheaper, whereas exports from other Union countries into the UK became more expensive. But the UK's exit from the ERM was no unmixed blessing, because it made its imports more expensive and increased foreign exchange risks for UK businesses. After the move to wide fluctuation bands in August 1993, turmoil in the ERM subsided. The new bands were so wide that the speculators had no clear target at which to aim. There were no dramatic currency adjustments in the following year. The French and Belgian francs and the Irish punt were soon back within the narrow bands. But in March 1995, the peseta and escudo were both devalued by 7% and 3.5% respectively. Suggestions for reform of the ERM have centred on the need for greater operational flexibility and for new mechanisms for joint action before crises develop ('fire prevention' rather than 'fire fighting'). But, arguably, the ERM is by no means a necessary building block for full EMU.

● TOWARDS A SINGLE CURRENCY

○ The Delors Report on EMU

In June 1988, the European Council in Hanover instructed Commission President Delors to head a committee to work out a plan for EMU. The Committee included the 12 governors of the national central banks and focused on practical issues relating to how EMU could be achieved. The report of the Committee (the *Report on Economic and Monetary Union* or Delors Report), presented in April 1989, favoured a phased approach to EMU, based on three stages. It recommended the creation of a European system of central banks and emphasised the need for greater co-ordination and convergence of economic and monetary policies. It did not go so far as to *explicitly* recommend a single currency, but its proposal for a currency area in which exchange rate parities would be irrevocably locked was a small step from this goal. The UK opposed the Report's main recommendations, on the grounds that they would require a massive transfer of sovereignty. At the European Council in Madrid in June 1989, a compromise was agreed: the date for the start of the first stage was set for 1 July 1990. An intergovernmental conference was convened to consider the later stages.

Table 10.2 Arguments For and Against Monetary Union

For

- faster and cheaper monetary transfers. Elimination of currency conversion (estimated by the Commission to be about 0.3–0.4% of Union GDP);
- reduction of business risk (in relation to trade and investment) through elimination of exchange rate fluctuations. Businesses can quote prices for goods to be sold elsewhere in the Union without the risk of profits being wiped out by currency movements;
- efficiency gains, due to factors 1 and 2, leading to increased cross-border competition;
- transparency of prices: consumers will know how much the same goods cost in each member state; firms and individuals will recognise the need for wage and price discipline;
- governments will no longer be able to use currencies as instruments of economic policy, for example, by printing more money or devaluing, to avoid tough and unpopular measures;
- lower inflation, due to the disciplines imposed on Union economies;
- the merger of financial markets could lead to economies of scale;
- it will give the EU greater weight in the international monetary system;
- it will foster the goal of political union, by establishing an additional common link between citizens of the Union;
- the alternatives are worse: for example, floating rates are inimicable to the goal of a single market; the ERM has serious flaws.

Against

- loss of national sovereignty over monetary affairs (for example, the power of national governments to change interest rates);
- loss of flexibility. The ability of governments to insulate their countries from adverse economic trends in other countries will be weakened;
- EU economies are too dissimilar for EMU to make sense: convergence of living standards in the EU is needed before a move to monetary union becomes feasible;
- the EU is not an optimum currency area, because it lacks wage flexibility, high labour mobility and sufficient fiscal transfers: for some countries, the adverse effects of EMU could outweigh its benefits. It would lead to more unemployment, because the effects of poor competitiveness could no longer be cushioned by a depreciating currency;
- it will divide the EU into 'insider' and 'outsider' countries (see below);
- monetary union constitutes an additional barrier for countries seeking membership of the EU (in particular, the countries of Eastern Europe);
- the effort and expense of monetary union is simply not worth it.

○ The Maastricht Schedule for EMU

The outcome of the IGC on EMU, together with the Delors Report, form the basis of the agreements on EMU reached at Maastricht. Prior to the summit, John Major floated a 'hard ECU' plan, for the ECU to exist alongside existing currencies as a parallel currency. This idea had already been rejected in the Delors Report and was dismissed as a non-starter by the other states.

The main thrust of the TEU's references to economic and monetary policy is towards ever closer integration. The Treaty sets out a timetable towards monetary union, a constitution for the Union's central bank and a set of convergence criteria for the economies of member states. The importance of prudent financial management, price stability and sound public finances constitute an underlying theme of the TEU programme for EMU. According to the Treaty, full EMU is expected to be achieved in three stages:

• **Stage 1** (1 July 1990 to 31 December 1993). The central elements of the first stage had been agreed prior to Maastricht. It embraced the abolition of remaining restrictions on capital movements, completion of the SEM, reduction of exchange rate fluctuations and greater co-ordination of economic and monetary policies. In March 1990, the Council agreed a convergence framework, involving adoption of an annual economic report and multilateral surveillance over member states' economic policies. Member states are required to regard their economic policies as a matter of 'common concern', and must co-ordinate them within the Council (Article 103, EC). Closer co-ordination and convergence of the economic performance of member states is monitored through the surveillance procedure, involving submission of reports from the Commission to the Council. If the economic policies of a member state are judged inconsistent with broad economic policy guidelines set by the Council, the Council may by QMV make recommendations to the state concerned. Before the start of Stage 2, the Council was also required (on the basis of a Commission report) to assess progress with regard to economic and monetary convergence and implementation of the SEM.

• **Stage 2** (from 1 January 1994). This transition period embraces closer alignment and convergence of member states' economies, moves towards independence by the central banks and the establishment of the European Monetary Institute (EMI). The EMI, based in Frankfurt, started its operations on 1 January 1994, with 200 staff. The EMI Council consists of an independent president (currently a Belgian, Alexandre Lamfalussy), plus the governors of the national central banks, one of whom is vice-president. The EMI is responsible for strengthening co-operation between the national central banks; strengthening co-ordination of monetary policies; monitoring the functioning of the EMS; facilitating use of the ECU and laying the foundations for later stages of EMU. Its resources consist of contributions from the central banks based on a weighting of 50% population/50% GDP. During this stage, the Commission and the EMI report to the Council on the progress made with regard to economic and monetary convergence, with particular reference to quantitative reference targets or 'convergence indicators' (Article 109j, EC), as shown in Table 10.3.

Table 10.3 The Numerical Convergence Indicators

- low inflation (an average of not more than 1.5% higher than that of the three best performing states in terms of price stability in the year prior to examination);
- low long-term interest rates (no more than 2% higher than the three best performing states in terms of price stability in the year prior to examination);
- a budget deficit of no more than 3% of GDP;
- a public debt ratio of no more than 60% of GDP;
- two years' currency stability within the ERM (a member's currency would have to be in the normal fluctuation margins of the ERM and without being devalued on its own initiative against the currency of any member state for at least two years).

The reports of the Commission and EMI are also required to take into account development of the ECU, results of the integration of markets, balances of payments; unit labour costs and other price indices. Only states meeting the necessary conditions can join Stage 3. On the basis of reports from the Commission and the EMI, the Council acting by QMV will assess whether member states meet these conditions. The Council will recommend its findings to the European Council. The EP will also be consulted and will forward its opinion to the European Council. The TEU requires the European Council acting by qualified majority vote to decide no later than 31 December 1996 whether a majority of members fulfil the conditions for the adoption of a single currency and whether it is appropriate to begin Stage 3 in 1997 (the 1997 date has now been ruled out by the European Council). If the date for beginning Stage 3 has not been set by 31 December 1997, then according to the TEU this stage must begin on 1 January 1999 (regardless of whether a majority of members meet the criteria). The UK and Denmark have separate protocols allowing them a choice as to whether to participate in Stage 3. The UK is not committed to move to Stage 3 without a decision of its government and parliament. Denmark may submit the issue to a referendum. Sweden is likely to allow its parliament to have the final say.

- **Stage 3.** This involves a move to irrevocably fixed exchange rates and to a single monetary policy for participating member states, leading to adoption of a single currency. In Stage 3, the Council will be able to impose sanctions on member states running excessive deficits. A European Central Bank, to be created by 1 July 1998, will take over the tasks of the EMI. The ECB will be independent, and will not take orders from EU institutions or member governments. It will not lend to national governments or to Commission organisations. It will have exclusive right to authorise the issue of bank notes within the single currency zone. The ECB and the national central banks will together form the European System of Central Banks (ESCB). The governing council of the ESCB will comprise members of the ECB executive board and the governors of the national central banks. The primary objective of the ESCB will be to maintain price stability. It will support general economic policies in the Union; define and implement monetary policy; conduct foreign exchange operations; hold and manage foreign reserves of members and promote smooth operation of payments systems.

○ Meeting the Convergence Criteria

The Maastricht schedule clearly did not allow for the crisis in the ERM, or for the severity of the economic recession in the early 1990s. In this period, the disparities between the convergence criteria and the economic performance of most member states raised serious doubts concerning the feasibility of the Maastricht schedule. In September 1993, John Major argued that these disparities meant that the 'mantra' of full EMU had all the potency of a rain dance. However, the Commission's annual economic report for 1995 argued that, providing additional efforts were made (particularly in the budgetary area) it was realistic to expect that a majority of countries could meet the EMU criteria by the TEU deadline (*European Economy*, no. 59, 1995, p. 19). The Report included a report on the progress made by member states in meeting convergence targets in 1994. It concluded that good progress was being made on price stability (8 out of 12 met the convergence target), but more progress was needed on government deficits, and debt (only Germany and Luxembourg met both the debt and deficit criteria). The Convergence Report recorded some improvement in *de facto* exchange rate stability (although three countries remained outside the ERM). The Report noted that none of the three new member states currently met all of the numerical convergence criteria, (due primarily to budgetary weaknesses) but predicted that all might do so by the target date.

According to some analysts, the convergence criteria were devised for political rather than economic reasons that is, to demonstrate countries' commitments to 'fiscal chastity', or, more cynically, to confine monetary union to a select club. Efforts by the poorer states to meet the criteria, by, for example, cutting public spending, could impose hardship on their peoples. Poorer states, therefore, are likely to continue to agitate for additional compensatory funding in support of convergence programmes. But the adverse effects of efforts to meet the criteria are by no means confined to poorer countries. The austerity programme introduced in France in the winter of 1995, leading to a wave of public sector strikes, was widely regarded as being at least partly attributable to efforts by the French government to meet its convergence targets. Arguably, some convergence criteria could be relaxed or even abandoned. For example, some leeway is allowed in judging fiscal and public debts. Similarly, the 'normal' fluctuation margins of the ERM might be reinterpreted to mean bands wider than ±2.25%. Similarly, if countries can show their public finances are moving in the desired direction, they might be permitted to proceed to the final stage. But the importance of adherence to the rules governing progress towards EMU was confirmed by the German constitutional court prior to the ratification of the TEU. This tough stance has subsequently been repeatedly reaffirmed by the German government (notably by German Finance Minister Theo Waigel, who caused a political storm in September 1995 by casting doubt on Italy's ability to meet the criteria). The German parliament will decide whether the convergence criteria have been fulfilled before German agreement to monetary union is secured.

The European Council in Cannes in June 1995 stated a firm resolve to prepare for a transition to a single currency by 1 January 1999 at the latest (thus effectively ruling out 1997 as a starting date), in strict accordance with the TEU's convergence criteria and procedures. The EMI president has also stated that the criteria must be strictly interpreted. Those favouring a tough line on convergence have tended to argue that, whereas the criteria should be regarded as sacrosanct, the date for the start of the third stage of EMU should not. This view, espoused for example by Chancellor Kohl and by the head of the German Bundesbank in 1995, led to speculation that the 1999 deadline might yet be abandoned, despite the fact that the European Council in Madrid in December 1995 reaffirmed the 1 January 1999 starting date.

O Technical Preparation and Name: Enter the 'Euro'

In May 1995, the Commission produced a Green Paper on the practical measures needed for a changeover to a single currency. The paper argued for completion of the changeover within four years of the decision to launch it. The paper rejected a 'big bang' approach, in favour of a gradualist strategy, which divided the changeover into three phases:

• **Phase A. Launch of EMU** (*1 year maximum duration*), commencing between the end of 1996 and July 1998. In accordance with TEU provisions, the decision will be taken to move to a single currency. It will be decided which countries qualify to participate. The European System of Central Banks (ESCB) and the European Central Bank (ECB) will be established. There will be intense preparation in the banking and financial sectors. Production of notes and coin will begin.

• **Phase B. Transitional Phase** (*three years' maximum duration*): the effective start of EMU and the emergence of a critical mass of activities. There will be irrevocable fixing of currency parities by the ECB, which will begin to operate a single monetary policy. National currencies remain in circulation, as the new currency is introduced, first for banking and other large transactions and then for the general public. A critical mass of users would thereby be created. A communications strategy aimed at the public will explain the benefits of a single currency and how it would work.

• **Phase C. Final Changeover** (*several weeks' duration*). For a transition starting date of 1 January 1999, this phase would commence in 2002. National notes and coins would be phased out and the new currency would become the sole legal tender.

The paper was broadly approved by ECOFIN and by the European Council in Cannes. The European Council in Madrid in December 1995 agreed that EMU will begin on 1 January 1999 and outlined the definitive blueprint for the introduction of the new currency: in early 1998, EU leaders will decide which member states meet the conditions for participation. The states which qualify will have their currency rates irrevocably fixed on 1 January 1999. The banknotes and coins of the single currency will begin to circulate by 1 January 2002 at the latest, with the national currencies of participating states completely withdrawn within six months of this date.

Until recently, it was generally thought to be virtually inevitable that the new currency would be called the ECU (or Ecu). However, in 1995 the German government and the Bundesbank challenged this assumption, by suggesting the name 'Franken' as an alternative to ECU. The value of the ECU has fallen substantially against the DM since 1979 and the name ECU does not inspire much confidence in Germany. But the Franken idea found little favour outside Germany. Other names were also suggested, such as 'Euro-Mark', 'Ducat', 'Florin' or 'Monnet'. This issue was finally settled at the European Council in Madrid, which decided on the name 'Euro'. ECOFIN has agreed that the largest value coin will be ECU 2 and that notes will range from ECU 5 to 500.

○ **Partial Monetary Union and the 'Insider/Outsider' Problem**

Although the formation of a single currency zone now seems almost certain, it is by no means clear how many member states will be able or willing to join it. The UK, Denmark and Sweden might opt not to participate and several countries may not meet the convergence targets. But the will to achieve monetary union remains very strong in several member states and also in the Commission and EP. For some countries, including France, EMU is a way of providing institutional checks on German economic power because, unlike the Bundesbank, the ECB is expected to have the interests of all member states at heart. The German government has consistently argued that political union must accompany monetary union, implying that there is an element of sacrifice in the decision to replace the DM with a Euro-currency. Past monetary unions (including the monetary unification of Germany in 1990) have been driven by political rather than by economic expedients.

Given the wide economic disparities between member states, a partial monetary union is a more realistic goal in the short term. However, a limited currency zone could lead to friction between zone 'insiders' and 'outsiders'. For example, insiders are likely to be suspicious that outsiders will seek to use their currencies to gain competitive advantage (for example, by devaluing in order to boost their trade and investment). Countries failing to meet the entry criteria may feel marginalised and fearful that they are being relegated to a second-class Union status. There seems a strong possibility, therefore that the creation of a partial monetary union would stimulate 'reluctant' outsiders to intensify their efforts to meet the entry requirements and would force 'willing' outsiders to seriously re-examine their decision to retain their own currencies. In the spring of 1996, various ideas for dealing with the insider/outsider problem were being canvassed, including the idea of a monetary pact between the two groups and the idea that outsiders should be obliged to participate in a revamped ERM.

FURTHER READING

Cobham, D., *European Monetary Upheavals*, Manchester University Press, 1994.
Commission, 'Convergence Report for 1994', *European Economy*, no. 59, 1995.
Commission, COM (95), 333, *One Currency for Europe – Green Paper on the Practical Arrangements for the Introduction of the Single Currency*, 1995.
De Grauwe, P., *The Economics of Monetary Integration*, Oxford University Press, 1994.
Kenen, P.B., *Economic and Monetary Union in Europe: Moving Beyond Maastricht*, Cambridge University Press, 1995.
Steinherr, A. (ed.), *Thirty Years of European Monetary Integration. From the Werner Plan to EMU*, Longman, Harlow, 1994.

# Chapter 11

Competition, Industrial and Research and Technological Development Policies

The Union's competition, industrial and RTD (Research and Technological Development) policies are perhaps best examined in conjunction for several reasons: developments in any one of these policies are likely to have major repercussions for the others. Each constitutes an important component of the European business environment. Each has implications for the ability of European firms to compete successfully in world markets. Each has been accorded a central role in the Union's strategy for economic growth, competitiveness and employment. Each has stimulated an ideological debate concerning the role of government in business and industry. In each case the problem of reconciling national and Union level policies has loomed large.

● COMPETITION POLICY

Articles 85–94 of the Treaty of Rome established competition rules designed to prevent or remove anti-competitive practices deemed incompatible with the common market. The main features of this policy are outlined below.

○ Anti-competitive Agreements

Article 85 prohibits agreements between undertakings which may prevent, restrict or distort competition, such as agreements which:
- directly or indirectly fix purchase or selling prices;
- limit or control production, markets, technical development or investment;
- share markets or sources of supply;

- apply dissimilar conditions to equivalent transactions with other trading parties;
- make conclusion of contracts subject to acceptance of supplementary obligations.

The Treaty invests the Commission with considerable investigatory and enforcement powers in relation to Union competition policy. The Commission has the power to order parties to terminate conduct illegal under Article 85, and can impose large fines of up to 10% of the world-wide turnover of the group to which the infringing firm belongs. In February 1994, the Commission imposed a record fine of ECU 104 million on 17 steel companies, including British Steel, for operating a cartel. But in more than 90% of cases, an agreement is reached before action needs to be taken.

Article 85 only applies if the agreement has a significant effect on competition within the Union. Exemption may be given if the agreement contributes to an improvement in production, distribution or economic progress, or if it benefits consumers (Article 85(3)). For example, an exemption has recently been given on the grounds that an agreement strengthened European industry in global markets. Parties to an agreement can seek a declaration (known as a *negative clearance*) from the Commission confirming that the agreement does not breach the competition rules. In an effort to increase the speed and to reduce the cost of decisions, *de minimis* notices and *block exemptions* have been introduced. *De minimis* notices set out criteria to assist companies to decide whether their agreement is likely to fall within the scope of Article 85. Block exemption regulations set out categories of agreement which fall within the exemption provision of Article 85. Agreements will not breach Article 85 if:

- market share as a result of the agreement is less than 5% of the total market in the area affected by the agreement;
- aggregate annual turnover of the undertakings is below ECU 200 million.

○ Dominant Positions

Dominant positions may enable firms to put pressure on suppliers or buyers. The ECJ has defined dominance as 'the ability to act to a significant extent independently of competitors, customers and ultimately of consumers' and has stated that an indication, even presumption, of dominance exists once a company achieves a 50% market share. Article 86 concerns abuse of a dominant position by one or more undertakings, through activities such as:

- the imposition of unfair selling or purchase prices;
- limiting production, markets or technical development to the prejudice of consumers;
- applying dissimilar conditions to equivalent transactions with other

trading parties;
* making the conclusion of contracts subject to supplementary obligations.

There must be a cross-border dimension before the Commission can act. It has been difficult for the Commission to prove that a dominant position has been abused. There have been about 15 times as many Commission decisions under Article 85 as under Article 86. The first referral under Article 86 did not occur until 1971.

○ Merger Control

The Treaty of Rome did not contain a provision dealing with mergers. Articles 85 and 86 of the Treaty proved inadequate to deal with mergers, even though in 1972 the ECJ ruled that Article 86 could be used to block a merger if it created a dominant position in a particular market. A wave of merger activity in the 1980s led to pressure to develop specific merger legislation. The Merger Control Regulation introduced in September 1990 prohibits cross-border mergers which would create or strengthen dominant positions. It gives the Commission power to block large-scale cross-border mergers and take-overs where:

(a) aggregate world-wide turnover is more than ECU 5 billion;
(b) aggregate Union-wide turnover of at least two of the undertakings exceeds ECU 250 million, unless one has more than two-thirds of its aggregate Union-wide turnover in one member state.

Firms are required to notify the Commission of their intention to merge, if a Union dimension is involved. The regulation gives the Commission investigative powers and powers to fine undertakings which fail to notify a merger or which supply incorrect information. Since 1990, the Commission's Competition Directorate (DG IV) has had a Merger Task Force. In its first five years of operation, it received 288 notifications, but only two attempted mergers were prohibited. The attempted take-over of Canada's de Havilland by Aerospatiale and Alenia-de Havilland was refused, because it would have given the merged company a market share of more than 50%. In 1994, the Commission prohibited a proposed joint venture in the German pay television market (the MSG Media Service case). The impact of the regulation has been limited by the high threshold before the Commission can examine deals. The Commission is currently seeking a cut in the threshold, but several member states are opposed to this.

○ State Aids

State aids are government subsidies to enterprises, such as direct payments, 'soft loans', debt write-offs, tax breaks, or guaranteed borrowing. In the

1980s, the Commission estimated that state aids within the Union averaged more than ECU 80 billion a year, or 2.5% of Union GDP, which was larger than the Community budget. Many key industries, such as railways, airlines, steel, shipbuilding and textiles receive state aids. In recent years, governments have come under pressure to provide rescue packages for troubled industries. However, governments have also been under pressure to cut state budgets. There are wide variations in the scale and pattern of state aids between EU countries. For example, Italy currently gives roughly three times as much as the UK in state aids.

State aids which distort, or threaten to distort, competition were banned by Article 92 of the Treaty of Rome (the coal and steel industries are covered by Article 67 of the ECSC Treaty). Article 92 covers aid which provides a firm with an economic advantage which it would not otherwise have received and which is capable of affecting trade between member states. However, it contains many exemptions, such as:

- aid having a social character;
- aid to alleviate natural disasters or other exceptional occurrences;
- aid granted to certain areas of the Federal Republic of Germany to compensate for economic disadvantage caused by the division of Germany;
- aid to promote the economic development of areas where the standard of living is abnormally low or where there is serious underemployment;
- aid to promote important projects of common European interest;
- aid to facilitate the development of certain economic activities or areas;
- other categories decided by the Council (by QMV) following a Commission proposal.

These exemptions are so varied as to provide the Commission with considerable discretionary powers. Article 93 of the Treaty sets out the procedures for decisions on state aids. All aid, other than assistance of up to ECU 50,000 over three years to any one firm, must be notified to the Commission. The rules on aids apply equally to the public and private sectors (in the case of the former, aid should not be given to state-owned companies if a private investor would not do so, given the same circumstances). An aid may be suppressed or modified by the Commission, subject to appeal by interested parties to the ECJ. The Commission has formulated three principles to guide decisions on aids:

- it should be part of a restructuring package (not a featherbedding exercise);
- it may be used as a 'breathing space' for industries with major social problems;
- it should not lead to an expansion of capacity.

The Commission's policy on state aids has arguably been lax. It has tended to approve restructuring packages without much scrutiny. The Commission took 527 decisions on state aids in 1994: of these cases, it raised no objections in 440, initiated proceedings in 40 but took negative decisions in only 3 (other decisions were taken in the remainder of cases). Control of aids has proved difficult for several reasons: it is often difficult to ascertain the true level of aid or to compare levels between countries; the number of Commission staff concerned with state aids is very small; unlike monopolies and mergers control, there is no parallel body to control state aids at national level. The Commission now favours a *one time last time* approach to state aids for ailing firms and industries, although this may well prove difficult to sustain in the face of strong pressures from governments and industrial lobbies.

● INDUSTRIAL POLICY

○ Goals and Development

In its broadest sense industrial policy embraces all government policies affecting industry (including, for example, environmental, energy and competition policies). However, it now tends to be defined more narrowly, to refer to government policies to foster and protect European industries, for example through:
- restructuring packages for ailing industries;
- support for 'sunrise' industries;
- support for small and medium-sized enterprises (SMEs);
- support for RTD programmes;
- protection of industries against 'unfair' foreign competition.

Elements of industrial policy can be discerned in both the ECSC Treaty, which includes references to intervention in the coal and steel industries, and the Treaty of Rome, which contains a reference to government support for industry. However, neither Treaty spelled out an industrial policy as such. The 1950s and 1960s were decades of economic growth in EC countries. Therefore industrial policy was not regarded as a key priority by member states.

The need to support Europe's industries became more widely recognised in the 1970s, as traditional industries declined and the competitive position of EU firms in world markets worsened. The perception of significant gaps between the industrial performance of the Union and of its principal competitors was a major factor precipitating the development of a European industrial policy in the 1980s. It also became widely accepted that some key industrial problems could only be effectively dealt with at European level. The importance of EU industrial policy is shown by the fact that an industry chapter (Title XIII, EC) was included in the TEU. EU support for industry is channelled through various mechanisms, such as the Structural Funds, the EIB and RTD framework programmes.

○   A Contentious Policy

The operation of an industrial policy is fraught with problems. For example, government intervention could do more economic harm than good. Financial aid might be given to prop up economically unviable enterprises. There will always be lobbies calling on governments to bail out ailing firms. It is by no means self-evident which industries or firms should be supported. The records of governments in 'picking industrial winners' has been poor. One strategy might be to encourage the emergence of large *Eurochampion* firms, able to take on the US and Japanese manufacturing giants in global markets (there are fewer very large businesses in the Union than in the US). This might be sought through encouraging mergers between EU firms or through financial support to boost firm size. According to its critics, the Eurochampion strategy has several flaws: it could reduce competition within the EU, by reducing the number of firms; it means that some firms (the potential Eurochampions) will be given preferential treatment; it could have a negative effect on the efficiency of Eurochampions because they may become reliant on subsidies.

There is by no means unanimity of view concerning the purpose of industrial policy and of the extent to which it is compatible with other policy objectives (for example, reconciling support for industry with the creation of a level playing field for business). There are significant variations in the industrial philosophies of member states. France has tended to favour an 'interventionist' industrial policy, involving commitment to national planning and assistance. By contrast, Conservative governments in the UK have severely curtailed industrial subsidies.

Industrial policy has caused fierce debates within the EU between those advocating state intervention and those arguing that industrial growth is best achieved through the operation of market forces. In recent years, the balance has shifted towards the latter (there is a privatisation wave throughout Europe) but advocates of intervention have fought a spirited rearguard action. Leon Brittan (1994) has argued that EU governments are moving towards a 'common diagnosis' of industrial problems. All are concerned about labour costs; all agree on the need to cut public spending; all agree on the need for more capital investment, RTD and training. The need for the Union's industries to pursue high-tech, high value-added activities has been widely accepted in principle. However, translating this diagnosis into concrete remedies is easier said than done.

● RESEARCH AND TECHNOLOGICAL DEVELOPMENT (RTD) POLICY

○ The EU's 'Technological Lag'

Both the Cecchini Report (1987) and the Commission's White Paper on *Growth, Competitiveness and Employment* (1993) identified *technological lag* as a major factor accounting for the EU's poor economic performance relative to its major competitors. High-technology products account for about one-quarter of Japan's exports, for almost a third of US exports, but for only one-fifth of those from Western Europe. Of the top 100 information technology (IT) companies in 1992, only 12 were European owned, and some of these 12 (Groupe Bull, Siemens Nixdorf and Olivetti) were making heavy losses. The main reasons often cited to account for the EU's technological lag are:

● **Low investment:** in 1991, total public, private, civil and military spending on RTD in the EC was ECU 104 billion (302 per capita) compared with ECU 124 billion (493 per capita) in the US and ECU 77 billion (627 per capita) in Japan, equivalent to 2% of GDP in the EU, 2.8% in the US and 3% in Japan. The EC had only 4 researchers and engineers per thousand of the working population compared with 8 for the US and 9 for Japan. There were also wide variations in the amounts devoted to research within the EU. RTD spending per capita in 1989 ranged from ECU 502 in West Germany to ECU 20 in Portugal (the figure for the UK was ECU 299). The White Paper advocated an increase in EU RTD spending from 2% to 3% of Union GDP.

● **Poor application:** both the US and Japan are currently better at producing tangible research outputs in the form of saleable products. Europe is stronger in pure science than in applied research and commercial applications, despite the fact that researchers in the EU produce more than three times as many scientific papers as their counterparts in Japan. The White Paper attributed this to inadequate links between universities and businesses and advocated greater emphasis on product development rather than on basic research.

● **Fragmentation:** duplication of research and failure to reap economies of scale have frequently been cited as major deficiencies. National RTD programmes predominate, with Union programmes accounting for only about 4% of EU spending on RTD.

○ The Development of RTD Policy

The idea of a European technological community was part of Monnet's 'Action Committee for a United States of Europe' programme in the 1950s and 1960s, but was not adopted. The development of the civilian nuclear power industry was boosted by the signing of the European Atomic Energy Community (Euratom) Treaty in 1957. But it was not until the late 1970s, when the problems of poor competitiveness and industrial decline in the Union became manifest, that the issue of RTD in the non-nuclear field began to be seriously addressed. In 1979, Vicomte Davignon, who had been appointed Commissioner with responsibilities for RTD in 1977, produced a document which criticised the fragmentation of the Union's research effort and which advocated an explicit industrial strategy for the Union. Davignon invited the heads of Europe's top electronics and IT companies to a round table discussion on this issue in 1979. Davignon's ideas provided the underpinning for the European research programmes created in the 1980s.

Union RTD programmes currently have several distinctive features. The idea behind all programmes is to encourage firms to 'think European': they support collaborative projects, involving partners from different member states; they are undertaken on a shared cost basis (the EU being responsible for up to half of total costs); research grants are awarded on a competitive basis (there are no national research quotas). In principle only projects involving fundamental research at the 'pre-competitive' stage are eligible for assistance. Product development and marketing remain the responsibility of private industry. This principle was established to prevent firms in receipt of research support from reaping unfair competitive advantages. But when research support is pre-competitive, it is difficult to judge its impact. Because of the problem of poor application of research results in the EU, there is a trend towards support for more market-oriented projects. The EU has its own joint research centre, located on five sites in Italy, Germany, the Netherlands, Belgium and Spain.

The current aim of EU RTD policy is not to transfer all research activities to the European level, but to promote projects which it would be more costly and less efficient to run at national level. The need to address the Union's technology gap is reflected in both the SEA and the TEU. The SEA places a strong emphasis upon the need for cross-border collaboration in RTD and gives the Commission the task of improving co-ordination of member states' RTD programmes. The Commission provides a centralised information service on EU RTD activities (CORDIS – the Community Research and Development Information Service). Since 1987, as a result of the SEA, EU RTD activities have been co-ordinated under framework programmes. The TEU (Title XV, EC) reinforced and extended the Union's role in RTD.

Table 11.1 outlines some major EU RTD programmes. By no means all European collaborative RTD projects have been confined to member states. For example, EUREKA, ESA (the European Space Agency), DIANE (Direct Information Access Network for Europe, a database), CERN (the European Centre for Nuclear Research), the European Science Foundation, COST (European Co-operation in the Field of Scientific and Technical Research) and JET (the Joint European Torus programme aimed at harnessing fusion energy) are pan-European ventures, involving both EU and non-EU countries. The Anglo-French Concorde project and the Airbus project (involving companies from France, Germany, the UK and Spain) have been developed outside the Union framework.

Table 11.1 Some Major RTD Programmes

ESPRIT (European Strategic Programme for Research in Information Technology) was launched in February 1984 to support the development, manufacture and use of IT products. Esprit claims that about one-fifth of the recent products of Europe's large electronics companies are based on technology deriving from Esprit projects;

RACE (Research and Development in Advanced Communications Technologies in Europe) aims to contribute to the introduction of Integrated Broadband Communication;

BRITE/EURAM (Basic Research in Industrial Technologies for Europe) aims to strengthen the competitiveness of European manufacturing industry in world markets. It focuses on applying new technologies to traditional industries (for example, vehicles, aeronautics and textiles);

SPRINT (Strategic Programme for Innovation and Technology Transfer) aims to improve the competitiveness of SMEs through technology transfer;

TELEMATICS provides funding for the development of a trans-European electronic information exchange infrastructure;

BIOTECH (Research and Technological Development in Biotechnology);

EUREKA (European Research Co-operation Agency), established in 1985, aims to improve Europe's performance in producing high-tech goods and services for world markets. It was proposed by President Mitterrand as a response to the US Star Wars programme. It is not an EU body: its membership comprises EEA members, Switzerland, Turkey and some East European countries. It is separate from the EU framework programmes. However, it is managed by the Commission. EUREKA projects, which are proposed and run by industrial firms, include 'JESSI' (semiconductor research) and 'EUREKA Audio-Visual' (promotion of a European high definition television). EUREKA's critics argue that it has a poor record in producing results in the form of commercially successful products.

○ **The RTD Framework Programmes**

These programmes are accorded a central role in the Union's RTD policy and provide insights into current RTD priorities. Their principal aims are:
• to ensure that there is sufficient expertise in main technologies;
• to enable European firms to reap economies of scale in RTD;
• to facilitate co-ordination of national RTD efforts, to avoid duplication;
• to narrow gaps in RTD spending between member states.

Table 11.2 The Fourth Framework Programme (1994–98)

Activity	ECU Million		
		EU 12	EU 15
1 – RTD & Demonstration Programmes		**10,686**	**11,434**
I. Information and communication technologies	3,405		
1. Telematics	843		
2. Communication technologies	630		
3. Information technologies	1,932		
II. Industrial and materials technologies	1,995		
4. Industrial and materials technologies	1,707		
5. Standards, measurement and testing	288		
III. Environment	1,080		
6. Environment and climate	852		
7. Marine sciences and technologies	228		
IV. Life sciences and technologies	1,572		
8. Biotechnology	552		
9. Biomedicine and health	336		
10. Agriculture and fisheries	684		
V. Energy	2,256		
11. Non-nuclear energy	1,002		
12. Nuclear fission safety	414		
13. Controlled thermonuclear fusion	840		
VI. Transport	240		
14. Transport	240		
VII. Targeted socioeconomic research	138		
15. Socioeconomic research	138		
2 – International Co-operation	540	**540**	**578**
3 – Dissemination & Exploitation of Results	330	**330**	**353**
4 – Training & Mobility of Researchers	744	**744**	**796**
TOTAL		**12,300**	**13,161**

Source: Commission.

The third programme (1990–94) was worth ECU 6.6 billion and the fourth (1994–98) is worth ECU 13.16 billion (adjusted from ECU 12.3 billion following the fourth enlargement, although the precise breakdown of the adjusted figure was not available at the time of writing). The fourth programme, reflects many ideas for 'technological awakening' contained in the Delors White Paper. The programme seeks improved transfer of technologies from universities to companies, through better dissemination and utilisation of research results, with particular emphasis on benefiting SMEs. It seeks to boost the Union's research effort in newer technologies, such as IT, biotechnology and eco-technology. It also seeks better integration of national, Union and pan-European research activities.

O Evaluation

The key role assigned to RTD in the Union's current strategy for growth and employment is an indication of its importance within the Union's policy portfolio. RTD policy has also become an important element of other Union policies (for example, competition, trade, industry, the environment, energy and trans-European networks). The impact of the Union's RTD policy is difficult to evaluate, not least because the Union is but one of several sources of funding for research projects and because of the difficulty in measuring research impacts. For example, a recent study of the EUREKA initiative concluded that EUREKA may well have had a 'synergising' effect upon Jessi (semiconductors) and the high definition television (HDTV) project, but that specific benefits were difficult to identify (Peterson, 1993). It is clear that the Union's RTD policy will not of itself solve the problem of the Union's 'technological lag'. But it is now firmly established as a key aspect of the Union's policy portfolio and, given the Union's commitment to the promotion of high-tech, high value-added industries, seems set to continue to grow in importance.

FURTHER READING

Bangemann, M., *Meeting the Global Challenge: Establishing a Successful European Industrial Policy*, Kogan Page, London, 1992.
Brittan, L., *Europe*, Hamish Hamilton, London, 1994.
Cecchini, P., *The European Challenge: 1992 The Benefits of a Single Market*, Wildwood House, Aldershot, 1988.
Commission, *Growth, Competitiveness and Employment*, White Paper, 1993.
Commission, *European Competition Policy*, 1994, Annual Report, 1995.
Peterson, J., *High Technology and the Competition State: An Analysis of the Eureka Initiative*, Routledge, London, 1993.
Sharp, M. and Pavitt, K., 'Technology Policy in the 1990s', *Journal of Common Market Studies*, vol. 31, no. 2, 1993, pp. 129–51.

 **Chapter 12**

Trans-European Networks

● WHAT ARE TRANS-EUROPEAN NETWORKS?

The Union is currently according high priority to the promotion of Trans-European Networks (TENs) programmes in the fields of transport, energy, telecommunications and environmental infrastructure. These programmes seek to connect the networks of member states, in order to create integrated, Union-wide networks. The importance of TENs to the aims of integrating the economies of member states and to economic growth was acknowledged in both the TEU and in the Commission's White Paper on *Growth, Competitiveness and Employment.* The European Council in Brussels in December 1993 established two TEN working groups, one on transport and energy (headed by Commissioner Henning Christopherson and comprising high ranking officials from member states) and the other on telecommunications (headed by Commissioner Martin Bangemann and comprising industrialists). The European Council in Corfu in June 1994 extended the Christopherson group's mandate to include environmental infrastructure. At Corfu, over forty separate TENs projects were agreed. These networks are also being extended beyond the Union, in particular to Central and Eastern Europe.

The Union is performing guiding and co-ordinating roles in relation to TENs programmes, although only a small proportion of the finance for TENs projects will come from the Community budget. The bulk of funds for these projects is expected to be provided by the private sector and by national governments, although the EIB and the newly created European Investment Fund have been accorded important roles. EU finance ministers recently proposed that the Union contribution to TENs should be limited to 10% of the overall cost. This chapter focuses on transport networks, although it also deals briefly with energy and telecommunications networks.

● THE COMMON TRANSPORT POLICY

◯ The Union's Transport Systems

The Union has one of the most developed groups of transport systems in the world. In EU 12, transport accounted for about 7% of Union GDP, for 5.6 million jobs (plus a further 2.5 million employed in the manufacture of transport equipment), for 40% of public investment and for almost 30% of energy consumption. As an industry, transport has been growing in importance in recent decades, due to increases in car ownership, cross-border trade and citizens' leisure time. Each member state has developed its own transport system within a national context and therefore EU transport systems tend to be poorly connected. There is so far little integration between the different transport modes: in EU 12, combined (or intermodal) transport accounted for only 4% of total goods transported.

Road transport is now the predominant mode of transport for passengers and freight. In EU 12, private cars accounted for 79% of all passenger journeys, compared with 9% for buses, 7% for rail and 6% for aircraft. For all types of inland traffic (national and international) road transport accounted for 89.5% of all goods transported, compared with 6.5% for rail and 4% for inland waterways. Air traffic, in terms of passengers carried, has more than tripled in the last two decades, whereas both rail and waterway transport have declined as a proportion of total transport use.

There are wide variations in the pattern and quality of national networks. Railway and motorway networks are dense in some countries but sparse in others. Belgium has the densest network of both rail and motorway networks. Germany's motorway network accounted for almost one-third of the EU network in 1990. Greece, Portugal, Spain and Ireland are relatively poorly served by road and rail links. Several countries have no inland waterways, but in the Netherlands about one-third of goods are transported by this mode.

◯ The Development of the Common Transport Policy (CTP)

Although the goal of a Common Transport Policy was set out in Articles 74–84 of the Treaty of Rome, until the 1980s little was done to achieve it. The reasons why a CTP has proved so difficult to develop can be summarised as:
- **vested interests:** the domination of some transport sectors by national carriers, which have an interest in defending near-monopoly positions;
- **diversity:** the difficulties involved in harmonising the different national transport networks. For example, in the rail sector, there are different sizes of rolling stock and of power supply. Each country currently has its own

air-traffic management system;
- **costs:** the enormous expense involved in developing a common transport infrastructure (for example, the building of roads, tunnels, railtracks, airports);
- **burden-sharing:** the 'who pays?' problem (should the financial burden fall primarily on the states directly affected by projects, or should costs be borne by all EU members?).

In 1982, the EP took the Council to the ECJ for failing to carry out its obligations under Article 74 of the Treaty of Rome: in a complex judgment in 1985, the Court ruled that, although references in the Treaty to the CTP were too vague to identify clearly what the Council's obligations were, the Treaty had nevertheless been infringed. The Court ruled that inland transport of goods and passengers should be open to all Union firms and recommended that the Council worked towards a CTP. Since the mid-1980s, the CTP has been shaped by four principal factors:
- **Environmental Policy.** Transport is never environmentally neutral. Member states are facing common transport problems, such as congestion, pollution, safety and energy consumption. A key feature of the EU's current transport policy is the extent to which it has become intertwined with environmental policy. The themes of environmentally friendly transport and of sustainable mobility are now integrated into the CTP.
- **The Impact of the Single European Market.** Peripheral regions could lose out on the benefits of the SEM because of poor transport links to prosperous regions. The SEM programme includes a wide range of measures to reduce barriers to the cross-border movement of goods and people and to increase cross-border competition in transport.
- **The Trans-European Networks Programme.** Underlying the TENs programme agreed at Maastricht was the recognition that the goal of a barrier-free Europe could not be achieved without further measures to tackle the problem of physical barriers, such as transport bottlenecks (for example, at Rotterdam), missing transport links and poor infrastructure. In April 1994, the Commission identified 126 road schemes, 11 rail links, 26 inland waterways and 57 combined transport links to be completed by 2010, at a cost of ECU 400 billion. By this year the EU should be linked by 58,000 km of roads, 70,000 km of railway lines, 12,000 km of inland waterways and 267 designated airports.
- **Enlargement.** The geographical expansion of the Union as a result of enlargement, and the Union's closer links with Eastern Europe, have increased the need for a pan-European approach to transport policy. As a result of the fourth enlargement, an additional 21 schemes were added to the TENs programme, at a cost of ECU 49 billion.

○ **The Current Aims of the CTP**

These were set out in a Commission White Paper in 1992: that is, to achieve a 'double integration' of national networks and of transport modes, in order to create a single trans-European network; to improve the EU's transport infrastructure; to use more energy-efficient, less-polluting modes; to improve safety and to provide citizens with a wider choice of transport. Measures to achieve these objectives include the interconnection of existing networks, unblocking bottlenecks, improving links with peripheral regions and with neighbouring countries; combining different transport modes; modernisation of equipment; research into new transport technologies; and measures to improve service quality. In July 1995, the Commission published its transport action programme for 1995–2000, which focused on three goals: improving the quality of the transport system; integrating transport policy into the SEM; and developing transport links with countries outside the Union.

After years of lying virtually dormant, the CTP is showing distinct signs of life. The TENs programme, if fully developed and if sufficient finance is forthcoming, will do much to create the backbone of an integrated Union transport system. But it is by no means certain that sufficient private and public sector capital will be raised to support this programme.

○ **Road Transport**

In recent years, EU road transport policy has focused on four issues:
1. The opening up of transport markets to cross-border competition. The Council agreed in June 1988 to liberalise road haulage by progressively abolishing national road haulage permits and quotas, so that carriers could engage freely in cross-border trade. National quota restrictions ended in 1993. On 1 January 1993, checks on goods crossing internal frontiers were abolished. A regulation on road cabotage (the ability of transport firms to trade *within* another member state, for example, for a German firm to transport goods from London to Birmingham) was adopted in 1994, but will not be fully complete until July 1998. There is now a Union-wide maximum weight for lorries (the UK, which has lower limits, is exempt from these regulations until 1998. Because of its special position as an international transit route, and its concern about environmental damage to Alpine passes, Austria will be able to place limits on heavy lorry traffic until 2004).
2. Integration of networks. A trans-European road network is planned for 2002, with the aim of connecting national networks and relieving road congestion. Cross-border networks include motorways and tunnels through the Pyrenees, a motorway connection between Lisbon and Madrid, and the Channel tunnel linking the UK and France. The planned road-building

programme should add an extra 15,000 km of new motorways by 2002.

3. Pollution. Road transport is responsible for 80% of CO_2 emissions from transport which contribute to global warming, as compared with 11% for air transport, 4% for railways and less than 1% for inland waterways. Environmental measures include the promotion of lead free petrol, harmonisation of environmental standards for new vehicles and encouragement to use alternative transport modes.

4. Safety. About 50,000 people are killed each year on EU roads. The TEU explicitly refers to measures to improve road safety. In 1986, the Commission drew up an action programme for road safety, including measures to improve road signs, vehicle safety and driver training.

○ Rail

There is no pan-European rail network as yet: for example, UK trains are narrower and lower than continental trains. The Eurostar trains, travelling via the Channel tunnel, have to cope with the different signalling and electric power systems of the British, French and Belgian rail networks. Spain, Finland, and ex-Soviet Union countries have different gauges to other European countries. Electrical power supply, breaking and signalling systems also vary. Investment in railways varies enormously from one country to another. Most rail industries in the Union are loss-making public monopolies, sustained by government subsidies. The EU is seeking to develop a high-speed, pan-European network linking most major European cities by 2015. About 30,000 km of high-speed track is planned for the next 25 years, covering Western and Central Europe. High-speed rail links are planned between London, Paris, Brussels, Cologne and Amsterdam, at a cost of ECU 8.5 billion. The Channel tunnel project, undertaken by an Anglo-French consortium (Eurotunnel), opened in 1994, linking Folkestone to Calais and providing rail services from an extensive network of terminals.

○ Air

The air transport industry has been notoriously resistant to effective deregulation, perhaps because a national airline is almost regarded as a symbol of nationhood. More than 95% of the 630 international routes in Europe are monopolised by one or two carriers. Regulated markets lead to limited consumer choice, higher fares and lower efficiency. The Commission estimated in 1994 that European airlines are 20% less competitive than US airlines. On many routes, scheduled air fares are 50% higher in the EU than in the US. Some governments continue to subsidise their national carriers. The EU has also provided subsidies for some airlines.

The EU has an 'open skies' policy to promote more competition in the airline industry. Until recently, co-operation was based around intergovernmental agreements rather than upon a common European approach. In 1986, the ECJ ruled that EC competition rules were applicable to this sector and that price-fixing agreements were illegal. Agreement on a partial liberalisation of air transport was finally reached in December 1987 and came into effect in January 1988. It provided for greater flexibility with regard to fares and traffic sharing, although it was limited to scheduled services between member countries and contained block exemptions. A new package agreed in 1990 extended the measures agreed in 1987. In June 1992, transport ministers agreed a third liberalisation package, to establish a single market in civil aviation. This covered scheduled, non-scheduled and cargo services. The UK and the Netherlands wanted a free market in air transport from the end of 1993, but some other countries favoured a six-year breathing spell to allow inefficient firms to cut costs. A four-year compromise was eventually agreed. From January 1993, EU charter airlines were able to compete freely on price and to compete throughout the EU, although air cabotage remains subject to restrictions until 31 March 1997 (the Azores and the Greek islands are exempt for ten years).

Despite these developments, the open skies objective is far from being fully realised. An official committee on air transport, known colloquially as the 'committee of wise men' produced a report in January 1994 entitled *Expanding Horizons*, which stated that the single aviation market existed in name only, because of subsidies, national preferences and other impediments to competition. It recommended that the EU pursue deregulation, privatisation and competition in this sector and that state aid should be phased out. EU Transport Commissioner Kinnock is currently resisting US attempts to sign bilateral open skies agreements with individual member states and is seeking to negotiate an agreement on behalf of the Union. In 1995, the Commission proposed an integrated air traffic management system, involving the creation of a network of 267 designated airports.

O Sea and Inland Waterways

The Union's merchant fleet has declined substantially, in both tonnage and market share. Maritime shipping was not included in the CTP. A common shipping policy was agreed in December 1986, to be established by 1993. This policy resulted in four regulations (on competition, on predatory pricing by third countries, on cargo reservations and on freedom to provide services) which took effect in 1987. The liberalisation of maritime cabotage was agreed in principle in 1991, but will take years to take effect. Maritime cabotage was deregulated in northern Union states from 1 January 1993.

Deregulation will occur in Spain, France, Italy and Portugal in the period 1995–99 and from 2004 for passenger and ferry services in Greece.

Although there has been a fall in the use of inland waterways, they still play important roles in transporting heavy industrial goods in some areas, notably the Rhine and its tributaries. The EU is seeking to reduce overcapacity in the industry, for example by providing financial aid for scrapping of vessels. Liberalisation embraces measures such as removal of cross-border controls on vessels and mutual recognition of crew licences.

● ENERGY AND TELECOMMUNICATIONS POLICY

○ Energy

Although the coal and nuclear industries were dealt with respectively in the ECSC and Euratom treaties, energy policy was not mentioned in the Treaty of Rome. The oil crises of the 1970s, prompted serious consideration of energy policy, by giving rise to concerns about security of supplies. Energy was not given a separate chapter in the TEU, although it is mentioned in various parts of the Treaty. The 1996 IGC will decide whether or not to extend the TEU to include an energy chapter.

The energy dependency of the EU is expected to rise from the current level of about 50% to about 70% by 2020. There are wide variations in energy resources, and patterns of energy use between member states. The current aims of EU energy policy are to open up energy production to competition, to interconnect energy networks, to make better use of existing capacities, to promote the export of energy technologies and to encourage use of non-polluting forms of energy. The EU has several energy programmes: for example, THERMIE is a programme to promote the use of energy technology; SAVE promotes energy efficiency and ALTENER renewable energy sources. The European Councils held in Corfu and Essen established a list of 10 priority projects involving the connection of gas networks and of electricity grids. The connection of EU supply lines with energy sources in Central and Eastern Europe is also regarded as a priority.

○ Telecommunications

The development of TENs in the telecommunications sector has centred on efforts to harmonise and liberalise the telecommunications industry and to promote European 'information highways'. The White Paper on *Growth Competitiveness and Employment* and the Bangemann Group's report (June

1994) both advocated measures to promote TENs in this sector.

The current aims of EU telecommunications policy are to achieve open markets, interconnected networks, interoperability of service and open access to networks for suppliers. As a result of recent policy developments and rapid technological change, the EU should in large measure have full competition in telecommunications markets by 1998. In May 1988 a directive was adopted on liberalisation of telecommunications equipment. This was followed in June 1990 by a directive on liberalisation of telecommunications services, although it contained many exemptions. The directive nevertheless required the Commission to draw up a review paper on the prospects for full liberalisation of these services. The review led to the Council calling on the Commission to take steps to achieve full liberalisation of voice telephony by January 1998, with exemptions for Luxembourg until 2000 and Greece, Ireland, Portugal and Spain until 2003. The Council also required the Commission to draw up the regulatory framework for the 1998 target by 1 January 1996. In November 1994, the Council decided to scrap all binding provisions on choice of infrastructure by 1998. The Commission has also developed measures to achieve full liberalisation of mobile communications and satellite, radio and TV broadcasting.

A key aspect of change in the telecommunications sector has been the convergence of telecommunications and information technologies. In September 1994, the Council approved a Commission action plan for the information society, based on the Bangemann Group's report on this subject. The plan embraced a broad range of proposals on information technology, telecommunications, television, RTD and education. But given the rapid pace of technological change in these fields, the appropriateness and effectiveness of EU measures to promote the information society remain to be seen.

FURTHER READING

Button, K., *Transport Economics*, Edward Elgar, Cheltenham, 1993.

Commission, COM (94), 440 and COM (94), 682, *Green Paper on the Liberalisation of Telecommunications Infrastructure and Cable TV Networks*, 1994.

Commission, COM (94), 34, *Europe's Way to the Information Society*, 1994.

Commission, COM (94), 659, *Green Paper: For a European Energy Policy*, 1995.

Commission, *Trans-European Networks*, The Group of Personal Representatives of the Heads of State or Government Report, 1995.

Curwen, P., 'Telecommunications Policy in the European Union, *Journal of Common Market Studies*, vol. 33, no. 3, 1995, pp. 331–60.

Kiriazidis, T., *European Transport: Problems and Policies*, Avebury, Aldershot, 1994.

Nijkamp, P., *Europe on the Move*, Avebury, Aldershot, 1993.

 **Chapter 13**

Environmental Policy

● DEVELOPMENT

○ The Main Factors Shaping EU Environmental Policy

The Treaty of Rome contained no provision for a Union environmental policy. Indeed, the initial impetus for the development of the Union was towards rapid industrial and agricultural growth, aims which might be perceived as potentially incompatible with environmental protection. However, since the beginning of the 1970s, the Union has developed an extensive range of policies on environmental issues, including more than 200 pieces of legislation. All EU policies are now required to take into account the environmental dimension. Environmental concerns are accorded high priority, for example, in the EU's policies on transport and agriculture and in its assistance programmes for Eastern Europe. Environmental policy was a key issue in negotiations for the fourth enlargement. Environmental considerations play an important role in all projects financed by the European Investment Bank. The EU regards itself as a major participant in international fora on global environmental issues.

The growing importance of EU environmental policy in the last two decades can be attributed to a combination of factors, such as the rise of the 'green' movement and acceptance of the need for cross-border collaboration on environmental problems because 'pollution knows no frontiers'. The development of an effective EU environmental policy has, however, been impeded by several key factors, viz.:

1. The wide variations in environmental standards within the EU. For example, Austria, Denmark, the Netherlands, Finland, Sweden and west Germany have much higher environmental standards than Greece, Portugal or Spain. In recent years, there has been a trend towards greater flexibility in

216

the application of Union environmental protection measures, providing that minimum requirements are met. The fourth enlargement has increased pressure for high environmental standards in the EU, because the new entrants generally have higher environmental standards than the EU requires. In cases where the Union is seeking to meet such high standards, the new entrants are allowed to maintain their standards. Where the EU has no plans to meet these standards, the new entrants are allowed to maintain their standards for four years (the situation will then be re-examined). Austria obtained approval to continue restricting the use of its Alpine passes by EU trucks until 2001 (until 2004 unless pollution levels fall by more than 40% by 2001).

2. **The fuzzy boundary between national and EU policies.** Some environmental matters (for example, the environmental consequences of domestic road projects) are restricted in their effects to a specific territory whereas others affect several countries and some have global implications, for example, the emission of chlorofluorocarbon (CFC) gases. The UK has argued that the EU has no right to be involved in every nook and cranny of domestic policy and that the UK alone should decide on the environmental implications of projects with no cross-border dimension.

3. **Environmental policy has often proved difficult to implement and enforce.** In EU 12, only Denmark escaped admonition by the ECJ for failing to apply EU standards with regard to environmental legislation. The EU's chief legislative instrument for the implementation of environmental policy has been the directive, which provides member states with leeway in relation to when and how Community laws are transposed into national law.

4. **Environmental problems shows no signs of abating.** The Commission report on the Union's 5th 'Environmental Action Programme' predicted that without a change in current energy demand, there could be a 25% increase in energy use in the EU between 1990 and 2010. Figures produced by Eurostat in June 1994 showed that carbon dioxide emissions from households (with the exception of east Germany) and from transport (with the exception of Denmark) were increasing throughout the Union.

5. **The problem of reconciling environmental priorities with other policies.** The adverse environmental consequences of some Union policies (for example, commitment to industrial growth, the CAP or transport projects) are by no means easy to eliminate. This has often led to tension between the Commissioner for the Environment and other Commissioners. The White Paper on *Growth, Competitiveness and Employment*, however, argued that the pursuit of high environmental standards (reflected for example in the development of new, cleaner technologies) could enable European industry to 'trade up' to higher value-added activities. It stressed the need to exploit positive synergies between industrial competitiveness and

environmental protection. 'Environmental optimists' tend to view environmental protection as a creator of jobs, whereas 'environmental pessimists' regard it as a threat to international competitiveness.

6. Burden-sharing. Environmental improvements can be very costly: this raises the question of how much member states are prepared to contribute to environmental renovation in EU countries other than their own.

O   The Impact of the SEA and the TEU

The SEA marked a watershed in the development of EU environmental policy, by providing the Union with an explicit statutory mandate in this field. Prior to this, Union environmental policy had to be legitimised through a liberal interpretation of certain general provisions in the Treaty of Rome (such as the preamble which refers to the goal of improving living and working conditions). The SEA added a title on environmental policy to the Treaty of Rome (Title VII), declaring its objectives to be:

1. preserving, protecting and improving the quality of the environment;
2. protecting human health;
3. prudent and rational utilisation of natural resources.

The Title stated that the Community would act when these objectives could be attained better at Community level than at national level, an implicit reference to the 'subsidiarity' principle. It also stated that environmental protection requirements will be a component of other Community policies. It allowed member states to adopt more stringent measures providing they are compatible with the Treaty of Rome (Article 130t). The TEU further strengthened the Union's role in environment policy and also made the nature of this role somewhat more explicit. It added a fourth policy objective, viz.:

4. promoting measures at international level to deal with regional or world-wide environmental problems.

The TEU also states that a task of the Community is the promotion of 'sustainable and non-inflationary growth respecting the environment' (Article 2, EC). It commits the Community to aim for a high level of environmental protection, taking into account regional diversity (Article 130r, EC) It also states that environmental protection requirements must be integrated into other policies. Prior to ratification of the TEU, Council decisions on environmental policy were based on the 'unanimity' principle. The TEU (Article 130s, EC) provides for qualified majority voting on most environmental issues, although in some areas, such as fiscal measures, town and country planning and measures significantly affecting choices between different energy sources, the unanimity principle still applies. The article in the TEU which could have the biggest impact on Union environmental policy is Article 3b on subsidiarity. The TEU also established the Cohesion Fund, which finances environmental and transport projects in the four poorest member states.

● PROGRAMMES AND POLICIES

○ The Environmental Action Programmes

From 1973, the Union has adopted a series of environmental action programmes. The programmes are indicative rather than legally binding. However, many items contained in the programmes are eventually translated into Community law, although often after considerable argument, refinement and delay. The first action programme set out to:
- foster environmental awareness in member countries;
- conduct impact studies in member countries;
- prevent or reduce pollution and noise nuisances;
- introduce measures for the management of waste;
- promote clean technologies.

It also led to the establishment in 1975 of the principle that those guilty of polluting the environment should be made to pay (*the polluter pays principle*), which was given legal force in the SEA (Article 130r(2), EEC). The second and third programmes consolidated and further developed the ideas contained in the initial programme. The fourth programme (1987–92) was closely linked to the policies on the environment contained in the SEA. In particular, it sought to integrate Union environment policy with other policies and to establish common standards for environmental protection. The fifth programme (1993–2000) signals a shift in emphasis in Union environmental policy in several ways: it emphasises that policy should be geared towards prevention rather than correction of environmental damage; it favours a shift from the traditional 'top-down' (or command-and-control) approach based on regulatory environmental legislation towards a 'bottom-up' approach. The new approach has two essential features: it seeks to involve a broader range of actors and to employ a broader range of policy instruments, including economic incentives to promote 'environmentally friendly' products and improved information and education. The programme focuses on five target sectors: industry, energy, transport, agriculture and tourism.

In line with guidelines laid down in the programme, the Commission is seeking to ensure that environmental requirements are fully taken into account as soon as Union policies are conceived. Each of the Commission's

Directorates-General is required to choose an official charged with the task of ensuring that the environmental effects of legislative proposals are taken into account. They are also required to provide an annual report on the environmental dimension to their activities. Any project liable to have an environmental impact is now subject to a *strategic environmental impact assessment*. An Information Directive which came into effect on 31 December 1992 seeks to improve public access to environmental information held by public bodies with responsibilities in this field. These bodies must provide information on request to any person at a reasonable charge. There is an appeals procedure in case of refusal or failure to respond.

○ **The European Environment Agency**

The European Environment Agency is the successor to the 'Corine' programme (1985–90), which was an experimental project on the collection and collation of information on the state of the environment and natural resources within the Union. The Agency is based in Copenhagen and has been established to collect and publish comparative data on environmental conditions in member states. It will publish a report on the state of Europe's environment every three years. It also prepares reports on the EU's environmental action programmes. The EP wanted the Agency to have an enforcement role, but the Council would not agree to this. Its functions may be extended to include involvement in the monitoring of EU environmental legislation and preparation of criteria for the award of environmental labels. However, its staff (47) is arguably too small to take on wider responsibilities. The Agency started operations in the spring of 1994. It has a management board comprising one representative from each member state, two from the Commission and two designated by the EP. Its work focuses on several priority areas, including air and water quality, waste management, noise emissions, hazardous substances and coastal protection.

○ **Examples of Specific Environmental Policies**

Water. Measures have been introduced in relation to drinking water quality, sewage treatment and the discharge of dangerous substances into rivers and seas. Several member states (including the UK) have been taken to the ECJ because of alleged breach of the 1980 Drinking Water Directive. A considerable proportion of the UK's water industry investment programme is directed towards meeting EU standards on water and sewage treatment. There are still major marine pollution problems, particularly in relation to the North Sea, the Mediterranean and the Baltic Sea. Various measures against marine pollution have been introduced, for example in relation to bathing water quality and the promotion of clean beaches. The EU publishes an annual report on EU bathing water standards. A blue flag is awarded to the cleanest beaches in the EU.

Waste. The reduction, processing and recycling of waste is now regarded as a key priority. In the EU alone, more than 100 million tonnes of municipal waste and 21 million tonnes of toxic waste are produced each year. The first directive on waste recycling was adopted in 1975. A new directive on the disposal of hazardous waste was adopted in December 1991. There are standards relating to the classification and labelling of dangerous substances and a voluntary scheme for labelling environmentally less harmful products. Over 80% of packaging waste in the EU is currently dumped. In December 1994, the Council adopted a directive on packaging waste: between 50% and 65% of such waste is to be recovered and recycled rather than dumped within five years (Ireland, Greece and Portugal have temporary exemptions). The 'eco-labels' scheme launched by the Commission gives a seal of approval to producers meeting environmental criteria (currently applicable to dishwashers and washing machines). LIFE is a new programme which funds specific actions on the environment, such as projects to promote nature protection clean technologies and waste management. It has a budget of ECU 450 million for 1996–99.

Air. Atmospheric pollution is a main cause of 'global warming' and of 'acid rain'. Policies on air quality include: the limitation of atmospheric pollution by industrial plants and by motor vehicles; a ban on the use of chlorofluorocarbons (CFCs) in aerosols; and measures to promote use of unleaded petrol. Carbon dioxide (CO_2) emissions, from the use of coal and petrol, contribute to 'global warming' through the so-called 'greenhouse effect'. Although the EU is seeking to maintain carbon dioxide emissions at their 1990 levels by the year 2000, the Commission noted in 1994 that only Denmark and the Netherlands had completed programmes to reach this stabilisation target.

The Commission has on several occasions proposed a carbon/energy tax (commonly known as an *eco-tax*) with the combined aims of increasing energy efficiency and reducing pollution. The tax would be weighted towards fuels with the highest carbon content (with a target tax of 10 dollars on a barrel of oil). Renewable or non-polluting energy sources would be exempt from the tax. However, the proposal has run into determined opposition from several member states, principally on the grounds that it would handicap European industry and would be very unpopular with EU citizens. In October 1994, environment ministers again failed to reach agreement on a strategy for reducing carbon dioxide emissions. In May 1995, the Commission submitted a revised eco-tax proposal, which in effect would allow member states to choose whether or not to adopt it.

● THE INTERNATIONAL DIMENSION

○ The Pan-European Dimension

Because pollution knows no frontiers, it is essential that EU environment policy has a wider European dimension. Conferences involving environment ministers of both EU and non-EU European countries are held on a regular basis. The first pan-European environmental conference in 1991 led to the Commission being asked to prepare a report on the state of the environment for the whole of Europe. The third conference, held in Lucerne in April 1993, agreed an environmental action programme for Eastern Europe. The fifth was held in Sofia in October 1995. The EU is assisting environmental renovation programmes in Eastern Europe in various ways. Environmental renovation and protection are integral components of the Union's aid programmes for the region. Association agreements signed with Central and East European states contain environmental provisions.

○ The Global Dimension

The EU has been active in developing policies in relation to global environmental issues, such as climate change, depletion, of the ozone layer and deforestation. The Council has confirmed its commitment to implementing 'Agenda 21', a non-binding UN action plan for sustainable development into the 21st century, agreed at the UN Conference of the Environment and Development held in Rio de Janeiro in June 1992. Cognisance is also taken of Agenda 21 in the 5th Action Programme. But the decision by France to resume nuclear testing in the Pacific in 1995, although vigorously condemned by the EP and criticised also by several Union governments, may well have had negative 'fall-out' on the Union's global image on environmental issues.

FURTHER READING

Commission, COM (92), 23, *Towards Sustainability*, 1992.
Commission, COM (95), 647, *The 5th Action Programme* (Draft Review), 1995.
Haigh, N., *EEC Environmental Policy and Britain*, Longman, London, 1990.
Holl, O. (ed.), *Environmental Co-operation in Europe*, Westview, Oxford, 1993.
Judge, D., *A Green Dimension for the European Community: Political Issues and Processes*, Frank Cass, London, 1993.
Lieferingk, J.D., Mol, A.P. and Lowe, P. (eds), *European Integration and Environmental Policy*, Belhaven Press, London, 1993.

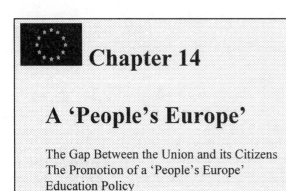

Chapter 14

A 'People's Europe'

● THE GAP BETWEEN THE UNION AND ITS CITIZENS

Although it is demonstrably true that European integration has touched the lives of all citizens of the European Union, in the vast majority of cases it has yet to touch their hearts and minds. It is probable that only a tiny minority of European citizens have an awareness of impact of Union policies on their lives, or even a basic understanding of how the Union operates. Although the Commission and the EP launched a joint campaign to encourage Europeans to vote in the elections to the EP in June 1994, voter turnout at 57%, was the lowest of the four direct elections held since 1979. The lack of public involvement in, and understanding of, Union affairs has been attributed to many causes, such as:

● **The domination of European affairs by political and technocratic elites.** European integration is still widely viewed as the concern of governments rather than of ordinary people. Eurosceptics attribute this to a desire of these elites to monopolise policy processes, or to deliberately hide their 'federalist' intentions from the European electorates. Euro-federalists, on the other hand, contend that levels of popular participation could and should be increased, by strengthening Union democracy and by increasing citizens' perceptions of the importance of the Union to their lives.

● **Lack of information about European affairs.** Although thousands of documents emanate from the Union every year, very few ever reach ordinary citizens. People are generally aware only of the aspects of the EU which affect them directly, such as cross-border shopping;

- **The Byzantine complexity of rules and procedures.** The Union's policymaking and implementation system, comprising a complex network of institutions and a vast web of technical rules and arcane procedures, is undoubtedly difficult to understand.
- **'Euro-jargon'.** The Union has developed a large vocabulary of technical terms (including more than 1,300 acronyms) which all but the most determined are likely to find off-putting.
- **The resilience of national identities.** Although the EU is seeking to encourage citizens to feel a sense of European identity, Europeans tend to think of themselves as citizens of a particular state rather than as European citizens *per se*. National, rather than European, issues still largely determine how people vote in elections to the EP.
- **Poor image.** If ordinary people think of the Union at all, they are likely to associate it with bureaucracy and waste. This poor image has been reinforced by a tendency of national politicians and the tabloid media to blame 'Brussels' for all national ills. Many national problems are falsely attributed to the European Union. 'Euromyths' and 'Euroscares' constitute a staple diet of stories about Europe in the British tabloid media. In an effort to counter these stories, the UK government periodically publishes a pamphlet debunking the more fantastic claims. Examples of these claims, taken from *Facts and Fairytales Revisited* (Foreign and Commonwealth Office, June 1995) are shown in Table 14.1. The real significance of such stories is not that they are demonstrably untrue, but that they derive from and reinforce the popular cartoon image of 'Brussels' as a rule-obsessed bureaucracy.

Table 14.1 Recent British Euromyths and Euroscares

- EU rules define snails as land-based fish;
- the Commission has produced a map of Europe on which the UK is labelled 'Mercia';
- the Commission has authorised a soap opera to promote the European ideal;
- EU rules prohibit square strawberries and curved cucumbers;
- feeding stale bread to swans is illegal under Community law;
- home-made cakes may no longer be sold in garden centres;
- the British army will be absorbed into a European army;
- pizza size is to be regulated by Community law;
- Brussels intends to 'harmonise' Christmas;
- the EU plans to outlaw beermats for being unhygienic;
- Community law will force UK motorists to drive on the right;
- herbal tea is to be classified as a drug.

● THE PROMOTION OF A PEOPLE'S EUROPE

○ The Goal of a 'People's Europe'

The need to bring European integration closer to ordinary people has been endorsed by several European Council meetings and is likely to figure prominently at the 1996 IGC. The notion of a Citizens' (or People's) Europe was endorsed at the European Council in Fountainebleau in June 1984. Following this meeting, a committee comprising representatives of heads of government and the Commission President, and headed by Pietro Adonnino, was appointed to explore ways of narrowing the gap between 'Europe' and the citizen. The Adonnino Committee's two reports were approved by the European Council in 1985. The reports advocated a raft of measures to foster the goal of a People's Europe, such as greater freedom of movement, promotion of European cultural, educational and sporting links, extension of citizens' rights and promotion of a European identity. But the sheer number and variety of specific proposals hardly served to clarify the notion of a People's Europe, which has remained rather vague and fuzzy. The promotion of a People's Europe is usually taken to comprise three elements, viz.:

- **promoting a European identity,** through the use of European symbols and the creation of a European citizenship;
- **enhancing public understanding of, and involvement in, the EU policy system,** by simplifying and opening up the decisionmaking process;
- **strengthening the European dimension of policies and activities,** through joint action on common problems and encouragement of cross-border links.

○ Promoting a European Identity

The EU already has many symbols of identity. The *European Flag* was chosen by the Council of Europe in 1955. It was not adopted by the Community until 1986. According to the Council of Europe, the number of stars was chosen as a 'symbol of perfection'. It will remain at 12, however many countries join the Union. The *European Anthem* (adopted in 1972) is the prelude to the 'Ode to Joy' from Beethoven's 9th Symphony. *Europe Day* (9 May, the date of the Schuman Declaration) was chosen by the European Council in Milan in 1985. The TEU established citizenship of the European Union (Article 8, EC), conferring rights and benefits, such as:

- the right to move and reside freely within the territory of member states (Article 8a);
- for EU citizens residing in another EU country, the right to vote and stand

as a candidate in elections to the EP and in municipal elections (Article 8b). A directive adopted by the Council in December 1994 set a deadline for the transposition of this right to vote in local elections at 1 January 1996 and limited candidature in local elections to office lower than mayor/deputy mayor;

- the right to petition the European Parliament. The EP's Petitions Committee examines complaints by citizens of discrimination by national authorities against EU citizens from another country (it received 1,352 petitions in 1994). Union citizens also have the right to raise cases of maladministration by any EU institution with an Ombudsman (Article 8d). The first Ombudsman, Jacob Söderman from Finland, was elected by MEPs in June 1995;
- stronger diplomatic protection outside the EU. Citizens have access to diplomatic and consular facilities of a member state other than their own if their own countries are not represented (Article 8c).

However, Union citizenship *complements*, but does not replace, national citizenship. Arguably, it largely falls into the category of 'concessions to foreigners' rather than genuine citizenship. It might also be argued that it is an attempt to create something artificially which can only develop naturally. Moreover, Europeans might even perceive Euro-citizenship as a threat to their national identities.

○ **Public Understanding of and Involvement in the EU Policy System**

The referenda held on the TEU in 1992 showed that public support for European integration could not be taken for granted. Throughout the EU, opinion polls also exposed widespread public ignorance about the contents of the Treaty. At the European Council in Edinburgh in December 1992, it was agreed that measures should be introduced by the Union to improve its openness, to simplify its procedures and to encourage dialogue with the public. This resulted in the adoption of a 'new approach' to information and communication policy and subsequent measures to increase the openness or 'transparency' of decisionmaking. In December 1993, the Council and Commission approved a code of conduct establishing general rules on the right of access to information from Union institutions. The code, reviewed every two years, sets out minimum requirements governing applications for information. Institutions can still refuse access to any document where disclosure could undermine the protection of the public or private interest, commercial or industrial secrecy, the Community's financial interests, or an institution's interest in the confidentiality of its proceedings.

The Commission's current information strategy for a People's Europe centres on the need to make information more widely available and easier for citizens to understand. Specific measures have included granting public access to all Commission documents (with exceptions relating to security) and making Union public data bases more user friendly. The Commission is encouraging 'active participation' of European citizens, by, for example, greater use of Green and White Papers, public hearings and conferences. Following the chastening experience of the TEU ratification process, the Commission is also seeking to encourage much wider participation in the discussions preceding the 1996 IGC than took place prior to Maastricht. But although such 'opening' measures are undoubtedly valuable, particularly to pressure groups, researchers and students, they hardly seem likely to have much direct impact on the general public.

○ **Strengthening the European Dimension of Policies and Activities**

Virtually all EU policies are expected to contribute in some way to the realisation of a People's Europe. Arguably, tangible policies are likely to have a bigger impact upon citizens' perceptions of the EU than symbols or information campaigns. The TEU extends the range and depth of the Union's involvement in various policy fields, such as education, culture, consumer policy and migration. Examples of the partial 'Europeanisation' of policies are given below.

● EDUCATION POLICY

There is no mention of education policy in the Treaty of Rome, although it does refer to 'training'. Although education remains primarily a national responsibility, the Commission has sought to promote the incorporation of a 'European dimension' into the education systems of member states. The main emphasis of Union 'education policy' is on voluntary co-operation. The TEU espouses educational objectives for the Union, but these are rather vague and are qualified by an explicit acknowledgement of member states' responsibility for the content of teaching and the organisation of education systems (Article 126, EC). EU education policy has centred on the promotion of inter-university co-operation programmes (of which there are currently more than 2,500) and the injection of a 'European dimension' into teaching. Substantial progress has been made on the mutual recognition of qualifications. University degrees and higher education diplomas awarded after at least three years' study are now recognised in all member countries (although in some cases aptitude tests are taken). There are other rules for more specialised diplomas and qualifications.

Until January 1995, when the SOCRATES and LEONARDO programmes came into force, there were six main EU education programmes: ERASMUS, LINGUA, COMETT, FORCE, PETRA and EUROTECNET. In June 1994, the Council agreed that these would be regrouped into two five-year action programmes: SOCRATES (action linked to universities, schools and establishments of higher education) and LEONARDO for vocational training. SOCRATES has a budget of ECU 850 million and LEONARDO of ECU 620 million for 1995–99. From 1995, all Union education programmes were open to participation by all countries in the European Economic Area.

SOCRATES promotes co-operation between educational institutions and provides funds for students to study at institutions outside their own countries. It supports actions in three spheres: higher education (a minimum of 55% of the budget), school education (a minimum of 10%) and 'horizontal actions' relating to language teaching, open and distance education and exchanges (a minimum of 25%). It took over the work of ERASMUS (which focused on cross-border inter-university co-operation and student exchanges) and LINGUA (language learning). It extended cross-border educational co-operation to schools, at nursery, primary and secondary levels, although the budget for school education is so far small. It also took over two other programmes: EURYDICE (promoting information exchanges on education systems) and ARION (study visits for educational specialists).

LEONARDO supports three strands of measures: support for members' vocational training systems and policies; promotion of innovation in training programmes; and support for language skills in vocational training. It covers activities supported by the COMETT, PETRA, FORCE and EUROTECNET programmes. COMETT (launched 1987) aims to improve training in advanced technology by fostering co-operation between universities and enterprises. In the second phase of the programme (1990–94), 11,000 European organisations were involved in 507 projects. PETRA (launched in 1987) is an action programme for the vocational training of people under 28. It provides for work experience or traineeships in another Union country. FORCE promotes continuing vocational training in the EU (for example, through exchange programmes between managerial staff). EUROTECNET seeks to promote innovation in the field of vocational training and technological change. In addition to its educational programmes, the Union also operates a Youth For Europe programme, which promotes exchange projects between young people between 15 and 25. About one-third of the Youth for Europe budget (ECU 126 million for 1995–99) is earmarked for those not having access to the other education programmes.

Union educational programmes, particularly in the fields of inter-university co-operation and student exchanges, have undoubtedly become established features of the education sectors of member states. But these remain essentially adjuncts to national educational systems rather than serious threats to them. A host of factors (not least the diversity of educational traditions, the enormous cost of education and 'subsidiarity') seem likely to ensure that education remains primarily a national responsibility.

● CULTURAL POLICY

The Union's cultural policy has two principal objectives: to foster regional and national traditions and to reinforce a sense of European identity. The TEU (Article 128, EC) states that the Community shall contribute to the flowering of the cultures of member states, while respecting their national and regional diversity. Specific cultural programmes include KALEIDOSCOPE (support for cultural events involving at least three member states); the MEDIA programme, which aims to promote a more integrated European audio-visual industry; and RAPHAEL, a cultural heritage programme. There is also a European Union youth orchestra. The European City of Culture programme established in 1985 is hosted by a different European city each year (Copenhagen 1996; Thessaloniki 1997). In order to promote links with the wider Europe, a programme of European 'cultural months' was established in 1990 (St Petersburg 1996; Ljubjana 1997). Some critics question the need for a European cultural policy, arguing that cultural developments should be left to the market or to the public sectors of member states. Nor is there unanimous agreement on the purpose and direction of cultural policy: for example, not all states share France's enthusiasm to counter American domination of the film industry.

● CONSUMER POLICY

Consumer policy affects citizens directly and tangibly, and therefore is an important aspect of the goal of bringing the Union closer to the European citizen. The TEU states that the Community 'shall contribute to a high level of consumer protection' (Article 129a, EC). The principal aim of the Union's consumer policy is to *complement* rather than replace national policies. There was no specific mention of consumer policy in the Treaty of Rome. Although a consumer protection unit within the Directorate-General for Competition was established in 1968, consumer policy remained undeveloped, due primarily to differences in national approaches, technical standards and product regulations. Several factors led to greater emphasis on consumer policy: the growth of the consumer movement in member states; the entry of the UK and Denmark, both of which had strong consumer traditions; and increasing recognition that the free market approach was insufficient to ensure high consumer standards.

In 1975, the Council agreed a programme for a consumer protection and information policy, based on five fundamental rights: protection of consumers' health and safety; protection of consumers' economic interests; the right to information and education; the right to redress; and the right to consumer representation and participation. It envisaged action to safeguard consumers' interests in foodstuffs, textiles, toys, credit and advertising. The second programme, launched in 1981, recognised two other objectives, the inclusion of the interests of consumers in all EC policies; and the promotion of dialogue between representatives of consumers, producers and distributors. The third consumer protection programme was launched in 1986 to coincide with the White Paper on the Single Market. The SEA (Article 100a) refers to a high degree of protection for consumers in Single Market legislation. The third programme introduced the 'new approach' doctrine, meaning that essential requirements would be specified in general terms, leaving the details to be developed by the standardisation bodies. An independent Consumer Policy Service was created by the Commission in 1989. European consumer 'infocentres' have been established in areas where there is significant cross-border traffic. The Commission has a Consumer Committee, comprising representatives from national consumer organisations and public bodies, to advise it on consumer policies.

● FREEDOM OF MOVEMENT

○ A Border-free Union?

The notion of a 'People's Europe' is probably most visibly manifested in the Union's policies on freedom of movement. Since 1985, EU passports have been replacing national passports. There are special channels for EU citizens at air and sea ports. There has been mutual recognition of driving licences since 1983. A directive in force from July 1996 abolished the need for EU citizens to change driving licences when residing in another EU country. Considerable progress has been made on the removal of restrictions on cross-border travel by Union citizens, including customs and excise checks on luggage and goods, although for various reasons governments have been reluctant to scrap intra-Union border controls altogether. The UK government argues that passport checks are the only effective way of distinguishing between EU citizens and others.

About five million EU citizens reside in a member state other than their own. Article 48 of the Treaty of Rome gave European workers the right of freedom of movement and to work in any member state, although Article 48 (4) specified that this did not extend to public service employment. The ECJ ruled in 1980 that this clause only applied to certain public posts, such as those conferring responsibility for safeguarding state interests (for example, the police, judiciary, army or diplomatic service). The SEA introduced measures to abolish various impediments to free movement for workers, such as qualifying periods for eligibility for employment. Those working in another member state require a residence permit valid for five years and renewable on request (they can only be refused a permit on the grounds of public policy, security or health). This right is extended automatically to the person's family. Citizens may stay to look for work in another member state for a 'reasonable' period (up to six months). They may continue to receive unemployment benefit from their home countries for up to three months, providing they register as jobseekers in the host country. They must possess an identity card and forms E303 (issued by the body responsible for paying unemployment benefit) and E119 issued by the health insurance authority.

It is now easier for EU citizens to move within the Union without losing benefit entitlements. Insurance contributions paid in another member state are taken into account when benefits are being assessed in the host country. Citizens may also receive certain benefits from the home country whilst living in another member country. Retired people may reside permanently in a member state in which they have lived for three years or have worked for one year. Citizens on short visits to other member states (of up to one year) are entitled to urgent medical and dental treatment at free or reduced cost, providing they obtain an E111 form. Students have a right to live in any member state, providing they can support themselves financially and are not a charge on the host country's social security system.

◯ The Schengen Agreement

This Agreement is separate from, but complementary to, EU policy to abolish border controls. It is a good example of a 'vanguard' integration project, involving a group of EU states. Only Union states can join 'Schengen'. Schengen provisions are compatible with Community law but separate from it. The Commission has observer status in the Schengen group. The Agreement commits the signatories to abolish internal land, sea and air border controls. Citizens of signatory countries should therefore be able to travel within the 'Schengen zone' as freely as US citizens within the US: for example, airports are required to treat passengers from other Schengen countries in the same way as domestic passengers. Airports are therefore regarded as internal borders for flights within the zone and as external borders for flights to or from other countries.

The Agreement originated from the Saarbrucken agreement between France and Germany in July 1984, which sought to abolish frontier controls between the two countries. The Benelux countries soon became involved and an agreement was signed by these five countries in Schengen (Luxembourg) in June 1985. Italy signed in November 1990 and Spain and Portugal in June 1991. Greece and Austria have also signed the agreement but have not yet begun to implement it (nor has Italy). Denmark, Sweden, Finland, the UK and Ireland are currently outside the system, although Denmark has observer status. Denmark, Sweden and Finland are part of a Scandinavian passport system allowing for free movement between Scandinavian countries, including Norway. Because the Schengen Agreement requires signatories to be members of the Union, the Scandinavian system would create complications concerning Norway's position if Denmark, Finland and Sweden joined. They are likely to join once an agreement is reached on this issue. The UK is currently sceptical about the ability of Schengen to achieve tight external frontiers. The UK's position is an obstacle to the entry of Ireland, because if Ireland joined and the UK did not, it could mean extra border controls between the two countries.

The Schengen Convention, signed in June 1990, sets out the rules concerning common treatment of non-EU nationals and the measures needed to replace internal border controls with a system of common controls, for example:

- tight controls against illegal immigration including checks on identity papers when entering the zone;
- applicants for asylum are not allowed to 'shop around'. If they are refused asylum in one Schengen country, they are deemed to have been refused in all;
- if the presence of a non-EU national is deemed illegal in one Schengen country, it is deemed illegal in all and he or she will be expelled from the Union (either to their home country or to a third country);
- movement towards a common set of visa requirements and exemptions in relation to visitors from outside the EU. Because of differences in national policies, there are currently three visa categories: some countries require no visa (for example, the US, Norway, Hungary); others require a single visa (for example, Turkey, China) and others (for example, Australia and Brazil) require visas for some Schengen states;
- non-EU nationals meeting common conditions for entry may travel freely within the Schengen zone for up to three months;
- exchange of information and co-operation between police and

immigration authorities.

The Schengen Information System (SIS) exchanges information between these authorities on illegal drugs, weapons and other undesirable commodities. Its main data base, located in Strasbourg, stores information on arrest warrants, missing persons, stolen documents and goods, and so on. It is not connected to Interpol, the police co-operation centre in Lyons. It is also separate from Europol, which is an EU body (see below).

The implementation of the Schengen Convention was delayed for five years because of various disagreements between the signatories. The main problems have centred on mechanisms for effective co-operation between police and immigration authorities, doubts about the effectiveness of external controls around 'Schengenland' and differences in domestic policies. In October 1993, all Schengen countries agreed to abolish border controls by December 1993, providing certain conditions were met, such as tighter checks on non-EU nationals entering the zone, extra vigilance concerning drug trafficking; and computerised linking of police and immigration authorities. However, concern about lax border controls meant that the target date was not reached.

The Convention came into force on 26 March 1995 although full implementation did not commence until 1 July. Seven countries agreed to participate (Belgium, the Netherlands, Luxembourg, Germany, Portugal, Spain and France), but in June 1995 France suspended full participation due to its concerns about internal security. Greece and Italy did not participate, due to problems concerning the control of coastal frontiers and delays in preparing for exchange of data between police forces. Austria's participation is scheduled to begin in 1997.

◯ Migration from Outside the EU

The number of people seeking to migrate to other countries has increased markedly in recent years as a result of wide disparities in wealth between rich and poor countries, the prevalence of war and other factors. There are at least eight million non-EU nationals resident in EU 15. People from outside the EU seeking to immigrate to EU countries are generally divided into two categories: *asylum seekers* (refugees from war or oppression) and *economic migrants* (those seeking to improve their economic situation). The latter are no longer welcome in any EU country and the sheer numbers of asylum seekers has led to the imposition of strict rules and curbs on asylum. The number of requests for political asylum in EU 12 increased from less than 60,000 in 1983 to more than 500,000 in 1993.

Each member state has developed its own immigration policies. However, growing recognition that EU countries face similar migration problems, combined with efforts to remove the EU's internal borders, has led to greater intergovernmental co-operation in this field. There has already been some standardisation of EU migration policy, In 1985, the Commission issued guidelines for a Community policy on migration. At the end of 1991, Union ministers adopted a 'host third countries' resolution, allowing for refugees to be returned to the country from which they came. To prevent migrants from 'shopping around', if an asylum seeker is refused asylum by one Union country, he or she is deemed to have been refused by all. A special declaration on asylum was attached to the TEU. The TEU placed visa policy within the EC pillar. The Treaty required the Council to adopt a common visa policy, with decisions taken by qualified majority voting, by 1 January 1996 (Article 100c, EC). However, the objective of a common visa policy has proved difficult to achieve, primarily because of disagreements between member states concerning the list of third countries to which visa requirements are to apply.

● CO-OPERATION ON JUSTICE AND HOME AFFAIRS

There is no common European legal zone, penal code or police force and no European equivalent of the US Federal Bureau of Investigation. Moreover, none of these seem likely to emerge for the foreseeable future, because judicial matters tend to involve inherently contentious and sensitive issues. European co-operation in policing and other judicial matters of 'common interest, such as customs co-operation and co-operation in security matters, preceded the TEU. For example, the TREVI Group was established in 1975 as an intergovernmental forum for co-operation in policing as a result of growing terrorism (TREVI is an acronym for 'Terrorisme, Radicalisme, Extrémisme, Violence Internationale'). Its brief was later broadened to cover general police matters and international crime such as drug trafficking.

The TEU codified and substantially extended co-operation in judicial and home affairs. Title IV of the TEU stated that member states should regard several matters in this field as of 'common interest': these included asylum policy, immigration policy, judicial co-operation in civil and criminal matters and preventing and combating drug trafficking and terrorism. Title IV work is supervised by the Justice and Home Affairs Council and prepared by the 'K4' Committee of senior officials and by COREPER. The Committee is supported by various subcommittees and working groups, comprising a very complex network. The TEU also established a European Police Office (Europol), charged with exchanging information on police matters on a Union-wide basis. In October 1993, the Council agreed that Europol and its first stage, the Europol Drugs Unit, would be sited in The Hague. The Drugs

Unit opened in February 1994 and is concerned with co-ordinating and analysing intelligence on drugs trafficking and associated money laundering.

Most of the TEU's provisions on JHA matters are proving difficult to implement, due to the complexities of the issues involved, the reluctance of member states to pool sovereignty in these policy areas and the cumbersome decisionmaking process associated with the pillars structure. The Commission, the EP and also some governments would like to see the abolition of the JHA pillar and the integration of JHA matters into a single Union framework. This issue will be considered by the 1996 IGC.

FURTHER READING

Close, P., *Citizenship, Europe and Change*, Macmillan, London, 1995.

Coenen, H. and Leisink, P., *Work and Citizenship in the New Europe*, Edward Elgar, Cheltenham, 1993.

Collinson, S., *Europe and International Migration*, RIIA, London, 1994.

Meehan, Elizabeth, *Citizenship and the European Community*, Sage, London, 1993.

Preston, J., *EC Education, Training and Research Programmes*, Kogan Page, London, 1991.

Rosas, A. and Antola, E., *A Citizen's Europe. In Search of a New Order*, Sage, London, 1995.

Smith, J., *Citizen's Europe*, RIIA, London, 1994.

 **Chapter 15**

The European Union in the Global Economy

● TRENDS IN THE GLOBAL ECONOMY

○ Why Global Economic Trends are Important to the Union

The European Union is the world's largest trading entity and has the world's largest market. It has less than 7% of the world's population but accounts for about a quarter of world GDP and for about two-fifths of world trade (if trade between EU members is included). The EU is also the world's largest importer of many goods, including agricultural products, textiles and clothing. Access to the EU's big market is therefore of crucial importance to many countries outside the Union. But the economic health of the Union also depends upon the ability of Union countries to compete successfully in world markets. According to the Commission, more than 12 million jobs in the EU depend directly on the export of goods. The EU economies are currently facing major challenges of adaptation, as a result of structural changes in the global economy – for example, growing international economic inter-dependence, rapid technological change, the decline of traditional industries and the rise of East Asian 'tiger economies'. Within the Union, there is currently a fierce debate about how to rise to these challenges. It will be useful, therefore, to examine the Union's external trading position in the context of global economic change.

○ Key Global Economic Trends

Perhaps the most fundamental trend in the global economy is towards the internationalisation of production, finance and markets (Table 15.1).

Table 15.1 Key Developments in the Global Economy

* **unprecedented growth:** in international trade, in foreign direct and indirect investment and in world production;
* **increasing international interdependence,** manifested in (1) and also in the growth of transnational production chains;
* **globalisation,** manifested in (1) and (2). The concept also embraces the notions of global markets, industries and products;
* **rapid industrial change,** manifested for example in the decline of traditional, and the rise of new, industries and production systems;
* **the communications revolution,** manifested for example in high-tech telecommunications and transport networks;
* **the emergence of new 'growth poles',** particularly in the Far East;
* **the spread of market-based economic systems,** for example, the integration of former communist states into the global economy and the global privatisation revolution;
* **the 'new protectionism':** for example, the widespread use of non-tariff barriers to international trade, such as 'voluntary export restraints' and anti-dumping legislation;
* **the growth of regional economic co-operation:** for example, attempts to create regional trading formations in North America, South America, Asia and Europe;
* **the rise of the green movement,** which constitutes a challenge to growth-oriented ideologies. It is affecting patterns of energy use, production processes and products.

A central role in the globalisation process is being played by foreign direct investment (FDI) by multinational companies (MNCs). These are companies which locate productive assets, such as factories or retail outlets, in more than one country. MNCs now control about one-third of the world's private sector productive assets, with a turnover greater than the total of world exports. A finished product is increasingly likely to contain components manufactured in several countries. This growth in 'international sourcing' has been attributed to a combination of factors, such as improvements in communications, the cross-border production chains operated by MNCs and to the rise in the number of states capable of producing high-quality goods.

The EU is both a major recipient and source of FDI (Table 15.2), although there is considerable variation in FDI flows from and to member states. In 1992, Germany and France accounted for about half of all EU direct investment into non-EU countries, whereas the UK received 43.6% of all direct investment into the EU by non-EU countries. Intra-EU direct investment (direct investment between member states) is also distributed very unevenly. In 1992, France and Germany were the source of about half of all intra-EU direct investment, whereas the UK, France, Belgium, Spain and the Netherlands were the largest recipients. Intra-EU direct investment grew from ECU 10.5 billion in 1986 to ECU 38 billion in 1992. The SEM programme is widely regarded as having provided a major, although by no means the only, stimulus to both inward and intra-EU direct investment.

Table 15.2 External Origins and Destinations of EU FDI (1990–92)

Outward from EU12 (ECU Million)			Inward into EU12 (ECU Million)		
Cumulative 1990/92		%	Cumulative 1990/92		%
US	21,112	34	US	26,559	35
Japan	1,689	3	Japan	8,151	11
EFTA	8,707	14	EFTA	21,445	28
Other Western industrialised states	8,628	14	Other Western industrialised states	7,238	9
ACP (excluding OPEC)	2,411	4	ACP (excluding OPEC)	1,547	1
Other developing states	12,349	20	Other developing states	8,405	11
Former communist states	3,637	6	Former communist states	1,608	2
Other countries	2,989	5	Other countries	2,822	4
Total	61,522	100	Total	76,775	100

ACP = African, Caribbean and Pacific countries (signatories to the Lomé agreements with the EU); OPEC = Organisation of Petroleum Exporting Countries.
Source: Eurostat, Europe in Figures, 1995.

International trade, often described as the engine of economic growth, has increased faster than world output in almost every year in recent decades. Between 1950 and 1994, world merchandise trade has increased 14 times, whereas world merchandise output increased 5.5 times, both in real terms (World Trade Organisation, 1995, p. 15). The growth in world trade is partly attributable to *trade liberalisation*: tariffs on manufactures have fallen from 40% at the end of the Second World War to less than 5%, although these falls have been significantly offset by the increase in *non-tariff* barriers to trade, such as import quotas and technical regulations. The geographical distribution of world production is very uneven. The EU, US and Japan account for about 15% of the world's potential labour force but produce about 70% of world GDP. But there is growing evidence that the balance of world economic power may be shifting towards Asia. The economies of Hong Kong, South Korea, Taiwan and Singapore have grown considerably faster than those of the Western developed economies in the past two decades. There is now a new generation of 'Asian Tigers' (for example Thailand, Malaysia and, most importantly, China). Integration of Eastern Europe into the global economy is also highly significant, particularly for the Union which has assumed special responsibilities for this region.

● EU TRADING PATTERNS

○ The Structure of EU Trade

The structure of EU trade falls into two categories: firstly, trade between EU countries (*intra-Union trade*) and secondly trade between EU countries and the outside world (*extra-Union trade*). Intra-Union trade (at about 60% of total EU trade) is significantly greater than intraregional trade in other parts of the world. For example, just over a third of Japan's exports go to the Asia–Pacific region and about a third of US exports go to North and South America. Union membership is likely to result in a substantial increase in the proportion of a country's trade accounted for by 'intra-Union' trade (Table 15.3). The expansion of intra-Union trade has largely been due to *intra-industry trade* (for example, where two countries both import and export machinery) rather than to increasing specialisation (for example, where one country would specialise in manufacturing and the other in food products).

Table 15.3 Intra-EU Trade in 1958 and 1992 (as % of Total Trade)

	Exports (%)			Imports (%)		
	1958		1992	1958		1992
Belgium/Lux	55.4		74.8	55.5		71.2
Denmark	59.3		54.5	60.0		55.4
Germany	37.9		54.1	36.3		54.7
Greece	50.9	48.2*	64.2	53.7	40.9*	62.7
Spain	46.8	53.3#	66.3	31.8	37.9#	60.3
France	30.9		63.0	28.3		65.6
Ireland	82.4		74.2	68.9		71.9
Netherlands	58.3		75.4	50.7		58.8
Portugal	38.9	62.5#	74.8	53.4	45.9#	73.6
UK	21.7		55.5	21.8		50.7
EU12	37.2		61.3	35.2		59.3

* = 1980; # = 1985; *Source*: Eurostat, 1994.

Prior to the fourth enlargement, EFTA was the EU's leading trading partner, accounting for almost a quarter of the EU's external trade. Trade with EFTA has been relatively harmonious, possibly because it is roughly balanced 'intra industry' trade. The US is the EU's single most important trading partner (Table 15.4). There have been a series of trade disputes between the EU and the US, but these have not resulted in an all-out trade war. Whereas the EU's trade with the US is broadly balanced, the Union has a substantial trade deficit with Japan (Figure 15.1). Almost all of the EU's imports from Japan are manufactured goods.

Figure 15.1 Trade and FDI Between the EU, US and Japan (in ECU Billion)

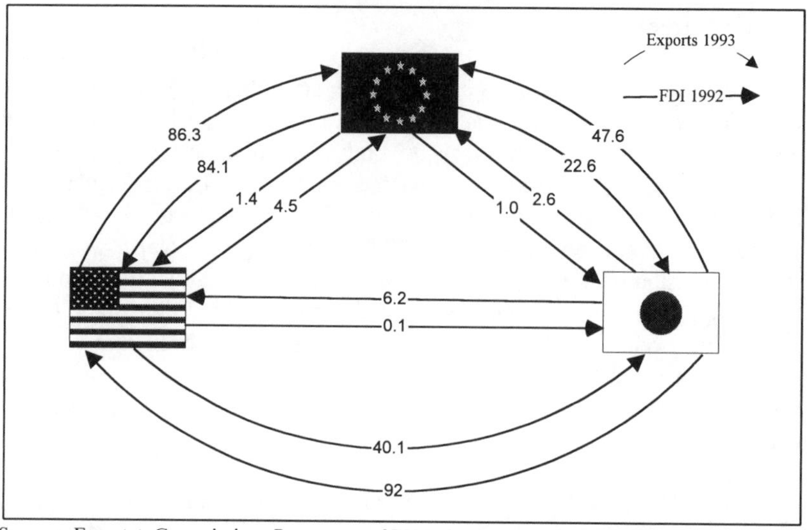

Sources: Eurostat; Commission, *Panorama of EU Industry 1994*, Brussels, 1995.

Table 15.4 The EU's Main Trade Partners (% of Total Extra-EU Trade)

Country	Exports (1993)	Imports (1993)
US	17.5	17.3
Japan	6.7	9.7
Switzerland	8.1	7.4
Austria	6.1	4.6
Sweden	4.3	4.8
Norway	2.1	3.6
Former Soviet Union	3.3	4.0
Other CEECs	6.6	5.2
ACP Countries	3.4	3.1
OPEC	8.4	8.4
Newly Industrialised Countries	7.0	6.4
China	2.3	4.1
Latin America	4.8	4.5

CEECs = Central and Eastern European countries. *Source*: Eurostat, *Yearbook*, 1995.

EU trade with the Third World consists largely of the export of manufactures and the import of raw materials, agricultural products and low-tech manufactures. The EU currently has a trade surplus with many developing countries and with many transition economies in Eastern Europe. Comparative data on the product compositions of EU, US, Japanese and

EFTA trade is shown in Table 15.5. About three-quarters of EU exports consists of manufactures, but the EU is also a substantial exporter of agricultural products.

Table 15.5 Comparison of Trade Patterns by Product Category (1993)

Product Category	Imports				Exports			
	EU	US	Japan	EFTA	EU	US	Japan	EFTA
Food, Drink,Tobacco	7.5	5.1	16.3	6.4	7.5	8.7	0.6	4.0
Crude Materials	6.2	2.8	11.8	4.0	1.9	5.3	0.6	4.3
Oils	0.4	0.2	0.2	0.2	0.3	0.3	0.0	0.1
Energy	13.1	9.8	20.5	6.1	3.2	2.1	0.5	9.2
Chemicals	7.0	5.1	7.3	11.7	13.0	9.9	5.6	13.1
Manufactured Goods	14.5	11.5	11.0	17.8	16.4	8.4	11.0	23.3
Machinery, Transport Equipment	31.0	44.0	17.0	34.5	42.6	48.4	72.0	31.9
Misc Manuf. Articles	16.8	18.1	13.8	18.7	13.2	11.7	8.0	13.5
Others	3.5	3.4	2.0	0.5	1.9	5.2	1.7	0.4
	100.0	100.0	100.0	100.0	100.0	100.0	100.0	100.0

Source: Eurostat, *External Trade*, 1995.

❍ The EU's Declining Position as a World Trader

The EU currently has a major problem of poor global competitiveness in many manufacturing sectors, such as vehicles, textiles and electronics. The EU's trading position would be much worse were it not for Germany's success as an exporter of manufactures. Germany has consistently had a trade surplus with most other countries, including the US and Japan, whereas several (including the UK) have had substantial trade deficits in recent years. EU imports of high-tech products have been growing at almost twice the rate of EU exports of such products. Conversely, the proportion of low-tech goods in EU exports has increased. Germany accounts for a substantial proportion of high-tech goods produced by the EU. The EU's poor external trade performance has been attributed to a variety of possible causes, for example to high labour costs, over-regulated labour markets, poor productivity, technological lag and 'unfair' competition from low-wage economies. In the 1980s, labour costs in the EU grew by 4% a year, compared with little increase in Japan and none in the US. The US and Japan spend less on welfare per capita, but higher proportions of their GDP on RTD, than the EU.

The White Paper on *Growth, Competitiveness and Employment* (1993) argued that EU industry must enhance industrial competitiveness by trading up to higher value-added activity (in new high-tech industries) rather than by trading down, meaning drastically reducing the wages of EU workers to the levels pertaining in Asian Tiger economies. This would not only be politically impossible, but would make no economic sense as the White Paper recognised. Another possible solution is that of *protectionism* (thereby insulating the EU economy from external economic pressures). For various reasons however (see below), this 'solution' would probably be worse than the disease. Another solution involves state aid for industry, in particular through financial support for ailing firms or for firms selected for their growth potential ('Eurochampions'). But state aids are not only costly to the taxpayer, they also cushion subsidised industries from market disciplines.

● EU TRADE POLICY AND TRADE RELATIONSHIPS

○ Responsibilities

EU trade policy derives from the Common Commercial Policy (CCP) established in Article 113 of the Treaty of Rome, which transferred tariff and general trade policy from the national level. The CCP embraces a common tariff regime, common trade agreements with third countries and uniform application of trade policy instruments. The Commission proposes trade policy under Article 113, but decisions are taken by the Council, mainly by qualified majority vote. Anti-dumping and countervailing duties decisions are now decided by simple majority; association agreements – negotiated under Article 238 – require unanimity. Several Commission DGs are involved in trade policy, in particular: DGI (External Economic Relations), DGVI (Agriculture), DGVIII (Development) and DGIV (Competition). This sometimes leads to confusion concerning the EU's negotiating position.

A committee of the Council (the '113 Committee') comprising national officials and permanent representatives meets regularly to consider trade negotiations and agreements. The EP has no automatic right to be consulted on trade agreements concluded under Article 113, although it is kept informed and its views on these agreements may be taken into account. Its assent is, however, required for 'association' (Article 238) and 'trade and co-operation' (Article 228) agreements and on several occasions it has used this power to block specific agreements.

Article 113 bestows on the Commission the competence to enter into negotiations on general trade and tariff policy with non-member countries. In the early 1990s, the Commission was engaged in seven sets of external trade negotiations: the Uruguay Round of GATT; the fourth Lomé Convention (aid and trade to 70 developing countries); the fourth multifibre agreement (MFA); the reform of the Generalised System of Preferences (GSP);

negotiation of the EEA agreement with EFTA; negotiation of association agreements with East European countries; and negotiations with Japan over market access. EU countries undoubtedly benefit in terms of 'clout' from this collective approach to external trade negotiations. But it also limits the independence of member states. The interests of member states in relation to external trade are by no means easy to reconcile, a problem which increases with every enlargement. For example, some member states have car industries to protect, whereas others do not. There have been fierce disagreements between EU countries over trade negotiations with the US and over the extent of market access to be granted to the new democracies of Eastern Europe.

The EU does not as yet have a fully common commercial policy, because member states still pursue national trade policies in some key areas. For example, export promotion is still largely a national responsibility. Member states can also apply for deviations from the CCP. The extent to which responsibility for external trade policy has been transferred from the national level is still not fully clear, despite a ruling by the ECJ in 1975 that the CCP covers all trade instruments. Since 1980 the Commission has negotiated on behalf of all member states in the GATT forum, even though it is the member states, not the EU, which are the contracting parties to GATT. EU states signed the GATT agreement in Marrakesh in April 1994 separately, and in accordance with the alphabetical order of GATT. The GATT deal had to be ratified by the Council, the EP and national legislatures.

As a result of its dissatisfaction with the agreement reached by the Commission in the Uruguay Round of GATT, France disputed the Commission's right to negotiate on trade on behalf of all members. In April 1994, the Commission asked the ECJ to examine the issue of responsibility. The Court gave its opinion the following November, ruling that the Community had exclusive powers in relation to trade in goods and in the cross-border supply of services. It confirmed that the Community had exclusive powers in the areas of trade in services and goods covered by intellectual property rights where Community legislation had achieved complete harmonisation or where there are provisions relating to the treatment of nationals of non-member countries. But in relation to other issues concerning services and intellectual property, it decided that responsibility is shared between the Community and member states.

○ Is the EU Protectionist?

The EU's posture towards the world is described in Commission literature as being 'open to the world and in solidarity with it'. However, the EU by no means practices open trade in relation to non-EU countries, as the list of protectionist instruments and preferential agreements below shows. The EU is hardly unique in practising 'managed trade' (a euphemism for protectionism). Moreover, the use of protectionist instruments has not prevented substantial import penetration of EU markets by Japan and the NICs. It has been argued that collective decisionmaking in relation to the CCP has a protectionist bias, because member states tend to support each others' protectionist demands on a *quid pro quo* basis: for example, one country will agree to support protection of the car industry, if another will agree to support protection of footwear. Nevertheless, some countries are less protectionist than others. The EU 12 'trade liberals' were the UK, Germany, the Netherlands, Luxembourg, Denmark and Belgium. By contrast, Spain, Portugal, Italy and France have tended to be the most protectionist. Sweden, Finland and Austria have pursued protectionist policies in services and agriculture, but less so in industrial products where they have a strong comparative advantage. Protectionist industrial lobbies are active both in Brussels and within member countries.

The principal protectionist argument is that free trade is not fair trade, because foreign competitors have unfair advantages, such as subsidies and lower labour costs. The consequence of opening EU markets to 'unfair' competition, according to the protectionists, is the destruction of European industries. The protectionist case is often buttressed by the 'breathing spell' argument, that European industries need to be shielded from foreign competition until they are fit to compete. It has also been argued that EU policies of 'social protection' (as enunciated in the Social Charter) can only work if cheaper foreign goods (produced in countries were social protection is minimal) are kept out of EU markets. The problem with protectionist solutions to adverse trade balances is that domestic industries have little incentive to become more efficient or to engage in restructuring, because they are shielded from external competition. Protectionism has certainly contributed to Eurosclerosis and at least partly explains why the EU has fallen behind its main competitors in the production of high-tech goods. Protectionist measures are likely to provoke retaliation, leading to a spiral of tit-for-tat actions. Moreover, enrichment of East Asia and of Eastern Europe through trade could create new opportunities for EU exporters.

○ **Instruments**

The EU has an armoury of instruments to facilitate 'managed trade', viz.:
• **The Common External Tariff.** The CET imposes a system of harmonised tariffs (about 9,500 tariff lines) on exports from outside the Union. Once the tariff has been paid in one EU country, an additional tariff does not have to be paid if the good is then moved to a second EU country.

- **Quantitative Restrictions.** Under Article 115 of the Treaty of Rome, a member state has been able to impose quantitative restrictions on imports from outside the EU, even if these imports have already entered the EU via another member state. If goods were free to circulate, then Japanese car manufacturers could attack the French car market via Denmark (which has no car industry to protect). In 1994, all national quantitative restrictions maintained by member states were removed and Union-wide quotas were introduced on seven product categories. A member state can still request the Commission to authorise a temporary suspension of certain products from Union treatment.
- **Anti-Dumping and Countervailing Measures.** 'Dumping' is (1) the export of goods below the cost of production or (2) charging different prices in different markets (below the price charged in the exporter's home country). Union-wide anti-dumping measures were introduced in 1990. Within the EU there are about 100 complaints and about 14 actions against dumping each year. The most affected sectors have been chemicals and electronics, but steel, cars, typewriters, photocopiers, printers, textiles, cement, fork lift trucks and flowers have all been subject to duties. In 1994, the Commission initiated 18 anti-dumping investigations and the Council imposed definitive anti-dumping duties in 14 cases. Industries must provide evidence of dumping and of its effects. Anti-dumping applications should normally be made by a trade organisation or by a company acting on behalf of a substantial proportion of producers (national or Union-wide). The Commission may then investigate and impose anti-dumping duties. Many investigations take more than 18 months. A provisional duty may be imposed before the investigation is complete. Many investigations are terminated following price undertakings. Anti-dumping restraints are normally agreed for 3 years and in general lapse after 5 (the *sunset clause*). 'Countervailing duties' are imposed when exporters are subsidised, to the damage of competitors in the home market. They have been used more sparingly than anti-dumping measures.
- **Safeguard Clauses:** that is, the imposition of restrictions on imports for a temporary period when exports are seriously injuring, or threatening to seriously injure, domestic industry. The threshold of injury is usually higher than in anti-dumping cases. In safeguard cases, a Commission decision can be referred for Council review within 90 days. It is limited to the duration of the injury or threat. The main product areas have been textiles, steel, machinery consumer electronics and vehicles. Union-wide measures were introduced in 1990.
- **Voluntary Export Restraints.** VERs are quota agreements aimed at limiting the amount of goods exported by one country into another. For example, many VER agreements have been reached between EU countries

and East Asian countries. Before 1993, countries imposing VERs on Japanese cars included France (a maximum of 3% of market share); Italy (2,500 cars, plus 750 commercial vehicles); Spain (1,000 cars plus 200 commercial vehicles); and the UK (11% of market share). A Union-wide agreement has been reached on car imports from Japan, with the aim of eliminating national restrictions and all restrictions by 1999 (whether from Japan or from Japanese 'transplants'). This is part of a breathing spell, to allow Europe's car makers leeway to improve their competitiveness. However, by 1995 there was still discord between the EU and Japan on the interpretation of this agreement.

• **Local Content Rules,** relating to the extent to which a product has been locally manufactured (as distinct from being imported). For example, France initially refused to recognise the Nissan Bluebird produced in Sunderland as a British car, because it did not have a high enough 'local content'. The internationalisation of production is making it increasingly difficult to determine the origin of goods. The EU has formulated a complex set of regulations concerning rules of origin.

• **Regulatory Policy** is often a byproduct of other objectives: for example, in relation to health or environmental standards.

◯ Trade Relationships

The bargaining power of the EU in trade negotiations with other countries varies considerably: the US has considerable negotiating strength, because it is a huge export market for the EU. The US was the EU's major protagonist in the Uruguay Round of GATT and eventually forced the EU to make concessions with regard to agricultural exports. The EU's adverse trade balance with Japan has enabled it to negotiate voluntary export restraints with Tokyo without fear of retaliation. The EU's trading relationship with EFTA countries has been the closest of all and has been based on reciprocal free trade agreements (the mutual elimination of tariffs and quantitative restrictions on manufactures), although the EU has held most of the aces in trade negotiations with EFTA. The EEA Treaty extended this relationship, but its significance was soon overtaken by the decision of several EFTA countries to seek entry to the Union. The Third World is too weak and divided to exert much clout in trade negotiations with developed countries.

The EU operates an elaborate system of preferential trading arrangements, based on a *hierarchy of discrimination*, or *pyramid of privileges*, in relation to market access. Thus trade barriers are applied selectively, depending on the country (or group of countries) concerned. Many of these arrangements embrace far more than trade objectives. For example, the trade aspects of the Lomé Convention are part of the EU's development policy. The 'trade and co-operation' and 'partnership and co-operation' agreements signed by the EU with countries of the former Soviet Union contain references to political co-operation. Carrot-and-stick trade weapons (withdrawal or extension of trade privileges) have been used to foster foreign policy objectives. An agreement leading to a customs union with Turkey was concluded by the EU–Turkey Association Council in March 1995. The EP made its approval of this agreement (required under the assent procedure) conditional upon improvements in Turkey's human rights record. The EP finally approved the agreement by 343 votes to 149 in December 1995. In 1995, the EU held up a trade agreement with Russia because of Russia's actions in Chechnya.

The Union has concluded a bewildering variety of trade treaties: some involve specific states and others groups of states; some are largely or entirely confined to trade matters, whereas others embrace additional forms of co-operation; some are fully reciprocal whereas in other cases, the EU offers more trade concessions than it receives. The Union's network of relationships is continuing to grow: for example, in December 1995, the Union signed a co-operation agreement with Mercosur (comprising Argentina, Brazil, Paraguay and Uruguay), the first international agreement between two customs unions. The previous month, the EU and twelve Mediterranean countries adopted the 'Barcelona Declaration', providing for a free trade area between the signatories by 2010. In agreements with developing and transition economies, the EU usually offers technical and financial assistance in addition to trade concessions. The main types of agreement are: trade agreements (Article 113, EC); trade and co-operation agreements (Article 228, EC); and association agreements (Article 238, EC). However, there are many variants within, and some overlaps between, these categories. In general, Article 238 agreements offer the closest and broadest relationships with the EU, involving trade privileges, co-operation and institutional links. Article 113 agreements tend to offer fewest privileges.

- **Examples of Article 238 Agreements**
the European Economic Area Agreement (see Chapter 9): this provides for the reciprocal free movement of goods, services, capital and people between the EU and the EFTA signatories. It also embraces co-operation in many non-economic fields;
'Europe' Agreements: these grant privileged, although by no means full, access to EU markets for Central and East European countries seeking closer links with the EU. Signatories tend to view these agreements as stages on the way to Union membership rather than ends in themselves (see Chapter 19);
the Lomé Convention: this is an agreement between the EU and 70 former colonies of member states in Africa, the Caribbean and the Pacific (see Chapter 16). Under the Convention these countries are granted almost duty-

free entry on industrial exports and agricultural exports on a non-reciprocal basis. Some agricultural products have guaranteed access. The Convention also provides technical and financial assistance. Despite these concessions, the share of ACP countries in EU imports has fallen in recent years;

Mediterranean Agreements: Turkey, Cyprus and Malta have association agreements with the EU. Agreements have also been signed with other Mediterranean countries (in the Middle East), granting them varying degrees of market access. They tend to be less generous than the privileges granted in the Lomé agreements, particularly in relation to agricultural products. They also include financial and technical co-operation. The Barcelona Declaration of November 1995 launched a 'Euro-Mediterranean partnership' based on the concept of association with twelve Mediterranean countries.

• **Examples of Article 228 Agreements.** Many co-operation agreements have been signed with developing and 'transition' countries. For example, 'trade and co-operation' and 'partnership and co-operation' agreements. They offer trade privileges and various forms of assistance, but tend to be less comprehensive and generous than 238 Agreements (see Chapter 19).

• **Examples of Article 113 Agreements.** These include both non-preferential trade agreements with developed countries and also preferential trade agreements with developing countries in Latin America, Asia and the Middle East. Some 113 agreements signed with developing countries also include financial and technical assistance under Article 235 (EC). The Generalised System of Preferences involves generalised reductions of import duties, without reciprocity, for imports from developing countries (subject to quantity ceilings). Most relate to industrial goods. They are less generous than Lomé agreements and are of value only to Third World countries excluded from other arrangements.

○ **The Implications for the EU of the Uruguay Round of GATT**

Until its replacement by the World Trade Organisation in January 1995, the General Agreement on Tariffs and Trade was essentially a forum established to facilitate the liberalisation of world trade. GATT operated on the principle of *non-discrimination*, which obliged GATT signatories to offer the same trade concessions to all members, although in practice there are many exceptions to this principle. GATT negotiations proceeded through forums known as Rounds. The seven Rounds prior to the Uruguay Round led to tariff reductions on manufactures of the major industrialised countries from approximately 40% to about 4.7%. The Uruguay Round was generally regarded as the most ambitious and wide ranging of all GATT Rounds. It sought to deal with the issues of agriculture, textiles, services, intellectual property rights and other sensitive sectors. The Round also grappled with the issue of the *new protectionism* (various non-tariff barriers to trade), whereas previous Rounds concentrated primarily on tariff reduction. Non-tariff barriers now constitute a more formidable obstacle to the liberalisation of international trade than tariffs.

The Uruguay Round was deadlocked for years, principally because of conflicts of objectives. For example, there were bitter disputes between the US and the EU over the liberalisation of trade in agriculture and services. The US threatened trade sanctions against EU countries unless they agreed to remove trade-distorting export subsidies from agricultural exports. The dispute over agriculture threatened to destroy the façade of unity between EU countries in the GATT negotiations, because France was less willing to make concessions on agriculture than other member states. After several periods of deadlock on this issue, a deal was eventually agreed, much to the chagrin of the French farm lobby, which accused the Commission of conceding too much. However, it is widely thought that the GATT deal will be beneficial to the EU as a whole. The final act of the Uruguay Round of GATT was signed in Marrakesh in April 1994. According to the GATT Secretariat in a report published in April 1994, market opening for industrial and agricultural goods (excluding services) could add \$235 billion a year to world income by 2002. It has been estimated that the gains from the removal of barriers in the services sector (for example, transportation, telecommunications), currently about a fifth of world trade, could also be high. About two-thirds of expected gains from liberalisation will accrue to developed economies, largely because of cuts in farm supports. The largest gainer from the Round is likely to be the world's largest exporter, the European Union.

FURTHER READING

Anderson, K. and Blackhurst, R. (eds), *Regional Integration in the Global Trading System*, Harvester Wheatsheaf, Hemel Hempstead, 1993.

Cline, W.R. (ed.), *Trade Policy in the 1980s*, Institute for International Economics, Washington DC, 1993.

Dyker, D., *The European Economy*, Longman, Harlow, 1992.

Hayes, J., *Making Trade Policy in the European Community*, St. Martin's Press, London, 1993.

Mayes, D.G. (ed.), *The External Implications of European Integration*, Harvester Wheatsheaf, New York, 1993.

Sinclair, P.J.N., 'World Trade, Protectionist Follies and Europe's Options for the Future. *Oxford Review of Economic Policy*, vol. 9, no. 3, 1993, pp. 114–25.

Wolf, M., *The Resistible Appeal of Fortress Europe*, Rochester Paper No. 1, Centre for Policy Studies, London, 1994.

World Trade Organisation, *International Trade. Trends and Statistics*, Geneva, 1995.

 **Chapter 16**

Development Policy

● PRINCIPAL FEATURES

The Union and its member states together provide more than two-fifths of aid for developing countries. This is more than the combined total for the US and Japan. However, less than 15% of EU aid is channelled through EU institutions. *Bilateral* aid remains the principal form of aid provided by EU countries to developing countries. Only Greece gives more aid via the EU than bilaterally. The EU's development policy is nevertheless of long-standing (dating from the Treaty of Rome) and embraces agreements with more than 100 countries. The TEU introduced a title on development co-operation (Title XVII) into the EC Treaty. This Title set out the main objectives of EU policy in relation to developing countries, viz.:

* sustainable economic and social development;
* smooth and gradual integration into the world economy;
* the campaign against poverty;
* developing and consolidating democracy and respect for human rights.

EU development policy derives from a mixture of enlightened self-interest and altruism. The Third World is the EU's biggest export market, taking over a third of EU exports. The EU is dependent upon the Third World for a wide range of food products and raw materials, such as tropical fruits, coffee, bananas, rubber, tin, copper, manganese and uranium. It obtains about 90% of its oil from the Third World. Moreover, a substantial amount of EU development aid returns to the EU in the form of contracts for EU firms. About three million jobs in the EU depend upon exports to developing countries. EU development policy also provides the EU with levers of influence in the world arena.

EU development policy has been shaped by Europe's imperial past. Four of the six original members of the Union (France, Belgium, the Netherlands, Italy) had colonial or ex-colonial links with territories outside Europe. At the time of the Union's formation, France was anxious to retain special relationships with its overseas colonies and therefore advanced the idea of 'association' between the Union and these territories. Articles 131–36 of the Treaty of Rome outlined this concept of association, which embraces trade concessions and development assistance. It was later formalised in the 'Yaoundé Convention' (signed in 1963 and 1969), a programme mainly directed at ex-French and Belgian colonies in Africa. Largely as a result of the accession of the UK, which has post-colonial ties with many developing countries, the Yaoundé Convention was superseded by the Lomé Convention in 1975. The EU's development policy has both 'regional' and global dimensions: the regional dimension embraces wide-ranging agreements with specific groups of countries – principally the 'Lomé', 'Mahgreb' and 'Mashreq' countries (see below). The global dimension embraces agreements affecting most or all developing countries. The policy consists of instruments such as trade preference, development finance and humanitarian aid.

The Council, the Commission and the EP each play important roles in EU development policy. The Council is the key decisionmaker and the Commission the proposer, negotiator and implementer of policies. The importance of the EP's role varies in relation to which particular aspect of development policy is being considered and upon the legal basis under which a proposal is introduced. For example, the European Development Fund (EDF), the main source of finance for EU development policy, lies outside the Community budget and therefore the EP's influence on this source of funding is limited. Since 1973, the EP has repeatedly sought to integrate the Fund into the Community budget (the goal of 'budgetisation'), but so far without success. Member states remain reluctant to lose control over the size of their EDF contributions. This reflects their determination to retain their own development policies. In recent years, attempts have been made to develop mechanisms for coordination between national and EU policies, in order to achieve 'complementarity' between them. The TEU allows the Commission to take initiatives to promote such co-ordination. The Council adopted a resolution on complementarity in June 1995, but so far the process of coordination remains at an early stage of development.

Despite these limitations, the EP takes a very active role in development policy, notably through its Committee on Development Co-operation, and has contributed to many development initiatives. The EP has repeatedly agitated for an increase in EU development aid and for the transfer of national development policies to the EU level. The EP's assent is required for certain types of external agreement with developing countries (for example, for co-operation and association agreements).

● THE LOMÉ CONVENTION

○ Origins and Development

This Convention is the centrepiece of the EU's development policy. Although the Union has an elaborate network of aid policies for other Third World countries, the signatories to the Convention are at the top of the EU's pyramid of privilege in terms of aid and trade benefits. The Convention is a formal, comprehensive and binding set of aid agreements between the EU and 70 developing countries in Africa, the Caribbean and the Pacific (the ACP countries). The first Convention was signed in 1975 in Lomé, capital of Togo in West Africa, between the Union and 46 developing countries. There are now 70 ACP countries, 47 in Africa, 15 in the Caribbean and 8 in the Pacific. About 40 of these are amongst the world's poorest countries. Of the 70 ACP countries, only Liberia and Ethiopia are not former colonies of a member state. Not all former colonies of European countries are included in Lomé. For example, India and Pakistan, although formerly part of the British empire, are not Lomé members. Lomé countries tend to have relatively small populations, the big exception being Nigeria. The Convention also includes 20 overseas countries and territories (OCTs) for which member states are still responsible. The Lomé agreements affect only about 12% of the total number of people in the Third World.

The EU emphasises that Lomé is based on partnership and dialogue. To facilitate this dialogue, three joint institutions have been established: an ACP–EU Council of Ministers, comprising ministerial representatives of EU and Lomé states, plus a Commission representative; an ACP–EU Committee of Ambassadors, comprising the permanent representative of each member state, a representative of the Commission and the heads of mission to the Union of each ACP state; and an ACP–EU Joint Assembly, comprising one elected representative from each Lomé country and an equal number of MEPs. The ACP–EU Council is the decisionmaking body; the Committee undertakes advisory, preparatory and monitoring work on behalf of the Council; the Assembly is a consultative body and meets twice yearly, alternately in a Union and an ACP country.

The fourth Lomé Convention was signed in December 1989, following 14 months of negotiations, and came into force in September 1991. The fourth Convention will last for 10 years, double the period of previous conventions. It is divided into two five-year cycles, with ECU 12 billion allocated to the first and ECU 13.3 billion to the second. The main emphasis of Lomé 4 is on long-term development, in particular upon private investment, the promotion of small businesses and environmental protection. It also places greater emphasis upon effective monitoring than previous conventions. The EU is seeking to shift the emphasis in Lomé from development aid to improving the competitiveness of ACP economies.

○ **The European Development Fund (EDF)**

The European Development Fund, which is central to the operation of Lomé, was established in 1958, as a result of provisions in the Treaty of Rome. The Fund is outside the Community budget and is financed directly by member states. Separate EDFs has been established for each Lomé Convention (for example, the 7th and 8th for Lomé 4). The percentages contributed by member states to the 7th EDF ranged from 25.96% for Germany to 0.19% for Luxembourg (the UK's contribution was 16.37%). EDF resources comprise both *programmable aid*, based on an indicative programme agreed with each ACP country or OCT, and *non-programmable aid*, which is not earmarked for any specific state.

Five specific funds operate through the EDF: STABEX, SYSMIN, emergency aid for disaster relief, refugee aid and structural adjustment aid. Funds for Lomé development projects are channelled through the EDF mainly in the form of grants (which, unlike loans, do not have to be paid back). Ninety per cent of the funds allocated to Lomé 4 is in the form of grants from the EDF (compared with about 70% for Lomé 3) and the rest in the form of loans and risk capital from the European Investment Bank. Sub-Saharan Africa receives more than 40% of EDF grants.

Table 16.1 Lomé Finance, 1975–95 (in ECU Million)

	Lomé 1	Lomé 2	Lomé 3	Lomé 4*
	1975–80	**1980–85**	**1985–90**	**1990–95**
STABEX	377	634	925	1,500
SYSMIN	–	282	415	480
Grants	2,150	2,999	4,860	7,995
Special Loans	46	525	600	–
Risk Capital	99	284	600	825
Total EDF	3,072	4,724	740	10,800
EIB Loans	390	85	1,100	1,200
TOTAL	3,462	5,409	8,500	12,000

* First cycle. Source: Commission.

There has been considerable wrangling between member states over the size of their contributions to the EDF. A mid-term review of Lomé 4 took place in 1994 and 1995. The review exposed serious differences between EU members on future contributions to the Fund, with France, supported by the Commission, seeking an increase of 30% in the Fund's size and several members (the UK and Germany in particular) strongly opposing increases. A figure of ECU 13.3 billion for the 8th EDF (1995–2000) was agreed at the European Council in Cannes. The UK reduced its contribution by 23%. The three new member states agreed to contribute ECU 880 million.

○   **The Main Policies and Instruments of Lomé.** These comprise:

• **Trade Co-operation.** About 99.5% of ACP exports have duty and quota free access to EU markets. This accounts for about 40% of the external trade of ACP countries. Funds are also provided for trade promotion and development. More than 95% of EU imports from ACP countries are primary products. Less than 1% of ACP agricultural exports are covered by the CAP (arguably CAP protectionism deters ACP countries from producing CAP products).

• **STABEX** (Stabilisation of Export Earnings). The commodities exported by many ACP countries are subject to dramatic price fluctuations in world markets. STABEX provides a cushion for eligible ACP states when their export earnings are reduced due to adverse market conditions, by guaranteeing them a minimum revenue from their exports of basic commodities to the EU. It offers grants for the least-developed countries and interest-free loans for the others. Under Lomé 3, STABEX funds totalled ECU 925 million. It now covers 49 products. Coffee accounts for about one-third of STABEX funds. Thirty two countries were entitled to receive STABEX transfers in 1993. Prior to Lomé 4, products covered must have accounted for at least 6% of the country's average earnings from the EU for the last four years (1.5% for the least-developed countries). Under Lomé 4, dependency thresholds have been lowered to cover products constituting 5% of an ACP country's total export earnings (1% for the least-developed, landlocked or island countries). STABEX has not always been adequate to cover drops in earnings, even though Lomé 4 increased its size by 62%.

• **SYSMIN.** This is similar to STABEX, but relates to countries dependent upon a specific mineral (accounting for at least 15% of export earnings over four years). Loans are given to countries suffering a drop in export earnings or production capacity. The main products covered are copper, cobalt, phosphates, manganese, tin, bauxite, alumina, iron ore, uranium and (in certain circumstances) gold. The bulk of SYSMIN aid is co-financed with other agencies (principally the EIB, World Bank (the International Bank for Reconstruction and Development) and the African Development Bank).

• **The Sugar Protocol** requires the EU to undertake to purchase specific quantities of cane sugar from ACP states at guaranteed prices, which are above world prices. The Protocol covers 1.3 million tonnes of ACP sugar, representing about two-thirds of ACP sugar exports. ACP signatories to the sugar protocol (19 in 1994) are each given a quota.

• **Technical and Financial Co-operation,** to assist industrialisation and rural development. It is financed through the EDF and the EIB. The structural adjustment facility is the main innovation of Lomé 4. 'Structural adjustment' provides financial support to assist countries undergoing economic reforms. In 1993, 42 countries were deemed eligible for structural adjustment aid.

Table 16.2 The Case For and Against Lomé

For
• it commits the EU to a long-term and comprehensive programme of development assistance;
• it has established formal mechanisms for dialogue on development issues between the EU and ACP countries;
• it provides a vehicle for dialogue and collaboration between EU member states on development issues;
• arguably, it has fewer strings attached than bilateral aid programmes;
• no ACP country has left the Lomé scheme.

Against
• it is an agreement among unequals; despite the EU's rhetoric about partnership, ACP states have weak bargaining power and have to accept what the EU is prepared to offer;
• the Commission lacks the analytical capacity to prepare strategic development programmes for 70 countries;
• the EU's distinction between ACP countries and the rest of the developing world is arbitrary and unfair;
• it perpetuates a 'dependency culture';
• the proportion of manufactures in ACP exports has not significantly increased under Lomé;
• the funds committed to Lomé have failed to keep pace with population growth in the ACP countries. For many Third World states debt rescheduling could make a bigger contribution to their development needs than current Lomé policies;
• rates of disbursement of aid have been slow;
• projects have tended to be insufficiently adapted to local conditions;
• projects funded through Lomé are inadequately monitored. More resources should be devoted to impact assessments of EU programmes;
• the development records of many ACP states have been poor. During Lomé 3, there was a significant decline in standards of living in many ACP states.

● EU AID OUTSIDE LOMÉ

Outside the Lomé framework, the EU has an extensive range of trade and aid agreements with developing countries in the Mediterranean region, Asia and Latin America. Some of the largest recipients of EU aid (for example, Egypt, Bangladesh and Turkey) are not Lomé members. Between 1992 and 1996, the Commission allocated ECU 12 billion for Lomé, ECU 4.4 billion for the Mediterranean area and ECU 2.7 billion for Latin America and Asia. Co-operation agreements between the EU and developing countries outside Lomé tend to be less generous than those offered to ACP countries.

The Mediterranean countries in North Africa and the Middle East are the most favoured outside Lomé. These embrace the 'Mahgreb' group (Algeria, Morocco, Tunisia, Libya and Mauritania) and the 'Mashreq' group (Egypt, Jordan, Lebanon and Syria). Agreements with these countries offer restricted, but non-reciprocal access to EU markets, plus financial and technical assistance. The EU has also concluded bilateral agreements with many Latin American countries and also multilateral agreements with 'Mercosur', the Andean Pact and other regional groupings. The main forms of aid applicable to developing countries outside Lomé (some of which also apply to ACP countries) are:

• **The Generalised System of Preferences.** The EU introduced GSP in 1971. It allows Third World states outside Lomé to export most of their industrial and other processed products to the Union, free of customs duties. However, the quantity of goods is subject to quotas and some products are largely excluded. GSP is also administratively very complex. The effects of GSP have in fact been very limited because exports from many Third World states are not competitive anyway. The main beneficiaries of GSP have been China, Brazil and the Asian Tigers rather than the poorest developing countries. The significance of GSP has been further reduced by the lowering of customs duties as a result of GATT agreements.

• **Development Projects.** In 1994, there were EU development projects in more than 100 countries. A new EU project, HORIZON 2000, has recently been established to increase aid levels for public health, poverty, aids prevention and food distribution networks.

• **The European Community Investment Partners (ECIP).** This scheme was set up in 1988 to assist EU private businesses to invest in developing countries in Asia, Latin America and the Mediterranean, through joint ventures and other means. By 1995, there were 60 eligible countries. ECIP allocations in 1994 totalled ECU 40 million.

• **Humanitarian Aid.** Humanitarian aid constitutes about one-fifth of the EU's total assistance to poorer countries, in the form of food and finance. It covers food aid and emergency aid, deriving from disasters such as drought, famine and human conflict. It is financed both through the EDF and the Community budget. The EU also channels humanitarian aid through UN agencies, such as the UN refugee agencies UNRWA (the United Nations Relief and Works Agency) and UNHCR (the United Nations High Commission for Refugees) and through international non-governmental organisations (INGOs). About 60% of EU food aid is given to non-ACP countries and is mainly supplied through international agencies and INGOs. Budget allocations for food aid amounted to almost ECU 600 million in 1994. ECHO, the European Community Humanitarian Office, was set up in April 1992 to provide a single service to manage all emergency humanitarian aid. In 1994, ECHO disbursed about ECU 764 million to more than 50 countries (ex-Yugoslavia received ECU 269 million and Africa ECU 324 million).

○ The Role of the EIB

Although the EIB's primary responsibility is to provide development finance for projects within the EU, it also provides loans to developing countries and to Central and Eastern Europe, as shown in Table 16.3.

Table 16.3 Geographic Breakdown of EIB Loans to Non-EU Countries

	1992		1993		1994	
	ECU m.	%	ECU m.	%	ECU m.	%
ACP/OCT	252	28	226	12	462	20
CEECs	320	36	882	47	957	43
Mediterranean	321	36	680	36	607	27
Asia/Latin America	0	0	99	5	220	10
TOTAL	893	100	1,887	100	2,246	100

Source: EIB.

● FUTURE DIRECTIONS

Pressures for change in EU development policy are emanating from several directions. The entry into the Union of Sweden, Finland and Austria could affect this policy in two ways: firstly, these countries are generous aid donors (giving more aid as a proportion of GDP than any EU 12 state). In this regard, the new entrants already set a salutary example to other countries and could add a powerful voice in favour of a substantial increase in levels of EU aid. Secondly, none of the new entrants had colonies outside Europe and may not support the 'ACP bias' in EU 12 development policy. They could, therefore, contribute to the emergence of a 'globalist' approach to EU development policy. This policy is also being shaped by the collapse of communism. Since the end of the cold war, there has been a tendency for aid donors (for example, the World Bank, the IMF, the EU and developed states) to add political and economic conditions, such as the promotion of good governance, human rights and prudent economic management, to aid packages. Although the fear of a 'big switch' in aid from the Third World to Eastern Europe has not yet proved well-founded, Eastern Europe has increased demands on EU aid resources. In the longer term, this could reduce the absolute amounts provided to the Third World. The Central and East European countries (CEECs) already account for a substantial proportion of EIB loans to non-EU countries, as Table 16.3 above shows.

It seems unlikely that national aid programmes will be superseded by EU programmes in the foreseeable future. Nevertheless, the need for greater co-ordination between the aid policies of the EU and of member states is increasingly recognised. Moreover, because development policy is an aspect of the EU's external relations, the emergence of a stronger common foreign and security policy would also enhance the prospects for the convergence of EU and national aid policies.

FURTHER READING

Babarinde, O., *The Lomé Convention and Development*, Avebury, Aldershot, 1994.
The Courier, bi-monthly publication on ACP issues.
Davenport, M. and Page, S., *Europe: 1992 and the Developing World*, Overseas Development Institute, London, 1991.
Grilli, E., *The European Community and the Developing Countries*, Cambridge University Press, 1994.
Herrman, R. and Weiss, D., 'A Welfare Analysis of the EC–ACP Sugar Protocol', *Journal of Development Studies*, vol. 31, no. 6, 1995, pp. 918–41.
House of Lords Select Comittee on the European Communities, *EC Aid and Trade Policy*, HL Paper 123, 1993.
Malek, M., *Contemporary Issues in European Development Aid*, Avebury, Aldershot, 1991.
Zartman, M., *Europe and Africa*, Lynne Rienner, London, 1993.

 **Chapter 17**

The Common Foreign and Security Policy

● THE DEBATE ON THE UNION'S INTERNATIONAL ROLE

○ From Civil Power to Superpower?

A combination of external and internal developments have increased the urgency with which member states have needed to seriously address the issue of the Union's international role. The end of the cold war confronted the Union with major foreign and security policy challenges: by unfreezing cold war institutional structures, the collapse of communism placed the Union's relations with Eastern Europe on an entirely new footing; it created new security threats, deriving from ethnic and border disputes in Eastern Europe; it changed the geopolitical situation in Europe and provided the Union with opportunities to play a major role in the reshaping of the European continent; it raised fundamental questions concerning the Union's status in the post-cold war international order; it made the pattern of the Union's external relations more complex and uncertain.

Those favouring deeper Union integration have tended to argue that the Union cannot be regarded as fully developed until it has a credible foreign and defence policy. The pursuit of deeper Union integration also has implications for the Union's external policy: for example, the abolition of internal frontiers requires member states to agree common approaches to questions of immigration from outside the Union. The issue of CFSP raises fundamental questions about the nature of the Union. Until quite recently, the EU was widely regarded as essentially a *civil power*, with an international role primarily concerned with external economic relations (that is, as an economic giant and political pygmy). Mrs Thatcher retained this civil power or 'trade area' view of the Union throughout her premiership. The civil power image of the Union is implicitly rejected in the TEU, which defines CFSP to include defence and envisages that a common defence policy might 'in time' come about. However, although in terms of its economic and military *potential*, the Union may have the capability to develop into a major international power in its own right, the Union's CFSP remains in an embryonic and fragile stage of development.

○ The Unclear Aims of CFSP

There are 'maximalist' and 'minimalist' conceptions of what CFSP should involve. The maximalist conception implies a unified, supranational foreign policy, with the EU eventually having its own foreign ministry and its own defence forces under a single command. The minimalist conception interprets CFSP as being limited to co-operation between member states on matters of mutual interest. At present the maximalist aim is highly unrealistic. Each member state still has its own foreign ministry and foreign policy; each has its own network of relationships with other countries, deriving from its history, national interests and geographical location. Recent crises in the Gulf and in the Balkans have exposed serious differences of viewpoint between member states on foreign policy issues. In recent years, member states have gone to war independently of the EU (the UK in the Falklands war; France and the UK, under the aegis of the UN, against Iraq). Moreover, the more states there are in the EU, the more foreign policy interests and viewpoints there are to reconcile.

Central to the issue of CFSP is that of *purpose*: is the ultimate aim to transform the EU into a 'superpower', capable of intervening in global crises and of competing with the US for global leadership? Even if agreement could be reached on this aim (a most unlikely prospect), the EU does not yet have the capability to perform a 'superpower' role. The EU countries would have to increase military spending by more than 2% a year to bring their combined military strength up to the US level. In 1993, the US spent 4.8% of its GDP on defence, compared with 2.6% for European members of NATO (NATO, 1995). Hill (1993) argues that a dangerous gap has opened up between Union capabilities and expectations in relation to CFSP, leading to unrealistic external policies. Moreover, several Union states remain at best unenthusiastic about the prospect of a fully blown CFSP. A more realistic current aim of CFSP is to enhance the ability of the member countries to agree common positions (that is, to 'speak with one voice') and to act more cohesively in international affairs.

Table 17.1 Arguments For and Against CFSP

For	Against
• Collectively, Union countries will be able to exercise greater clout in international affairs.	• Differences in foreign policy interests, deriving from geography and history.
• The development of the Union is creating common international interests amongst Union members.	• Foreign and security policy are core functions which governments are reluctant to relinquish.
• The potential for instability in post-cold-war Europe requires a common approach.	• There are major problems in co-ordinating foreign policy positions.
• It is a logical phase in the development of the Union.	• Several member states are at best lukewarm about CFSP.

○ The Union as an International Actor

A case can be made for the view that the EU is already a major international actor. Member states have operated a formal, albeit very loose, system of co-operation in foreign policy for over two decades. There have been many examples of co-ordinated foreign policy actions between member states (for example, the application of common sanctions policies to South Africa, Argentina, Iraq and Serbia). About 150 states now have diplomatic missions accredited to the EU. The EU has observer status at the United Nations, and in some UN institutions, such as the UN Economic Commission for Europe, the United Nations Conference on Trade and Development (UNCTAD), the United Nations Industrial Development Organisation (UNIDO) and the United Nations Educational, Scientific and Cultural Organisation (UNESCO). It has special status in the OECD. It has signed more than 50 international agreements and many bilateral agreements with non-EU states. It has a network of diplomatic missions in many non-EU countries. It has formal links with most of the world's poor countries. The Commission negotiates the Union's external trade agreements. In 1989, the Group of 24 industrialised countries ('G24') gave the Commission the mandate to organise and co-ordinate G24 assistance for Eastern Europe.

Although most of these relationships are linked to economic matters, they also tend to have a strong political dimension: for example, important political conditions tend to be attached to EU trade and aid relationships. But despite this formidable portfolio of external relationships, the EU is still widely regarded as a lightweight in international affairs. President Jacques Santer has acknowledged that progress on developing CFSP since Maastricht has been disappointing. The strengthening of the Union's CFSP is therefore regarded as a major priority by the Union's integration deepeners. This issue will figure prominently on the agenda of the 1996 IGC.

● THE DEVELOPMENT OF CFSP

○ From European Political Co-operation to CFSP

In 1969, an EC heads of government meeting in The Hague requested EC foreign ministers to consider ways of enhancing co-operation between member states in the field of foreign policy. As a result, European Political Co-operation (EPC) was established in 1970, without a Treaty basis. EPC was a framework for concerted action by EC countries in the field of foreign policy, involving intergovernmental communication, consultation and mutually agreed common action. It was a limited step towards a common foreign policy rather than a great leap forward. The system developed in an *ad hoc* way and operated outside the EC's institutional structures and legislative processes, on the basis of consensus between governments. There was no voting and its provisions were non-binding. Nor did it cover military aspects of security. In order to enhance policy continuity, a 'troika' arrangement has operated since 1974, by which the last, current and next holders of the Council presidency consult with each other on foreign policy matters. EPC operated a Political Committee, comprising Political Directors in the Ministries of Foreign Affairs of member states. The Commission was represented at all EPC meetings. The presidency of the Council kept the EP informed of subjects discussed in EPC.

EPC was given recognition in Title III of the SEA, which stated that member states would endeavour jointly to formulate and implement a European foreign policy. The Treaty led to the formation of a small EPC Secretariat. EPC led to the adoption of common positions on many issues, including major foreign policy questions concerning the Middle East, Eastern Europe and South Africa. Cynics argue, however, that EPC largely resulted in a plethora of vaguely worded declarations (usually after key events had occurred) and little action. The absence of a defence component also weakened the credibility of EPC. EPC never opened a dialogue with communist Eastern Europe. The Gulf crisis of 1990–91 also exposed wide differences in the contributions member states were prepared to make to the military campaign to oust the Iraqi army from Kuwait. EPC was formalised and extended in the TEU, but was subsumed under the heading of CFSP (effectively replacing the term EPC). A Union CFSP was established by Article J of the TEU, as one of the three pillars of the European Union.

Article J.2 of the TEU requires member states to co-ordinate their action in international organisations and to uphold common positions in international forums. As under EPC, CSFP is based on intergovernmental co-operation and lies outside the Community framework. The main differences between EPC and CSFP are that CSFP covers defence issues and strengthens the Union's commitment to the development of *joint action* in foreign and security policy. Under the TEU, CFSP entails a commitment to the eventual framing of a common defence policy which might in time lead to a common defence, but issues with defence implications are not subject to joint action.

○ CFSP Decisionmaking Structure and Organisation

Although the TEU formalised the role of the European Council in CFSP agenda setting, it is the Council (in the form of the General Affairs Council made up of Union foreign ministers) which is the principal decisionmaking body in relation to CFSP. The Council is empowered to define common positions and to decide on matters which are to be the subject of joint actions. The General Affairs Council meets monthly, but also holds additional meetings when considered appropriate. All significant decisions in the Council are taken by unanimity, except for procedural questions and in cases when, by mutual consent, a decision is taken to use qualified majority voting. It is the Council presidency rather than the Commission which represents the Union on CFSP issues and which is responsible for the implementation of common measures. Under Article J.5, the Council presidency is responsible for practical implementation of joint actions (see below), assisted where necessary by representatives of the previous and next member state to hold the presidency, in association with the Commission.

The Council is assisted in its CFSP role by a network of groups, that is, by COREPER; by senior foreign officials from member states (collectively known as the Political Committee), who prepare CFSP work for COREPER and the General Council; by the Correspondents Group (other foreign ministry officials who perform liaison and preparatory work not dealt with initially by the Political Committee); and by various working groups comprising high-ranking diplomats and Commission representatives. The TEU absorbed the EPC Secretariat into the Council's General Secretariat.

Although the Commission is 'fully associated' with CFSP, it does not have the exclusive right to initiate proposals. However (unlike under EPC), it may submit CFSP issues and proposals to the Council. It therefore shares initiative rights with member states. The Commission does not perform a monitoring role in relation to CFSP. In the Santer Commission, responsibility for external relations is divided amongst several Commissioners. The Commission maintains delegations in more than 100 countries and in several international organisations. These links tend to be reciprocal: most non-EU countries maintain official missions to the Union in Brussels. However, these have not replaced the bilateral diplomatic missions between member states and other countries. The TEU requires member-states' missions and Commission delegations to co-operate with each other in the interests of unity. In addition to its central role in external trade negotiations, the Commission is also a key actor in the Union's relations with developing countries and with the transition economies of Eastern Europe. The European Council can declare that certain aspects of CSFP should be the basis of joint action (Article J.3 of the TEU). Joint action must receive unanimous approval, meaning that states have a veto, except in fields where they agree unanimously to surrender this veto. In this event, decisions on specific issues can be made by qualified majority. Article J.3.6 allows members states to act unilaterally on areas covered by joint action in urgent cases, with the proviso that they have regard to the general objectives of the joint action and keep other member states informed. Article J.3.7 allows members to opt out of a joint action providing the action is not thereby undermined. Joint actions so far have included humanitarian aid to Bosnia, support for the transition to democracy in South Africa, the 'Stability Pact' in Europe (see below) and support for the Middle East peace process.

Union level democratic control of CSFP remains very weak. Under CFSP, as under EPC, the EP's role is largely confined to advice. However, the TEU requires the Council presidency to consult the EP on the 'main aspects and basic choices' of CFSP and to take the EP's views into consideration. The EP must be kept regularly informed by the presidency and the Commission of developments in CFSP. It can ask questions of, and make recommendations to, the Council on CFSP issues. It holds an annual debate on progress in implementing CFSP. The EP is not content with this limited role and would like a much greater input into CFSP decisions. It also favours the abolition of the CFSP pillar, greater use of majority voting, common embassies and a review of EU representation on the UN Security Council. CFSP is likely to be a very contentious issue at the 1996 IGC. Some EU members, supported by the Commission and the EP, are seeking the introduction of QMV in relation to CFSP. This idea, however, is likely to be strongly opposed by some member states. Aspirants for membership of the EU have been left in no doubt that they must accept CFSP as defined in the TEU. Prior to entry, Austria, Finland and Sweden accepted that their accession should strengthen rather than weaken the Union's capacity to act effectively in foreign and security policy. But all three have post-war traditions of neutrality which may inhibit them from taking an active role in CFSP. Conversely, some Central and East European countries, if admitted to the Union, might well prove to be enthusiastic participants in CFSP.

● POST-COLD WAR SECURITY STRUCTURES IN EUROPE

○ Key Questions

The end of the cold war raises several fundamental issues concerning European security. Firstly, what is to be the function of NATO following the demise of the Soviet threat? Secondly, can the European Union develop its own defence capability, either distinct from, or in partnership with, the Atlantic alliance? Thirdly, how should members of NATO and of the Western European Union respond to requests for membership by former communist countries? Fourthly, to what extent should the European Union assume a 'trouble-shooter' role in relation to the ethnic and border disputes resulting from the collapse of communism in Eastern Europe? There are two ways in which a security system appropriate to a post-cold war environment might be built: existing institutions can be adapted to suit new conditions, or new 'purpose-built' organisations can be created. In the security field, there has been a tendency to make use of existing institutions, in particular NATO, the Western European Union and the Organisation for Security and Co-operation in Europe (OSCE), formerly known as the Conference on Security and Co-operation in Europe (CSCE). This *ad hoc* approach has meant that security policy currently involves a complex web of institutions with overlapping functions and memberships (see Figure 17.1 and Table 17.2).

Figure 17.1 'Variable Geometry' in Europe's Security Architecture

	NATO		**OSCE**	
US Canada				
EU	**WEU**		Albania	Bosnia-H
Belgium			Armenia	Croatia
Denmark (O)	Iceland (AM)		Azerbaizan	Cyprus
France	Norway (AM)		Belorus	Liechtenstein
Germany	Turkey (AM)		Georgia	Macedonia (O)
Greece			Moldova	Malta
Italy			Kazakhstan	Monaco
Luxembourg			Kyrgyzstan	Slovenia
Netherlands			Russia	San Marino
Portugal			Tajikstan	Switzerland
Spain			Turkmenistan	Vatican City
UK			Uzbekistan	Yug.Fed (S)
	Czech Rep.(AP)		Ukraine	
Austria (O)	Estonia (AP)			
Ireland (O)	Lithuania (AP)			
Finland (O)	Latvia (AP)			
Sweden (O)	Bulgaria (AP)			
	Hungary (AP)			
	Poland (AP			
	Romania (AP			
	Slovakia (AP)			

O = Observer; AM = Associate Member; AP = Associate Partner; S = Suspended

Table 17.2 The New Security Framework

	NATO	NACC	PFP	WEU	OSCE	CE
Belgium	y	y	y	y	y	y
France	y	y	y	y	y	y
Denmark	y	y	y	o	y	y
Germany	y	y	y	y	y	y
Greece	y	y	y	y	y	y
Ireland	n	o	n	o	y	y
Italy	y	y	y	y	y	y
Luxembourg	y	y	y	y	y	y
Netherlands	y	y	y	y	y	y
Portugal	y	y	y	y	y	y
Spain	y	y	y	y	y	y
UK	y	y	y	y	y	y
Austria	n	o	y	o	y	y
Finland	n	o	y	o	y	y
Sweden	n	o	y	o	y	y
Iceland	y	y	y	am	y	y
Liechtenstein	n	n	n	n	y	y
Norway	y	y	y	am	y	y
Switzerland	n	n	n	n	y	y
Cyprus	n	n	n	n	y	y
Malta	n	n	y	n	y	y
Turkey	y	y	y	am	y	y
Albania	n	y	y	n	y	y
Armenia	n	y	y	n	y	n
Azerbaizan	n	y	y	n	y	n
Belorus	n	y	y	n	y	n
Bosnia-H	n	n	n	n	y	n
Bulgaria	n	y	y	ap	y	y
Croatia	n	n	n	n	y	n
Czech Rep.	n	y	y	ap	y	y
Estonia	n	y	y	ap	y	y
Georgia	n	y	y	n	y	n
Hungary	n	y	y	ap	y	y
Latvia	n	y	y	ap	y	y
Lithuania	n	y	y	ap	y	y
Macedonia	n	n	n	n	o	o
Moldova	n	y	y	n	y	y
Poland	n	y	y	ap	y	y
Romania	n	y	y	ap	y	y
Russia	n	y	y	n	y	y
Slovakia	n	y	y	ap	y	y
Slovenia	n	o	y	n	y	y
Tajikistan	n	y	n	n	y	n
Turkmenstan	n	y	n	n	y	n
Ukraine	n	y	y	n	y	n
Uzbekistan	n	y	y	n	y	n
Yug.Fed.	n	n	n	n	s	n
US	y	y	y	n	y	n
Canada	y	y	y	n	y	n

Organisations

NATO = North Atlantic Treaty Organisation
NACC = North Atlantic Co-operation Council
PFP = Partnership for Peace
WEU = Western European Union
OSCE = Organisation for Security and Co-operation in Europe
CE = Council of Europe

Categories

European Union

EFTA

Mediterranean' States

Ex-Communist States

North America

Abbreviations

y = yes
n = no
o = observer status
am = associate member
ap = associate partner
s = suspended

A system of *complex interdependence* seems to be emerging, linking security structures and regions A key question is whether these organisations (especially NATO and the WEU) duplicate or complement each other.

○ The Western European Union

The WEU is a good example of a low-profile institution which been revitalised by the end of the cold war. It has its origins in the Brussels Treaty of 'Economic, Social and Cultural Collaboration and Collective Self-Defence' (March 1948), concluded between Belgium, France, the Netherlands, Luxembourg and the UK, when the main concern of its signatories was the prospect of German rearmament. The exercise of the military responsibilities of the Treaty were transferred to NATO in 1949. The Treaty was subsequently modified by the Paris agreements of October 1954, which enabled Germany and Italy to join (following the refusal of the French National Assembly to ratify the European Defence Community Treaty). The Paris agreements introduced the 'Western European Union' title and explicitly referred to the promotion of European integration as a WEU goal. Between 1954 and 1973, the WEU helped to integrate the FRG into the Atlantic alliance. It also played a role in Franco-German *rapprochement*, through the arbitration of the Saar issue.

There was a slowing down of its activities between 1973 and 1984. But the potential of the WEU to play a more important role in European security was recognised in various proposals for 'deeper' European integration which emerged in the early 1980s. The US decision in 1983 to launch the 'Star Wars' programme without consulting Europe encouraged EU countries to consider the need for a stronger European dimension to European security. The WEU was relaunched in Rome in 1984, at a meeting of WEU foreign and defence ministers, when it was agreed to hold two meetings of foreign and defence ministers a year. In October 1987, the WEU ministerial council adopted a 'platform on European security interests', which set out the WEU's future programme, based around giving European integration a security dimension and reinforcing the European pillar of the Atlantic alliance.

The declaration on the role of the WEU agreed at Maastricht viewed the WEU as both strengthening the European pillar of the Atlantic alliance and as the defence component of the future European Union. A commonly used metaphor is that the WEU is a 'hinge' linking the US and Europe, through complementarity rather than rivalry with NATO. At Maastricht, member states outside the WEU were invited to join or become observers, although there is no obligation to join. In June 1992, the foreign and defence ministers of WEU member states, meeting in Bonn, issued the 'Petersberg Declaration', which set out the guidelines for the WEU's future development:

it pledged support for conflict prevention and peacekeeping efforts in co-operation with the CSCE (now OSCE) and the UN Security Council.

The WEU is currently made up of 10 countries: the UK, France, Germany, Italy, Spain, Portugal, Belgium, the Netherlands, Luxembourg and Greece. Spain and Portugal joined in 1990. In November 1992, Greece became a member and Ireland and Denmark became observers. Norway, Iceland and Turkey became 'associate members'. Nine Central and East European countries also became 'associate partners' at a ceremony in Luxembourg in May 1994. In 1995, Austria, Finland and Sweden became observers. Observers may attend WEU Council meetings and are invited to working-group meetings where they may, on request, speak. Associate members may take a full part in Council meetings and its working groups. They may associate themselves with the decisions of member states and can take part in WEU military operations. Associate member status excludes security guarantees. Associate partner status involves various forms of consultation and co-operation, but also excludes security guarantees. The Ministerial Council of the WEU and representatives from the nine associate partner countries have endorsed a policy document containing preliminary ideas for a 'Common European Defence Policy'. The WEU's 'variable geometry' therefore embraces the following: *members* (all are also members of NATO and the EU); *observers* (members of NATO and/or of the EU); *associate members* (NATO but not EU members); and *associate partners* (neither NATO nor EU members).

The WEU has a Council of Ministers (the WEU Council) and a Permanent Council. The WEU Council meets at least twice a year in the capital of the country holding the one-year presidency. The Permanent Council, chaired by the WEU Secretary-General and supported by a Secretariat with a staff of about 100, is responsible for day-to-day management. The WEU Secretariat was based in London until January 1993, when it moved to Brussels. A 'planning cell', set up to strengthen the WEU's operational role, was established in October 1992. The cell has compiled a list of forces answerable to the WEU (FAWEU). The WEU has a parliamentary assembly established in 1954 (consisting of members of national parliamentary delegations to the Council of Europe's Consultative Assembly). It meets in Paris twice yearly. WEU chiefs of defence staff now meet twice yearly and on an *ad hoc* basis. The WEU has also established a dialogue with East European military forces. The WEU chiefs of staff met during the Gulf crisis for the first time since 1954. The WEU played a role in the co-ordination of member states' naval units deployed in the Gulf (Operation *Cleansweep*). In ex-Yugoslavia, ships and aircraft under the control of the WEU have helped to monitor the UN embargo on Serbia-Montenegro. The WEU is currently active in the Adriatic, the Danube (helping to enforce the UN embargo) and in the EU's administration of Mostar in Bosnia. But the conflict in ex-Yugoslavia also exposed the current limitations of the WEU. Actions by the WEU in the conflict have been overshadowed by those of NATO, which remains the world's most powerful and credible military alliance.

◯ The 'Eurocorps'

If a 'European army' is ever established, its origins might well be traced back to Franco-German co-operation in the field of defence. The Eurocorps, which might eventually become the future defence arm of the WEU, became operational in 1994. It currently comprises one French and one German division plus contingents from Belgium, Spain and Luxembourg. Other EU members, however, have so far declined to participate. Eurocorps is expected to operate in situations outside the remit of NATO, or where NATO has decided not to act. Eurocorps falls under NATO command where defence of NATO territory is required. The Eurocorps is still in a nascent stage and its future role remains unclear.

◯ NATO and the WEU

NATO was established in 1949 as an alliance against the threat of a Soviet attack on Western Europe. Far from being wound up following the end of the cold war, NATO remains very much 'in business'. It is currently in the process of developing new roles and is also likely to expand its membership (currently 16), to include some former communist countries. Its key role in a post-cold war world may be to ensure stability in the wider Europe, by protecting democracy and stability, especially in Europe's southern and eastern flanks. NATO has a Council (comprising permanent representatives of each member state, meeting weekly), an International Staff, a Secretary-General (a senior international statesman, who chairs Council meetings) and an extensive network of committees and planning groups. There is also a North Atlantic Assembly, comprising nominees from the parliaments of member states. The Assembly, meeting twice yearly, is independent of NATO, but acts as a link between the parliaments of member states and the Alliance.

Many European states remain keen to maintain the transatlantic link between the US and Europe which NATO provides. This might be achieved through a merger of NATO and the WEU. Others would prefer the WEU to gradually take over the role of NATO, thereby reducing the US role in European defence. In October 1991, prior to the Maastricht summit, France and Germany and the UK and Italy produced contradictory proposals on

European defence: the Franco-German proposal sought to downgrade NATO by beefing up the WEU, whereas the UK–Italian proposals for the WEU were based on the continuation of a strong NATO role. There is already improved co-operation and co-ordination between WEU and NATO. In 1992, the Independent European Programme Group (IEPG), a forum aimed at achieving co-operation in arms procurement and comprising European member nations of NATO, was dissolved and its functions transferred to the WEU. The January 1994 NATO summit called for a European security and defence identity (ESDI), involving both NATO and the WEU. NATO is also working out ideas for common joint task forces (CJTFs), involving both NATO and WEU military capabilities. There could be a partial merger between NATO and the WEU, in which their capabilities remain separable rather than separate (meaning that they would retain their potential for independent action). However, this could simply confuse matters, by duplicating chains of command. The relationships between these two organisations in post-cold war Europe have yet to be clearly defined.

○ The Expansion of NATO?

An issue of pressing importance is how East European countries can be integrated into West European or transatlantic defence structures. Many of these countries are actively seeking membership of NATO. Existing NATO members have hardly welcomed these overtures with open arms. NATO membership for these countries could embroil existing members in military conflicts in Eastern Europe. To admit some but not others would create a new division in Europe. A specific reason for this caginess has been a fear of antagonising Russia. In Warsaw in August 1993, Boris Yeltsin gave approval to NATO membership to East European states, but under Russian army pressure subsequently argued that East European security should be jointly guaranteed by NATO and Russia. NATO has a 'gradualist' policy in relation to the admission of new members. In January 1994, NATO leaders declared that they expected and would welcome NATO expansion, but without setting a timetable or identifying future applicants. The alternative is to offer the CEECs institutionalised dialogue and collaboration with NATO.

After the failed Soviet coup in August 1991, NATO issued a declaration that the security of Eastern Europe was 'inseparably linked' with that of the Atlantic alliance. In October 1991, US Secretary of State James Baker and the German Foreign Minister Hans-Dietrich Genscher proposed that a 'North Atlantic Co-operation Council' be formed, to institutionalise East European participation in the non-military activities of NATO. The NACC came into existence in December 1991. It currently includes 38 countries: 16 NATO members, the former Warsaw Pact countries, Albania and all successor states of the Soviet Union. Austria, Finland, Slovenia and Sweden have observer status. The Council consists of the foreign ministers or other representatives of member states, meeting at least once a year. Ideas are being developed for collaboration between NATO and the CEECs, such as offers of training for military personnel. Another possibility is that NACC members could participate in joint peacekeeping and peacemaking operations. NACC might also serve as a 'waiting room' for prospective members of NATO.

At the NATO summit in Brussels in January 1994, President Bill Clinton launched the Partnership for Peace initiative, based on the idea of a more extensive degree of collaboration between NATO and other countries than envisaged in the NACC agreements. Invitations to negotiate PFP agreements were sent to all former Warsaw Pact countries, including Russia and other former Soviet republics. By June 1995, 26 countries had signed, including Russia. Austria Finland and Sweden have also joined PFP. PFP has been established within the framework of NACC. It does not offer security guarantees, but PFP signatories are able to consult with NATO if they feel their security is threatened. PFP goes beyond dialogue and co-operation and involves participation in political and military bodies at NATO headquarters. PFP allows for variation in the scope and level of participation in co-operative activities by each partner. Joint NATO/PFP exercises are also conducted.

○ The Organisation for Security and Co-operation in Europe

The OSCE (known as the CSCE until January 1995) is the only current pan-European institution to which all European countries belong. It was created in the early 1970s to promote East–West dialogue, during the period of *détente* between the West and the Warsaw Pact countries. The OSCE now has 53 members. The cold war was formally wound up at a CSCE summit in Paris November 1990, which led to the signing of the Paris Charter for a New Europe. The Charter established the Council of Foreign Ministers of the CSCE, together with a Committee of Senior Officials, a Secretariat in Prague, a Conflict Prevention Centre in Vienna and an Office of Democratic Institutions and Human Rights (ODIHR) in Warsaw. The OSCE is essentially a forum which provides regular opportunities for members to discuss, and co-operate on, security issues. It has established preventive diplomacy missions in Estonia and Latvia and also has missions in Kosovo, Sanjak and several other trouble spots. It has been involved in withdrawal of Russian troops from the Baltic; in crisis management in Moldova; in conflict resolution in Nagorno-Karabakh and Chechnya; and in sanctions assistance missions in the Balkans. Its main asset is its pan-European and pan-Atlantic membership. Its main drawback is that it is viewed as little more than a talking shop. The fact that decisions have to be unanimous limits its scope for effective action. A Russian suggestion in 1994 that the OSCE could become an 'umbrella' for all security organisations in Europe found no support amongst NATO allies.

⟲   The Council of Europe

Based in Strasbourg, the Council was established in May 1949, following the Hague Congress (see Chapter 1). Its principal aims are to maintain the basic principles of human rights, pluralist democracy and the rule of law and to enhance the quality of life for European citizens. It is not a military organisation and statutes do not allow it to become involved in defence issues. It nevertheless has an important contribution to make to stability in Europe through its promotion of democratic values and human rights. It has a Committee of Ministers and a Parliamentary Assembly. The Council has concluded about 140 intergovernmental conventions and agreements, including the Convention on Human Rights. Several former communist states have now been admitted to the Council, including Russia (in January 1996), despite misgivings about Russia's actions in Chechnya.

●   THE EU AS A EUROPEAN TROUBLE-SHOOTER?

The will and ability of the EU to develop a credible CFSP has been put to severe test in post-cold war Europe, no more so than in the Balkans, where arguably Union diplomacy has been tried and found badly wanting. This is not to deny the successes of CFSP. Thus the EU has established mechanisms for dialogue with the East European countries on CFSP issues. In May 1994, the EU hosted a conference in Paris on 'stability in Europe', with particular reference to the problem of ethnic disputes. Forty of the 53 members of the OSCE attended the Conference, which led to the launching of the 'Stability Pact in Europe' in March 1995. The Pact, which is monitored by the OCSE, is primarily designed to contribute to peace and stability in Eastern Europe. In May 1994, the EU Foreign Affairs Council agreed to a request of the Bosnian Federation to administer the Bosnian town of Mostar for two years. Because of its economic and political leverage (stemming not least from the desire of many East European countries to enter the EU), the Union has been able to play a moderating role in the region. Thus the EU has helped to secure a peaceful resolution of a dispute between Slovakia and Hungary. In 1994, the Council issued 110 CFSP statements, and adopted 9 joint actions (for example, humanitarian aid for Bosnia, support for Middle East peace) and 8 common positions (for example, the embargo on Serbia and Montenegro).

But these achievements seem somewhat paltry when measured against the EU's failure to prevent or halt the civil war in ex-Yugoslavia, or its attendant horrors of 'ethnic cleansing'. In 1991, the Foreign Minister of Luxembourg, Jacques Poos, one of a 'troika' of EU foreign ministers charged with the task of resolving the developing crisis in Yugoslavia, optimistically referred to this crisis as 'Europe's hour'. The EU made earnest efforts to mediate between the warring factions: it organised several peace conferences and played a major role in drafting peace plans. Each of these plans collapsed, due to the failure to secure the agreement of the warring sides. By the autumn of 1995, and in particular following the acceptance by the belligerents of a US-brokered peace plan for Bosnia (the Dayton Accord), the EU had effectively been relegated to a secondary, supporting role in the conflict resolution process. The EU is currently seeking to play a major role in the post-war reconstruction process in the region.

The conflict proved Europe's inability to solve its problems on its 'own' (meaning without the military and diplomatic muscle of the United States). It also exposed the limitations of the WEU, which in large measure was relegated to a minor military role in the conflict, whereas NATO's role became of key importance. Arguably, the EU's floundering performance as peacemaker in ex-Yugoslavia had as much to do with the complexity and intractability of the problem as with the EU's own shortcomings. But, with the benefit of hindsight, the conflict in ex-Yugoslavia exposed flaws in the EU's capacity to act effectively and coherently in international affairs, viz.:

• **the phenomenon of 'chain gang diplomacy',** where one state takes unilateral action and virtually forces others to follow suit: the clearest example of this was the German decision to recognise Croatia, Slovenia, and later Bosnia (France and the UK urged caution). German unilateral, and arguably precipitate, recognition of Croatia and Slovenia gave an impression that Germany was determined to pursue its own foreign policy goals;

• **the unwillingness or inability of the EU to back tough words with tough action:** the crisis exposed the gulf between the ability of EU countries to agree on broad statements of principle, and their inability to enforce their decisions (or even to agree on operational questions);

• **conflicts of interest and viewpoint:** serious splits developed between member states on policy towards Bosnia, in particular with regard to the arms embargo and use of air strikes. For example, Germany and Greece have different perspectives on Balkan issues. Greece refused to countenance the recognition of Macedonia unless it changed its name. In 1994, the Commission asked the ECJ to issue an emergency order ending Greece's unilateral trade embargo against Macedonia.

Perhaps the most important lesson arising from recent EU involvements in civil conflicts and international crises is that EU objectives need to be more precisely defined and matched more closely with capabilities. The contributions made by EU countries to the 'Rapid Reaction Force' for Bosnia in 1995 stretched the military capabilities of the participating states. But even if the EU's military capability was to be greatly enhanced, the problem of how to achieve greater coherence in CFSP would still have to be solved.

FURTHER READING

Buchan, D., *Europe: The Strange Superpower*, Dartmouth, Aldershot, 1993.
Ginsberg, R.H., *Foreign Policy Actions of the European Community: The Politics of Scale*, Lynne Rienner, Boulder Co., 1989.
Hill, C., 'The Capability-Expectations Gap, or Conceptualising Europe's International Role', *Journal of Common Market Studies*, vol. 31, no. 3, 1993, pp. 305–28.
Laffan, B., *Integration and Co-operation in Europe*, Routledge, London, 1992.
NATO, *NATO Handbook*, NATO Office of Information and Press, Brussels, 1995.
Nuttall, Simon, *European Political Co-operation*, Oxford University Press, 1992.
Redmond, J. (ed.), *The External Relations of the European Community: The International Response to 1992*, St. Martins Press, New York, 1992.
Rummel, R. (ed.), *Toward Political Union – Planning a Common Foreign and Security Policy in the European Community*, Westview Press, Boulder Col., 1992.

 **Chapter 18**

The Enlargement of the Union

● WHY ARE SO MANY COUNTRIES SEEKING ENTRY?

Under the terms of Article 237 of the EC Treaty and Article O of the TEU, any European democracy has a right to apply for membership of the European Union (although neither Article defines what a 'European' country is). Until recently, enlargement could be dealt with at a fairly leisurely pace: the first enlargement did not occur until 1973, when the UK, Ireland and Denmark acceded. Greece acceded in 1981 and Spain and Portugal in 1986. In each case, there had been long preparatory periods before entry. Greece signed an association agreement with the Community in 1961 and applied in 1975. Spain signed an association agreement in 1970 and applied in 1977. Portugal was a member of EFTA and also applied in 1977. The accession of Austria, Finland and Sweden was preceded by shorter preparatory periods. At least 15 countries are currently seeking entry into the EU, raising the prospect that future enlargements will be unprecedented in their scale and pace. The following reasons have frequently been suggested to explain the rush to join the Union:

● **Guaranteed Access to EU Markets.** Although the EU has repeatedly denied that the SEM has protectionist objectives, removal of trade barriers between EU countries is likely to boost intra-EU trade at the expense of trade with the outside world. Non-EU firms, therefore, could lose business through *trade diversion*. Association agreements give countries preferential access to EU markets, but do not grant them complete and unqualified access.

● **Insider Participation.** Only members are allowed to participate in the EU's decisionmaking processes. Non-members with substantial trading links with the EU have no right to a say in EU decisions of vital concern to them (for example, competition policy).

• **Fear of Marginalisation** and isolation from major developments in Europe. In Eastern Europe, the entry motive is often expressed as part of a wider aspiration to 'rejoin Europe'.

• **Access to Resource Transfers.** If fully integrated into the EU, East European countries, Malta, Cyprus and Turkey would be net beneficiaries from the Community budget (the reverse is true for EFTA countries).

• **EU Entry is Likely to Boost Inward Investment,** as the post-entry increase in FDI in Spain and Portugal shows.

• **The Removal of Cold War Prohibitions on Entry.** The end of communist rule removed a barrier to the entry of East European states. The issue of neutrality was also a formidable obstacle to the entry of Austria, Finland and Sweden during the cold war era.

• **The Disappearance, or Receding Attraction, of Alternatives to EU Membership.** Comecon is dead. EFTA is probably dying.

• **Panic of the Closing Door** – the fear of being left behind in the rush to join. Late applicants are likely to find themselves at the back of a long queue.

● THE FOURTH ENLARGEMENT

With the exception of access to budgetary transfers, all of the reasons for the rush to join the EU outlined above applied to Austria, Finland and Sweden. Given the importance of EU markets for EFTA exports, EFTA countries could not remain indifferent to the SEM programme. More than half 'EFTA 7's' exports went to, and more than half its imports came from, the EU. The response of the EFTA states to the challenge of the SEM was to seek to negotiate an agreement which would give them as many of the potential benefits of the big market as possible. They therefore enthusiastically embraced Delors' offer to form a European Economic Area with the Union.

From the beginning, the EEA was perceived by some EFTA statesmen as a kind of 'EU ante-chamber', or staging post on the road to full EU membership. At the start of the negotiations, the then ministerial chairman of EFTA, Wolfgang Schüssel (Austrian Minister of Foreign Affairs), stated that he regarded the EEA as 'the fastest train to Brussels'. For others in EFTA (and for some in the Union), the EEA negotiations were viewed as a means of shelving the entry issue. However the negotiations had the effect of accelerating applications for full membership, partly because of the EU's tough negotiating stance and partly because they were similar in many respects to full entry negotiations. Applications by EFTA countries for Union entry could hardly be opposed on grounds of unsuitability or unreadiness.

These countries are amongst the richest in the world, in terms of per capita GDP; all have high standards of social and environmental protection; all are politically stable; all have relatively small populations (five EU12 states had larger populations than the combined population of 'EFTA 7').

By the time the EEA came into force on 1 January 1994, negotiations for the entry of Austria, Finland, Norway and Sweden into the EU were at their final stage. The negotiations began in early 1993 and were completed in the spring of 1994. They were conducted in parallel, but each application was judged on its merits. In each applicant country there was a strong 'anti-entry' lobby. In general, business groups tended to favour entry whereas farming, fishing and environmental groups tended to oppose it. The issue of neutrality was an important factor in three of the four states. Domestically, the four governments sought to promote the idea of entry by arguing that it was a means of improving, or at least safeguarding, living standards and of avoiding marginalisation. The four's agricultural sectors were more subsidised and protected than those of the EU.

The main issues in the negotiations for Austria's entry were trans-alpine routes, budgetary transfers and alpine farming. The end of the cold war, instability in Russia, the decline of Finnish trade with the ex-Soviet republics and rising unemployment encouraged Finland to take a closer look at the Union. Norway previously applied in 1969 and was accepted for membership in 1972. However, it withdrew its application following a referendum. Norway has done well economically since its decision not to join the EU in 1972. Therefore, fears of missing the EU boat were still widely regarded as unfounded. Spain insisted on access to Norway's fishing grounds, provoking the Norwegian response of 'not one fish'. A complex deal was eventually struck, based around access already granted in the EEA agreement. Referenda on entry were held in each of the applicant countries in 1994. The votes in favour of entry were: 66.4% in Austria, 56.9% in Finland and 53.1% in Sweden. Only the Norwegians rejected entry, albeit by a narrow margin, with 52.2% voting against.

The accession of Austria, Finland and Sweden increased the EU's population by 6.2% (from 348.6 million to 370.4 million), its GDP by about 7%, its GDP per capita by about 1% and its area by 37%. It extended the boundaries of the EU to the Arctic Circle and to the borders of Russia. It increased the number of working languages from 9 to 11. All EU legislation dating back to 1952 is being published in the languages of the new member states. 'EU 15' comprises 5 large and 11 medium-sized or small countries. There are several important institutional and policy implications of the fourth enlargement. It extended the period between which each country holds the rotating Council presidency from 6 to 7.5 years. It increased the number of votes in the Council from 76 to 87 and raised the number of votes needed to block decisions based on QMV from 23 to 26 (see Chapter 4). The new entrants have 11 votes out of 87, over twice as many as they would be entitled to if votes were allocated strictly in accordance with population size.

The new entrants are net contributors to the Community budget, although by less than was originally estimated. There will be a rebate on entrants' budgetary contributions for the first three years of membership (amounting to ECU 3.6 billion between 1995 and 1998), in order to offset the effects of alignment of the entrants' higher farm prices to EU levels. A regional aid programme has been introduced for the remote and sparsely populated regions of the Nordic countries and for Austria's Burgenland region.

The new entrants are required to phase out subsidy programmes which conflict with the CAP. They sought to ensure that entry would not be at the price of lowering their standards in relation to the environment, consumer safety and other policies. A deal which in effect enables the new entrants to maintain their high environmental and safety standards was therefore agreed. The new entrants indicated that the TEU provisions on common foreign and security policy were broadly acceptable. Austria's application in 1989 was made on the understanding that Austria would maintain its neutral status. But the concept of neutrality has changed in the post-cold war era and all three new entrants now have observer status in the Western European Union.

It is possible that the new entrants could provide the UK with much needed allies on a number of important institutional and policy issues. They may resist reforms which they perceive as leading to an erosion of sovereignty. They may also adopt similar positions to the UK on international trade issues. They may align themselves with other rich 'Northern' states in opposing increases in resource transfers to poorer EU members. Nordic traditions of open government might also contribute to greater transparency in EU decisionmaking.

● EU POLICIES TOWARDS ENLARGEMENT

○ **Problems**

The EU has hardly welcomed recent overtures for entry with open arms, for several reasons. A greatly enlarged, more heterogeneous, membership could slow down the pace of integration, by making the objectives of political, economic and monetary union more difficult to achieve. Unless very long transition arrangements are negotiated, the entry of the East European countries and Turkey would require a massive expansion of the Community budget. Many potential entrants have large farm sectors, which would strain the CAP to breaking point. East European entrants would provide stiff competition for existing members in key industries such as agriculture, textiles and steel. If East European countries and Turkey were admitted, there could be a flood of economic migrants into the EU's richer states. Enlargement also raises crucial issues of effective Union governance: admission of several very small states may require changes in the basis of representation in EU institutions.

○ **Deepening versus Widening**

The debate between those wishing to give priority to pursuit of deeper integration between member states and those wishing to give priority to widening the EU's membership intensified following the end of the cold war. The main arguments in this debate are outlined in Table 18.1.

Table 18.1 Deepening versus Widening

The Case for Deepening
• the momentum of integration must be maintained, otherwise the whole process will stall;
• there is a danger of an 'accession avalanche.' It is better to create strong foundations for the EU before allowing others in;
• premature entry of East European countries would impose a heavy burden on the Community budget;
• precipitate widening could make the EU more inward looking, as it sought to deal with the problems arising from its heterogeneous membership;
• extensive widening would exacerbate conflict within the Union, by increasing the number and range of problem issues.
The Case for Widening
• it is inevitable that many other European states will join the EU at some point. It therefore seems reasonable to delay further deepening, so that new members can play a full role in the EU's development;
• the EU would no longer be confined to Western Europe, and would become a truly European formation;
• not to widen would be to betray the principles on which the EU was founded (that is, it is open to any democratic European state);
• not to widen would be to miss an historic opportunity created by the end of the cold war to end the division of Europe once and for all;
• widening will increase the EU's 'clout' in international affairs;
• it will create new business opportunities, by creating a bigger SEM.

A key issue between wideners and deepeners is that of *motive*: for example, deepeners have accused wideners of pursuing a hidden agenda, aimed at slowing down processes of deepening and at transforming the Union into a loose confederation. Conversely, wideners have accused deepeners of insularity – that is, of failing to adjust to post-cold war realities and of perceiving 'Europe' to mean 'Western Europe'. Both sides can claim some victories in this debate, because both widening and deepening are on the EU's current agenda. The extent to which widening and deepening are compatible, however, remains highly debatable.

⟁ A Strategy for Enlargement.

The unprecedented scale of applications for EU entry has forced the EU to give serious consideration to the development of a coherent strategy to replace its erstwhile *ad hoc* approach to enlargement. It is now widely recognised that a mistake was made in the 1963 association agreement with Turkey, which virtually promised Turkey entry at some future date.

The emerging strategy of enlargement seeks to address two central questions: the *conditions* for membership and the *time-scale* at which enlargement should proceed. Article F of the TEU effectively attaches political conditions to membership, by affirming that the principle of democracy, and respect for human rights are fundamental characteristics of the Union. The European Council in Copenhagen in June 1993 reaffirmed these conditions. Applicants must also agree to accept the *acquis communautaire*. The *acquis* now embraces the TEU, including its provisions in relation to foreign and security policy. Moreover, enlargement must not jeopardise the 'forward movement' of EU integration. The European Council in Copenhagen also attached economic conditions in relation to applications from Central and Eastern European countries.

Various strategies for future enlargement have been suggested. For example, prospective members might be admitted in selected groups (for example, firstly the Mediterranean 'orphans' and then some Central European states) – the *wave approach*. This is a variant of the 'concentric circles' model of enlargement once advanced by Jacques Delors. Those in the inner circles have brighter entry prospects than others, as shown in Figure 18.1. The EU has insisted that each country's application must be considered on its merits and must involve separate negotiations. But although the fourth enlargement involved separate negotiations with each applicant, these took place in parallel. The declaration of the European Council in Madrid in December 1995 expressed the hope that accession negotiations with former communist countries and with Malta and Cyprus would also begin in parallel.This should not be taken to mean, however, that all applicants will be admitted in a single wave, a most unlikely prospect. The Commission is required to present an opinion on individual applications after the completion of the 1996 IGC, which is unlikely to complete its work until well into 1997.

Figure 18.1 A Concentric Circles Model of Future Enlargement

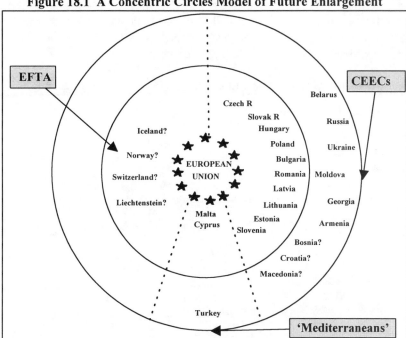

Another possibility is that applicants could be asked to join a separate organisation, closely linked to the EU, as a necessary prelude or preparation for full entry (the *waiting-room approach*). The European Economic Area is often cited as having the potential to perform this function. Another suggestion is that East European countries could be encouraged to set up their own 'Economic Union', with the possibility that the Western and Eastern 'Unions' would merge once disparities in economic performance and wealth levels between them had narrowed (the *parallel integration approach*). Some countries might also be offered *partial membership* (for example, entailing exclusion from the CAP, from the Structural Funds and from provisions on migration). But prospective members are unenthusiastic about these options, because they are wary of being fobbed off with a form of second-class membership.

● FUTURE ENTRANTS?

○ Potential Members

Potential members (Map 18.1) can be roughly divided into three categories:
* residual EFTA states (Iceland, Norway, Switzerland and Liechtenstein);
* former communist Central and East European states (CEECs, some of which have signed Association ('Europe') Agreements with the EU);
* the Mediterranean group (Malta, Cyprus and Turkey).

Map 18.1 The Enlargement of the EU: Potential Future Members

Poor aspirant countries are likely to face the most formidable entry problems, for three reasons: their economic situation tends to be worse even than that of Greece, the EU's poorest member; the EU is still struggling to cope with the budgetary implications of the admission of three poor countries in the 1980s; poor countries will have major difficulties in meeting the obligations of membership as a result of the EU's commitment to EMU. Conversely, the world is now moving at a faster pace and therefore the snail's pace of past enlargements is no reliable guide to future trends.

○ Residual EFTA

Norway, Switzerland and Iceland could probably enter the Union quickly, if they opted to do so. The result of the Norwegian referendum in November 1994 effectively ended the possibility that Norway would join the EU in the near future. A 'no' vote in the Swiss referendum on the EEA in December 1992 had the same effect in relation to Switzerland. Switzerland has a very long history of avoiding European entanglements. It is not even a member of the United Nations. Its economy is already highly intermeshed with the EU economy (being the EU's third-largest trading partner). Large companies and banks tend to favour entry (Swiss banks and insurance companies already have many subsidiaries in the EU, and all major EU banks have branches or subsidiaries in Switzerland) but there is strong opposition to entry from some other groups, including farmers.

If Norway opted to join, Iceland could be pulled towards entry via a Nordic 'domino effect' and in order to secure the same access as Norway to the EU's market for fish (Iceland depends upon fishing for about 80% of its exports). Although EU membership is currently opposed by all main parties, recent polls show that about 50% of Icelanders favour applying. It is a NATO member, and therefore neutrality is not an issue. Liechtenstein has a population of only 30,000 and is too small to join as a full member. It joined the Council of Europe in 1978 and became a full member of the UN in 1990. It joined GATT in 1994. EU membership would compromise its position as a tax haven and could lead to immigration problems. It may be satisfied with membership of the EEA, which it joined in May 1995.

○ The CEECs

On 1 April 1994, Hungary became the first ex-communist country in Eastern Europe to formally apply for EU entry. By January 1996, eight other CEECs (Poland, Romania, Slovakia, Estonia, Latvia, Lithuania, Bulgaria and the Czech Republic) had also submitted applications. All CEEC applicants are looking for a firm date for commencement of entry negotiations.

Eurobarometer surveys have repeatedly shown the peoples of Eastern Europe favour closer links with the EU (see, for example, *Eurobarometer*, no. 5, 1995). Several East European countries have also taken practical steps to improve their chances of entry, such as moves to bring their technical standards in line with EU standards and participation, or attempted participation, in organisations closely associated with Western Europe. There has also been substantial realignment of the external trade of Eastern European countries towards the EU.

The EU has been reluctant to commit itself to early membership for the CEECs. It is clear that the 'absorption capacity' of the EU could be a major obstacle to early CEEC entry. With an average GDP per capita of about one-third of the EU average, large agricultural sectors and major problems of regional and industrial maldevelopment, entry of these countries in their present state would wreck the Community budget and also EU agricultural, regional and social policies. Nevertheless, strong pressure for early entry emanating from several CEECs has forced the EU to give serious consideration to the issue of Eastern enlargement.

Several recent European Councils have addressed the issue of Union entry for CEECs with Europe Agreements. The European Council in Copenhagen in June 1993 offered these countries entry as soon as they are able to assume the obligations of membership. In June 1994, the European Council in Corfu instructed the Commission to prepare a report outlining an accession strategy for associated CEECs. The report, which was presented to the European Council in Essen in December 1994, accorded the Europe Agreements a central role in the accession process, by stating that they should form the basis of closer relations between the Union and associated countries.

In May 1995, the Commission published a White Paper on the subject of Eastern enlargement, focusing on the measures thought necessary to adapt the economies of the CEECs to the Single European Market. Its *pre-accession strategy* for associated CEECs included proposals for economic alignment, requiring CEECs to take measures to bring their standards and administrative structures in line with EU practice. The White Paper did not, however, include a specific timetable for membership. Nor did it deal with the problems of agriculture, environmental or social policy, except where these were directly related to 'internal market' issues. The strategy was accepted by the European Council in Cannes in June 1995. The emerging EU policy on CEEC entry seems to be based on the following five principles:

- acceptance that some CEECs will eventually enter the EU;
- differentiation: the entry prospects of some CEECs are considerably brighter than others. There are wide variations between CEECs in relation to their economic prospects, political stability, population size and historical ties with Western Europe;

- political conditionality: criteria include political stability, maintenance of democracy and respect for human rights;
- the Union's 'absorption capacity', taking into account budgetary and trade implications and also the need to maintain the momentum of European integration;
- the CEECs will be required to make substantial adjustments to make their economies compatible with the SEM.

○ The Implications of an Eastern Enlargement

A recent study by Baldwin (1994) has shown that the entry of even the most suitable CEECs would be highly problematic. If admitted, the 'Visegrad 4' countries (Hungary, the Czech and Slovak Republics and Poland) would receive substantially more from the Structural Funds than the four poorest countries in EU 15. Baldwin estimates that the 'V4' countries would need to grow by 10% a year to be budget neutral and that their entry would add ECU 58 billion to the EU budget by 1999, requiring a 60% increase in budgetary contributions. The accession of V4 would also bankrupt the CAP. The V4 are 2.5 times as 'agricultural' as the EU 12 average. Many other CEECs are between 4 and 7 times as agricultural. Eastern entrants would almost certainly seek to build coalitions of interest in the Council, to exert pressure for budgetary increases. However, assessments which point out the potential economic burdens for the EU of an Eastern enlargement have been criticised for not given sufficient consideration to the possibility of fast economic growth in the CEECs, or to the possibility of radical reform of the Community budget (Hopkinson, 1995).

When negotiations for the entry of these countries do commence, it seems inevitable that countries and interest groups within the EU will demand major safeguards: these demands will emanate from farmers, from representatives from the regions, from the EU 15 'poor four' (with which the V4 would be competing for Structural Funds), from sensitive industrial sectors, such as steel and textiles, and from EU countries worried about migration.

○ Factors Affecting CEEC Entry Prospects

Table 18.2 provides a snapshot of some key qualifying and disqualifying factors. It includes highly subjective and disputable assessments and therefore it is no more than a rough guide. Moreover, the 'positive scores' by no means provide exact indicators of entry prospects: for example, Russia's population size would present a major obstacle to Russia's entry even if all other scores were positive.

Table 18.2 Some Factors Affecting the Entry Prospects of CEECs

	Economy	Size	Democracy/ Human Rights	'Europe' Agreement?	At Peace?	Positive Score
Albania	✕	✓	✓	✕	✓?	3?
Armenia	✕	✓	✓?	✕	✕	2?
Belorus	✕	✓	✓	✕	✓	3
Bosnia	✕	✓	✕	✕	✕	1
Bulgaria	O	✓	✓	✓	✓	4
Croatia	O	✓	?	✕	✕	1?
Czech R.	✓	✓	✓	✓	✓	5
Estonia	✓	✓	✓	✓	✓	5
Georgia	✕	✓	?	✕	✕	1?
Hungary	✓	✓	✓	✓	✓	5
Latvia	✓	✓	✓	✓	✓	5
Lithuania	✓	✓	✓	✓	✓	5
Macedonia	✕	✓	✓	✕	?	2
Moldova	✕	✓	✓	✕	?	2?
Poland	✓	✕	✓	✓	✓	4
Romania	O	O	✓	✓	✓	3/4
Russia	✕	✕	✓?	✕	✓?	2?
Slovakia	O	✓	?	✓	✓	3?
Slovenia	✓	✓	✓	✓	✓	5
Ukraine	✕	✕	✓	✕	✓	2
Yug. Fed.	✕	✓	✕	✕	✕	1

Key: ✓ = yes, good or *generally* satisfactory;　✕ = no or poor; O = 'middling'; ? = no clear answer possible.

O　**Alternatives to Membership?**

The formidable obstacles to EU entry by the CEECs in the short to medium terms raises the question of alternatives to full membership, such as:

A. partial membership;

B. membership of an EU waiting-room organisation;

C. a pan-European trade zone incorporating elements of A and B.

A. Partial Membership? Some previous enlargements have involved long transition periods for new entrants (for example, Greece, Spain and Portugal were not fully integrated into the CAP. There were quotas on Iberian iron and steel for 7 years and restricted migration rights for 5 years). However, previous entrants were given full access to the Structural Funds. In 1991, Frans Andriessen, EU External Affairs Commissioner, advanced the notion of affiliate membership for the East European states, which would offer membership benefits without holding up the process of integration. Affiliates would have membership of the Council in certain areas, and representation in the EP. CEEC entrants might be given full access to the SEM, but could be excluded for several years from access to the Structural Funds and the CAP (together accounting for about 80% of the Community budget). Restrictions might be placed on CEEC exports of agricultural products, steel and textiles because of low labour costs in CEEC countries. Migration might also be restricted. But the exclusion of CEEC countries from access to the Structural Funds and the CAP would, in the light of the EU's aim to narrow regional imbalances within the Union, be a glaring anomaly: it would mean that although poor regions in Western Europe would receive regional aid, the Eastern regions would not. Restrictions on access to EU markets would also be highly controversial and would run counter to the EU's SEM objectives.

B. A Waiting Room? For example, membership of the EEA might constitute a useful intermediate stage on the road to full membership. At the time the EEA Treaty was negotiated, it was widely acknowledged that the EEA could at some point be widened to embrace the East European states. The EEA involves participation in the SEM, but exclusion from the CAP, the Structural Funds and representation in Union institutions. But aspirants for EU membership tend to be dismissive of such ideas, viewing them as distractions from their goal of rapid and full entry into the Union.

C. A Pan-European Trade Zone? Baldwin (1994) favours the creation of a Pan-European trading system with three concentric circles: the EU, the EEA and an 'AAA' (Association of Association Agreements). The AAA would comprise the EU plus CEECs with association agreements, The system would create a free trade zone for industrial goods. It would give enterprises in CEECs access to other CEEC markets It could stimulate the production of labour-intensive goods in the East, enabling EU members to concentrate on the production of high-tech, high value-added goods. There would also be an Organisation for European Integration (OEI) for countries regarded as most suitable for entry. The OEI would enable members to participate in the SEM, but would exclude them from the CAP and Structural Funds. The main advantage of the OEI would be that it would replace the current *ad hoc* system with a comprehensive set of agreements. But many CEECs might view this scheme as a distraction from their primary goal of EU entry.

○ **Associated CEECs**

Amongst the CEECs, Hungary is a leading contender for early entry. It has a relatively small population, and is vigorously pursuing policies of privatisation, marketisation and 'western-reorientation'. It has also received the lion's share of foreign direct investment into Eastern Europe. Hungary was the first CEEC to join the Council of Europe. Hungarian exports to Western Europe now exceed those to Eastern Europe. Two-thirds of Hungarian trade is with EU countries now that Austria has acceded.

The Czech Republic has made remarkably fast economic progress since 1990. It has reoriented its trade towards Western Europe, and has received substantial FDI. President Vaclav Havel has argued that, in reorienting themselves towards the West, Czechoslovaks and other East Europeans were seeking to return to 'a certain civilisation, a certain political culture'. Although less developed than the Czech Republic, Slovakia is still closely associated with it. Its prospects of early entry largely derive from these close links. Poland is also a major front-runner. The EU is now Poland's most important trading partner. About half of Poland's exports currently enter the EU. The size of Poland's population could be an obstacle to early entry. Poland could present the EU with fierce competition in some sectors (not least agriculture) if granted full market access. Bulgaria and Romania are economically too weak, and possibly too unstable politically, to be ranked in the same entry category as the V4. Association agreements with the Baltic republics and Slovenia were completed in 1995. Slovenia's geographical position and its rapid economic progress put it in the 'fast lane' towards entry. The Baltic republics are also making good economic progress. Their small populations mean that they could be fairly easily absorbed.

○ 'The Rest'

The chances of early entry for other CEECs currently seem very remote. Most are too poor and many too politically unstable for serious consideration. Most will probably have to settle for alternatives to membership, such as preferential trading agreements or association agreements containing only the vaguest reference to future entry. Russia and Ukraine (with populations of 147 million and 51 million), would be very difficult to absorb, even if they made substantial progress in reform. Russia, Georgia, Moldova and Armenia are currently unacceptable on political grounds: internal divisions within both Georgia and Moldova have erupted into civil war; Armenia is at war with Azerbaizan. Albania is wretchedly poor and undeveloped. With the exception of Slovenia, all successor states of former Yugoslavia are currently ruled out on political grounds, although their prospects could improve sharply if a lasting peace settlement in the Balkans is achieved.

○ Turkey and the 'Mediterranean Orphans'

Turkey's association agreement (1973) contained a reference to eventual Turkish membership of the Community, but without specifying a date. Turkey is generally recognised as being the most secularised of all Muslim countries. It formally applied for membership in April 1987. In December 1989, the Commission issued a negative opinion on Turkey's application, on the grounds that Turkey would be a major institutional, political and financial burden to the Union, at least for the foreseeable future. Turkey is regarded as an unappealing prospect for several reasons: it has a large population; it is poor and underdeveloped (with a GDP per capita of less than half of the EU's poorest member); Turkey has a poor human rights record (particularly in relation to its treatment of its Kurdish minority). It has an unresolved dispute with Greece over Cyprus. Turkey's status as a 'European' country is by no means generally accepted in the EU. The Commission's opinion nevertheless recognised Turkey's geopolitical importance and favoured appropriate steps to 'anchor it firmly within the future architecture of Europe' (see 'Europe and the Challenge of Enlargement', *Bulletin of EC*, supplement 3/92). Since 1973, there has been duty-free access of Turkish industrial goods, excluding textiles. A customs union between the EU and Turkey came into effect on 1 January 1996. Turkey may end up with a form of 'super-associate' status rather than full membership.

Negotiations for the accession of Malta and Cyprus will begin six months after the end of the 1996 IGC. Malta applied in 1990. It has a GDP per capita lower than the Union average, but with a population of only 350,000, it would hardly overburden the Structural Funds. It has been linked to the EU since 1971 by means of an association agreement. If admitted, Malta would benefit from various EU subsidies. About 75% of its trade is with the EU. The Commission produced a favourable opinion on Malta's application in June 1993, but urged it to undertake economic reforms in the fields of taxation, banking and trade. Cyprus also applied in 1990. It has had an association agreement with the EU since 1973. It has a small population and a higher GDP per capita than some poorer EU members. But the *de facto* partition between Turks in the north and Greeks in the south is a potential obstacle to entry. The Commission's opinion on its application stated that Cyprus had a 'European identity' and was suited to membership, if its inter-communal dispute could be resolved. In the case of Malta and Cyprus, the Commission raised the issue of the implications for EU institutions of the admission of very small countries.

● THE IMPACT OF ENLARGEMENT ON THE UNION

○ Enlargement and the 1996 IGC

The European Council in Corfu established a clear link between enlargement and the 1996 IGC. Enlargement will undoubtedly be accorded much greater importance at this IGC than was the case at the Maastricht summit. No new accession negotiations will be entered into until after the completion of the IGC. For example, decisions on majority voting, on the representation of small states and on the size of the Commission are to be taken prior to any accession negotiations. Acceptance by the Commission of a multispeed Europe derives in large measure from recognition of the fact that enlargement will inevitably increase the diversity of the Union's membership. In its report to the IGC Reflection Group (see Chapter 4) the Commission has stated that it will not support any dilution of the Union's *acquis* as a result of enlargement. It seems far more likely that aspirant countries will be required to adjust to the EU than the other way round.

○ Towards the Pan-Europeanisation of European Integration?

Although some CEECs have excellent prospects of entry into the Union, the entry prospects of others seem at best remote. This does not necessarily mean, however, that there will be a clear demarcation between an enlarged Union and the rest of Europe. It seems more likely that the Union and European countries outside it will become increasingly intermeshed in pan-European ventures of various kinds, such as trans-European networks and RTD programmes. Moreover, the agreements signed between the EU and non-associated CEECs are recognised to be stages on the road to deeper co-operation, perhaps leading eventually to a free trade zone encompassing virtually the whole of Europe. Intermeshing could well mean that the boundaries of the Union will become increasingly rough-edged and fuzzy.

FURTHER READING

Anderson, K. and Blackhurst, R. (eds), *Regional Integration and the Global Trading System*, Harvester Wheatsheaf, Hemel Hempstead, 1993.

Baldwin, R.E., *Towards an Integrated Europe*, Centre for Economic Policy Research, London, 1994.

Commission COM (95), 163, *White Paper on preparation of the associated countries of Central and Eastern Europe for integration into the Internal Market of the Union*, May 1995.

Commission, *Europe and the Challenge of Enlargement*, Bulletin Supplement 3, 1992.

Hopkinson, N., *The Eastern Enlargement of the Union*, Wilton Park Paper, 91, HMSO, 1995.

Laurent, Pierre-Henri, 'Widening Europe: The Dilemmas of Community Success', *Annals of the American Academy of Political and Social Science*, no. 531, January, 1994, pp. 124–40.

 **Chapter 19**

The European Union's Relations with the New Eastern Europe

● THE UNION'S SPECIAL RELATIONSHIP WITH EASTERN EUROPE

The collapse of communism in Eastern Europe was so sudden and unexpected that little prior attention had been given by the Union to the question of its future relationship with the region in a post-cold war world. During the communist period, official contacts between the Union and the Soviet bloc had been minimal, due to ideological hostility and low levels of trade. With the exception of Yugoslavia and Romania (which had trade agreements with the Union), communist East European countries were at the bottom of the Union's system of trade preferences. But even before the cataclysmic events in Eastern Europe in the autumn of 1989, the Union had accepted special responsibilities for the region. Following decisions taken at the 'G7' summit in Paris in July 1989, the Commission was given responsibility for co-ordinating Western aid to Poland and Hungary. This was later extended to include other Central and East European countries (CEECs).

The EU's assumption of a special relationship with the CEECs can be justified in terms of enlightened self-interest: for reasons of geographical proximity, the EU would find it difficult to insulate itself from the consequences of economic collapse and political instability in Eastern Europe. The Union shares land borders with several CEECs (Finland with Russia; Germany with Poland and the Czech Republic; Austria with the Czech and Slovak Republics, Hungary and Slovenia; Italy with Slovenia); as noted in Chapter 18, the peoples of Eastern Europe have strong aspirations for closer links with the Union. Because of its potential political and economic leverage, the Union could play a major role in ensuring that anti-democratic forces in the CEECs do not gain the upper hand. The region also offers substantial trade and investment opportunities for EU companies. Several EU countries currently have substantial trade surpluses with Eastern Europe. EU exports to the region could increase substantially in the next decade, particularly if East European living standards rise. The region's problems of environmental degradation also pose a threat to Western Europe, as the Chernobyl nuclear disaster in 1986 showed. For the Union, therefore, its relationship with the new Eastern Europe contains a mixture of opportunities, benefits, threats and costs, viz:

Opportunities and Benefits	**Threats and Costs**
• *trade benefits (new markets);*	• *trade threats to EU industries;*
• *new investment opportunities;*	• *diversion of FDI to Eastern Europe;*
• *opportunities to contribute to reshaping of Europe;*	• *distraction from deepening of EU integration;*
• *possible cuts in defence spending;*	• *possible embroilment in conflicts;*
• *closer links with the East.*	• *a 'mass migration' threat;*
	• *financial costs of aid packages.*

● EU AID POLICIES FOR THE REGION

○ Main Features

Several distinctive features of the EU's relationship with the new Eastern Europe can be discerned: the EU has shown a preference for *bilateral* arrangements with CEECs. There is no equivalent of the Lomé Convention for Eastern Europe. The EU's trade policy towards the region has been referred to by Baldwin (1994) as 'hub and spoke bilateralism', in that the East European countries are connected to the EU hub by separate agreements. These bilateral deals exhibit a 'pyramid of privilege' in relation to aid and trade concessions. CEECs with association (or Europe) agreements are at the apex of the pyramid whereas those lower down have (or may be eventually be offered) trade and co-operation agreements. The EU has consistently emphasised that CEEC recipients of EU trade and aid concessions must remain committed to democratic governance and respect for human rights. Perhaps the most important factor shaping the Union's relationship with the CEECs has been the interplay between the EU's desire to assist the reform process in the region and powerful constraints on the extent of assistance actually rendered. Critics of EU policy towards the region point to the gulf between the EU's magnanimous rhetoric and its actual performance. They point to the reluctance of the EU to fully open up its markets to East European industries. They complain that the EU seems to be concerned to keep Eastern Europe at 'arm's length' through strict restrictive immigration and trade agreements. The EU has imposed a wide range of restrictions on CEEC exports, including sector-specific quotas and anti-dumping and countervailing duties. They condemn EU foot-dragging with regard to requests of CEECs for Union membership.

In its defence, the EU could accuse the CEECs of having unrealistic expectations concerning the extent of Western assistance. It is now generally accepted that the West has no intention of providing aid to Eastern Europe on the scale of the Marshall Plan, the US aid programme which helped Western Europe get back on its feet in the early post-war years. Not only would the amounts required to bankroll Eastern Europe's regeneration be prohibitive: unlike the recipients of Marshall Aid, the CEECs are developing market economies almost from first principles. Several CEECs have shown a remarkable ability to reorient their external trade towards the EU. The CEECs have a comparative advantage in a substantial range of goods, such as agricultural products, steel, chemicals, textiles, clothing, footwear, glass and cement. Arguably, some EU industries are too vulnerable to be opened up completely and suddenly.

○ CEEC Access to EU Markets

Before the collapse of communism, the EU employed a phalanx of tariff and non-tariff barriers to keep out East European goods. The changes in Eastern Europe brought about by Mikhail Gorbachev resulted in the signing of bilateral trade and economic co-operation agreements of modest scope between the Union and several East European countries between 1988 and 1990. The agreements lifted some quotas and quantitative restrictions but did not contain tariff preferences. The end of 'soft markets' in the region (that is, guaranteed markets via Comecon) has made it necessary for these countries to seek new outlets for their goods. It was agreed at the special European Council in Dublin in April 1990 that Association (Europe) Agreements should be offered to certain CEECs. Not only do these offer more generous terms than the earlier agreements, they also contain explicit political provisions. These are also known as *second-generation* agreements because they replace the agreements signed between 1988 and 1990. In each of the Europe Agreements, the CEEC's aspiration to join the EU at some unspecified date is explicitly recognised. By 1995, the EU had signed Europe

Agreements with Hungary, Poland, the Czech and Slovak Republics, Bulgaria, Romania, the Baltic republics and Slovenia. Each is valid for ten years. Such Agreements have to be ratified by the EP and by the national parliaments of the member states. They consist of four elements: promotion of freer trade between the signatories; industrial, technical and scientific co-operation; financial assistance; and a mechanism for political dialogue.

Each Europe Agreement establishes an Association Council comprising ministerial-level representatives, plus an association committee of civil servants. The Agreements grant the CEECs free trade in industrial goods over ten years. Market access provisions are weighted in favour of the CEECs in that the EU has agreed to reduce its import barriers more quickly than the East European signatories. It is envisaged that when the East European economies are significantly closer to the EU level, negotiations will begin for the free movement of persons, services and capital. Unlike the EEA Treaty, there is no formal commitment in the Agreements to acceptance of the *acquis communautaire*, although Associates are required to act to ensure that their future legislation is compatible with it.

Negotiations for the Agreements have led to fierce haggling over details, due to pressure by EU industrial and agricultural lobbies. The lobbies argue that the lower labour costs and lower environmental standards in the CEECs give these countries unfair trade advantages. In the Agreements, sensitive industrial sectors are subject to transitional arrangements. The Agreements also contain safeguards against disruption of EU markets. Mainline agricultural items (cereals, beef, lamb, dairy products) remain protected by the CAP. In May 1993, anti-dumping duties were imposed on steel pipes from Hungary and Poland, despite the fact that the Agreements had eliminated quotas for steel. The European Councils held in Copenhagen and Corfu both endorsed a more rapid opening of the EU's market than anticipated in the agreements and favoured early-warning mechanisms before anti-dumping or similar measures were introduced. In its first transition report in 1994, the European Bank for Reconstruction and Development (EBRD) (see below) identified the EU as the main threat to East European exports and investment and made the following criticisms of the Agreements:

- they include contingent protection measures, in the form of vaguely defined 'safeguard clauses', which enable the EU to impose restrictions on a range of imports;
- they do not significantly alter the regulations governing anti-dumping;
- they set high local content rules of 60% for exports from Eastern Europe (that is, at least 60% of the product must be of local origin).

The Commission was authorised by the Council to negotiate Partnership and Co-operation (PCA) agreements with the ex-Soviet republics to supersede the 1989 agreement with the Soviet Union. These countries (excluding the Baltic states) are unlikely to be offered full association agreements in the near future, because such agreements now routinely contain references to future EU membership for the CEEC partner. A PCA falls somewhere between a trade and co-operation agreement and a Europe Agreement, in that there is explicit reference to political co-operation. PCAs, embracing trade, economic and political matters, have already been signed with Ukraine and Russia. It is envisaged that talks on a free trade area with the signatories to PCA agreements will begin in 1998. Trade and co-operation agreements with the Baltic states were signed in 1992 and came into force in the spring of 1993. In January 1995, these were superseded by free trade agreements. Europe agreements for the Baltic states and Slovenia were negotiated in 1995.

○ **Financial and Technical Assistance Programmes**

It is difficult to assess the amount of financial assistance rendered by the EU to Eastern Europe, for various reasons: aid by no means emanates from a single source. In addition to aid channelled through EU institutions, member states have their own aid programmes for the region (for example, the UK has its 'Know-How' Fund). The member states also contribute to the work of the multilateral agencies, such as the World Bank, the IMF and the EBRD. Well-publicised announcements of aid do not necessarily result in actual disbursements, because these have frequently involved 'repackaging' of what has already been promised. A distinction must also be made between aid in the form of loans, which have to be paid back, and grants, which do not. The grant component of aid to the region has been small. Whereas about 88% of Marshall Aid was in the form of grants, less than 10% of aid for Eastern Europe falls into the category.

Requests for aid from Eastern Europe coincided with increased budgetary pressures on the EU. Nevertheless, Eastern Europe has received more aid from the EU and its member states than from any other source. The Commission estimates that between 1990 and 94, the EU and its member states provided ECU 38.7 billion to Eastern Europe, more than two-thirds of the total from the G24 countries. By September 1993, the EIB had lent ECU 1,308 million to Eastern Europe. In November 1993, the Council agreed in principle to lend up to ECU 3 billion over three years to ten CEECs. The main focus of EU technical assistance has been on transmission of 'know-how', through training programmes. The PHARE and TACIS programmes are the main channels for EU aid to the region, contributing about 70% of technical assistance to CEECs. PHARE (Poland and Hungary: Aid for Economic Restructuring) has kept its original name, even though it now includes 12 CEECs.

Table 19.1 Finance Provided by PHARE in 1993

Country	ECU Mn	Sector	ECU Mn
Albania	49	Agriculture	17.0
Bulgaria	85	Developing private sector	93.4
Estonia	22.5	Financial sector	56.0
Hungary	85	Environment and nuclear safety	77.5
Latvia	29.5	Social development, employment,	45.5
Lithuania	39	health	
Poland	208	Education, training, R & D	173.9
Romania	100	Infrastructure	326.4
Slovak R.	40	Public administration & institutions	81.9
Slovenia	24	Humanitarian aid	30.0
Czech R.	60	Democracy, civic society, NGOs	6.2
Macedonia	25	General technical assistance	55.5
Multi-country	86	**Total**	**963.3**
Other	109.5	*Source:* Commission, *General Report (1994)*	
Total	**963.3**		

In 1994, the PHARE programme amounted to ECU 963 million and TACIS (Technical Assistance to the Commonwealth of Independent States) to ECU 510 million. The programmes, financed through the Community budget, embrace technical assistance, infrastructure investment and humanitarian and emergency aid. There are a number of specific support programmes, such as TEMPUS (Trans-European Mobility Programme for University Studies), OUVERTURE (inter-regional co-operation) and the PHARE and TACIS Democracy Programme. PHARE operates through indicative programmes agreed between the Commission and the government of the recipient state. Action programmes for specific projects are then developed. The operation of the programmes has been widely criticised for being slow and bureaucratic (leading to long gaps between applications and disbursements).

• THE EBRD

Although it is not a European Union institution, member states played a key role in the creation of the European Bank for Reconstruction and Development (EBRD) in 1990. The proposal for a new bank for Eastern Europe was first mooted by President Mitterrand in October 1989, and was discussed at the European Council in Paris in December. The Bank was envisaged as a principal institutional vehicle for Western aid to Eastern Europe. The US was originally doubtful about the need for a new agency, but resigned itself to the fact that it would probably be created with or without its support. At its inception there was haggling over who should be its president and where it should be sited. In May 1990, members voted for a London base. The Bank's articles of agreement were signed in Paris on 29 May 1990. Its first president was a former advisor to President Mitterrand, Jacques Attali. The Bank has a membership comprising both EU and non-EU states, plus several non-European states and two institutional members (the European Commission and the European Investment Bank). The EU bloc (with its two institutional members) has a majority of votes.

The EBRD is the fourth major area-based development bank, the others being those for Africa, Asia and Latin America. It is a hybrid institution, in that it is partly a development bank and partly an investment bank. The Bank lends at market rates to countries in the region committed to economic reform, multiparty democracy and pluralism. It was agreed that the Bank would have an initial capital of ECU 10 billion and would direct its lending primarily towards the private sector. Sixty per cent of its lending is for the private sector and 40% for public sector infrastructural projects. The Bank has a 'Triple A' credit rating which allows it to borrow in international capital markets on favourable terms. It operates in 25 countries.

The Bank opened in the spring of 1991. However, there has been much criticism of its role and capabilities. Critics have argued that it merely duplicates the functions of the World Bank, the International Finance Corporation and the EIB; that it is a prime example of post-cold war 'tokenism' and that it merely diverts attention from the need for Western countries to open their markets to East European exports. By the end of 1993, signed commitments amounted to only ECU 2.8 billion, and disbursements only ECU 556 million. In 1993, Attali resigned, following a *Financial Times* exposé of lavish spending on the EBRD's headquarters. He was replaced by a professional banker, Jacques de Larosière, who has increased the number of professional bankers by about 25% (to about 250). The Bank is also seeking to increase its on-the-ground presence in the region but it remains to be seen whether it can salvage its somewhat tarnished reputation.

● PROSPECTS FOR EASTERN EUROPE

Communist systems exhibited a common pattern of resource misallocation, enterprise mismanagement, technological stagnation, indifference to product quality and low environmental standards. Several years have now elapsed since the East European revolutions and a clearer picture is now emerging of the CEEC's problems and prospects (Table 19.2).

Table 19.2 Prospects for Eastern Europe

The Optimistic View

- most CEECs have relatively small populations. Excluding the ex-Soviet republics, the combined population of the East European states is only 136 million (for Eastern Europe as a whole, it is about 400 million);
- a powerful reformist mood. Even though reform communist parties have done well at the polls recently (for example, in Poland, Lithuania, Hungary and Bulgaria), they are committed to the introduction of market economies. Many East Europeans favour a reorientation to the West and do not fear Western cultural and economic influences;
- most of the East European states have relatively low foreign debts:
- the East European states are more industrialised than most Third World countries (in fact, they are overindustrialised). They are less vulnerable to product price volatility than many countries in the Third World;
- low labour costs, being on average about one-tenth of West European levels. The region also has a relatively well-educated workforce;
- the West may be more likely to be generous with aid, because of cultural affinity, geographical proximity and strategic interest;
- several have made remarkable progress in reorienting their external trade towards Western markets and in attracting FDI;
- the entrepreneurial spirit, long suppressed by communism, has re-emerged alive and well in some parts of the region.

The Pessimistic View

- the limited volume of capital flows. Western commercial banks and MNCs have been very cautious and selective in their lending and investment policies to Eastern Europe; private investment flows and official aid are concentrated in a few CEECs;
- the willingness, and capacity, of Western countries to assist the reform process in the region should not be overestimated;
- 'absorption capacity'. Even if financial aid was given on a massive scale, can Eastern Europe absorb it? Are there enough commercially viable projects into which lending can be channelled?
- unrealistic expectations. Reforms require major behavioural and attitudinal changes, in addition to financial support;
- currency problems. Hard currency shortages have led to barter deals becoming a major element in the trade of some CIS countries;
- ethnic conflict, an unwanted side-effect of communism's demise, remains a threat to the transition process in several CEECs. In the post-cold war era, there have been armed conflicts in the Balkans, Georgia, Moldova, Russia (Chechnya) and between Armenia and Azerbaizan.

The euphoria which accompanied the end of communist rule has long since been replaced by more sober assessments of the region's future. It will probably take several decades for most of the CEECs to 'catch up' with the West European market economies. However, some CEECs (for example, the Czech Republic, Hungary, Slovenia and Poland) have made considerable progress in pursuit of their transition goals. The private sector now accounts for well over half of the GDP in many CEECs.

Although there is no consensus on the most appropriate strategy of development for transition economies, it is possible to identify common ingredients of the reform strategies adopted by CEECs, viz.: the holding of democratic elections; the liberalisation of prices; the liberalisation and reorientation of external trade; institutional restructuring at all levels; the creation of a legal framework for a market economy (for example, property and company laws); the restructuring and privatisation of state enterprises; the removal of budget support from enterprises; the creation of new tax systems; the creation of social safety nets for the disadvantaged (for example, the unemployed and pensioners); and policies to attract foreign direct investment. The drive towards closer links with the European Union must also be regarded as a major common ingredient of CEEC transition strategies. The nature of the Union's response to Eastern Europe's 'great transformation' has major implications both for the transition countries and for the Union itself. It is to be hoped that the Union will rise to this challenge.

FURTHER READING

Baldwin, R.E., *Towards an Integrated Europe*, Centre for Economic Policy Research, London, 1994.

Dyker, D., The National Economies of Europe, Longman, Harlow, 1995.

European Bank for Reconstruction and Development, *Transition Report*, 1994.

Gros, D. and Steinherr, A., *Winds of Change: Economic Reform in Eastern Europe*, Longman, Harlow, 1995.

Kennedy, D. and Webb, D., 'The Limits of Integration: Eastern Europe and the European Communities', *Common Market Law Review*, vol. 30, no. 6, 1993, pp. 1095–1117.

Kramer, H., 'The European Community's Response to the New Eastern Europe', *Journal of Common Market Studies*, vol. 31, no. 2, 1993, pp. 213–44.

Pinder, J., *The European Community and Eastern Europe*, Pinter, London, 1991.

Van Ham, P., *The EC and Central Europe*, Pinter, London, 1993.

Bibliography

● OFFICIAL PUBLICATIONS

A vast range of information is published by the Union on virtually every aspect of its activities. The Office for Official Publications of the European Communities (OOPEC) based in Luxembourg is the principal source of official information, but most EU institutions also disseminate material. Information leaflets of various kinds are available (usually free) from Commission and EP offices in member countries. The Commission's London Office publishes *The Week in Europe* and *Background Reports*. A more comprehensive range of publications is held in European Documentation Centres. There are about 40 EDCs in the UK, mainly in University libraries. EDCs receive copies of all publications issued by OOPEC. The Commission's DG X has produced a free video guide to information sources in the EU. A newsletter, *EUR-OP News*, is published four times a year by OOPEC. OOPEC also publishes a guide to EU information sources. The library of the European Commission compiles a monthly bibliography of recent EU publications. The following list, which is far from comprehensive, contains information about some of the most widely used official publications and sources.

Bulletin of the European Union: published 10 times a year by the Secretariat-General of the Commission, it provides an account of the Union's recent activities. Supplements to the *Bulletin* are published on significant issues;

CELEX: The offical data base of Community law;

COMEX: external trade statistics of the EU and member states;

Commission Documents are generally known as COM documents. These set out the Commission's viewpoint on Union matters and include proposals for legislation, plus analytical reports of various kinds;

Competition Policy Newsletter, published quarterly by the Commission;

The Courier, reports on EU relations with ACP countries;

Court of Auditors produces special reports;

Court of Justice. Legal Bibliography of European Integration (annual);

Directory of Community Legislation in Force, published twice yearly;

Economic Report, published annually by the Commission;

Environmental Research Newsletter, published twice yearly by the Commission;

EP News, newsletter published by the European Parliament;

ESC Opinions and Information Reports, published in the C section of the *Official Journal (OJ)*. There is a monthly *ESC Bulletin*;

Eurobarometer reports on public opinion in the EU (twice yearly);

EUROPA, the European Commission's Internet server, can be found at: http://www.cec.lu;

European Dialogue, published bi monthly by the Commission, informing East European countries on EU policy;

European Economy: published quarterly, by the Commission;

European File: about 20 Commission pamphlets a year on specific topics;

European Parliament Briefing, published by the European Parliament;

Eurostat: the Statistical Office of the European Communities provides statistical information for the Commission and all the citizens of Europe. For example, it produces *Basic Statistics, Europe In Figures* (annual) and *Rapid Reports* (about 50–55 issues a year on a variety of subjects). There is a Eurostat Information Office in Luxembourg and a data shop in Brussels;

Factsheets on the European Parliament and the Activities of the European Communities, published by the European Parliament;

Frontier Free Europe, monthly Commission newsletter on the SEM;

General Report on the Activities of the European Union, published annually by the Commission, provides summaries of institutional and policy developments;

Green Europe, quarterly, on agriculture and rural policies;

Official Journal of the European Communities (OJ) is published on most working days, divided into the following sections: *L series*: Legislation containing the full text of all legislation and acts the EU is obliged to publish and information on other legal acts; *C series*: Communications, Information and Notices. It covers proposals for legislation; written questions put by Parliament; ECU exchange rates; reports on cases before the ECJ; EU job vacancies and other official notes; *S series*: Supplements, containing notices of public works and public supply contracts open to competitive tender; *Annex*: debates in the EP;

Panorama of EU Industry is a detailed annual review by the Commission of the situation of the manufacturing industries in the EU;

Review of the Council's Work, published annually by the Council;

Scad Bulletin: a weekly bibliographic guide to principal EU publications and documents;

Social Europe: published thrice yearly by the Commission;

Treaties are published by the OOPEC.

● OTHER SOURCES

○ Independent Guides to EU Activities

Various guides are produced, for example:

Agence Europe, daily reports, Agence Internationale d'information pour la Presse, Brussels.

Annual Report on the Activities of the European Community, published by the *Journal of Common Market Studies*, Blackwell, London.

Annual Review of European Community Affairs, Brassey's, London.

Annual Review of European Community Affairs, Centre for European Policy Studies, Brussels.

European Access (bimonthly), Chadwyck-Healey, Cambridge.

European Trends, Economist Intelligence Unit, London.

The European Companion, published annually by Dod's, London.

○ Journals

Many academic journals in the social and legal sciences publish articles on European affairs. The following have a specific European focus:

Common Market Law Reports, Sweet & Maxwell, London.

Common Market Law Review, Kluwer, Dordrecht.

Euromoney, Euromoney, London.

European Journal of Sociology, Cambridge University Press.

European Law Review, Sweet & Maxwell, London.

European Urban and Regional Studies, Longman, Harlow.

Journal of Common Market Studies, Blackwell, Oxford.

Journal of European Public Policy, Routledge, London.

Journal of European Social Policy, Longman, Harlow.

West European Politics, Frank Cass, London.

○ Books

Anderson, K. and Blackhurst, R. (eds) (1993), *Regional Integration and the Global Trading System*, Harvester Wheatsheaf, Hemel Hempstead.

Archer, C. (1994), *Organising Europe: The Institutions of European Integration*, Edward Arnold, London.

Arter, D. (1993), *The Politics of European Integration in the Twentieth Century*, Dartmouth, Aldershot.

Artis, M. and Lee, N. (eds) (1994), *The Economics of the European Union: Policy and Analysis*, Oxford University Press.

Baldwin, R.E. (1994), *Towards an Integrated Europe*, Centre for Economic Policy Research, London.

Begg, D. (1993), *Making Sense of Subsidiarity*, Centre for Economic Policy Research, London.

Brittan, L. (1994), *Europe*, Hamish Hamilton, London.

Buchan, D. (1993), *Europe: The Strange Superpower*, Dartmouth, Aldershot.

Bulmer, S., George, S. and Scott, A. (eds) (1992), *The United Kingdom and EC Membership Evaluated*, Pinter, London

Burgess, Michael (1989), *Federalism and European Union*, Routledge, London.

Cecchini, P. (1988), *The European Challenge: 1992 The Benefits of a Single Market*, Wildwood House, Aldershot.

CEPR Annual Report (1993), *Making Sense of Subsidiarity*, London.

Church, C. and Phinnemore, D. (1994), *European Union and the European Community: A Handbook and Commentary on the Post-Maastricht Treaties*, Harvester Wheatsheaf, Hemel Hempstead.

Cockfield, Lord (1994), *The European Union: Creating the Single Market*, Wiley, London.

Coffey, P. (1994), *The Future of Europe*, Edward Elgar, Cheltenham.

Colchester, N. and Buchan, D. (1990), *Europe Relaunched: Truths and Illusions on the Way to 1992*, Economist Books, London.

Collinson, S. (1994), *Europe and International Migration*, Pinter, London.

De Grauwe, P. (1994), *Economics of Monetary Integration*, Oxford University Press.

Dyson, K. (1994), *Elusive Union: The Process of Economic and Monetary Union in Europe*, Longman, Harlow.

El-Agraa, A. (1994), *The Economics of the European Community*, Harvester Wheatsheaf, Hemel Hempstead.

Flynn, J. (1994), *European Law: A Question of Interpretation*, Butterworth, London.

George, S. (1994), *An Awkward Partner, Britain in the European Community*, Oxford University Press.

Ginsberg, R. H. (1989), *Foreign Policy Actions of the European Community: The Politics of Scale*, Lynne Rienner, Boulder, Col.

Gold, M. (1993), *The Social Dimension: Employment Policy in the European Community*, Macmillan, London.

Grahl, J. and Teague, P. (1990), *1992 – The Big Market*, Lawrence & Wishart, London.

Greenwood, S. (1992), *Britain and European Co-operation Since 1945*, Oxford, Blackwell.

Haas, E.B. (1958), *The Uniting of Europe*, Stanford University Press.

Johnston, M.T. (1994), *The European Council. Gatekeeper of the European*

Community, Westview Press, Boulder, Col.

Keohane, R.O. and Hoffman, S. (1991), *The New European Community*, Westview Press, Boulder. Col.

Kirchner, E. (1992), *Decision-Making in the European Community*, Manchester University Press.

Laursen, F. and Vanhoonacker, S. (eds) (1992), *The Intergovernmental Conference on Political Union*, Martinus Nijhoff, Dordrecht.

Lipgens, W. (1986), *The History of European Integration* (2 Vols), Oxford University Press, London.

Lodge, J. (ed.) (1993), *The EC and the Challenge of the Future*, 2nd Edition, Pinter, London.

Mayes, D.G. (ed.) (1993), *The External Implications of European Integration*, Harvester Wheatsheaf, New York.

Michalski, A. and Wallace, H. (1992), *The European Community: The Challenge of Enlargement*, Royal Institute of International Affairs, London.

Milward, A.S. (1987), *The Reconstruction of Western Europe 1945-51*, London, Methuen.

Milward, A.S. (1992), *The European Rescue of the Nation-State*, Routledge, London.

Nugent, N. (1994), *The Government and Politics of the European Union*, Macmillan, London.

Pinder, J. (1991), *The European Community and Eastern Europe*, Pinter, London.

Pinder, J. (1991), *The European Community*, Oxford University Press.

Sbragia, A.M. (ed.) (1991), *Euro-Politics: Institutions and Policymaking in the 'New' European Community*, Brookings Institution, Washington DC.

Smith, J. (1994), *Citizen's Europe*, Royal Institute of International Affairs, London.

Smith, M. and Stirk, P. (1993), *Making the New Europe*, Pinter, London.

Spicer, M. (1992), *A Treaty Too Far*, Fourth Estate, London.

Stirk, Peter (1989), *European Unity in Context: The Inter-War Period*, Pinter, London.

Swann, D. (1995), *The Economics of the Common Market*, Penguin, Harmondsworth.

Wallace, W. (ed.) (1990), *The Dynamics of European Integration,* Pinter, London.

Weatherill, S. and Beaumont, P. (1993), *EC Law*, Penguin, Harmondsworth.

Westlake, M. (1994), *A Modern Guide to the European Parliament*, Pinter, London.

Wistrich, E. (1994), *The United States of Europe*, Routledge, London.

Young, J.W. (1993), *Britain and European Unity, 1945–1992*, Macmillan, London.

Index

Note: Institutions and organisations are listed under their abbreviations or acronyms when these are well known. A full list will be found on pp. xii–xvii.